EUROPEAN DIPLOMATIC HISTORY

1789–1815

Steven T. Ross received his Ph.D. from Princeton in 1963. He subsequently carried out research in Paris, and he is presently an Associate Professor of History at the University of Texas. His former publications include several articles and reviews for scholarly journals.

EUROPEAN DIPLOMATIC HISTORY 1789–1815

FRANCE AGAINST EUROPE

BY STEVEN T. ROSS

ANCHOR BOOKS
DOUBLEDAY & COMPANY, INC.
GARDEN CITY, NEW YORK
1969

The Anchor Books edition is the first publication of
EUROPEAN DIPLOMATIC HISTORY 1789–1815:
FRANCE AGAINST EUROPE

Anchor Books edition: 1969

Library of Congress Catalog Card Number 68–27135

Printed in the United States of America
First Edition

CONTENTS

LIST OF MAPS

INTRODUCTION

European rulers and diplomats have always sought to protect and expand the power of their states. By the middle of the seventeenth century concern for the security and aggrandizement of the state overshadowed all other considerations. The state embodied its own ends. No treaty was too solemn to break, no engagement too binding to violate, and no moral principle too absolute to ignore if it ran contrary to the reason of state. Rulers recognized no law higher than their own interests and accepted no limitations upon their pursuit of power save those imposed by material conditions and the counter-greed of others. Pretexts for an onslaught against a rival changed over the decades, but the primary concern of statesmen—the interest of the state—remained inviolable.

In the course of the perpetual struggle for security and conquest powerful rulers have attempted to establish a continental and at times a world-wide hegemony. Faced with extinction, other powers have responded by temporarily putting aside their own ambitions and rivalries, banding together to defeat the aggressor, and then attempting to establish a balance of power in which no single state could threaten the sovereignty of the rest. Such attempts, however, have usually failed, for after an interval of peace, the original aggressor state has regained its strength and resumed its march of conquest, or a new power has drawn the sword against Europe.

During the first half of the seventeenth century the Hapsburg dynasty lost its predominant position in Europe while Bourbon France, recovering from decades of civil strife, again became a major power. Cardinal Richelieu, the chief architect of the French revival, pursued a foreign policy designed to weaken both the Austrian and Spanish Hapsburgs. He gave diplomatic and financial support to princes engaged in hostilities against the

Hapsburg Emperor of Germany, and in 1635 he intervened directly in the Thirty Years' War. Although Richelieu did not live to see his policy fulfilled, at the war's end France and her allies emerged victorious after more than ten years of bitter fighting.

The Peace of Westphalia, signed in October 1648, dealt a serious blow to Hapsburg power. Spain had to recognize the independence of the United Provinces, and the Emperor agreed to grant complete sovereignty to the hundreds of states within the Holy Roman Empire and made important territorial concessions to Sweden and France. War between France and Spain continued until 1659, but in that year the Spanish signed the Peace of the Pyrenees, by which they sacrificed several strategically located areas. In addition the Spanish agreed to a marriage between the heir to the French throne and a daughter of their own monarch, thereby giving the Bourbons a dynastic claim to the whole of the Spanish Empire. The treaties of Westphalia and the Pyrenees thus marked a significant shift in the balance of power away from Madrid and Vienna toward Paris.

A second important development during this period was the effort of dynastic monarchs to enhance the strength of their governments in domestic affairs. Throughout the Continent, rulers attempted to reduce all elements of society, particularly the feudal nobility, to obedience to the royal will. A popular reaction against the chaos caused by the numerous political and religious conflicts of the late sixteenth and early seventeenth centuries strengthened the hand of the princes, for many individuals and social groups came to regard a powerful central government as the only guarantee of domestic tranquillity. Supported by popular opinion, rulers began to wrest power from their noble subjects by taking local governmental authority out of their hands and placing it under the control of a centralized bureaucracy.

Among the most assiduous practitioners of the art of

centralization were the Bourbon monarchs of France. The struggle between the crown and its mighty aristocratic vassals had been a central theme of French history for many centuries. In the sixteenth century powerful kings had attempted to strengthen their central administrative apparatus at the expense of the traditional rights and privileges of the nobility, but their successes had been largely undone during periods of regency, inept government, and aristocratic reaction that frequently followed their deaths. The demise of Henry II in 1559 had ushered in a period of violent civil strife as cliques of nobles aligned themselves with religious factions and fought to gain control of the queen regent and her feeble sons. The first Bourbon king, Henry IV, managed to restore a large measure of royal authority, but the succession of a minor in 1610 allowed the aristocrats to regain power and influence.

Upon assuming personal control of affairs of state in 1617 Louis XIII and his chief adviser, Richelieu, resumed the traditional royal policy of attacking the powers and prerogatives of the aristocracy. The Cardinal broke the independent power of the Huguenots and forced the nobles to pull down their fortified castles. He then challenged aristocratic control of the countryside by reducing the authority of the noble provincial governors and transferring the bulk of their administrative tasks to the intendants, a corps of royal bureaucrats recruited from the middle class. Cliques of great nobles tried several times to force him from office, but the Cardinal foiled all the conspiracies and prevented the fractious peers from regaining control of the central government.

After Richelieu's death in 1642, his policy was nearly undone, for the death of Louis XIII in the following year left the country in the hands of still another weak regency, and the nobles seized their opportunity to attempt to recapture the royal government. Cardinal Mazarin, Richelieu's successor, tried to continue the policy of enhancing the power of the crown, but the hereditary magistrates of the Paris *parlement* successfully challenged his fiscal policy and then insisted upon a general reduction of royal authority. The great feudal lords quickly joined the revolt of the "nobles of the robe," and from 1648 to 1653 France underwent still another interval of turmoil.

Fortunately for the crown, the rebel factions lacked internal cohesion. The *parlementaires* soon deserted the feudal aristocrats, who also lost the support of the lower classes by calling upon Spain for armed assistance. Lack of popular backing plus divisions within the noble ranks enabled the crown to crush the rebellion. Consequently, when Louis XIV assumed personal direction of his kingdom in 1661, he was able to employ the general popular reaction against the forces of factionalism and disunity in a massive effort to fulfill his predecessors' policy of centralization.

For more than half a century Louis was the personification of royal power and prestige. Endowed with charm, great common sense, and the absolute conviction that his actions had divine sanction, the hard-working monarch both reigned and governed. He was determined to create a powerful centralized state, and all segments of society felt the impact of his will. Louis was quite successful in limiting the influence of the nobility. He forced the semisovereign *parlements* to relinquish their ancient privilege of demanding changes in royal edicts before registering them as part of the law of the land, and he forbade the provincial estates to meet without royal sanction. The magnificent palace at Versailles also served a political purpose, for it not only enhanced Louis's own glory but also attracted the nobility to the royal presence, where the King could check their intrigues and flatter their vanity by means of lavish gifts and sinecures. Deeply enmeshed in the elaborate court life that became the marvel of all Europe, the aristocrats became progressively less influential in the councils of government, where Louis and his middle-class officials conducted the vital affairs of the realm. Louis did not completely destroy the power of the French nobility. Aristocrats retained their wealth and social prestige, and individual noblemen continued to hold high office within the ranks of the central administration. Nevertheless, the nobles had for the moment become the reluctant but obedient servants of the monarch.

In addition to weakening the nobles Louis sought to strengthen his kingdom by improving its economic and military situation. Colbert, the King's financial adviser, restored the depleted treasury and reorganized the keeping of public accounts on a more efficient basis. To stimulate economic activity Colbert abolished many of the vexatious internal tariffs and improved the country's road and canal network. The state also took a direct hand in founding new industries by establishing its own enterprises and by supplying inducements in the form of loans, tariff protection, monopolies, and tax benefits to businessmen who were willing to set up commercial or industrial ventures of their own. One important result of these policies was to increase the government's tax revenues, and this increased tax yield in turn enabled the crown to finance a series of extensive military reforms.

At the accession of Louis XIV the French army was badly organized and inefficient. Military units were the private property of noblemen who raised them and bargained with the King to determine their conditions of service. Under the skillful guidance of Le Tellier and Louvois the army was transformed from a private preserve of the aristocracy into a professional force belonging to the monarch. Louvois also suppressed fraudulent contractors, equipped and armed soldiers at the government's expense, and imposed uniform standards of drill and training. Although he did not abolish the system of purchasing commissions, Louvois did establish a parallel promotion schedule that enabled poor but talented officers to advance on a basis of merit. These and other reforms gave Louis the largest, best-equipped, and best-led army in Europe.

The creation of internal order and stability did not, however, lead to international peace, for Louis was determined to use his wealth and his new army to seek glory, prestige, and power in foreign lands. In 1667 the Sun King hurled a powerful expedition into the Spanish Netherlands (Belgium), thereby opening a series of wars that were to last for more than forty years. Louis's expansionist policies followed two main lines. The first was to push French frontiers north into the Low Countries and east into the Rhineland and the Franche-Comté. The second aspect of the Grand Monarch's designs was his desire to obtain the crown of Spain for his dynasty. Philip IV of Spain had died in 1665, and his successor, Charles II, was sickly and childless. Louis had a legal claim to the Spanish inheritance resulting from his marriage to a daughter of Philip's at the time of the peace of 1659. These two policies were linked, for assaults on outlying Spanish provinces not only strengthened French frontier defenses but also served notice on the court of Madrid that Spain could obtain peace and security only by accepting a Bourbon overlord. Had Louis achieved his goals he would in all probability have been able to create a universal monarchy, for the combined resources of France and Spain would have given him such power that all other states would have had to bow to his will.

In the 1660s only those rulers directly threatened by French arms offered resistance. Other statesmen had their own foreign and domestic problems and were at first not fully aware of the threat posed by French expansion. However, as Louis's armies advanced against feeble opposition the Dutch grew alarmed, for they regarded the Spanish Netherlands as a vital buffer zone between themselves and France. Consequently, they formed with Sweden and England the first of the coalitions designed to resist French aggression. Unwilling to risk a large-scale war against a league of great powers, Louis in May 1668 agreed to relinquish his conquests except for a number of fortified towns in Belgium. But far from restoring peace and tranquillity, the treaty of 1668 merely convinced him that it was necessary to cripple Dutch power as a prelude to further conquests.

In the following years Louis proceeded to isolate the Dutch diplomatically, thus avoiding the prospect of fighting against a coalition, and bribed the King of England to join him in an invasion of the United Provinces. In 1672 Louis launched a major war by invading Dutch territory. The Dutch, however, staved off immediate destruction by flooding their country and overthrowing the bourgeois oligarchs in favor of William of Orange. In William they found a leader as capable and resolute as Louis himself. He quickly aroused the rulers of Europe to the dangers of French aggression and created a new anti-French coalition that forced Louis to accept still another compromise peace in 1678. France obtained more towns in Flanders and the entire Franche-Comté, but Louis had to abandon his scheme of destroying Dutch independence.

He did not, however, relinquish all his aggressive designs. After his setback in the Low Countries, the Sun King turned his attentions to Germany. In Alsace, legally a part of the Empire, French officials annexed many regions including the large and wealthy city of Strasbourg. To prevent the German princes from combining against France, Louis encouraged the Ottoman Turks to renew their assaults upon central Europe. In the spring of 1683 a huge Turkish army marched on Vienna, whereupon Louis proposed a truce between himself and the Empire on the basis of the *status quo*. Because such a truce would have left France in possession of the territories she had recently taken, the Emperor refused to consider it. Louis then invaded the Spanish Netherlands and took the fortress of Luxembourg, and the Emperor, unable to fight the Turks and the French simultaneously, reluctantly agreed to a twenty-year truce in the west. Signed in 1684, the truce guaranteed to France the retention of her latest conquests.

Meanwhile, the war in the east was going badly for the Turks. They failed to take Vienna, and in the following years the Emperor in league with Poland and Venice unleashed a major counteroffensive. Imperial troops penetrated deep into the Balkans, and Louis realized that the Emperor, strengthened by the acquisition of vast territories and millions of new subjects, would eventually return to the west and attempt to undo the terms of the truce of 1684. The Sun King, therefore, decided to strike while his foe was still tied down in the east. He wanted to make good his claim to part of the Palatinate, install his own protégé as Archbishop of Cologne, and force the Emperor to transform the truce into a permanent peace recognizing French supremacy in the Rhineland. Consequently, in the fall of 1688 Louis ordered his armies to invade Germany.

He had, however, miscalculated, for the German princes decided to resist sooner than make further sacrifices. The League of Augsburg, a defensive organization formed by Bavaria, Saxony, and the Palatinate in 1685, took the field. Spain, Sweden, and the United Provinces came to the League's assistance, and the Emperor withdrew troops from the Balkans for a campaign on the Rhine. The Glorious Revolution in England added still another state to the anti-French ranks, for the new King was none other than William of Orange. He was able to convince the Parliament to declare war on Louis, and by 1690 all the major European powers had banded together in a Grand Coalition.

The war lasted until 1697, but neither France nor the coalition was able to gain a decisive victory, and the antagonists finally concluded a compromise peace. The Ryswick Treaty obligated Louis to recognize William as King of England, and the Dutch obtained a line of barrier forts in the Spanish Netherlands. France evacuated the Low Countries and Luxembourg but retained her

Alsatian annexations. Although the War of the League of Augsburg did not put an end to French aggression, it nevertheless marked a decisive stage in the international relations of Europe: England had become an anti-Bourbon power, and for the first time *all* the leading states had united in a common war against the Grand Monarch.

The death of Charles II of Spain on November 1, 1700, presented Louis with his last and his greatest opportunity to achieve his dream of European hegemony. The continental powers had been attempting to solve the problem of the Spanish succession for many years. Both the Austrian Hapsburgs and the Bourbons had valid dynastic claims to the entire inheritance, but England and the United Provinces were reluctant to see a major power obtain all of the Spanish domains. However, the efforts of the maritime powers to devise an acceptable solution to the succession issue all failed. An attempt to give Charles's empire to a minor third power collapsed upon the death of the prospective heir, a Bavarian prince, and arrangements to partition Spanish territories foundered upon Vienna's refusal to accept anything less than the entire inheritance. The Spanish nobility also opposed partition. They cared little who ruled them as long as their empire was preserved intact. Years of defeats at French hands had convinced them that they could retain their holdings only with French support, and they decided to throw themselves into the arms of their ancient foe. The Spanish aristocrats, therefore, convinced their dying monarch to leave all his possessions to Philip of Anjou, a grandson of Louis XIV, with the provision that if the Bourbons rejected any part of the succession all of it would then pass to an Austrian prince.

Although he did not want to alarm other powers and force them to devise still another coalition, Louis did not wish to refuse the Spanish offer, for he realized that any attempt at partition would lead to war with both Austria and Spain with no guarantee of support from the maritime states. On the other hand, by accepting the Spanish inheritance he would have Spain on his side in the inevitable clash with Austria, and by careful negotiation he hoped to be able to convince the British and Dutch to remain neutral. More important, perhaps, than these considerations was the fact that the Spanish succession offered the Sun King a unique opportunity to fulfill all his desires for glory and power. With Spain and her vast colonial holdings in the hands of his dynasty no other power could stand against him. Consequently, on November 24, 1700, Louis proclaimed his grandson King Philip V of Spain.

At first only the Austrians disputed the Bourbon succession at Madrid, but Louis soon aroused the other powers against him. By occupying the Dutch barrier forts, opening negotiations with his grandson for the transfer of Belgium to France, and depriving English and Dutch merchants of their commercial privileges in Spanish ports, he convinced other rulers that he was planning to direct France and Spain as a single political unit. William then opened talks with the Hapsburgs to reconstruct the Grand Coalition, and on September 7, 1701, England, the United Provinces, and Austria concluded an alliance with the objectives of partitioning the Spanish Empire and separating the crowns of France and Spain forever.

The ensuing War of the Spanish Succession was for France a disaster. The balance of armed might had altered since the 1690s, for Louis's best generals had either died or retired from active service while the forces of the coalition had gained in numbers and experience. Furthermore, the coalition had at its disposal two of the greatest generals of the age—Marlborough and Eugene. These two brilliant field commanders proceeded to inflict a series of devastating defeats upon the armies of the Grand Monarch, and by 1709 France was on the brink of total collapse. Desperate for peace, Louis offered enormous concessions to the allies. He agreed to recognize the Protestant succession in England, restore the barrier forts to the Dutch, surrender Alsace to the Emperor, abandon Spain's colonies, and ask Philip to abdicate. The allies, however, were not satisfied and insisted that Louis give them bases in France for use in renewed hostilities if Philip refused to leave Spain. This last condition Louis rejected, for it was tantamount to total capitulation. In desperation he issued an appeal to his subjects for continued support of the war, reinforced his shattered armies, and held back the allied forces for the rest of the year. Louis reopened peace talks in 1710. He renewed his earlier concessions and even went on to offer to subsidize an allied expedition to drive his grandson from Madrid. Confident of victory, the allies refused to accept these terms and demanded that Louis send a French force to Spain to depose Philip. Again Louis resorted to arms and continued to hold the allies at bay until growing war weariness and divisions within the Grand Coalition convinced the belligerents to end hostilities.

The treaties of Utrecht and Rastadt, signed in 1713 and 1714, did not satisfy all the members of the coalition, but they did effectively put an end to the threat of Bourbon hegemony. The treaties left Philip as King of Spain, but extracted the guarantee that the crowns of France and Spain would never be united in the hands of a single monarch. Furthermore, Spain had to relinquish the Spanish Netherlands, Milan, Sardinia, and Naples to Austria and surrender Sicily to Savoy. England took Gibraltar and Minorca and obtained a commercial foothold in Spanish America. Louis had to give up Newfoundland, Acadia, and St. Kitts Island to the British, recognize the rights of the Hudson's Bay Company in Canada, and dismantle the naval installations at Dunkirk. The peace settlement thus created a balance of power in which no single state, especially France, could threaten the sovereignty of the others.

From the defeat of the Grand Monarch's final bid for supremacy until the wars of the French Revolutionary Era a new strategic and diplomatic situation prevailed in Europe. After 1713, the major powers enjoyed a general equality of military and economic strength with the result that no ruler was ever strong enough to attempt to establish a universal hegemony. Monarchs naturally continued their pursuit of glory and power, but because no one of them was able to achieve a preponderance of force, they had to content themselves with somewhat more limited objectives. Seizing a province or a colony from a weak state or depriving a major power of a valuable territorial possession became the objectives of war and diplomacy. Instead of trying to destroy each other, rulers tried to increase their strength by making specific territorial and commercial gains while at the same time striving to reduce the power of their rivals. As in previous eras, however, they continued to concern themselves primarily with the interest of their states, and technological conditions and mutual suspicion and hostility remained as the only real checks upon their ambitions.

The structure of eighteenth-century society placed a number of limitations upon the arts of war and diplomacy. Since the European economy was essentially agrarian, rulers lacked the industrial base necessary to equip a mass army. To obtain the revenues needed to build an armed force monarchs, whenever possible, excluded the productive classes—the bourgeois and peasantry—from military service, thereby further reducing their pool of available manpower. Consequently, the armies of the Old Regime were relatively small forces drawn from limited segments of the population—the officers from the aristocracy and the rank and file from the unemployed, beggars, and vagrants. The inability of any ruler to create a mass army resulted in a military stalemate among the major powers and made it difficult to achieve sweeping and decisive results by means of military operations.

The armament available to commanders also reduced the effectiveness of warfare. Weapons were noted for their short range, slow rate of fire, and lack of accuracy. To obtain effective firepower armies fought in close-packed linear formations, and to train men to operate under this tactical system was a long and expensive process. Rulers were, therefore, reluctant to send their troops into major engagements because casualties were invariably heavy, and it was exceedingly difficult and costly to rebuild a shattered professional force. Consequently, eighteenth-century warfare was highly formalized and consisted mainly of sieges and maneuvering. Decisive battlefield encounters were the exception, not the rule. War was thus less devastating than it had been during the religious conflicts of the sixteenth and seventeenth centuries and less destructive of human life than the total wars of more recent times. On the other hand, Old Regime warfare frequently failed to yield decisive results, thereby calling into question war's utility as a means of state policy.

Mutual suspicion and hostility among the competing states was still another factor that imposed a check upon the ambitions of individual statesmen. Since no ruler wanted another to increase his power, a unilateral act of aggression became almost impossible. If a king attacked a rival, other powers, wishing to participate in the spoils of victory or desiring to prevent the aggressor from making new conquests, would intervene. Thus a monarch wishing to indulge in the royal sport of power politics had always to consider the position of other interested parties. Consequently, most eighteenth-century wars were clashes of rival coalitions, and the victorious group divided the spoils equally.

The coalitions were not, however, permanent alliances, for as a prince's specific objectives changed so did his friends and foes. Thus while individual rulers in the post-Utrecht period abandoned plans of attaining hegemony, states acting alone or in conjunction with other powers continued their search for security and aggrandizement. After 1714 Spain, in order to regain her Italian possessions and provide employment for the sons of Philip's second wife, became an aggressive power. France, desiring an interval of peace in order to rebuild her fortunes and forces, joined her former foes, England, the Dutch Republic, and Austria, in a successful effort to halt the Spanish. When Spain capitulated in 1720, Austria took Sicily and gave Sardinia to Savoy in order to build a firm barrier against the possibility of renewed Spanish aggression. By 1733, however, Spain and France were allies once again and fought Austria and Russia during the War of the Polish Succession, in which each group sought to impose its own candidate on the Polish throne, and the Bourbon coalition also tried to seize Austrian provinces in Italy. Both coalitions showed a total lack of concern for the desires of the Poles and Italians, for if the great powers respected the independence of other leading states, they regarded weaker states as natural objects of prey.

The accession of Maria Theresa to the Hapsburg throne opened a new round of hostilities. In 1740 Frederick II of Prussia invaded Silesia. He was quickly joined by France, where ambitious nobles convinced Louis XV to abandon his minister's policy of avoiding major continental wars, and also by Spain and Bavaria. The rulers of these states planned to seize the bulk of Maria's lands and reduce the Hapsburg dynasty to the status of a minor central European principality. At that time, however, England was engaged in a maritime and colonial war with France and Spain, and to divert Franco-Spanish strength from the overseas conflict the British came to the support of the Austrians. The War of the Austrian Succession lasted until 1748. It involved all the major powers, whose troops fought not only in Europe but also in the Americas and India. The peace settlement, moreover, was short-lived, and within a decade after the peace of Aix-la-Chapelle the powers were again involved in a major conflict. During the Seven Years' War, 1756–63, England battled France and later Spain for maritime and imperial supremacy. Meanwhile, on the Continent, Frederick II resisted the efforts of Austria, Russia, and France to destroy his kingdom. To tie French forces down in Europe and protect Hanover, England gave Prussia financial and military support and the two conflicts merged into another world-wide struggle.

After the Peace of Paris monarchs paused to restore their armies and replenish their treasuries and then resumed their never-ending search for power. Prussia and her former enemies, Austria and Russia, instituted the first of the partitions of Poland in 1772. Three years later a rebellion in Britain's North American colonies gave France and Spain an opportunity to seek revenge for their earlier defeats. The Bourbon states sent military and economic aid to the American rebels and a few years later declared war on England. Most of the major powers supported the French and Spanish, but during and after the American Revolution they continued to dispute each other's attempts at aggrandizement. Prussia resisted Austrian efforts to gain control of Bavaria. The three eastern powers competed among themselves for a paramount position at Warsaw, and Austria and Russia combined in a scheme to dismember the Ottoman Empire. Prussia opposed them and renewed ties with England. The Prussians and British crushed a rebellion against the ruler of the United Provinces in 1787 and voiced common opposition to the Austro-Russian plan to partition Turkey. Thus at the outbreak of the French Revolution the great powers were still engaged in pursuing their own special objectives.

Yet despite the numerous wars of the eighteenth century and the changes wrought by these conflicts no power ever became strong enough to launch a unilateral bid for supremacy. The balance of power established at Utrecht was modified in the following decades but was never completely upset. The general equality of strength among the major states of Europe prevented any one of them from threatening the independence of the others.

Only radical political and social changes that would enable a ruler to tap a wider range of human and material resources than was possible under the old order could lead to a drastic change in the balance of power. Without the introduction of new techniques European diplomacy remained confined within a state system composed of sovereign powers that struggled constantly for new subjects and provinces, yet avoided any truly revolutionary changes. No power ever made an attempt to establish a continental hegemony. Specific acquisitions and equal compensations were the watchwords of the diplomats of the *Ancien Régime.*

In the course of the wars of the Old Regime Austria suffered important defeats but retained her status as a great power. Vienna had to relinquish many of her provinces in Italy to Spain, and Frederick II of Prussia was able to seize and retain Silesia. On the other hand the Hapsburgs foiled the attempt to dismember their empire and wrested large blocs of territory from Turkey and Poland, which to some degree offset their losses in Italy and Germany. Spain's status, like Austria's, remained basically unchanged in the eighteenth century. Despite a number of salutary reforms introduced by the Bourbons Spain never recovered her status as a first-rate power. The Spanish recaptured Naples and other regions in Italy but failed to regain Gibraltar and in the New World made further concessions to the British. Spain thus remained a fairly important but declining force in European diplomacy.

The rise of Prussia and Russia into the ranks of the great powers was a development of critical importance for the diplomats of the eighteenth century and for the future history of Europe. By the first decades of the eighteenth century the Hohenzollern dynasty had succeeded in creating a large and efficient military machine. Frederick the Great then proceeded to use this army to wrest Silesia from Maria Theresa. In the years following his successful aggression Frederick was able to prevent the Austrians from destroying his kingdom, thereby assuring his status as one of Europe's leading powers. Meanwhile in Russia after centuries of weakness and isolation, Peter the Great began the process of modernizing and Westernizing. He also launched successful expansionist wars against Sweden and Turkey, and his successors, though lacking his energy and imagination, were nevertheless able to profit from his innovations. They also continued his expansionist policies, and by the 1720s the wishes of St. Petersburg had to be included in the calculations of Western statesmen.

As Prussia and Russia enhanced their positions other states declined both in power and prestige. The chaotic aristocratic Polish Republic could offer no effective resistance to her more powerful neighbors. Poland became a pawn in the hands of foreign powers and incapable of pursuing an independent foreign policy. Sweden, after her defeat in the Great Northern War of 1699–1721, also sank into insignificance. Russia took most of Sweden's Baltic provinces, and the Swedes never recovered their former status. Largely because of its own internal corruption the Ottoman Empire never again threatened Europe after 1683. Attacked by the Austrians and Russians, Turkey slowly but inexorably retreated from the Balkans and the coasts of the Black Sea, and although they managed to stabilize their Balkan frontier in 1739, the Turks remained thereafter an object of the ambitions of other powers rather than an active force in continental affairs.

Of all the leading European states England was probably the most successful. British naval might expanded throughout the century, and in colonial affairs England defeated her rivals and obtained a dominant position in North America and the East Indies. By contrast the French consistently failed to enhance their power. On the Continent the Bourbon monarchs were unable to impose their candidate on the Polish throne; their attempt to dismember the Hapsburg Empire came to nought; and their attack on Prussia also collapsed. On the high seas the French never successfully challenged the might of the British fleets, and in colonial affairs France lost extensive and valuable possessions to England. The only major acquisitions France made during the eighteenth century were Lorraine and Corsica, relatively small prizes considering the men and money expended.

Even the one major French victory over the English had disastrous results for the Bourbon monarchy. French military, naval, and economic assistance played a major role in the final success of the American Revolution, but after 1783 England continued to reign as the world's leading naval power and dominated the bulk of the trade with the new American nation. The French monarchy, on the other hand, had in the course of the war amassed a huge debt, and this debt contributed directly to the growing economic plight of the crown. The royal government's attempts to solve their financial crisis coupled with the nobility's refusal to sanction any major reform of the taxation system were in turn the events that led to the outbreak of the Revolution.

Social tensions in France had been increasing for many decades. After the death of Louis XIV in 1715, the regency had allowed the aristocrats to regain political power within the structure of the royal administration. Nobles obtained high office, and the *parlements* recovered their former privilege of demanding changes in edicts before registering them. Furthermore, the nobility gained new strength and cohesion when the feudal lords merged with the newer judicial aristocracy of the *parlements;* by the middle of the eighteenth century the two branches of the aristocracy had fused into a single united caste. Louis XV tried to curb noble power by abolishing the *parlements*, but in 1774 Louis XVI restored the magistrates to office. After this victory, the nobles continued to expand their power. In 1781 they secured passage of a law excluding commoners from the officer corps. By the late 1780s all the bishops in France were of noble extraction; all the intendants came from the aristocracy, and nobles dominated the major royal councils. The nobility also retained their special economic privileges such as freedom from most personal taxation and the enjoyment of feudal dues and rents from their estates.

In the later decades of the century, however, the middle classes, conscious of their wealth and talent, became increasingly frustrated by the crown's refusal to admit them to positions of political power and social prestige and by the nobility's successful efforts to restrict admittance into their caste. Criticisms of the *status quo* launched by the *philosophes* gave the middle classes intellectual justification for their socioeconomic demands. The *philosophes* undermined many of the traditional moral and philosophic sanctions of the old order and strengthened a growing conviction that society not only could be but should be reformed.

The lower social classes were also growing restive by the 1780s. The peasants objected to remnants of the feudal agrarian system, which persisted even in the late eighteenth century. Efforts of the nobles to revive and collect feudal dues that had lapsed centuries before served to heighten and intensify peasant discontent. An economic recession in the last years of the Old Regime made these impositions even more burdensome and added further to agrarian unrest. Furthermore, agrarian and urban wage laborers and the artisans and shopkeepers viewed with alarm the rising cost of food, which came at a time of growing unemployment and declining wages.

In this context of growing discontent the crown in order to solve its dire fiscal predicament proposed a series of tax reforms in an attempt to force the privileged orders to contribute their fair share to the royal treasury. The nobles, however, resisted and then proceeded to use the government's plight to increase their own power within the state. In 1787 and 1788 the aristocrats with the support of the lower classes stymied all the royal government's efforts to institute reforms. Finally in the summer of 1788 the King surrendered to the privileged orders and agreed to summon, for the first time since 1614, an Estates General. A body of three chambers representing the clergy, the nobles, and the commoners, the Estates General was to solve the crown's financial dilemma and reform the laws of the kingdom.

The united front of aristocrats and commoners that had defeated the King soon broke down, for the nobles showed that although they were willing to resist the crown they were not going to share their power with the lower classes. On September 23, 1788, the *parlement* of Paris stipulated that at the forthcoming meeting the Estates should vote by order instead of allowing delegates to cast their ballots individually. Since the upper ranks of the clerical order came from the aristocracy, the vote by order would have allowed the nobility to control the Estates, and thus enable the aristocracy to control all of France.

The declaration of September 23 put an immediate end to the alliance between noble and commoner, for the middle class became aware of the real ambitions of the privileged caste and resolved to institute reforms in its own socioeconomic interests. Thus when the Estates General met in May 1789, the bourgeois delegates of the Third Estate were prepared to resist the pretensions of both the nobles and the monarch and were determined, with or without royal sanction, to write a new constitution for the nation.

By the summer of 1789 the middle-class deputies with the support of the peasants and urban masses succeeded in wresting political initiative away from the crown and the aristocracy. The revolutionaries frustrated all attempts at counterrevolution, and by the fall of 1791 they had completed their task of transforming France from a theoretically absolute state into a constitutional monarchy. The men of '89 also abolished most of the remnants of the manorial system, subordinated the Church economically and politically to the civil authorities, established fiscal equality by abolishing all special economic privileges, and opened civilian and military posts to all on a basis of talent rather than birth. But despite these accomplishments the Revolution did not end in 1791, for many people refused to accept the new order.

Thousands of noblemen, many of whom fled the country after 1789, were determined to destroy the constitutional regime. Aristocratic *émigrés* sought foreign intervention while many of those who remained in France began to organize armed insurrections. Louis, his queen, and the court also opposed the Revolution, and while refusing to co-operate with the nobles, the court faction engaged in conspiracies of its own. The vast majority of the higher clergy and about half of the parish priests formed a third antirevolutionary clique. Opposed to the legislation which had reduced the temporal power of the Church, this group launched an extensive propaganda campaign against the government. Meanwhile elements which had originally supported the Revolution were deserting the cause of constitutional government. Within the ranks of the middle class some wanted to revise the Constitution in a conservative manner while others wanted to make the government more democratic. Furthermore, the Constitution, by placing economic restrictions on the right to vote, had disenfranchised almost half the adult male population, and these "passive citizens" were willing to co-operate with the middle-class democrats in order to attain political equality. The Revolution was thus destined to pursue a course of continued factional clashes and violence.

By 1792 foreign war was to complicate and influence the pattern of internal strife and upheaval. To protect their revolution and their nation the French were to devise a new and revolutionary scheme of military organization that would enable them to marshal the human and material resources of the entire country. A new style of tactics was to make the new citizen army into the most formidable fighting force in Europe. The French were to defend their own land and, after successful counterattacks, carry their banners into the heart of the Continent. Thus the diplomacy of the Revolutionary Era was to witness the collapse of the system of sovereign states contending with but not destroying one another and the start of a new French attempt to establish hegemony. Ironically, the revolution that produced such new departures in the domestic affairs of France was also to witness the revival of an older style of diplomacy. As in the days of the Grand Monarch, revolutionary France by a series of domestic reforms was to attain such power that she could threaten to dominate the rest of Europe.

EUROPEAN DIPLOMATIC HISTORY

1789–1815

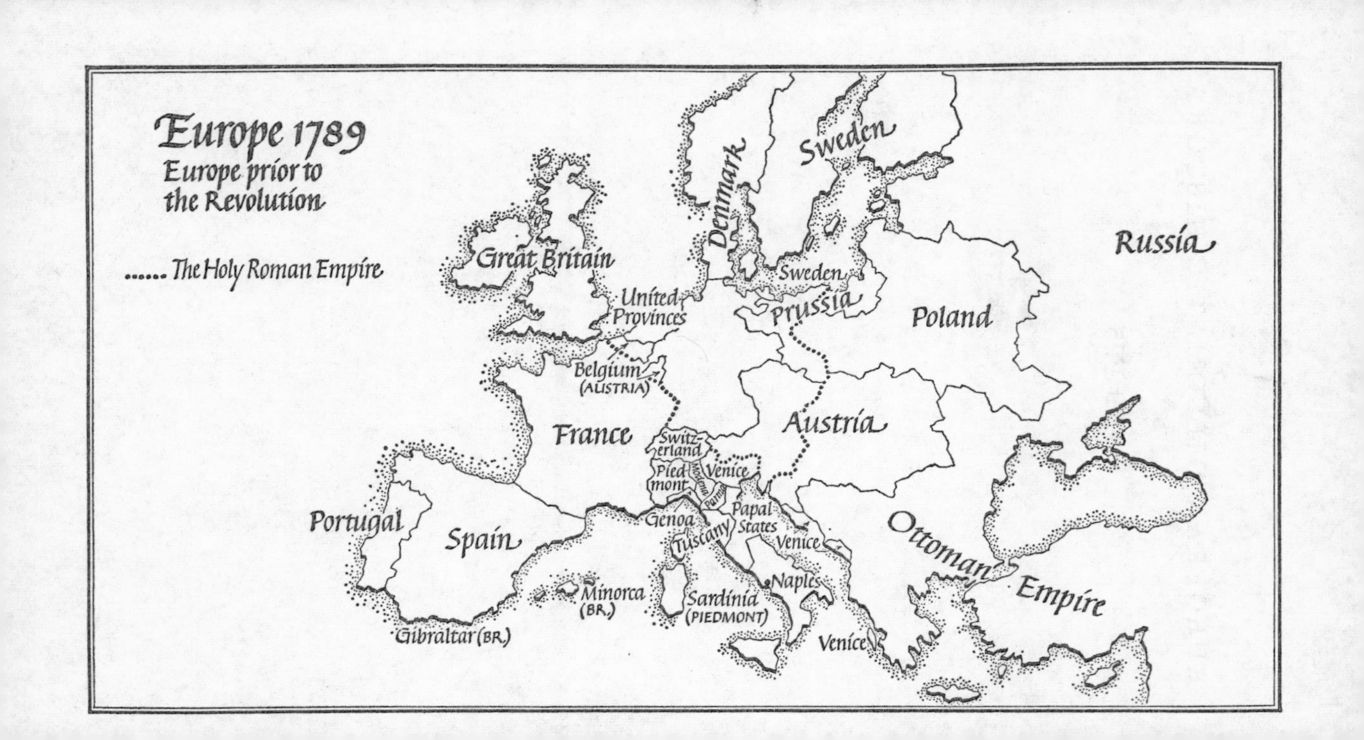
Europe 1789
Europe prior to the Revolution
...... The Holy Roman Empire
Russia
Sweden
Denmark
Great Britain
Sweden
Prussia
Poland
United Provinces
Belgium (AUSTRIA)
Austria
France
Switzerland
Piedmont
Venice
Modena
Parma
Papal States
Genoa
Tuscany
Venice
Naples
Sardinia (PIEDMONT)
Minorca (BR.)
Gibraltar (BR.)
Portugal
Spain
Venice
Ottoman Empire

CHAPTER 1

THE COMING OF WAR

In the spring of 1789, observers of the French Revolution did not suspect that within three years France would go to war with the major powers of Europe. Nor did they predict that the conflict would last for more than twenty years. Literate Europeans greeted the initial phases of the Revolution with friendly curiosity and sympathy. Illustrious Germans including Kant, Humboldt, Fichte, and Herder expressed their admiration for the Third Estate's efforts to attain liberty. Bentham, Wordsworth, Price, Fox, Stanhope, and many other English intellectuals and politicians approved of the National Assembly's policy of establishing a constitutional regime.[1] The sovereigns of Europe, though unwilling to apply the doctrines of the Revolution in their own lands, realized that Louis XVI's domestic problems reduced French influence in international affairs and consequently looked with some favor upon the upheaval in France.[2]

News of the more violent aspects of the Revolution—the storming of the Bastille, the peasant uprisings, and the October Days—caused a sharp division in public opin-

[1] For a discussion of European opinion on the French Revolution, see R. R. Palmer, *The Age of the Democratic Revolution* (Princeton, 1964), II; Jacques Godechot, *La Grande Nation* (Paris, 1956), I; J. Droz, *L'Allemagne et la Révolution française* (Paris, 1949); F. Valjavec, *Die Entstehung der politischen strömungen in Deutschland 1770–1815* (Munich, 1951); and P. A. Brown, *The French Revolution in English History* (London, 1918).

[2] See A. Sorel, *L'Europe et la Révolution française* (Paris, 1885), I; J. Holland Rose, *William Pitt and the Great War* (London, 1911); A. W. Ward and G. P. Gooch, *The Cambridge History of British Foreign Policy* (Cambridge, 1912), I; C. de la Rivière, *Catherine II et la Révolution française* (Paris, 1895); and A. Beer, *Joseph II und Kaunitz* (Vienna, 1873).

ion. Many backers of the initial phases of the Revolution turned violently against it. Edmund Burke's *Reflections on the Revolution in France* appeared in November 1790 and quickly attained wide circulation in England and on the Continent. German writers began to attack the "democratic rabble" and "mob rule" which, they assumed, prevailed in France.[3] On the other hand, events in France convinced many that political and social change was possible in their own lands. Insurrection erupted in Liège, in August 1789. A successful rebellion forced the Austrians to evacuate Belgium at the end of the year. Serfs in Electoral Saxony rose in rebellion in 1790, and Rhenish peasants refused to pay their manorial dues. English political clubs revived demands for the reform of Parliament, and Irishmen started to advocate changes in the *status quo*.[4] Paris meanwhile became the rendezvous for radical exiles from all corners of Europe, who joined the non-French democrats who had come to Paris before 1789 in calling for international revolution.

Fearing further development of revolutionary ferment, monarchs soon dropped their detached attitude toward the upheaval in France and initiated measures to halt the spread of subversive propaganda. The Duke of Bavaria banned the French semiofficial journal *Le Moniteur* from his domains. The court of Madrid ordered the seizure of all books and newsletters coming from France and

[3] See J. Steven Watson, *The Reign of George III* (Oxford, 1960); J. Dechamps, *Les Iles britanniques et la Révolution française* (Brussels, 1949); and L. Krieger, *The German Idea of Freedom* (Boston, 1957).

[4] For works on revolutions outside of France see Palmer, *Age of the Democratic Revolution;* S. Tassier, *Les démocrats belges de 1789: étude sur le Vonckisme et la Révolution brabançonne* (Brussels, 1930); P. Stulz and A. Opitz, *Volksbewegungen in Kursachsen zur zeit der französischen Revolution* (Berlin, 1956); W. T. Laprade, *England and the French Revolution* (Baltimore, 1909); W. P. Hall, *British Radicalism 1789–97* (New York, 1912); R. B. McDowell, *Irish Public Opinion 1750–1800;* and R. Jacob, *The Rise of the United Irishmen, 1791–1794* (London, 1937).

placed all resident Frenchmen under police surveillance. The King of Sardinia forbade Masonic lodge meetings, and in the spring of 1791, the Pope condemned the ecclesiastical reforms of the National Assembly.

Having struck out against inflammatory proselytism, rulers began to contemplate the next logical step—the destruction of the Revolution in France. Appeals from aristocratic *émigrés* and from the French court for aid in launching a counterrevolution bolstered the resolve of the European chancelleries by demonstrating that important groups in France would welcome foreign intervention.

Led by the King's brother, the Count of Artois, noblemen had been leaving France since July 1789.[5] After journeying through Belgium, the Rhineland, and Switzerland, Artois prevailed upon his brother-in-law, King Victor Amadeus III of Sardinia, to grant him refuge at Turin. There, the Count established a counterrevolutionary Central Committee. The members, including Artois, were united in their hatred of the Revolution and were determined to strike it down. Although they lacked experience in the complexities of political life and engaged in constant internal squabbles for power and influence, Artois did manage to impart a minimum sense of discipline, and the *émigrés* were soon hard at work devising means to free the King and to provoke armed revolts in the provinces. Agents penetrated France to recruit supporters. The Committee's adherents laid plans to spirit Louis from Paris and use him as a figurehead to spark the counterrevolution. The King, however, not wishing to be a pawn in his brother's hands, refused to co-operate with the aristocratic conspirators. Consequently, the plot faltered, and in February 1790 the government discovered, arrested, and executed the leader of the Parisian counterrevolutionaries. Artois's agents had better success

[5] For a statistical study of emigration see Donald Greer, *The Incidence of Emigration During the French Revolution* (Cambridge, Mass., 1951).

in the provinces. Aristocrat-inspired riots broke out at Toulouse in April 1790, at Montauban in May, at Nîmes in June, and at Lyons in July. Artois then drew up plans for a general insurrection which involved co-ordinated risings in southeastern France coupled with an *émigré* invasion. The government, however, uncovered these plans in December 1790 and captured many of the plotters. Undaunted, Artois and his followers continued to seek the destruction of the Revolution and to this end redoubled their appeals to foreign powers. Artois had already requested armed assistance from Joseph II, Holy Roman Emperor, ruler of the Hapsburg domains, and brother of the French queen. After Joseph's death in 1790, Artois called upon his successor, Leopold II, to invade France, overthrow the Assembly, and restore the power of the aristocracy.

While the aristocrats were plotting against the Revolution, Louis XVI and Marie Antoinette were also sending out secret appeals to their fellow monarchs for armed assistance. As early as November 1789 Louis had secretly informed Charles IV of Spain of his repudiation of all of his concessions to the Third Estate. Early in 1790, a secret agent of the court journeyed to Vienna with Louis's denunciation of the National Assembly. Finally, in October 1790, Louis commissioned the Marquis de Breteuil, an experienced diplomat and a former minister and personal friend of the queen, to secure the intervention of foreign powers against the Revolution. Not wishing to be thrown upon the mercy of a victorious aristocracy, the King warned Vienna not to co-operate with the *émigrés* and devised a counterrevolutionary plan of his own. Louis intended to sneak out of Paris and take shelter with loyal army units on the eastern frontier. Foreign powers would then conduct threatening military demonstrations. Louis, at this point, would "negotiate" with the foreign powers, "prevent" an invasion, and insist upon a full restoration of his authority as the price of continued security. In December the court began its preparations for the escape to the frontier.

In addition to aristocratic and royalist appeals, diplomatic disputes between France and a number of Rhenish princes and the papacy provided further excuses for foreign intervention in French domestic affairs.

By applying in 1790 the laws dealing with the abolition of feudalism and the nationalization of church lands to Alsace, the French Government antagonized many German rulers. France had taken control of Alsace in 1648, but many secular and clerical princes in Germany had retained title to Alsatian estates. In addition, German bishops had continued to wield ecclesiastical authority in the province. Consequently, when the National Assembly declared that its laws applied to Alsace, the Electors of Treves, Mainz, and Cologne, the Bishop of Basel, the Duke of Württemberg, and the Margrave of Baden immediately protested. The Assembly denied the princes' legal claims and instead offered cash compensation, which the princes refused. The princes then called upon the Empire to reassert its rights in Alsace and in December 1790 Leopold supported their claims.

The diplomatic clash with the papacy centered upon the fate of Avignon, a papal enclave on the Rhône River. Radicals in Avignon had expelled the papal legate and requested annexation to France. In the summer of 1791 the French occupied Avignon to quell the riots which had erupted between aristocrats and patriots. Finally, in September, France, with the consent of most of the population, annexed the former papal residence. The monarchs of Europe grew alarmed at the implications of this action, for the French were emphatically asserting the right of peoples to decide their own fate regardless of existing treaties and conventions. Furthermore, France had tacitly expressed a willingness to assist and absorb any region whose inhabitants started a rebellion.

Thus, by the end of 1791, the powers of Europe had numerous motives and excuses for intervening in French affairs. Fear of revolution, appeals for armed support by the *émigrés* and the court, and diplomatic clashes over Alsace and Avignon—any or all of these issues were a call to action. Yet war between France and Europe did not occur for another two years because the French sought to keep the peace, and the great powers had more pressing diplomatic problems.

Deputies in the National Assembly who supported the Revolution and the supremacy of the legislative branch of government wanted a long span of pacific foreign relations in order to complete and stabilize internal reforms. They realized that war would only strengthen the King's hand, for he was still the commander in chief of the armed forces. They also feared that foreign war would produce civil war, since counterrevolutionary elements would co-operate with the state's enemies in order to destroy the new regime. Finally, they knew that France was unprepared for a major conflict. Many noble officers had deserted their posts, the loyalty of those remaining was doubtful, and discipline in lower ranks was collapsing. The patriots could not rely upon the mercenary regiments, and the National Guard lacked proper training.[6] Thus, supporters of the Revolution realized that war could well lead to military collapse and the triumph of counterrevolution.

French diplomacy during the first two years of the Revolution gave ample proof that the Assembly as a whole sought to avoid war. In the spring of 1790, Spain seized several English ships in Nootka Sound on the Pacific coast of North America. William Pitt, George III's first minister, demanded reparations, and when Madrid refused, Britain began to prepare for war. Charles IV then appealed to his ally, Louis XVI. The Assembly, however, refused to risk war to protect Spanish colonial interests in North America, and on May 22, 1790, the

[6] L. Hartmann, *Les officiers de l'armée royale et la Révolution* (Paris, 1903).

deputies made the King's right to declare war subject to legislative approval and issued a decree assuring the world that France would never undertake a war of conquest. In August the Assembly created a Diplomatic Committee to supervise the Minister of Foreign Affairs and the monarch and prevent them from leading the nation into dangerous alliances. The Assembly then offered further proof of its pacific intentions by refusing to assist revolutionary groups in Belgium and Liège. Finally, it handled the problems of Alsace and Avignon with great caution, offering a cash compensation to the German princes and delaying the annexation of Avignon until several months after Pius VI had condemned the Revolution.

Despite their sympathy for Louis and distaste for revolutionary principles, the European powers were at first unwilling to intervene in French affairs, for they had far more pressing problems. In 1787, Catherine II of Russia had gone to war with the Ottoman Empire. Joseph II joined her in 1788. The two monarchs sought the total destruction of Turkish power in Europe. Catherine planned to establish a Greek Empire at Constantinople under her grandson's rule and transform Moldavia and Wallachia into a second satellite state. Joseph hoped to obtain the Ottoman provinces in the western Balkans. The war, however, went badly. After hard fighting, the Austrians managed to take Belgrade but could advance no farther. The Russians stormed the port of Ochakov on the Black Sea but soon afterward their advance also ground to a halt. It was soon apparent that the Turks were capable of continued resistance, and their ability to stave off defeat gave other powers the time and opportunity to intervene.

England desired to keep Russia away from the Mediterranean, and Prussia always opposed Austrian expansion. In 1779, the Prussians had halted an Austrian attempt to annex Bavaria, and in 1785 had frustrated Vienna's plan to exchange Belgium for Bavaria. Moreover, England and Prussia had worked together in 1787 to crush a revolution in the Netherlands, and at the end of 1788 the two powers were prepared to resist Russian and Austrian expansion. In addition, Gustavus III of Sweden was anxious to profit from Catherine's involvement in the Ukraine and Balkans to regain some of his country's lost Baltic provinces.

In June 1788, Gustavus, with the tacit support of England and Prussia, declared war on Catherine. Meanwhile, the Prussians worked diligently to undermine the Hapsburg Empire by offering support to the internal and external foes of Joseph II. Prussian officers secretly helped Belgian revolutionaries organize their armed forces; Frederick William began to contemplate the possibility of sending aid to Hungarian aristocrats, who were vigorously resisting Joseph's drastic reforms of the serf system; a Prussian army moved into Silesia and made ready to march into Hungary or Bohemia; Berlin gave diplomatic support to the Polish Patriot Party, a group seeking to establish a stable government able to resist Austrian and Russian pressure; and finally, in January 1790, Prussia concluded a treaty with the Ottoman Empire whereby the two powers agreed to fight for the complete liberation of Turkish territory. Thus, by the first months of 1790, Prussia was prepared to launch a major war against Austria or to force Vienna to grant huge concessions in return for peace.

Pitt, however, refused to follow his ally's initiatives, for he wished to restore the *status quo* in eastern Europe, prevent Russian and Austrian expansion, and consequently, he was also unwilling to fight for Prussian aggrandizement. Furthermore, the emergence of the Nootka Sound dispute with Spain made him even more anxious to avoid hostilities elsewhere. Consequently, he told Berlin that his government would support no Prussian moves likely to cause a war in eastern Europe. In April 1790, he offered his country's good offices to mediate between Austria and Prussia and restore the prewar *status quo.* Leopold accepted the British offer as a means to extricate himself from a dangerous diplomatic situation and gain time to restore order within his empire. Deserted by his major ally, Frederick William reluctantly also agreed to negotiate.

In July 1790, Prussian and Austrian diplomats met at the small Silesian town of Reichenbach, where the Prussians attempted to salvage something from the collapse of their grandiose schemes by proposing a series of complex territorial exchanges. Austria would take some Turkish provinces and return Galicia to Poland. In return the Poles would give Danzig, Thorn, and Posen to Prussia. The Poles, however, refused to relinquish any territory, and the British, unwilling to allow Prussian expansion in the Baltic, also opposed the exchanges. Prussia, therefore, had no choice but to accept Pitt's plan of restoring the *status quo.* Leopold also accepted the British position and signed an armistice with the Sultan in September. He then made his peace with the Magyar aristocracy by abandoning most of Joseph's reforms and at the end of the year sent his troops to reoccupy Belgium and Liège.

Catherine, however, ignored the other powers, concluded a peace with Sweden, and continued her war against the Turks. Pitt then began to consider direct intervention, and Frederick William, still seeking some territorial gain, associated himself with the new British policy. In March 1791, Pitt, seconded by Berlin, sent an ultimatum to St. Petersburg demanding withdrawal from Ottoman territory. In London, however, the parliamentary opposition raised a tremendous outcry against Pitt's bellicose stand. Encouraged by the Russian ambassador, they insisted that a Balkan war was irrelevant to Britain's real interests, and forced the government to abandon its policy. Catherine was thus able to conclude her campaigns successfully. Her armies invaded Moldavia and Wallachia, defeated the Turkish forces, and in August she signed a preliminary peace with the Sultan. The

Turks gave Ochakov to the Empress and allowed her to advance her western frontier to the Dniester River. These terms were later incorporated into a final treaty signed at Jassy on January 19, 1792. By her successful defiance of England and Prussia, Catherine had gained new lands and freed her army for use against the Poles, who had in May 1791 created a new constitution which established a stronger, more centralized regime.

By the time the eastern crises were over, Pitt had preserved the integrity of the Ottoman Empire; Poland had strengthened its government; Leopold had restored order within his domains; and Catherine had moved her frontiers farther west. Frederick William, however, had gained nothing, had spent vast sums on mobilization, and found himself diplomatically isolated. Consequently the Hohenzollern monarch decided to adopt an entirely new diplomatic stance.

In his constant search for new souls and provinces, Frederick William planned to use the revolution in France as a lever to obtain an alliance with Leopold and new territories in the west. As early as September 1790, he had proposed joint intervention to Leopold. In return for the restoration of Louis XVI's power, Prussia asked for the duchies of Berg and Jülich and suggested that Austria take equivalent compensation from France. Leopold had been too involved with his domestic and international problems to take this proposal seriously, but in the spring of 1791 he was willing to listen to renewed Prussian offers.

His readiness to contemplate an alliance with his recent foe was based upon a number of factors. First of all he realized that his unilateral peace with the Turks had ruptured his alliance with Catherine and that a league with Prussia was the only way to prevent a Russo-Prussian combination. Leopold was also concerned with the fate of Poland. He knew that Catherine intended to destroy the new Polish constitution, and he wanted to secure Prussian support in preserving Poland as a counterweight to Russian influence in eastern Europe. Finally, Leopold was becoming increasingly apprehensive over the course of events in France. His concern with the erosion of the Bourbon crown's power derived not only from his dynastic connections with the French ruling house but also from his diplomatic situation. Austria and France had been allies ever since 1756, but although the alliance had never been broken, it had virtually ceased to function after 1763. Leopold realized that if he restored the Bourbon monarchy, Louis would have to remain dependent upon his savior. Leopold would then be in a position to revive the alliance and become the senior partner in it. He would also be able to employ France as a counter to Prussia in the west while using Prussia to preserve Poland and check Russia in the east.

On June 11, 1791, Leopold met with Bischoffswerder, a trusted agent of the Berlin court, to discuss the terms of an alliance. The Emperor and the Prussian diplomat agreed to a preliminary defensive alliance including a provision for mutual aid if either contracting party experienced internal rebellions. The two powers also decided to guarantee Polish independence and committed themselves to a joint effort to form a European concert to regulate affairs in France. Finally, Leopold agreed to a personal meeting with the Prussian monarch at the Saxon town of Pillnitz in August. Leopold, at this point, was anxious to conclude a final treaty with Frederick William because he had received a letter from Marie Antoinette informing him of the royal family's imminent flight from Paris, and he wanted to be in a position to aid Louis's counterrevolution with a multipower military demonstration to terrorize the Assembly.

As the time for the Austro-Prussian meeting approached the need for concerted action grew more urgent than ever, for Louis's attempt to launch a royalist coup had turned into a fiasco. Louis and his family had escaped from Paris on the evening of June 20. Heading toward loyal army units on the eastern frontier, the royal coach lumbered along at seven miles per hour. Cavalry pickets sent to escort the royal party got lost, and on the evening of June 21 a postmaster halted the royal party in the provincial town of Varennes. Government officials placed the King under arrest and escorted him back to Paris under guard.

In the capital, news of the sovereign's flight and capture provoked a major outburst of antiroyalist sentiment. Most of the deputies, however, preferred to retain Louis as King, for they realized that if they deposed him, they would have to grant political rights to the less affluent sections of society where republican sentiment was the strongest. The Assembly also feared that any steps against the crown would bring foreign intervention. Consequently, when a crowd gathered on the Champ de Mars on July 17 to demand Louis's deposition, the National Guard fired on it and dispersed the meeting. The Assembly, dominated by the moderate Feuillant faction, then proceeded to suppress republican agitation and after accepting the fiction that Louis had been a victim of kidnappers, restored the King to his throne. Yet despite the triumph of the moderates, France was more deeply divided than ever. Many Feuillant leaders began to demand conservative revisions of the Constitution, while radicals called for a second revolution.

In addition to deepening political and social conflicts within the nation, the Varennes incident and its aftermath also brought French affairs to the front of the international scene. Leopold was especially concerned about the growth of antimonarchical sentiment in France not only because of the blows struck against the principles of monarchy but also because the weakening of the French Government would deprive Austria of a potential ally. The Emperor therefore acted quickly in an effort to frighten the Assembly into preserving the throne. From Padua on July 6, he appealed to the crowned heads of Europe to take common action to save the Bourbon monarchy. On July 25, Leopold signed the preliminary June agreements and set off to join Frederick William at Pillnitz. The two monarchs had thus publicly agreed upon the necessity of direct intervention to combat the Revolution.

Despite his calls for action Leopold nevertheless pursued a cautious and moderate policy at Pillnitz. He wanted to strengthen Louis's position, but he realized that bellicose moves might rouse the French populace to fury and lead to the complete destruction of the monarchy. Furthermore, the Feuillant leaders informed him that they would retain Louis in office if the powers did not increase tensions by adopting a threatening stance. Leopold also realized that if he resorted to arms, Prussia would join him and demand compensation either in France, Germany, or Poland. Not wishing to strengthen Prussia at the expense of his own actual or potential friends, Leopold concluded that he had further reason to avoid war. His objective at Pillnitz, then, was to devise a policy statement pacific enough to satisfy the French moderates yet sufficiently strong to frighten the radicals and keep Prussia loyal to its new Austrian alliance.

In the first days of the conference Leopold rejected a proposal from Artois, who by his insistence had virtually compelled Leopold to invite him to the conference. The Count called upon the Emperor to proclaim a regency for France coupled with preparations for invasion, a policy which might well have produced a violent reaction in France—precisely the result that Leopold wanted to avoid. The Austrian and Prussian rulers then proceeded to devise a common declaration, which they issued on August 27. The Pillnitz Declaration announced that the predicament of the French King was an object of common concern to all of the European courts. Leopold and Frederick William expressed the hope that the other powers in conjunction with Austria and Prussia would seek the most effective means to restore the liberty of the French sovereign. "Then and in that case," the declaration concluded, Berlin and Vienna would implement the policy of the European congress.[7]

The statement fulfilled Leopold's desires, for although it sounded quite belligerent, the call for agreement among all the major powers rendered it largely meaningless. Leopold knew full well that all the powers would never agree on a common course of action and that he would not in fact have to intervene in France. Furthermore, a secret article of the Pillnitz Declaration committed both parties to support the candidacy of a member of the Saxon ruling family for the Polish throne. Thus Pillnitz produced a seeming triumph for Leopold's foreign policy. He had kept Prussia tied to his own policy in the west and gained additional security for Poland. Finally, the declaration of August 27 was at least in part responsible for a temporary stabilization of French political life.

After Pillnitz, the French Constituent Assembly did restore Louis to his throne, and on September 14 the King accepted the new Constitution. Louis then proceeded to adopt the policy of ruling as a constitutional monarch and even ordered his brothers to return home. The King evidently sought to increase his popularity before undertaking an attempt to alter the Constitution in his favor at a later date.[8] Despite Louis's motives, his policy did have the immediate effect of producing greater tranquillity, and when the Constituent Assembly adjourned at the end of September many observers

[7] The full text of the declaration including the secret articles appears in Leopold Neumann, *Recueil des traités et conventions conclus par l'Autriche* (Leipzig, 1855), I.

[8] Feuillet de Conches, ed., *Louis XVI, Marie Antoinette et Madame Elizabeth,* IV, p. 99. The Queen never did accept the Constitution and on two occasions, October 19 and November 2, called upon the Emperor for an armed congress. For the moment, however, neither Louis nor Leopold paid much heed to her. See Ibid., pp. 212–14 and 230–31. See also A. R. von Arneth, ed., *Marie Antoinette, Joseph II, und Leopold II ihr Briefwechsel* (Leipzig, 1866).

hoped that the Revolution was finally over. Leopold was highly satisfied at the turn of events in France and suspended all projects of intervention. On November 12 Count Kaunitz, the Austrian Foreign Minister, issued a circular letter to his ambassadors stating that the French people had become more moderate and that Louis XVI was secure.

But while both Leopold and Kaunitz believed that the policy of threatening to intervene had produced stable conditions in France, they had gravely miscalculated the temper of the French populace. Most Frenchmen missed the significance of the qualifying phrase in the Pillnitz Declaration. Rather, they regarded the declaration as a clear threat of war in the near future. *Emigré* statements representing invasion as imminent strengthened this assumption. Finally, in the winter of 1791, numerous political factions in France became anxious to capitalize on the growing war psychosis, for they believed that a foreign war would provide an excellent means of their attaining political power at home.

When the Legislative Assembly met for the first time in October 1791, 130 deputies registered as members of the Jacobin Club. The Jacobins wanted to liberalize the Constitution by giving political rights to the lower class, and many of them advocated war with the Hapsburgs. Jacques Pierre Brissot, an ambitious lawyer, journalist, and deputy from Paris, led the prowar Jacobins. Brissot and his followers felt that war would be profitable for the businessmen, merchants, and financiers who supported their clique. The Brissotins also realized that if they could convince the public and the Assembly to support their militant foreign policy the King would have to appoint a Brissotin ministry. Furthermore, war would enable the government to take drastic measures against the domestic enemies of the Revolution and would force the monarch to reveal his true attitude toward the new regime. If, as Brissot suspected, Louis was hostile to the Constitution, the Assembly could depose him and establish a republic. Finally, Brissot felt that a successful war against Austria would enhance French power and win continued popular support for his clique.[9] For Brissot, war was a means to destroy the counterrevolution, liberalize the regime, increase national power, and secure his own faction's future.

Other groups in the Assembly were ill prepared to resist Brissot's calls for action. The 264 Feuillant deputies were deeply divided among themselves. Some wanted to preserve the domestic and international *status quo;* others desired to crush the radicals and restore a large measure of royal authority, and some were not adverse to war if they could then turn the army against their foes at home. The 345 independent deputies were suspicious of the King, believed that foreign courts were preparing to invade France to fulfill the Pillnitz Declaration, and were ready to follow politicians who called for harsh measures against the enemies of the nation.

The first overt move in the Brissotin campaign to produce a foreign war was a resolution of November 29, calling upon the King to summon the Elector of Treves to dissolve armed *émigré* bands assembling in his domains. The Brissotins assumed that the Elector would appeal to Leopold, that Leopold would support him, and war would follow.

The radicals would not, however, have convinced the Assembly to pass the resolution without the support of another prowar clique led by the Marquis de Lafayette and the Count of Narbonne. These two generals had

[9] Brissot and his collaborators have often been referred to as Girondists or the Gironde because several of Brissot's important followers came from the department of the Gironde. In the 1790s, however, the terms Brissotin and Rolandist (collaborators of the Rolands, who were in turn allies of Brissot) were more common. Use of the word Girondist to apply to all the prowar radicals and foes of Robespierre was a postrevolutionary development. In fact, Brissot did not lead a unified party. Rather, he was a leading figure in a loose, shifting coalition of like-minded politicians. See M. J. Sydenham, *The Girondins* (London, 1961).

originally supported the Revolution but by 1791 had come to desire a more conservative regime. Supported by a number of Feuillants, they wanted to launch a limited war against the Rhineland princes and, after a short triumphal campaign, turn their troops against domestic radicals. After restoring a large measure of royal authority, Lafayette and Narbonne expected to become the powers behind the throne. For tactical purposes they decided to lend their essential support to Brissot's followers and joined them in calling upon Louis to threaten Treves.

To the surprise of both groups Louis responded quickly and favorably to their resolution. On December 9 he appointed Narbonne Minister of War and on December 14 announced to the Assembly that he had sent an ultimatum to Treves giving the Elector the choice of dispersing the *émigrés* within one month or war.

Louis accepted the bellicose policy of the Brissotins because he too had come to regard a war as the best means of attaining political power at home. The growth of radical sentiment had convinced him that his policy of ruling as a constitutional monarch until public opinion shifted in his favor was doomed to failure. He therefore decided to support the warlike factions, but in contrast to the Brissotins and the generals' clique, Louis wanted not victory but defeat for French arms. He hoped that an armed congress of major powers would defeat his armies and force the people to turn to the crown as a mediator. Louis would then save France from invasion in return for a complete restoration of royal authority. In order to force the powers to act, he sanctioned the ultimatum to Treves, and on the same day, he ordered one of his secret agents to inform the Emperor that he wanted the Elector to reject the French demands.[10]

Meanwhile antiwar groups fought a desperate but losing battle to keep the peace. In the Jacobin Club Maxi-

[10] See J. Flammermont, *Négociations secrètes de Louis XVI et du baron Breteuil, décembre 1791–juillet 1792* (Paris, 1885).

milien Robespierre, a lawyer from Arras, former member of the Constituent Assembly, and advanced democrat, argued that foreigners would resist armed missionaries and that war, far from being a triumphal parade, would lead to long and bitter campaigns. He castigated Brissot for co-operating with the generals, said that Frenchmen should concentrate upon domestic reform, and predicted that war would inevitably lead to the establishment of a military dictatorship.[11] He failed, however, to sway the Jacobins. Brissot's glittering promises of easy victory, profit, and power influenced the radical deputies far more than Robespierre's prophecies of disaster, and they continued to support the policy of war with the Hapsburgs. A few Feuillants tried and failed to convince the King and their own colleagues that continued peace was essential for the security and stability of France. The pro-war factions were thus able to carry a proposal through the Assembly calling for the mobilization of several field armies.

Leopold's policy inadvertently strengthened the bellicose elements in France. Because his diplomatic agents in France had failed to keep him informed of the true nature of French public opinion and of the shift of the political balance of power, the Emperor continued to believe that he could avoid war, terrorize the radicals, and strengthen the moderates by assuming a threatening diplomatic stance. Consequently, on December 21, Leopold informed the French Government that the Elector of Treves had agreed to disband the companies of armed *émigrés* but added that, in the future, the Austrian army would protect the German princes against French aggression.[12]

[11] G. Michon, *Correspondance de Maximilien et Augustin Robespierre* (Paris, 1926), I, pp. 140–41; and M. Bouloiseau, G. Lefebvre, and A. Soboul, eds., *Oeuvres de Maximilien Robespierre* (Paris, 1953), VIII, pp. 47–64.

[12] *Archives des Affaires Etrangères* (hereafter *A.A.E.*) *Correspondance politique* 363. This volume contains the official diplo-

The policy of threats, so successful at the time of Pillnitz, failed to intimidate the Legislative Assembly. In fact, most of the deputies regarded the Austrian note as an effort to dictate the nation's foreign and domestic policy. The Assembly, therefore, proceeded to grant increased funds for the army and called upon Antoine de Lessart, the moderate pro-Feuillant Foreign Minister, to implement a Brissotin policy of sending special envoys to Prussia and England. At Berlin the agents were to win over international opinion by offering command of the French forces to the Duke of Brunswick—one of Europe's most famous generals and an acknowledged sympathizer with the Revolution's ideals—and convince Frederick William to remain neutral in any Franco-Austrian war. The mission to London was to propose an Anglo-French concert to regulate European affairs.[13] On January 14, 1792, a prowar deputy proposed that France call upon the Emperor to state, by March 1, whether or not he intended to abide by the alliance treaty of 1756 and renounce projects to form a European concert against France. The French would construe an unsatisfactory reply or no reply at all as a declaration of war.[14]

The Foreign Minister, an advocate of peace, replied to the Austrian note on January 21. He rejected the Emperor's attempt to intervene in French affairs but assured him that France wanted peace. The Assembly, however, was not satisfied with de Lessart's mild position. Following the lead of the prowar factions, the representatives, on January 25, proceeded to adopt the bellicose proposals of the fourteenth, thereby increasing international tension and furthering the drift toward war.[15]

---

matic correspondence between France and Austria as well as the official decrees of the Assembly and the correspondence between the French Foreign Minister and the ambassador in Vienna.

[13] Brunswick turned down the French offer while England promised nothing more than neutrality in case of war.

[14] *A.A.E. Correspondance politique* 363.

[15] Ibid.

The Emperor meanwhile continued to play into the hands of the warlike groups in Paris by seeking to organize an armed congress which would overawe the French radicals. On January 17, Leopold ordered the mobilization of forty thousand men and pressed the Berlin court to conclude a definitive alliance treaty. Prussia, anxious for a war that would provide the opportunity to exterminate the Revolution and seize indemnities, agreed and on February 2 concluded an alliance with Austria. The treaty stipulated that the parties would provide mutual protection against third-power aggression and internal rebellion. It also guaranteed a free constitution for Poland. This provision, by stipulating *a* free constitution rather than *the* Constitution of May 1791 left the way open for interference in Polish affairs. Leopold disliked this provision, but he had to consent to it in order to gain Prussian agreement to another article of the treaty whereby both courts agreed to promote a European concert to regulate French affairs.

Having secured Prussia's support, Leopold replied to the moderate French note of January 21. The Austrian statement of February 14 denounced the Parisian radicals and declared that Austria and Prussia would work together to protect Europe from revolution and restore Louis to his rightful place as head of the French state.[16]

Once again Leopold failed to intimidate the French. In fact, his note dealt a mortal blow to the moderates. The independent deputies rallied behind the Brissotins and demanded immediate action against Austria. Narbonne, after assuring the deputies that the nation's armies were fully prepared for action, began to press his fellow ministers for a declaration of war.[17] He also demanded that Louis purge his cabinet of royalists and advocates of continued peace. In a surprise move the King demanded Narbonne's resignation on March 9. This did

[16] Ibid.

[17] *Rapport fait par le ministre de la guerre L. de Narbonne à l'Assemblé Nationale le 11 janvier 1792* (Paris, 1792).

not, however, mark a shift in royal policy. The King still wanted a war, but he sought to prevent the outbreak of hostilities, retain the support of the moderates who opposed Narbonne, and keep the radicals from power until the Austrians and Prussians were fully prepared to come to his rescue.

The Brissotins and the generals' clique quickly struck back. They accused the Foreign Minister of complicity in a royal plot against the Constitution and launched impeachment proceedings against him. Other moderate ministers, wishing to avoid the same fate, hastened to resign. To avoid the ire of the left and retain his throne until the foreign courts intervened in his favor, Louis felt he had no alternative except capitulation to the left. He therefore confided the foreign affairs ministry to Charles François Dumouriez.

A former soldier and diplomat, Dumouriez intended to wage a brief victorious campaign and then use his army to restore royal authority. His policy differed from that of the other generals in two respects. First of all, Dumouriez expected that he, rather than Lafayette or Narbonne, would guide the destiny of France after the military coup. Secondly, Dumouriez wanted to wage his war in Austrian Belgium instead of in the Rhineland, for he dreamed of creating a state of his own in Flanders. His desire to fight in the Low Countries and his need for domestic popular support led him to conclude a tactical alliance with the Brissotins. He therefore proceeded to engineer the appointment of Brissot's collaborators to the finance and interior ministries. The accession of Dumouriez and the Brissotins to ministerial rank marked the final triumph of those factions that sought a war against the Hapsburgs. Conversely, the cause of the antiwar moderates and left became hopeless.

Meanwhile, events outside of France contributed to the inevitable drift into war. On March 1, 1792, Leopold II died after a brief illness. His son and heir, the twenty-four-year-old Francis II, was less prudent, less experienced in foreign affairs, and more bellicose than his father. He soon transformed Leopold's policy of intimidation into one of deeds and informed the Prussian King that he was willing to contribute fifty thousand men to a joint campaign against France.

At this juncture, Catherine's determination to undo the Polish Constitution of 1791, Frederick William's desire for new territories, and Francis' need to secure rapid Prussian consent to his plans for war forced Austria to abandon its policy of preserving a strong independent Poland. The Russian Empress in February had invited Frederick William to participate in a joint congress to regulate Polish affairs. Frederick William then decided to insist on compensation for the costs of a western campaign at Poland's expense, and on March 12 told Catherine that his government would co-operate with her on matters pertaining to Poland. Francis, in turn, realized that he would have to abandon the Poles if he were to obtain Prussia's help against the French. In an attempt to find equivalent indemnities for his own state, Francis on March 21 gave his preliminary consent to a Russo-Prussian partition of Poland and proclaimed his interest in reviving the old Belgian-Bavarian exchange plan. Although the Hapsburgs and Hohenzollerns signed no formal treaty settling the question of future indemnities, both powers were for the moment satisfied and proceeded to ready themselves for action in the west.

Already, on March 18, Kaunitz had delivered a note to the French ambassador. The note, written in reply to the French demand of January 25 for a statement of future Hapsburg policy, declared that Vienna would not abandon plans to form a concert to regulate affairs in France. This message crossed a letter from Dumouriez demanding that Vienna repudiate schemes for intervention.[18] After this bitter exchange, war became imminent. Additional communications between Paris and Vienna were

[18] *A.A.E. Correspondance politique 363.*

mere formalities to set the stage for the actual outbreak of hostilities. On March 27 Dumouriez demanded a response to earlier questions concerning Austria's intentions, and Kaunitz replied that his note of the eighteenth was his final answer to all French questions. Early in April Austria and Prussia agreed to confide the supreme command of their field armies to the Duke of Brunswick and began to plan the actual invasion of France. Meanwhile, Dumouriez told the Council of Ministers on April 16 that Francis II had definitely broken the alliance of 1756 and was intent on war. France, he said, had no choice but to resort to arms and he asked for a declaration of war. On April 20, 1792, Louis appeared before the Legislative Assembly and requested the declaration. That evening after a brief debate the deputies voted overwhelmingly for war.

The French Government issued its declaration of war against Francis in his capacity as the King of Bohemia and Hungary in an attempt to confine hostilities to a clash between itself and the Hapsburgs while the states of the Empire remained neutral. The plan failed, for Prussia quickly mobilized and agreed to join Austria in an invasion of France. The two powers planned to march on Paris in July.

The war, which was to last almost without interruption until 1815, producing extensive changes in the political and diplomatic structure of Europe, did not, ironically, begin as a clash between two crusading ideologies. Nor was the commencement of hostilities marked by an effort of a single power to attain continental hegemony. The French did not take the field seeking to conquer and revolutionize all of Europe. Rather, various factions regarded a foreign war as a useful tool to obtain power at home. The desire to export the Revolution was at best a secondary motive, and the Brissot clique, Louis XVI, Lafayette, Narbonne, and Dumouriez were concerned primarily with the domestic power struggle.

Until Leopold's death, Austria was very reluctant to fight. Leopold had been concerned primarily with the security of his own domains. He had supported a liberal reforming group in Poland and conservative factions in France in efforts to shore up regimes which would be useful to him diplomatically. When he tried to intervene in internal French affairs, he was less concerned with the safety of the Bourbons and the principles of royal authority than with his own power in international affairs. Leopold's policy of verbal intervention failed, and the less able Francis II inherited a dangerous and explosive situation. As prowar factions gained strength in France, the Emperor came to the conclusion that only military intervention could preserve the Bourbons. Frederick William of Prussia, although opposed to revolutionary ideology, declared war on France not to defend the principles of legitimacy but to reap territorial and economic gains. Catherine of Russia also opposed the Revolution and encouraged Austria and Prussia to destroy the Assembly. Catherine's major concern, however, was to involve Berlin and Vienna in a war in the west, thereby gaining for herself a free hand in Poland. Thus, for the crowned heads of Europe, the war began as a continuation of traditional power politics and not as an ideological crusade.

The belligerents fully expected that the ensuing war would be brief and that at the end of hostilities statesmen would sit down at the conference table to decide the fate of provinces, people, and governments. Nobody really believed that April 20, 1792, was to mark the opening of twenty-three years of unrelenting hostilities.

CHAPTER 2

ON THE BRINK OF DEFEAT

Nine days after the declaration of war, French armies marched into Belgium and into a series of catastrophic defeats. On the first day of operations, the soldiers of the Army of the North sighted Austrian cavalry pickets, panicked, and fled back across the frontier after killing one of their own generals, who tried to stem the retreat.[1] The total collapse of the French offensive revealed that their regiments that took the field with such high confidence were in fact tragically unprepared for war.

Despite the claims of generals and politicians the army in the spring of 1792 lacked men, training, and competent leaders. On paper the French forces numbered 150,000 regulars, 101,000 volunteers raised in 1791, and 87 additional volunteer battalions mobilized in 1792. In reality, field commanders could find only 94,700 men ready for action.[2] Even these troops lacked training, for discipline had declined among the regulars, and the volunteers had not fully learned the arts of war. A serious shortage of officers made it virtually impossible to train the rank and file in the field. By the spring of 1792 over 50 per cent of the officer cadre, most of whom were of noble birth, had left the country. With the exception of the artillery corps, which contained many bourgeois officers who remained loyal to the Revolution, the service arms were drastically short of experienced leaders.[3] The

[1] For an excellent study of the first months of the war see A. Chuquet, *La première invasion prussienne* (*11 Août–2 Septembre 1792*) (Paris, n.d.).

[2] *Ministère de la Guerre Etat-Major de l'Armée Archives Historiques* (hereafter referred to as *Min. de la Guerre A.H.*), *ordres de bataille des armées en campagne, 1792–1815, carton* X^p3.

[3] See S. Wilkinson, *The French Army Before Napoleon* (Lon-

armed forces were thus unable to serve as an effective instrument of aggressive national policy, and their ability to protect the nation from foreign conquest was, at best, minimal.

In the summer of 1792, France's salvation came not from the efforts of her leaders but rather from the failure of her foes to act rapidly and decisively. Francis and Frederick William spent vital months discussing the division of the spoils of victory and neglected the immediate problem of compelling the submission of their primary enemy.

The two rulers had previously agreed that Prussia would obtain compensations in Poland while Austria would engineer the Belgian-Bavarian exchange. In April, the two courts had not yet worked out the precise details of these territorial changes, and in the following month Catherine of Russia threw their calculations into complete disarray. Determined to overturn the Polish Constitution of 1791, the Tsarina in collaboration with some reactionary Polish magnates sent a hundred-thousand-man army into Poland. By July 22 the Russians had forced the King of Poland to surrender and were in complete control of the country.

Catherine's coup alarmed Berlin and Vienna, for Frederick William feared the loss of Polish compensation, and Francis gloomily contemplated the possibilities that Russia would keep all of Poland, thereby upsetting the power balance in the east, while Prussia demanded indemnities in Germany, thus destroying the *status quo* in the west. Consequently, Austria and Prussia began a feverish round of negotiations with Russia and each other in a desperate attempt to resolve the Polish question before it was too late to launch a summer campaign against France.[4]

---

don, 1915), and M. Lauerma, *L'artillerie de campagne française* (Helsinki, 1956) for discussions of emigration and the state of the various services.

[4] For a complete study of the Second Partition see R. H. Lord,

On July 14, 1792, as crowds in Paris celebrated the anniversary of the fall of the Bastille, the last coronation of a Holy Roman Emperor took place at Frankfurt. Five days later Austrian and Prussian diplomats met at Mainz to solve the vexing issue of compensation for the expense of the forthcoming campaign in France. Both sides quickly agreed to the general principle of equal indemnities, but clashes over details soon beclouded this accord. Austria felt that Prussia's claims to Polish provinces were too extensive, and the Prussians objected to the Austrian demand for Ansbach and Bayreuth in addition to Bavaria. Furthermore, both sides began to deal separately with Russia on the Polish question.[5] The failure to agree on compensations and the secret dealings with Catherine led to mutual suspicion in the Austro-Prussian coalition, and the ultimate fate of Poland loomed so important that Berlin and Vienna decided to keep the bulk of their armies at home instead of sending them against France. Although the Prussian army numbered over 170,000 men, Frederick William committed but 42,000 men to the war in the west. Francis, with about 200,000 troops, used only 70,000 of them to fight the French.[6] Even with the addition of 5500 Hessians and 4500 French *émigrés*, the allied force numbered only 97,000. These troops had to accomplish the Herculean tasks of defeating the French armies, taking Paris, restoring Louis XVI, and keeping order until a final settlement. Thus, mutual

---

The Second Partition of Poland (Cambridge, 1915). See also K. Lutostanski, *Les partages de la Pologne et la lutte pour l'indépendance* (Paris, 1918).

[5] See Lord, *The Second Partition*. The Hapsburg policy is put forth in the documents edited by A. R. von Vivenot, *Quellen zur Geschichte der Deutschen Kaiserpolitik Oesterreichs* (Vienna, 1873), III. On Russian policy, see the editorial comments of F. Martens, *Recueil des traités et Conventions conclus par la Russie avec les puissances étrangères* (St. Petersburg, 1875), II.

[6] *Archives Nationales* (hereafter referred to as *A.N.*) *AF II carton 281 dossier 2346* contains an official account of the campaign of 1792.

suspicion, concern over Poland's fate, and fear of Russian policy in the east imposed a long delay upon the Austro-Prussian invasion and led the two courts to retain the bulk of their armies at home.

Negotiations, suspicion, and vacillation prevented the Austrian and Prussian armies from crossing the French frontier until August 19. Despite the fact that the campaigning season was well advanced and that a rapid march on Paris was vital, the lack of decisive leadership at governmental levels was reflected in the field command. The Prussian contingent, though well trained and bearing the formidable reputation earned under Frederick the Great, encumbered itself with a huge, slow-moving supply train. Its artillery was numerically weak and the material obsolescent. The Duke of Brunswick, the Prussian commander and commander in chief of the whole allied force, had learned the art of war during the days of the Great Frederick and preferred cautious marches and sieges to decisive field encounters. His advanced age—he was fifty-seven—served only to increase his cautious approach to warfare. Furthermore, his pro-French sympathies probably posed a psychological barrier to a rapid and decisive approach to the campaign. The Austrian corps of thirty thousand men that accompanied the forty-two thousand troops of the Prussian invasion force also followed the cautious approach to campaigning common to most Old Regime armies.[7] Thus, even after entering France, the allied expeditionary corps advanced at a pace that was slow even by eighteenth-century standards.

Allied procrastination led indirectly to the collapse of one of their chief political goals—the restoration of royal authority in France. By the time Brunswick entered France, the French had already destroyed the remnants of the Bourbon regime. In June, Louis, in an attempt to

[7] See Chuquet, *La première invasion,* and Kellerman's account of the Valmy campaign in A.N. *AF III carton 281 dossier 2346.*

hold the radicals in check until the allies liberated him, dismissed the Brissotin ministers and Dumouriez and appointed in their place a moderate Feuillant ministry. The Brissotins retaliated by appealing to the Parisian populace, which was suspicious of the King and alarmed by the rising cost of living. Once the sans-culottes were mobilized it was impossible to restrain them. Continued inflation, the Brunswick Manifesto threatening the destruction of Paris if anyone harmed the royal family, and Lafayette's denunciations of the radicals served only to arouse further the ire of the Parisian sections. The Feuillant ministry fell on July 10, and the Brissotins undertook secret talks with the court in order to regain power. Since they hoped to return to office in alliance with the crown, the Brissotins abandoned their allies and tried to halt the popular movement, but it was too late. After the Assembly refused to suspend the King and arrest Lafayette, the sans-culottes, supported by volunteers who were passing through Paris on the way to the front, rose in rebellion. They seized control of the city government, established an insurrectionary commune, and on August 10, 1792, stormed the Tuileries. Louis fled his palace while at the front in northeastern France Lafayette sought refuge with the Austrians, who promptly threw him into prison. The leaders of the second revolution then forced the Assembly to suspend the monarch and call elections for a National Convention that would decide Louis's fate and write a democratic constitution for the nation.

Ironically, the Revolution of August 10 marked the defeat of those factions which had sought to use foreign war as an avenue to domestic power. Hostilities, however, continued and an interim regime, consisting of the Parisian Commune and a Provisional Executive Council of the defunct Legislative Assembly, guided the destiny of France until the National Convention could constitute itself.

The leading figure in the provisional regime was Georges Jacques Danton. Despite his checkered past, which included shady financial dealings and contacts with the court, *émigrés,* and the Duke of Orléans, Danton, a brilliant orator with a talent for rapid and bold decision, had become a leading radical spokesman, and as representative of the Commune he dominated the Provisional Executive Council. At this juncture the government had to make a crucial decision. The Prussians and Austrians were advancing, and the French armies seemed unable to stop them. Many members of the government wanted to abandon Paris and retreat to the Loire. Danton, however, insisted upon meeting the allies in eastern France and holding Paris at all costs. He knew full well that Paris was the heart and soul of the Revolution and that its loss would lead to the complete collapse of the national defense and to the destruction of the New Regime. With the nation's fate in the balance Danton successfully resisted all proposals to retreat and convinced his colleagues to stand and fight in front of Paris. Reinforcements began to flow to the field armies; the government started to requisition arms, horses, and other vital commodities, and special civilian commissioners joined the armies to check on the loyalty of the officers and encourage the men. Under Danton's direction the government geared itself for a desperate effort to halt the slow but inexorable advance of Brunswick's army.[8]

The allied army had finally begun to move. Brunswick planned to push through Luxembourg, cross the Meuse, and then march directly on Paris. On August 23 the garrison at Longwy capitulated to the Prussians after a siege lasting only a single day, and by August 29 Brunswick's army stood before the fortifications of Verdun. Unprepared for long resistance, the defenders surrendered on September 2. The loss of Verdun deprived the

[8] For a discussion of the origins of the civilian commissioners see J. Godechot, *Les Commissaires aux armées sous le Directoire* (Paris, 1938), I; and H. Wallon, *Les représentants du peuple en mission et la justice révolutionnaire dans les départments* (Paris, 1899), I.

French of the Meuse River barrier, and Dumouriez, who had gone to the front after his dismissal from the foreign ministry, fell back to the passes of the Argonne Forest, the last natural obstacle between the allied armies and Paris.

On September 12, however, Austrian troops broke through one of the passes, thereby splitting the French front. Dumouriez then abandoned the Argonne and moved his entire force south to the small village of Sainte-Menehoulde. From his new position he could await reinforcements from Alsace led by General François Kellermann and threaten Brunswick's flank and rear if the Prussians attempted to advance directly on Paris. On September 19 the Duke ordered his army forward. His objective was to push south, destroy the French field army, and then march on Paris.

As the Prussian advance guard probed through the fog on the morning of September 20 they came under French artillery fire near the town of Valmy. Kellermann, with thirty-six thousand men and fifty-eight cannon, had arrived from Alsace and bivouacked around Valmy in order to block any Prussian attempt to strike at Dumouriez's left flank and cut him off from Paris. Brunswick then brought up his main force of thirty-four thousand and prepared to assault the French position.

After an initial artillery barrage, Brunswick sent his infantry forward. Had the Prussians reached the French lines they could in all probability have shattered the ill-trained French foot soldiers, but Brunswick had not taken into account the effectiveness of Kellermann's field artillery. The gunners, the best-trained and -disciplined element in the entire French army, poured a withering barrage into the Prussian assault lines. The Prussians wavered and finally retreated. The Duke's artillery then took up the battle and in the early afternoon destroyed a French munitions cart. Kellermann's infantry began to waver, but his artillery quickly resumed its fire. The infantrymen resumed their posts, and when the smoke from the explosion cleared, the Prussians could see that the French lines remained unshaken. Unwilling to risk his men against a second French cannonade, Brunswick canceled all further attacks.

About three hundred French and two hundred Prussians died at Valmy. The opposing infantries never fired a shot, and the whole battle hinged on a single brief artillery duel. Nevertheless, the clash at Valmy was decisive. Brunswick did not attack again and ten days later withdrew toward the Meuse. The Battle of Valmy justified Danton's insistence upon defending Paris and saved the Republic, which had come into existence as the guns were thundering less than a hundred miles away. While the battle raged at Valmy, the National Convention had met for the first time in Paris, and two days later the deputies proclaimed that France would henceforth be a republic.

As the French celebrated their first military victory, new divisions arose to plague the Austro-Russian coalition. As the Prussians limped back toward the Meuse, Dumouriez, hoping to enhance his personal prestige by convincing them to evacuate France and perhaps even make peace and form an anti-Austrian alliance, sent out feelers for negotiations. The Prussians responded favorably, but when Frederick William learned of the proclamation of the Republic he broke off the preliminary talks on September 28. The fear that Dumouriez would attack his army, which was badly weakened by dysentery, convinced the Prussian King to resume talks on the following day. The government at Paris had meanwhile learned of their general's initial diplomatic overtures and although they suspected Prussian motives, they felt it was worth the effort to try to come to terms with one of the Republic's major enemies. The Executive Council therefore gave Dumouriez full powers to treat with Prussia. Talks proceeded until the fourth week of October, but at the end of this period France and Prussia were still at war. The Prussian ruler had never really intended

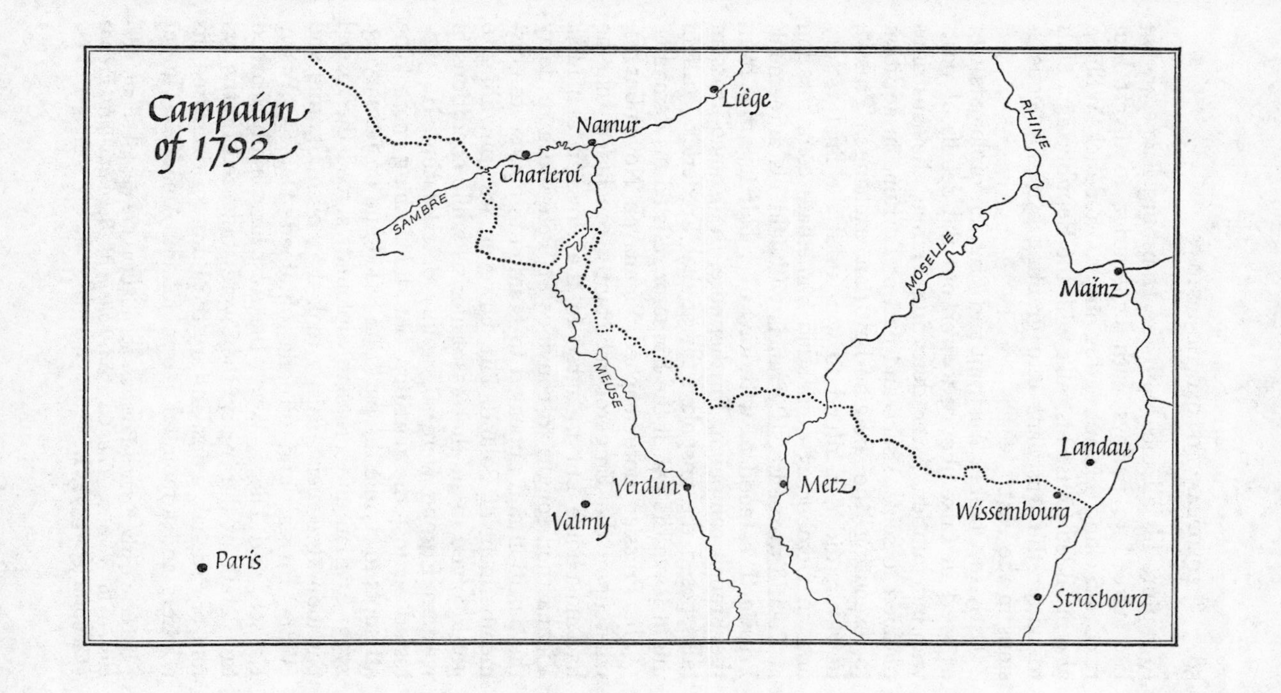
Campaign of 1792
Liège
Namur
Charleroi
SAMBRE
MEUSE
Verdun
Valmy
Paris
Metz
MOSELLE
RHINE
Maïnz
Landau
Wissembourg
Strasbourg

to rupture his alliance with the Hapsburg Emperor. He had agreed to parleys with Dumouriez to divert him from attacking his retreating army. Frederick William also intended to use his talks with the Republic as a club to batter the Austrians into granting extensive concessions in the east.[9]

Early in October Austrian and Prussian diplomats met at Merl in Luxembourg to iron out the details of postwar indemnities. After defeating France, the Austrians planned to seize Alsace and part of Lorraine in addition to executing the Belgian-Bavarian exchange. Prussia, however, did not intend to wait until the final victory and on October 25 demanded immediate compensation at Poland's expense. If Francis withheld his agreement, Prussia threatened to withdraw over half its army from the French campaign. Furthermore, the Franco-Prussian talks posed the unspoken threat that Frederick William might leave the war if the Emperor resisted his demands.

The Prussian note reached Vienna on November 20, whereupon the Emperor reluctantly concluded that he had no choice but to agree to the Prussian demands. Vienna then sought to convince St. Petersburg to delay the partition and appealed to London to oppose the dismemberment of Poland. Pitt, however, was unwilling to get involved in another eastern crisis while conditions in western Europe were so rapidly deteriorating. He protested against the partition but did nothing more. The attempts to stymie the partition failed and on January 23, 1793, Russian and Prussian diplomats signed the formal partition agreement. Russia took the Polish Ukraine and White Russia, and Prussia obtained Danzig, Posen, Kalisch, and Thorn. When the Austrians finally learned the details of the treaty, they were staggered by the extent of Prussia's gains. In fury the Emperor dismissed his advisers and appointed Baron Johann Amadeus Thugut

[9] These early Franco-Prussian negotiations are described and discussed in S. Biro, *The German Policy of Revolutionary France* (Cambridge, 1957), I.

as Foreign Minister. A secretive, withdrawn individual, Thugut was an experienced professional diplomat. He had served his Emperor in posts ranging from Constantinople to Naples. Totally devoted to the interests of the House of Hapsburg, he was willing to betray his allies, deal with his foes, and trample upon the rights of neutrals if only he could glean new power for his master. Thugut's immediate concern was to redress the balance of power with Prussia, and he began to seek for new provinces at the expense of either Poland, Venice, or France. The Hapsburgs thus came to regard their Hohenzollern allies as a major rival at precisely the moment when the French republicans unleashed several major offensives designed to liberate the Republic's soil and break the coalition.

General Adam Philippe Custine, leading a force of seventeen thousand men, advanced into the Rhineland at the end of September. He occupied Spire and took Worms on October 4. Custine's men encountered virtually no resistance. Local princes and their courts fled and among the ordinary inhabitants of the Rhineland nobody manifested a desire to fight and die for the old order. Townsmen in Mainz even refused to aid the local garrison, and the city surrendered on October 21. By the end of the month the French held all of the Rhineland south of the Moselle plus Frankfurt.[10]

Meanwhile, on the Franco-Sardinian frontier, the armies of the Republic overran the Sardinian provinces of Nice and Savoy. As in the Rhineland, nobody appeared willing to fight to preserve the Old Regime, and in many instances the French-speaking inhabitants of the two

[10] For a description of Custine's campaign see *Min. de la Guerre A.H., Mémoires historiques* (hereafter *M.h.*), *Armée du Rhin journal général des opérations 28 septembre 1792 jusqu' au 8 janvier 1794 322;* and R. W. Phipps, *The Armies of the First French Republic, The Armées de la Moselle du Rhin de Sambre-et-Meuse de Rhin-et-Moselle* (London, 1929). R. R. Palmer, *The Age of the Democratic Revolution* (Princeton, 1964), II, Ch. XIV, has a discussion of the Rhinelanders' reactions to the French invasion.

provinces greeted the French soldiers as friends and liberators.

The main French offensive took place in Belgium, where Dumouriez, leading forty thousand troops, marched on Mons at the end of October 1792. An Austrian force of fourteen thousand men took up defensive positions in a semicircle in front of Mons. On November 6 the French attacked the Austrian position at the small village of Jemappes. Covered by one hundred cannon, the infantry rushed forward in dense columns using numbers, shock, and *élan* to overcome their disciplined foes, who continued to employ the old linear-style tactics. Time and again Austrian volleys shattered the columns, but each time they re-formed and resumed their advance. The persistent French attacks finally broke into the Austrians' positions, and to avoid total annihilation, the Austrian commander abandoned Jemappes. He fell back behind the Meuse in order to regroup, and all of central Belgium lay defenseless.

Dumouriez quickly took advantage of his victory, and by November 14 his army had entered Brussels. By the end of the month the French tricolor flew from the walls of Louvain, Antwerp, and Liège. In little more than two months after their defensive victory at Valmy, the French had succeeded in mounting highly successful offensives of their own. They now had to decide how to govern their sudden acquisitions and devise plans for the ultimate disposition of the occupied provinces.

When establishing provisional administrations in conquered lands, the French sought to ease their tasks by working with individuals and groups who looked with favor upon the Revolution. In fact, the French had been dealing with foreigners who shared their ideals prior to unleashing their fall offensives.

Although counterrevolutionary publicists asserted that the French had created an international organization designed to subvert European civilization, such a bureau never existed. There were, however, numerous individuals who held French ideas because they found themselves in a socioeconomic situation similar to that which prevailed in Old Regime France. At first the French ignored them, but as war drew near the Brissotins, to assure the populace that victory was inevitable, began to assert that revolutionary ideals would spread throughout Europe. When the French armies advanced people everywhere, according to Brissot, would rise, overthrow their masters, and greet the Gaulic hosts as liberators. Shortly after the declaration of war, the Assembly created a Belgian Legion and later raised a Swiss, German, Savoyard, and Dutch corps. These units consisted of refugees who hoped to revolutionize their native lands with French assistance. Furthermore, the French Government in the spring of 1792 had a definite internationalist tinge. Brissot had traveled widely outside of France. The Foreign Minister had lived in Liège for many years, and Miranda, the army's second-in-command, was a Venezuelan.

However, despite any tendencies toward internationalism, the French never lost sight of their own national interests and never subordinated diplomatic and military reality to the crusading spirit. The refugee legions, for example, served only against states that had gone to war with France, and the French did not recruit legions for use against neutral states. The Batavian (Dutch) unit was an exception, but in this instance the Assembly officially named it the Free Foreign Legion so as not to alarm the Dutch Government, which was still neutral. Despite their distaste for monarchy, French leaders were quite willing to negotiate with individual kings and sought to convince Frederick William to leave the war. Thus in formulating policy for conquered regions the French guided themselves by concentrating on their own national interests and the realities of power while paying lip service to revolutionary principles.

On November 19, 1792, the Convention issued the First Propaganda Decree promising aid and friendship for all peoples who wished to attain liberty. Far from being a call to universal revolution, the decree was, in reality, a response to the requests of Belgian and Rhenish democrats who were assisting the French armies and wanted protection against counterrevolutionary reprisals. It was meant to reassure these democrats that it was safe to collaborate with France, but it did not apply to states that remained at peace with the Republic. The Foreign Minister even assured the English and Swiss that the proclamation excluded neutrals from its scope.[11]

Meanwhile, in Belgium, Dumouriez was seeking to create an independent republic with himself as protector. To win broad popular support he proposed that the Belgians proceed with the creation of their own government. The Convention, though ignorant of the general's scheme, nevertheless approved his suggestion, feeling that a friendly Belgian regime would ease the tasks of the army, alarm the Hapsburgs, and force Francis to negotiate. Belgian democratic clubs then chose delegates to work with French military authorities.[12]

Dumouriez, however, soon came into conflict with the Belgian democrats and the Convention. In his search for popular backing, he forbade his generals to requisition supplies and instead purchased them from local contractors. Lacking cash to pay the businessmen, the general tried to raise a loan from the Belgian clergy. In return, he promised to preserve their manorial dues and tithes. He also proposed an invasion of the United Provinces in order that he might later evacuate them in return for Dutch recognition of his rule in Belgium.[13]

His plans, however, went badly: The Convention for-

[11] See *A.N. AF II carton 57 dossier 219*, which contains instructions to the envoy in England emphasizing the importance of retaining Britain's neutrality.

[12] See S. Tassier, *Histoire de la Belgique sous l'occupation française en 1792 et 1793* (Brussels, 1934). *A.N. DP II carton 4* and *carton 5* contain reports from government agents which point out the necessity of creating a provisional government in Belgium to assist the French forces.

[13] *A.N. DP II carton 5* contains a report on Dumouriez's financial transactions.

bade him to enter the United Provinces; local leaders refused to pick him as the ruler of an independent Belgium, and the loan from the clergy failed to produce sufficient funds to supply his army. The unpaid, ill-fed, and poorly clothed volunteers began to desert, and the government in Paris began to suspect Dumouriez's loyalty.

To restrain Dumouriez and other ambitious generals and at the same time solve the problem of financing the war effort, the Convention, on December 15, 1792, issued its Second Propaganda Decree. The decree stated that when French forces entered enemy lands, commanders would proclaim the abolition of tithes and feudal dues, abolish aristocratic privilege, convoke primary assemblies that would organize interim governments, and confiscate the property of the ruling prince, the Church, and the aristocrats. The generals were then to issue assignats (paper money) for the purchase of supplies, using the confiscated property as security. The intents of this declaration were to ease the army's task of administering its conquests by securing the co-operation of pro-French groups, force those groups most opposed to the Republic to bear the costs of the war, and prevent generals from becoming too independent by prescribing a specific course of action for them.[14]

In Belgium the reaction to the decree was largely unfavorable. The inhabitants were reluctant to accept French assignats, and a Belgian Convention elected in December called for a restoration of the old social system. Local democrats, therefore, concluded that their best hope for retaining power and avoiding reprisals lay in joining France. Paris also concluded that an independent Belgian state would be dominated by the Republic's foes and that annexation was the best solution. In February 1793, Danton and Lazare Carnot stated that France had a historical right to her natural frontiers—the Rhine,

[14] *Réimpression de l'ancien Moniteur* (Paris, 1840), XIV, pp. 703 and 755.

the Alps, and the Pyrenees. The Convention in November had already annexed Savoy and Nice in order to protect pro-French elements, deny the provinces to the Republic's enemies, and strengthen the national frontiers. The French followed a similar policy in Belgium. In March 1793 primary assemblies under the supervision of French officers requested annexation. Piece by piece the Convention incorporated Belgium into the Republic. The Convention also annexed the Rhineland after a Rhenish Convention requested union with France.[15]

The French had thus passed rapidly from a policy of creating prorepublican provisional regimes to one of outright incorporation. Concern for national security, a desire to limit the influence of military men, and the need to finance the war at the expense of the state's enemies, rather than an attempt to create a world-wide revolution, dictated the Convention's policies. The expansion of France's frontiers was, however, to be ephemeral, for as the deputies were issuing the decrees of annexation, the enemies of France suddenly threw the Republic on the defensive.

The entrance of new powers into the war against France struck a major blow at the Republic's diplomatic and military position. England was the first major power to join Austria and Prussia. Despite his hostility to the Revolution, Pitt at first sought to remain neutral, but French policy in Belgium alarmed him. When the French, in order to win the support of Belgian businessmen, opened the Scheldt River to commercial navigation, England and the United Provinces objected. The Westphalia treaties of 1648 had closed the Scheldt to destroy Antwerp's commerce, and when the French reopened the river, the Stadtholder asked Britain for assistance in case of further hostile French moves. Pitt gave

[15] *A.N. AF II carton 3 dossier 15* contains instructions to the military to organize Belgian assemblies. See also Tassier, *Histoire de la Belgique*, pp. 305–9, and P. Sagnac, *Le Rhin français pendant la Révolution et l'Empire* (Paris, 1917).

an affirmative reply, and on November 29 William Grenville, the Secretary of State for Foreign Affairs, informed the French Government that continued British neutrality depended upon the withdrawal of the First Propaganda Decree and the closing of the Scheldt. On December 2 Pitt called up the militia and on the twentieth obtained parliamentary approval for the addition of twenty thousand men to the fleet. A few days later the Cabinet halted shipments of grain and other raw materials to France.[16]

The French tried to keep England out of war. They informed London that the opening of the Scheldt was not meant to be a hostile act and that the decree of November 19 did not imply that France would give aid to any and all seditious elements. These efforts failed, however. On January 11 and again on January 15, the French envoy in London reported continued British preparations for war. The execution of Louis XVI on January 21, 1793, sent a shudder of horror through the upper classes of Europe. The Bourbon rulers of Spain and Naples were outraged, other crowned heads became indignant at what they regarded as an unjust and inhumane process, and the action of the revolutionary courts convinced many who were already hostile to the new French regime that their opposition was moral and necessary for the salvation of the European social order. Individual responses to the death of the French King did not, however, seriously alter the policies of Europe's statesmen. Whether or not they were personally moved by the execution, they continued to pursue the special interests of their states. They did not unite in a crusade against the French Republic. Rather, they continued to follow their current policies virtually without interruption. Nor did

[16] For discussions of British foreign policy, see J. H. Rose, *William Pitt and the Great War* (London, 1912); A. W. Ward and G. P. Gooch, *The Cambridge History of British Foreign Policy 1783–1919* (London, 1922), I; and S. Watson, *The Reign of George III* (Oxford, 1960).

the King's death seriously alter French diplomatic procedures or objectives. The foreign ministry had changed little during the earlier years of the Revolution. There was of course some shifting of personnel, especially in the upper grades of the foreign service, but most of those in the lower ranks and not a few ambassadors continued to serve the Revolution. By the time the King perished the revolutionaries had already elaborated their strategic and diplomatic objectives and Louis's death did not seriously alter them. Thus the powers of Europe, revolutionary and conservative alike, used the execution as propaganda or justification for policy decisions, but the act itself did not materially alter any state's diplomatic decision.

Pitt used the execution of Louis as an ostensible reason for going to war with France, but his real considerations were the desire to check the Republic's expansion into the Low Countries and the hope of attracting the prowar Whig faction into his parliamentary coalition. On January 24, he ordered the French envoy to return home, thereby rendering further negotiations impossible.[17] This action in turn convinced the Convention that war was inevitable and that France should strike first in order to gain all the military advantages possible. On January 31, the government ordered Dumouriez to invade the United Provinces, and on February 1, 1793, the Convention declared war upon England.

England and the United Provinces were but the first of a long list of powers that entered the war in 1793. After the death of Louis XVI, the Spanish Bourbons concluded that the old Paris-Madrid alliance could never be revived. Madrid was also unwilling to allow the British a completely free hand in disposing of the French overseas colonies and therefore put an end to talks with the Republic. Paris had hoped to keep Spain neutral by means of these negotiations but when they failed, the

[17] See the reports of the French envoy for January 8, 11, 15, and 24 in *A.A.E. Correspondance politique* 586.

Convention on March 7 declared war. The states of Italy, pushed by the great powers and fearing French expansion, also joined the growing coalition. Tuscany, Venice, Parma, and Modena declared war on France. Portugal, one of England's oldest allies, also entered the ranks of the anti-French alliance. George III of England brought his German patrimony, Hanover, into the coalition, and in April the Imperial Diet went to war with the Republic.

Britain quickly became the leading force in the First Coalition by concluding alliances with most of its members. Treaties with Austria, Prussia, and Spain called for mutual co-operation in forming war plans and diplomatic policy. The British also provided subsidies to several lesser powers, the start of a policy that was to last until the fall of Napoleon. Despite numerous internal problems and conflicting ambitions, the First Coalition was quite formidable, placing more than 250,000 men in the field.[18] Furthermore, the very existence of the coalition meant that France was diplomatically isolated and had to fight for its survival alone.

Major military reverses added to the Republic's problems in the spring of 1793. Dumouriez had entered Dutch territory in February while Miranda protected his right flank by attacking Maestricht. Coburg, the Austrian commander, gathered forty thousand men behind the Roer River and on March 1 attacked Miranda. He achieved complete surprise, routed the French, and drove them back to the vicinity of Louvain. Coburg's advance in turn exposed Dumouriez's flank, and Paris ordered him to evacuate Holland and return to Belgium to cover Brussels. On March 18 Dumouriez tried to stop Coburg's march on the Belgian capital at Neerwinden, but his attack failed. He returned to Louvain, where the Austrians defeated him again three days later.[19]

[18] *Min. de la Guerre A.H., Ordres de bataille des armées en campagne, 1792–1815, carton Xp3.*

[19] See R. W. Phipps, *The Armies of the First French Republic, The Armée du Nord* (London, 1926) for a description of the French defeats in Belgium.

Seeing his plans to gain control of Belgium undone, Dumouriez made a desperate bid for power by transferring his loyalty to the Austrians. He concluded an armistice with them on March 25. The Austrians agreed to halt their advance at the French frontier while Dumouriez marched on Paris and restored the monarchy. The Convention, already suspicious of the general's motives, sent the War Minister and three commissioners to the front with instructions to remove Dumouriez from command. The general, however, arrested the delegation, turned them over to the Austrians, and called upon his troops to turn against the Republic. The soldiers rejected the appeal, and on April 5, Dumouriez with a small band of adherents fled to the Austrian lines. Dumouriez's treason, despite its failure, was a severe blow to the French morale.[20] In addition, Dumouriez had evacuated a number of important positions before his desertion, thereby adding to the demoralization of the defeated army and worsening the nation's over-all strategic position.

Coupled with the French collapse in the Low Countries was a renewal of Prussian military activity on the Rhine. Brunswick's troops retook Frankfurt at the beginning of December, and on March 21, 1793, the Prussians forced their way into the Rhineland. Brunswick then drove toward the French frontier, and by April the French had evacuated most of the Rhineland. A garrison in Mainz held out against the Prussian army, but the bulk of the French forces was engaged in seeking to prevent an invasion of Alsace.

While pursuing military operations, representatives of the major powers met in Antwerp on April 8 to arrange a division of the spoils of the expected victory. Coburg issued a declaration assuring the French that the coalition had no intention of seizing any of their territory, but the other delegates, including the Austrian representative,

[20] On Dumouriez's treason and some of its effects see *A.N. AF II carton 69 dossier 279.*

immediately rejected his pronouncement. The British, despite claims that they sought only to resist French expansion and restore the balance of power, laid claim to several French colonies. To convince Vienna to drop the exchange plan and retain Belgium as a check to French expansion, Pitt advocated enlarging the area by the addition of the French cities of Lille and Valenciennes. The Austrians at first insisted upon their right to execute the Belgian-Bavarian exchange, but Pitt was adamant that Vienna retain her Belgian provinces. The issue was not settled at Antwerp, but in discussions held later in London, when the Austrians, anxious to retain England's friendship to offset the Prusso-Russian entente, agreed to abandon the exchange. At London they also agreed to retain Belgium and extend its frontiers south to the Somme River. Finally, Vienna reserved the right to further compensations at French expense. Meanwhile at Antwerp Prussia and Austria remained divided over the fate of Poland, and Frederick William refused to employ his forces with full vigor until Francis recognized the Second Partition. This Francis refused to do. The first major allied conference thus revealed serious disagreements within the alliance, but the coalition's cause still looked promising: The French army was in disarray and allied armies were ready to invade France.

From the North Sea to the Meuse, 110,000 Austrian, English, and German troops prepared to assault the fortified cities in northern France. In the Rhineland, 42,000 Prussians and 24,000 Austrians threatened the Republic's eastern departments. Some 50,000 Spanish troops stood ready to attack across the Pyrenees, and 20,000 Sardinians intended to recapture Savoy and advance to the Rhône. To defend itself the Republic had over 300,000 troops, but many were ill trained, lacked food, clothing, and weapons, and suffered from low morale.[21] France

[21] *Min. de la Guerre A.H., Ordres de bataille des armées en campagne, 1792–1815, carton* X^{p}3, and *Min. de la Guerre A.H., Armées de la République situations générales, 1791–1802, car-*

thus found herself in a position far more serious than the one the year before.

The campaign of 1793 began in the north, the most crucial of all the war zones. The French sought to dislocate Coburg's forthcoming offensive by launching two general attacks on the first of May. The allies repulsed both offensives and unleashed their own drive on May 23 by advancing on Valenciennes, driving off the French field army and isolating the garrison. In June Coburg continued his slow, meticulous advance into northern France while the Spanish crossed the Pyrenees to threaten Roussillon and the Sardinians moved through the Alps.[22]

In July Coburg captured Condé and forced the Valenciennes garrison to surrender. The Prussians took Mainz in the same month. French defenses continued to crumble in August. Coburg defeated the French field army near Cambrai. The French then fell back to Arras, leaving the route to Paris open except for a small garrison in Cambrai. Coburg, however, was reluctant to dash for Paris while French garrisons and a field army were in a position to threaten his rear. Perhaps he remembered Brunswick's misfortunes and Valmy. In any case, he allowed the Duke of York, with thirty-seven thousand English, Dutch, Hessian, and Hanoverian troops, to advance on Dunkirk while he moved against Quesnoy. Coburg's caution had thus temporarily spared the Republic, but the allies stood deep in French territory, and the nation was still in a desperate position.

Major internal counterrevolutionary insurrections further undermined the Republic's security. The Vendée, a wild and desolate area in western France, had long been the scene of antirevolutionary sentiment. Led by the

---

ton B[1]*245*. See also *A.N. AF II, carton* 9 *dossier* 55, and Vivenot, *Quellen*, III, p. 353.

[22] Accounts of the campaign of the summer of 1793 appear in Phipps, *The Armée du Nord;* E. Bourdeau, *Campagnes modernes* (Paris, n.d.), I; and J. W. Fortescue, *A History of the British Army* (London, 1915), Vol. 4, Part 1.

Marquis de la Rouerie, nobles in Brittany, Normandy, and the Vendée had created a secret counterrevolutionary organization in 1791. The authorities had destroyed the association in January 1793, but many individual sections had survived. In the spring of 1793, these groups were waiting for a favorable opportunity to strike at the central government. Most priests in the Vendée had refused to take the oath to the Civil Constitution of the Clergy, and added their voices to the swelling chorus of hostility to the republican regime. The peasants, loyal to their priests and antagonistic to the republican middle class of the numerous towns scattered throughout the region, were a third source of counterrevolutionary strength.[23] Ever since 1790 there had been sporadic outbreaks of violence directed against government officials and backers of the Revolution, but in the winter of 1793, the Convention took steps that caused the various counterrevolutionary elements to coalesce and institute a general uprising.

On February 24 the Convention called for a levy of 300,000 men to bolster the armies at the front. News of the draft law reached the western departments on March 10, and on the eleventh bands of peasants began to attack government officials and bourgeois republicans. By March 13 the entire Vendée, except for the larger towns, was in the hands of rebels. Led by the local chieftains like Cathelineau and Stofflet, the peasants fought to protect their religion and resist conscription. Local nobles then joined the revolt and transformed it into a counterrevolutionary movement. By March 20 the nobles had welded the diverse bands into a Catholic and Royal

[23] For the background of the revolt of the Vendée see C. Tilly, *The Vendée* (Cambridge, 1964); C. Tilly, "Some Problems in the History of the Vendée," in *American Historical Review* (October 1961), LXVII; J. Godechot, *La Contre-révolution* (Paris, 1961), Ch. XI; and A. Goodwin, "Counter-Revolution in Brittany. The Royalist Conspiracy of the Marquis de la Rouerie 1791–1793," in *Bulletin of the John Rylands Library*, XXXIX (1957).

Army, which waged a highly effective guerrilla war against government forces. In April the rebels defeated a major expedition; early in June they captured Saumur, and by mid-June the Catholic and Royal Army was threatening Nantes.[24] With a peak strength of about sixty thousand men, the Vendean irregulars posed a constant threat to Paris and forced the government to divert valuable troops to the bitter tasks of counterinsurgency.

Royalist bands also operated in Brittany and Normandy. Favoring a constitutional monarchy, these Chouan bands worked in small units and were less dangerous than the Vendeans. Nevertheless, they also forced the government to employ men needed at the front in campaigns of internal repression.

A third wave of rebellions, led by supporters of Brissot's faction, dealt another major blow to the Republic's security. In late May and early June, Robespierre and his faction, in league with the Parisian sans-culottes, defeated Brissot's clique, placed many of its members under arrest, and gained control of the National Convention. Brissotin supporters did not, however, accept their exclusion from power. Arrested deputies escaped and fled to the provinces along with other sympathetic representatives. There they proceeded to rally the departments for a war on Paris.

By June 7, several departments in Normandy and Brittany had joined the federalist revolt. Local authorities in Bordeaux, Toulouse, Nîmes, and Marseilles also took up arms against the Convention. In July Toulon joined the federalist ranks, but local royalists first supported the rebellion and then captured it. Aristocratic officers of the Mediterranean fleet took over the defense of Toulon and

[24] For military operations in the Vendée see Paret, *Internal War* (Princeton, 1961); J. J. M. Savary, *Guerres des Vendéens et des Chouans contre la République française* (Paris, 1824–25), I; P. Bourniscaux, *Histoire des guerres de la Vendée et des Chouans* (Paris, 1819), I; and E. Gabroy, *La Révolution et la Vendée* (Paris, 1925), I.

asked the coalition for assistance. In August Admiral Hood led a British fleet into Toulon's harbor and disembarked fifteen hundred men. Later, another thousand British, three thousand Sardinian, and fourteen thousand Spanish and Neapolitan troops arrived to support the six-thousand-man royalist force. Hood issued a proclamation stating that he was holding the city until the Count of Provence, who claimed the throne as Louis XVIII, re-established the monarchy.[25] The allies had thus gained an important foothold in southern France. Corsica also joined the rebellion, and in Lyons, royalists took control of a federalist-inspired insurrection. By the summer of 1793, over half of the departments were in open rebellion against the Convention.

France was in dire straits by that summer, and the Convention had to face the enormous problems involved in fighting a foreign war and a civil conflict simultaneously. The First Coalition, on the other hand, had many problems of its own, chief among them the clashing ambitions of its members. Counterrevolutionary forces within France also worked under many hardships. The differing elements, royalists, constitutionalists, and federalists, rarely worked together. Furthermore, the royalist guerrillas in the west refused to leave their native provinces for a march on Paris. Still, the coalition and the counterrevolutionaries had won a series of striking victories. If they could organize a coherent set of political objectives and an effective military strategy before the Convention could organize its resources, victory would be theirs. In the fall of 1793, victory was to go to the side that most effectively mobilized its economic and human material.

[25] For the federalist revolts see R. M. Brace, *Bordeaux and the Gironde 1789–1794* (Ithaca, 1947); Godechot, *La Contre-révolution,* Ch. XII; and *Min. de la Guerre, A.H., M.h., Précis historique sur le siège de Toulon en 1793 400.*

CHAPTER 3

TRIUMPHS OF THE REPUBLIC

In the summer of 1793 republican leaders successfully dealt with the problems of internal anarchy, foreign invasion, and civil strife. While the allies remained suspicious of each other and failed to co-operate effectively, the French evolved an efficient central government and mobilized their economic and human resources for war. In the fall of 1793 they halted the allied advance into France and crushed the domestic counterrevolution. In 1794 the Republic attacked and won a series of major victories.

In 1793 a prerequisite for survival was a central regime able to organize and direct the activities of its subordinate officials and citizens, but as the French armies retreated on all fronts the government was singularly unsuited to the task of rallying the nation for massive resistance. Factional disputes divided the National Convention; ministers of the Provisional Executive Council frequently opposed the policies of the nation's elected representatives, and local authorities were often reluctant to take orders from Paris.[1]

On January 1, 1793, the Convention had created a Committee of General Defense to improve the efficiency of the government, but this large and unwieldy body of eighteen and later twenty-five members had little real power. In the spring military setbacks and Dumouriez's treason compelled the Convention to create a more authoritative supervisory body. The deputies, on April 6, 1793, established a Committee of Public Safety and au-

[1] See R. R. Palmer, *Twelve Who Ruled* (Princeton, 1941) for an excellent description of the problems facing the leaders of France in 1793.

thorized it to observe and accelerate the actions of the executive ministers, suspend ministerial decrees if necessary, and issue emergency decrees of its own.

Dominated by Danton, the Committee failed to stop the allied armies or repress internal insurrections. Furthermore, Danton's attempt to negotiate with the coalition at a time when France had little to offer in return for peace made many deputies suspicious of his ultimate objectives. Some even began to suspect him of royalist sympathies. On July 10 the Convention removed him from office and began to appoint the men who were to guide the nation's destinies for the next crucial eleven months.

With Maximilien Robespierre as their leading figure the twelve men who served on the Committee of Public Safety were a good cross section of the politically active segments of French society. The twelve included five lawyers, two army officers, two authors, an ex-noble, an actor, and a former Protestant pastor. Prior to the Revolution all of them had been successful in their chosen careers and in 1793 were hard-working, reasonably honest, patriotic, and determined to lead the Republic to victory. Of course, they did not agree on all issues. For example, some of them supported the demands of the sans-culottes for price controls and direct popular democracy, others opposed popular revolutionism, and a third group favored a measure of social democracy while establishing firm national discipline. Temperaments clashed, and personal antagonisms also divided the twelve. Still, they realized the necessity for a minimum of co-operation and quickly set to work to transform the Committee of Public Safety into an autonomous organization capable of controlling the Convention, the ministers, the armies, and the French people.[2]

[2] Palmer, *Twelve Who Ruled,* supplies biographical data on all the members of the Committee. There are numerous biographical works on the individual members, including J. M. Thompson, *Robespierre,* 2 vols. (Oxford, 1953); A. Mathiez, *Etudes Robe-*

On October 10, 1793, the Convention, realizing the necessity of providing France with an effective directoral body, agreed to place the Committee in charge of the nation's war effort by declaring that the French Government was revolutionary until the peace. This decree delayed indefinitely the implementation of the Constitution written in June, and gave the Committee extensive executive authority. The law of October 10 empowered the Committee to nominate generals and oversee the actions of ministers and other constituted bodies. The Convention, compelled by the need to create an effective central government, thus empowered the Committee to become the supreme regulating institution of the nation.[3]

On December 4, 1793, the Convention agreed to a further extension of the Committee's power. At this time the deputies declared that the Committee was to supervise the activities of all public functionaries. The law ordered ministers to report to the Committee every ten days, forbade local authorities to alter or interpret government orders, reduced the power of officials in the departments, and replaced locally elected district and communal officers with national agents who were directly responsible to the twelve. Finally, the decree placed the conduct of diplomacy in the hands of the Committee. Known as the "Constitution of the Terror," the law of December 4 coordinated all previous emergency decrees and defined the nature of revolutionary government. The Conven-

---

spierristes, 2 vols. (Paris, 1917–18); E. N. Curtis, *Saint Just, Colleague of Robespierre* (Cambridge, 1935); L. Gershoy, *Bertrand Barère, a Reluctant Terrorist* (Princeton, 1962); M. Reinhard, *Le Grand Carnot,* 2 vols. (Paris, 1950–52); and R. R. Palmer, "Fifty Years of the Committee of Public Safety," in *Journal of Modern History,* XIII (1941).

[3] The text of this and other decrees may be found in A. Aulard, ed., *Recueil des actes du Comité de Salut Public avec la correspondance officielle des représentants en mission,* 28 vols. (Paris, 1891–1907), VII (which covers the period 22 September–24 October 1793). See also J. H. Stewart, *A Documentary Survey of the French Revolution* (New York, 1951), pp. 479–81.

tion, acting through the Committee of Public Safety, established itself as the sole center of authority in France. Local officials and all other governmental organs became servants of the central regime, and the Committee functioned in a manner much like that of a modern war cabinet. Ultimately responsible to the Convention, the Committee had the delegated authority to make necessary executive policy decisions.

The last step in the development of the Committee's paramount position came on April 1, 1794, when the Convention abolished the Council of Ministers and replaced it with a dozen commissions that reported directly to the Committee of Public Safety. The decrees of October 10, December 4, and April 1, coupled with periodic purges of opponents, enabled the Committee to act as the Republic's chief policy-making body.

To increase their control over the provinces and organize the war effort, the twelve expanded the system of employing special agents, representatives on mission, armed with plenary powers. The Convention had begun to use such officials in March when it sent two deputies to each department to hasten the 300,000-man levy. In April special deputies had helped organize the defense of the frontier forts, and on April 9 the government sent three deputies to each field army to supervise the conduct of the generals, improve morale, and hasten the incorporation of volunteers into existing units. These deputies had extensive powers. They could spend public funds, carry out requisitions, and even suspend suspects, including generals. They could not only relieve generals from command but also arrest them.[4]

On May 7 the Committee defined the tasks of the representatives on mission as speeding up recruitment, securing logistical support for the armies, and informing Paris of local conditions in the provinces. The Committee

[4] H. Wallon, *Les représentants du peuple en mission et la justice révolutionnaire dans les départments* (Paris, 1889), I; and Aulard, *Recueil des actes,* III and IV.

also told the agents that they were not merely aides of the field commanders and that they should take an active role in planning and executing military operations. In August the Committee sent a new wave of delegates to the provinces and armies to supervise conscription and organize war production.

The representatives on mission acted as an important link between Paris and the departments and also assured the obedience of the military to civilian authority. Members of the Committee frequently went on missions themselves, thereby enhancing the prestige of the other representatives and emphasizing the importance of the system of direct control from Paris. Working with the Committee of General Security, a political police, the Revolutionary Tribunal, and local revolutionary societies, the special delegates enabled the Committee of Public Safety to exercise effective control over the nation's energies and resources.

One of the Committee's most important achievements was to enlarge and reorganize the armies. To obtain more men and satisfy the demands of the Parisian popular spokesmen who were calling for a mass armed rising against the enemies of the Republic, Robespierre and his colleagues resorted to general conscription under government supervision, thus combining the desires of the sansculottes with the requirements of military efficiency. On August 23, 1793, the Convention adopted the famous *levée en masse* decree, which stated that "henceforth until the enemies have been driven from the territory of the Republic, the French people are in permanent requisition for army service." The general conscription act ordered single men between the ages of eighteen and twenty-five to join the army, married men to work in arms factories and logistic services, women to serve in hospitals, and old men to act as propagandists.[5] In con-

[5] The full text of the decree is to be found in Stewart, *Documentary Survey*, pp. 472–74, and in Aulard, *Recueil des actes*, VI.

trast to the *levée* of February 24, which called up a limited number of men, the *levée en masse* sought to organize the entire populace for total war.

Carnot, a dour, hard-working former engineer officer, directed the application of the conscription acts of February and August and brought thousands of new men to the armies. From 361,000 men in February 1793, the armies grew to 670,900 by January 20, 1794. By April there were 842,300 men under arms; in May, 869,000; in June, 893,000; and in August, 1,075,600.[6] By the fall of 1794, the field armies had a grand total of 1,108,300 men, of whom 850,770 were immediately available for combat.[7]

The Committee also organized its vastly enlarged armies into effective tactical formations. By a decree of February 21, 1793, the Convention abolished all distinctions between the regular troops and conscripts and reorganized the infantry into demibrigades consisting of one regular and two volunteer battalions. The regulars were to instill discipline in the volunteer units; the volunteers were to encourage the regulars with their *élan*. Naturally the system did not work perfectly, for there were not enough regular battalions to go around, and many regular units had absorbed a large number of conscripts to replace combat losses. The government often used volunteer battalions raised in 1791 in place of regulars, and some demibrigades consisted entirely of draftees. Nevertheless, the new system worked well enough to bring about a marked improvement in the combat effectiveness of the army as a whole. The law also established the number of demibrigades at 196, but the necessities of the current campaign forced the government to delay the execution of the decree until the following year. Individual commanders introduced the new units into their armies in 1793, but it was not until January 8, 1794,

[6] *Min. de la Guerre A.H., Armées de la République situations générales 1791–1802 carton B¹244.*

[7] *A.N. AF II carton 212 dossier 1808, récapitulation générale des armées de terre.*

that the government established the use of the demi-brigade in all of the armies.[8]

At the same time, army commanders began to organize several demibrigades, plus supporting artillery and cavalry units, into combat divisions. The division could march and fight either as a single unit or as part of a larger force, thereby giving commanders greater flexibility in planning and executing operations.[9]

French tactics on the battlefield also improved. By 1793 generals had already abandoned the linear formations of the Old Regime professional armies because the volunteers and conscripts lacked the training necessary to deliver and withstand measured volleys of musketry. By trial and error, front-line commanders gradually devised tactics designed to minimize the lack of discipline and take advantage of their soldiers' numbers and *élan*.[10]

Republican officers first sought to carry enemy positions by throwing their men forward in massed assault columns, but soon discovered that, although the columns attained occasional successes, they suffered heavy losses, and that well-drilled regulars frequently halted them. Commanders also noted that soldiers would often advance on their own and fire on the enemy individually. Officers then began to protect their columns with a screen of light infantry. These skirmishers would cover the main columns and snipe at the enemy formations.[11]

[8] *Min. de la Guerre A.H., Organisation générale de l'armée, 1793, carton X^8^4.*

[9] S. T. Ross, "The Development of the Combat Division in Eighteenth Century French Armies," in *French Historical Studies IV*, No. 1 (1965).

[10] On the evolution of French infantry tactics see R. Quimby, *The Background of Napoleonic Warfare* (New York, 1957); S. Wilkinson, *The French Army Before Napoleon* (London, 1915); P. Paret, *Yorck and the Era of Prussian Reform* (Princeton, 1966); and J. Colin, *La tactique et la discipline dans les armées de la Révolution* (Paris, 1902).

[11] Paret, *Yorck*, points out that Old Regime armies also employed light infantry, but only for specialized and limited missions. The

Once the light infantry had weakened the enemy, battalion columns, forty men wide and twelve ranks deep, would move forward. Depending upon the immediate tactical situation, the column would deploy as light infantry and reinforce the skirmishers, deploy into a rough linear formation, form a square to fend off cavalry attacks, or charge and attempt to shatter their opponents' line. With his ability to fight both as a light infantry man or as part of an assault unit, the French soldier became a formidable warrior. An excellent artillery corps and tactical formations that allowed flexibility on both the individual and unit level increased the effectiveness and striking power of France's citizen soldiers.

Finally, the Committee developed a cadre of leaders loyal to the Republic and able to use the new armies effectively. The representatives on mission removed inefficient and disloyal officers from command and frequently executed them. Individuals of proven loyalty and talent received immediate promotion. Of course, not all who were removed were guilty as charged. Nor were all of the battlefield promotions successful. But given the tense and trying circumstances, the Committee and its delegates succeeded in finding an able group of military leaders.

In contrast to the Old Regime army, where a majority of the officers were of aristocratic descent, the new republican army drew most of its officers from the ranks of the middle classes. Some had previous military experience as enlisted men, NCOs, or junior officers in the Royal Army, others had served in the National Guard, and some had obtained their training as ordinary soldiers

---

French used skirmishers as an integral part of their tactical system. See Jourdan to General Duquesnoy, 14 October 1793, in *Min. de la Guerre A.H., Correspondance Armées du Nord et des Ardennes, 1–19 Octobre 1793, carton B¹20.* In his message, Jourdan told his subordinate that the untrained volunteers were well suited to function as light infantry and that the army should employ large numbers of skirmishers.

in the revolutionary forces. By the fall of 1793, the Committee had created a group of generals who were to carve a permanent niche for themselves in the annals of warfare. Napoleon Bonaparte, Jean Baptiste Jourdan, Louis Lazare Hoche, Jean Charles Pichegru, André Masséna, Jean Victor Moreau, Louis Nicolas Davout, and Guillaume Brune form but part of the list of famous leaders who became generals in 1793.[12]

The republican generals were young—their average age was thirty-three. Most of them lacked strategic ability because they had little or no formal military training. On the other hand, they were excellent tacticians—aggressive, brave, willing to learn by trial and error, and determined at all costs to triumph.

While expanding and reorganizing the military forces, the Committee also began to mobilize the national economy. Their objective was twofold. First of all, the government had to equip its armed forces. Secondly, the Committee had to pacify the Parisian sans-culottes, who were vociferous in their demands for price controls. Economic regulation would, therefore, protect the government's purchasing power while simultaneously satisfying the lower classes.

The government instituted its policy of economic control in May with the passage of a law establishing maximum grain prices. In July the Convention issued a decree prescribing the death penalty for those who withheld goods from market in order to drive up prices. In August the Convention forbade the export of capital and articles of prime necessity without a special license, created public granaries, and placed price controls on fuel, salt, and tobacco.[13] To limit inflation further, the government de-

[12] For biographies of the French generals see G. Six, *dictionnaire biographique des généraux et admiraux français de la Révolution et de l'Empire*, 2 vols. (Paris, 1934). For a discussion of the social origins of revolutionary generals and of methods of promotion see G. Six, *Les généraux de la Révolution et de l'Empire* (Paris, 1947).

[13] For general studies of French economic life during the Revo-

monetized all assignats bearing the royal portrait and transformed the state debt into permanent rents. The creditors collected a fixed annuity from these rents, but they could not redeem them. Early in September the Convention instituted a forced loan and on September 29 established a general maximum, setting prices and wages throughout the nation.[14]

In addition to controlling prices and wage levels, the Committee of Public Safety took a direct hand in war production. Government workshops established in Paris began to produce muskets and by 1794 turned out 750 weapons per day, almost as much as the combined production of the rest of Europe. Privately owned foundries and powder mills received government orders and worked to capacity, and the Convention granted thirty million livres to the Committee of Public Safety for use in establishing new plants. Representatives on mission helped entrepreneurs expand their factories. They also requisitioned convents, churches, and other national buildings and transformed them into powder mills and gun-making shops.[15] The Committee drafted workers for

---

lution see O. Festy, *L'agriculture pendant la Révolution française* (Paris, 1947); S. E. Harris, *The Assignats* (Cambridge, 1935); R. G. Hawtrey, *Currency and Credit* (London, 1919); E. Levasseur, *Histoire du commerce de la France* (Paris, 1912), II; F. L. Nussbaum, *Commercial Policy in the French Revolution* (New York, 1923); and R. B. Rose, "The French Revolution and the Grain Supply," in *Bulletin of the John Rylands Library*, XXXIX (1956). On the development of economic controls see Stewart, *Documentary Survey*, pp. 441–45 and 469–72, and *A.N. AF II carton 77 dossier 571*, which contains lists of import and export permits.

[14] See Palmer, *Twelve Who Ruled*, Ch. X, for a description of the French war economy. Stewart, *Documentary Survey*, pp. 492–501, contains the texts of the forced loan and the General Maximum Law.

[15] See *A.N. AF II carton 27 dossier 217*, which contains orders for the establishment of new plants, contracts for weapons, and requisitions. *A.N. AF II carton 214^A dossier 1835* also contains contracts and plans for industrial expansion to produce more rifles.

the arms plants and requisitioned privately owned weapons, horses, shoes, and clothing. Even the scientists served the war effort by training workers, seeking improved production techniques, and experimenting with new weapons.[16] Most war production remained in private hands, but the Committee subjected it to its own control in matters of price, quantity, and quality. The government thus geared the French economy to the necessities of the fight for national survival.

The Committee of Public Safety also redefined and clarified the Republic's foreign policy. First of all, it abandoned all attempts to co-operate with foreign revolutionaries. The twelve saw that non-French radicals had failed to give material assistance to the Republic in 1792 and 1793 and concluded that further efforts to work with them would lead only to useless complications. Consequently, in April the Convention renounced all attempts to intervene in the domestic affairs of other states and in June instructed its representatives abroad to take no part in local politics.[17] The government decided that it would no longer seek out and co-operate with local radicals and would make no further efforts to establish pro-republican regimes in conquered territories. On September 15 the Committee directed its generals to observe the ordinary rules of war in occupied regions. It instructed army commanders to disarm the inhabitants, take hostages, and levy contributions. The government later established commissions to seize all movable wealth and send it back to France.[18] The French retained the idea of forcing privileged classes to disgorge their wealth

[16] See *A.N. AF II carton 214^B dossier 1839*. This dossier contains requisitions of manpower and material for work in war industries and orders to scientists to find and publish the most modern production techniques.

[17] *A.A.E. Mémoires et documents 652.*

[18] *Min. de la Guerre A.H., Correspondance Armées du Nord et des Ardennes, 16–30 Septembre 1793, carton B¹19* contains the order for conduct in conquered regions. It is dated 18 September 1793.

for the benefit of the Republic, not because of any ideological predilection, but simply because it was easier to take from them than from the poor. Furthermore, the Committee was in case of necessity perfectly willing to force the lower classes to contribute their share. In late 1793, then, the Republic abandoned all the idealistic overtones which had characterized the policy of '92 and made no pretense about its overriding concern for France's own national interests.

In its relations with other states, the Committee pursued a policy calculated to strengthen morale at home and improve the nation's diplomatic security. The government put an end to all efforts to negotiate publicly with the enemies of France, partly because the Committee felt that public talks would strengthen the followers of Danton, who favored negotiations. The twelve also feared that public talks would undermine the nation's morale, weaken the war effort, and, at the same time, hinder secret diplomatic activity.[19]

The Committee was, of course, fully prepared to pursue the interest of the French state by all the traditional methods of power politics. Robespierre and his colleagues, assisted by the professionals in the foreign office, realized that England and Austria were the Republic's most dedicated, determined, and dangerous foes and concluded that France had to concentrate its efforts primarily against these two powers. Robespierre, aware of the rivalries among the allied powers, decided to try to detach Prussia from the coalition. He also wished to convince the Turks to attack the Austrians and Russians, persuade minor states in Germany and Italy to leave the war, and cajole Sweden, Poland, and the Ottoman Empire to form a League of Armed Neutrality to off-balance

[19] *A.A.E. Mémoires et documents 321* contains an order, dated April 21, from the Committee to the commander of the Army of the North, telling him to cease peace talks since their continuation would undermine both morale and secret diplomacy.

Britain's domination of the seas.[20] The Committee's foreign policy sought to divide the coalition and enable the Republic to concentrate its strength against its major enemies.

France in the summer of 1793 resembled a fort with a garrison reduced to squabbling factions trying to withstand the assaults of many hostile armies. In the fall, one group of defenders seized power and, by persuasion and force, welded the others into a coherent, united army. The new leaders treated those who disagreed with them as traitors, whatever their motives, since dissidents threatened the unity of the garrison and helped the attackers. The commanders, therefore, destroyed them. The defenders then rushed to protect their fortress against external foes and prepared to launch a vast sortie of their own.

Divisions within the ranks of the assailants materially strengthened the French. Angered and humiliated by their setback in Poland, the Austrians were determined to offset Prussian gains by obtaining equivalent compensations in the west. To pacify the British, Thugut had promised to retain Belgium, adding to it French Flanders as far south as the Somme River. To check Prussia, he secretly planned to seize Alsace and Lorraine and then exchange these provinces for Bavaria. At the same time, Thugut sought a *rapprochement* with Russia in order to split the Russo-Prussian alliance. Vienna, therefore, recognized the Polish partition treaty insofar as it applied to Russia, and began tentative talks for a renewal of the Austro-Russian alliance of the 1780s. To gain new lands, Thugut was willing to mislead his allies as to his ultimate objectives and to seek an alliance against a member of the coalition. The war against

[20] A report from the Foreign Minister to the Committee on July 1, 1793, set forth the divisions within the coalition. It appears in *A.A.E. Mémoires et documents 321.* The Committee's foreign policy was set forth later in the year in a position paper found in *A.A.E. Correspondance politique 651.*

France was less important to Austria than the search for new provinces.

Like their Austrian rivals, the Prussians were concerned primarily with their own expansion, and Frederick William regarded his participation in the war against France more as a bargaining instrument to force concessions from Vienna than as a crusade against revolutionary subversion. Growing Polish resistance to foreign domination caused the Hohenzollern King to pursue a very cautious policy in the west. Berlin announced that with the reconquest of Belgium, Prussia's obligations under the treaty of 1792 were fulfilled, and that the Prussian army would not participate in additional campaigns without a British subsidy. Frederick William then left the Rhine and returned to Berlin, where he could better follow events in Poland, and ordered his generals in the Rhineland to avoid large-scale actions against the French.[21]

Even the British, founders and paymasters of the coalition, failed to devise an effective strategy, because Pitt's government neglected to define clearly its political and military objectives. Pitt himself was torn between the alternatives of attempting to crush the Republic by means of land campaigns, and using England's naval might to blockade the French coasts and capture the Republic's colonies. Within his cabinet, Lord Grenville, the Foreign Secretary, advocated a continental policy while Henry Dundas, the Secretary of State for War, favored the imperial strategy of seizing the French colonial possessions.[22] Pitt never fully adopted either

[21] See S. Biro, *The German Policy of Revolutionary France* (Cambridge, 1957), I; and P. Sagnac, *Le Rhin français pendant la Révolution et l'Empire* (Paris, 1917). For more general studies see H. Holborn, *A History of Modern Germany 1648–1840* (New York, 1966), and M. Philippson, *Geschichte des preussischen Staatswesens vom Tode Friederichs des Grossen bis zu den Freiheitskriegen,* 2 vols. (Leipzig, 1880–82).

[22] For studies of British foreign policy see E. D. Adams, *The Influence of Grenville on Pitt's Foreign Policy 1787–1798* (Wash-

course, with the result that British strategy failed to produce decisive results in any theater of war.

British forces in Flanders and Toulon were insufficient to play a major role in defeating the French. Furthermore, Pitt's limited military contribution on the Continent weakened England's influence in the coalition. Overseas, Pitt found the French West Indies to be an overwhelming temptation and soon became involved in an expensive and futile campaign to conquer Saint Domingue (Haiti), the wealthiest possession in the French Empire. In 1789 revolution had come to Saint Domingue, and the planter aristocracy and lower-middle-class whites had struggled for power. Additional complications arose when the free mulattos sought and failed to attain equality. The white planters had armed Negro slaves and used them to crush the mulattos, but in the summer of 1791 many of these armed slaves joined a major servile insurrection. Hundreds of whites fled to neighboring British West Indian colonies, where their tales of the slave rising alarmed British officials. To prevent similar revolts in English colonies, Pitt increased his forces in the West Indies to nineteen battalions. The outbreak of war with France, plus continued appeals of French plantation owners for assistance, convinced Pitt to expand his military commitment in the Caribbean.[23]

In April 1793 the British occupied Tobago and in September a small detachment landed in Saint Domingue. In November seven thousand additional troops sailed

ington, D.C., 1904); C. Matheson, *The Life of Henry Dundas, First Viscount Melville, 1742–1811* (London, 1933); J. H. Rose, *William Pitt and the Great War* (London, 1912); and A. W. Ward and G. P. Gooch, *The Cambridge History of British Foreign Policy* (Cambridge, 1922), I.

[23] The following works supply the background for the history of Haiti: L. Deschamps, *Les Colonies pendant la Révolution: La Constituante et la réforme coloniale* (Paris, 1898). T. L. Stoddard, *The French Revolution in San Domingo* (Boston, 1913) is useful despite its racist bias. C. L. R. James, *The Black Jacobins* (New York, 1938) presents a Marxist view of the revolution in Haiti.

from England with the mission of seizing all French colonies in the West Indies. The rebellious slaves had meanwhile found a leader who was a match for any European general of his time. A former house slave, Toussaint Louverture had joined the revolt of 1791 and co-operated with the Spanish, who owned half of Saint Domingue. He soon came to realize that if victorious, the Spanish and English would restore slavery, and when the Convention abolished slavery he switched sides. Toussaint then fought to obtain freedom for himself and his followers. He was not interested in supporting the foreign policy of the Republic, but he nevertheless performed a great service for France by tying down thousands of English troops thousands of miles away from the decisive continental battlefields.[24] By dividing his forces, Pitt inadvertently gave the Republic an additional advantage in the fall campaigns.

On the French frontiers the coalition matched its strategic dispersal of effort with a similar tactical disarray. The Duke of York's British forces marched on Dunkirk while Coburg's Austrians attacked the forts in northern France. In the Rhineland, Austrian and Prussian units failed to co-operate, and neither force co-ordinated its actions with those of the armies in Flanders.

Carnot took advantage of allied disunity by rushing reinforcements to Flanders, and ordered General Jean Houchard, a battle-scarred veteran of the Royal Army who remained loyal to the Revolution, to lead fifty thousand men to the relief of Dunkirk, telling him to attack immediately despite the fact that he was not fully prepared, because the national morale required a victory.[25] Houchard then abandoned a plan to capture Furnes and encircle the allied army in favor of a direct thrust toward

[24] For the course of the war and revolution in Haiti see R. Korngold, *Citizen Toussaint* (New York, 1944), and C. Moran, *Black Triumvirate* (New York, 1957).

[25] *Min. de la Guerre A.H., Registre de l'état-major genéral, 18 août 1793 continuée jusqu' au 1 Octobre suivant, carton* B^1*110.*

Dunkirk. On September 6 his columns attacked Hanoverian posts protecting the British siegeworks, but they failed to penetrate the Duke's position. Houchard attacked again on September 8. Covered by light infantry, the French columns advanced against the allied posts around the village of Hondschoote and broke through the Hanoverian lines. That evening the Duke of York abandoned his siege trenches and fell back to Furnes. Houchard followed and took Menin on September 13.[26] But Coburg, who had just taken Quesnoy, sent reinforcements to Flanders and retook Menin, whereupon the Committee removed Houchard because of his failure to destroy the Duke's army. Assuming that his errors, which helped the coalition, were conscious ones, the government later tried and executed the victor of Hondschoote.[27]

The Battle of Hondschoote, despite its limited results and despite Houchard's tragic end, was, nevertheless, a turning point in the war. The French citizen army had halted an allied offensive and demonstrated to themselves and to the nation their ability to fight and to win.

In October the French switched their main efforts to the Sambre River area in northeastern France, where Coburg was attempting to capture Maubeuge for use as an advanced base for a march on Paris. The Committee attached enormous importance to Maubeuge's salvation. The fortress was a strategic key to north-central France, and the populace of Paris was so insistent on further

[26] See Houchard's report to the war minister in *Min. de la Guerre A.H., Correspondance Armées du Nord et des Ardennes, 1–15 Septembre 1793, carton B¹18.*

[27] For the order removing Houchard from command see *Min. de la Guerre A.H., Correspondance Armées du Nord et des Ardennes, carton B¹19.* The French removed many officers from command, including Jourdan, Hoche, and Bonaparte. Some, like Custine, perished. In dangerous circumstances, governments often react strongly to any apparent threat to their security. For example, during the American Civil War a congressional committee hunted for disloyal officers and even sent special agents to watch field commanders.

victories that failure to relieve the city might lead to another revolutionary *journée* and the destruction of the Committee. So important was the forthcoming campaign that Carnot himself went to the front to assist and supervise General Jourdan, one of the Committee's new middle-class generals and the new leader of the Army of the North.

While Carnot directed the requisition of supplies, Jourdan gathered a striking force of forty-four thousand men, organized them into three columns covered by skirmishers, and led them toward the village of Wattignies, an important position in Coburg's siege lines.[28] On October 15 Jourdan attacked, but the Dutch and Austrian forces repulsed his columns. The French attacked again on the sixteenth. They suffered three thousand casualties, but one of the columns stormed and held Wattignies. Although his forces were still largely intact, Coburg, shaken by the violence of the French assault, decided to retreat. On October 17 he abandoned the siege of Maubeuge and fell back into Belgium.[29] For the French, Wattignies was decisive. Jourdan, it is true, did not destroy the Austro-Dutch army, but in halting a second allied offensive, the Army of the North gave the nation renewed confidence in the prospects of victory, security from invasion for the rest of the year, and time to complete its military and economic mobilization.

On the other fronts, the French also managed to halt allied offensives. In the Rhineland the Prussians had taken Mainz and by late October were attacking Landau. The Austrians had also moved forward, taking Wissembourg and forcing the French back to Strasbourg. After Wattignies, Carnot sent reinforcements to generals

[28] *Min. de la Guerre A.H., Correspondance Armées du Nord et des Ardennes, carton B¹20,* and *Min. de la Guerre A.H., M.h., Mémoires militaires du Maréchal Jourdan, campagne de 1793 608¹.*

[29] See Jourdan's report to the Convention and his report to the War Minister in *Min. de la Guerre A.H. carton B¹20.*

Hoche and Pichegru, commanders of the French forces in the Rhineland and Alsace. Attacks launched in November failed, but in early December the two generals combined their forces, drove the Austrians out of Alsace, and recaptured Wissembourg. Their success in turn uncovered the Prussian flank and at the end of the month the Duke of Brunswick gave up the siege of Landau and retreated toward the Rhine. French troops also drove enemy forces from Savoy, and along the Pyrenees constant counterattacks stemmed the Spanish advance and forced them to give up their efforts to take Perpignan. By the end of 1793 the French had turned back all attempts to invade their territory and were preparing to carry the war into enemy lands in the spring.

Meanwhile, within France, republican forces succeeded in defeating counterrevolutionary movements. The federalist revolts collapsed quickly. Many departments voluntarily restored the authority of the Convention, while others capitulated with little resistance. By early autumn only the Vendée, Lyons, and Toulon continued to fight against the Republic.

Fighting in the Vendée was exceedingly bitter since both sides commonly shot prisoners and killed civilian opponents. In June the Catholic and Royal Army failed to take Nantes, but a series of unco-ordinated republican expeditions proved unable to crush the rebels. In the late summer the garrison of Mainz, having capitulated to the Prussians, returned to France on parole. To obtain the right to return to France the garrison commander had agreed to refrain from fighting the allied armies, but since nothing was said about using the garrison within France, the Committee sent it to the Vendée, and in mid-September it began to advance into the center of the rebellious region. Royalist commanders hurled all their available men against the republican columns and by September 22 succeeded in halting their advance. The republicans then reorganized their forces, forming a new Army of the West of thirty-two thousand men. In October the Army of the West began a new advance into the Vendée, moving inland from the coast. At the same time other detachments entered the Vendée from the south and east.

On October 16, thirty-five thousand royalists attacked the Army of the West at Cholet. Republican troops slaughtered the peasant guerrillas and forced the remnants to flee the Vendée. Accompanied by thousands of civilians, the royalists crossed the Loire River into Brittany on October 18. The Bretons, however, failed to join their rebellion, leaving the Vendeans with but one choice —to capture a port and obtain arms and supplies from a British squadron that was sailing to their aid. On November 13 the rebels tried to take Granville, but the garrison repulsed them. In desperation the Vendeans fled back toward their homes. Republican forces sent detachments to block the passages over the Loire while large columns pursued the desperate royalists. The Army of the West caught and defeated the rebels near Le Mans and, on December 23, annihilated the remnants of the Catholic and Royal Army at Savenay. Escapees from this debacle made their way back to the Vendée and resumed small-scale partisan warfare, but they were no longer a serious military threat to the Republic.

In the Rhône Valley republican forces invested Lyons on September 17. After a lengthy bombardment, the city fell on October 9. Republican authorities then instituted an extensive purge of royalists and federalists, slaughtering foes of the government in wholesale lots. The fall of Lyons in turn enabled the Committee to increase pressure on Toulon. In November General Dugommier, assisted by Major Napoleon Bonaparte, his artillery commander, organized an attack on the allied positions. By December 18 the French infantry had seized positions from which Bonaparte's guns could bombard the harbor. That evening the British blew up the arsenal, burned a number of captured French ships, and evacuated the port. On the morning of December 19, French troops entered Toulon.[30] By the end of the year the Republic had effectively destroyed the power of its internal enemies.

As the Committee made ready to launch a series of major offensives in the spring of 1794, deepening rivalries within the allied camp weakened the forces of the coalition. The fate of Poland continued to be the major cause of interallied dissension, and Austro-Prussian rivalry in the east severely limited the coalition's effectiveness in the west.

To many Poles, the Second Partition and the presence of Russian troops on their soil was insupportable. Great nobles, gentry, and burghers began to form secret resistance organizations, and these cells gradually established contact with each other and with patriots who had gone into exile after the Second Partition. One prominent exile, Thaddeus Kosciuszko, went to Paris to seek French aid, but aside from expressions of sympathy, he obtained nothing from the Convention. Undaunted, resistance groups in Poland prepared for action and chose Kosciuszko as their leader.[31]

Meanwhile in Warsaw, the Russian garrison commander, having obtained fragmentary information concerning revolutionary preparations, began to arrest suspects and disbanded several Polish regiments. The Poles decided that they had to act before the Russians destroyed their organization, and in March 1794, a regi-

[30] On the fall of Lyons see Palmer, *Twelve Who Ruled*, Ch. VII. On the general question of executions see D. Green, *The Incidence of the Terror During the French Revolution* (Cambridge, 1935). On the recapture of Toulon see the 1852 French staff study, *Min. de la Guerre A.H., M.h., Précis historique sur le siège de Toulon en 1793 400*. For a more recent account see D. G. Chandler, *The Campaigns of Napoleon* (New York, 1966), pp. 15–29.

[31] For the background of the Polish Revolution see H. de Montfort, *Le drame de la Pologne: Koscuiszko 1764–1817* (Paris, 1945); J. Godechot, *La Grande Nation* (Paris, 1956), I, pp. 182–87; and R. R. Palmer, *Age of the Democratic Revolution* (Princeton, 1956), II, pp. 146–56.

ment near Cracow launched the insurrection. Kosciuszko returned to Poland on March 24 and issued a call for a general rising. On April 4, with a force of regulars and scythe-armed peasants, he defeated a small Russian detachment, and news of his victory convinced many to join the insurrection. Warsaw drove out its Russian garrison on April 16, and as the Russians withdrew to the Ukraine to await reinforcements, Vilna joined the rebellion.

Despite the initial victories the Polish revolt was doomed. In June the Prussians sent fifty thousand men into Poland while the Russians collected a large force for a march on Warsaw. Furthermore, the Poles lacked firm unity. One group of rebels, led by the King and conservative nobles, wished only to eliminate foreign domination. A second faction, consisting of petty nobles, army officers, bureaucrats, and professional men, sought to institute extensive social reforms, and some of them even advocated emancipation of the serfs. To unite both groups, Kosciuszko attempted a compromise which granted the serfs personal freedom but retained the manorial system and personal labor obligations for peasants remaining on estates owned by nobles. The result of this plan was to alarm the conservatives and disappoint the reformers and peasants at the moment when the eastern powers were preparing to destroy Poland's independence.

The Prussians first advanced on Cracow, taking Poland's ancient capital in mid-June. By July 2 the Prussian army stood in front of Warsaw. The Prussians then tried and failed to storm the city. Catherine had refused to aid the Prussian assault because she wanted to conquer Warsaw with her own armies. After their defeat, the Prussians fell back, and the Russians advanced. On October 10 a Russian corps defeated the main Polish army and captured Kosciuszko; on November 4 the main Russian army entered the outskirts of Warsaw, and on the sixth the city surrendered.[32] The Polish Revolution was over, but the extinction of Poland's independence was to cause bitter dissension among the eastern courts.

Even before the collapse of the Polish rising, Catherine had decided upon the elimination of Poland from the map of Europe. The Empress, however, did not want to strengthen Prussia further by allowing Berlin a major share of the spoils. She therefore decided to arrrange the final partition with Austria in order to check Prussia and win Hapsburg approval of a revival of her project for dismembering the Ottoman Empire. The Prussians insisted upon retaining Cracow and advancing their frontier to the Vistula. The Russians rejected these demands, and the Austrians sent over twenty thousand men to Galicia to give credibility to their demands for Cracow and extensive territory in southwestern Poland. Rounds of talks and threats continued throughout the year. On January 3, 1795, Austria and Russia signed the Third Partition treaty, whereby Austria and Russia took most of Poland, leaving a small portion, including Warsaw, to Prussia. The treaty also included an Austro-Russian alliance against Prussia in case Frederick William tried to alter the partition agreement by force. The Prussians refused to accept the treaty, and a final settlement of the Polish issue was not reached for more than a year.

Austro-Prussian rivalry over the dismemberment of Poland in turn had a significant impact on the western battlefields in 1794. The two courts retained over seventy thousand troops, vitally needed in Belgium and the Rhineland, in the east. Austrian negotiations with Russia angered and alarmed the Prussians. Frederick William therefore refused all but minimal co-operation in the west and even began to contemplate a separate peace with France. The coalition thus had to meet French at-

[32] M. Kukiel, "Kosciuszko and the Third Partition," in *Cambridge History of Poland* (Cambridge, 1941), and K. Osipov, *Alexander Suvorov* (New York, 1941). Suvorov led the Russian forces that took Warsaw.

tacks at a time when its own forces were deeply divided.

In planning the forthcoming campaign, the Committee of Public Safety chose to make its major effort in Belgium. The French had already decided that Austria and England were their most implacable foes and that the Republic could obtain peace only by crushing their most bitter enemies in battle. Since the British and Austrians had their main field armies in the Low Countries, the Committee felt that it had to seek a decision in that area. Furthermore, the Committee was aware of the growing Austro-Prussian hostility over Poland and hoped that Prussia would eventually leave the war. By fighting in Belgium and limiting their blows against the Prussian forces in Germany, the French sought to encourage those groups in Berlin which advocated a separate peace with France. Military considerations also influenced the government's strategy. The largest allied armies served in the Low Countries, and Carnot knew that if the Republic triumphed in Belgium it could then easily defeat its enemies on other fronts.[33]

In February 1794 Carnot began to concentrate reinforcements in northern France, and informed his field commanders that the armies of the Republic were to prepare to strike decisive blows against two or three critical positions.[34] The allied lines, consisting of a series of closely linked fortified posts, ran from Ypres on the Channel through Denain and Valenciennes to the Meuse. The line then followed the Meuse to Namur and ran from there to Treves. Over 150,000 English, Dutch, Austrian, and German troops held the posts and served in the mobile field armies. For his offensive, Carnot decided

[33] As early as July 1, 1793, the Foreign Minister noted the growing hostility between Austria and Prussia. See *A.A.E. Mémoires et documents 321.* Carnot decided to launch offensives in the north on February 2, 1794. See *Min. de la Guerre A.H., Inventaire analytique, Armées du Nord et des Ardennes, janvier–mars 1794.*

[34] E. Charavany, *Correspondance générale de Carnot* (Paris, 1908), IV, pp. 279–80.

to launch massive attacks against the allied flanks while standing on the defensive in the center. He ordered the 75,000-man left wing of Pichegru's Army of the North to take Ypres and Ghent and then wheel east on Brussels. Thirty thousand troops of Pichegru's command were to hold the French center and pin down as many allied units as possible. On the right, a composite force of 64,800 men drawn from the armies of the North and Ardennes, and from Jourdan's Moselle Army, was to drive on Charleroi and Namur. The Committee told both its generals to seek a decisive encounter in the field, to avoid sieges, mask enemy garrisons with a minimum number of troops, and defeat, pursue, and exterminate the main allied forces.[35]

The allies, despite their lack of unity, also organized a spring offensive. The Austrians promised French territory to Sardinia, claiming Milan in return, and the British arranged to pay Prussia a subsidy in exchange for the participation of sixty-two thousand Prussian soldiers in the forthcoming campaign. The Prussians, however, refused full co-operation because of their rivalry with the Austrians, thus forcing Coburg to operate without needed reinforcements. The allies, therefore, fell back upon their earlier strategy of attacking the fortresses in northern France in order to wear down the Republic's armies and open the routes to Paris.[36]

Coburg opened his offensive against the French center on April 17. He planned to take Le Cateau and Landrecies and then move on Cambrai, the last major bastion between his forces and Paris. By April 26 he had succeeded in surrounding Landrecies and driving off a

[35] Charavany, *Correspondance*, pp. 382–83; see also the Committee's instructions to Jourdan of May 23 in *Min. de la Guerre A.H., M.h., Mémoires militaires du Maréchal Jourdan Campagne de 1794 608²*.

[36] For negotiations concerning the subsidy to Prussia and the Austrian rejection of this plan see Vivenot, *Quellen*, IV, pp. 100–1, 107–12, and 121–23.

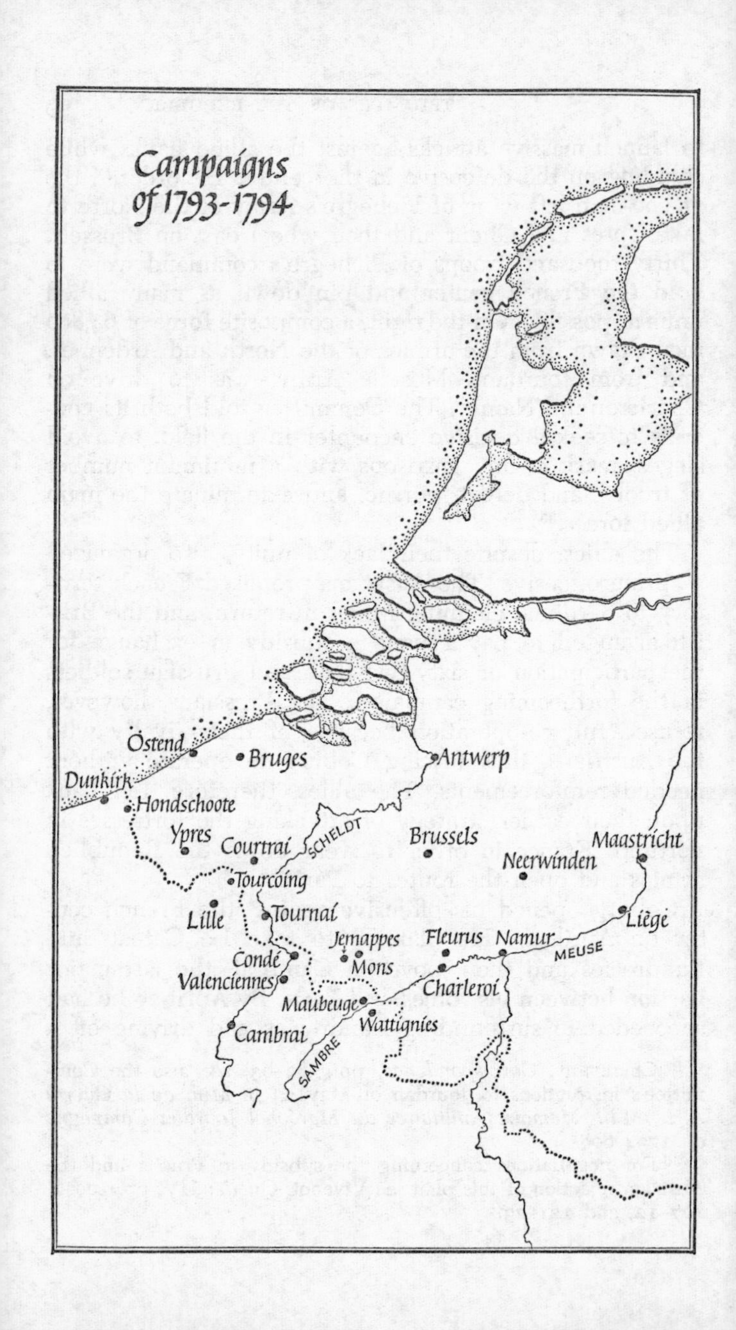
Campaigns of 1793-1794
Ostend
Bruges
Antwerp
Dunkirk
Hondschoote
Ypres
Courtrai
SCHELDT
Brussels
Maastricht
Neerwinden
Tourcoing
Lille
Tournai
Liège
Jemappes
Fleurus
Namur
Condé
Mons
MEUSE
Valenciennes
Charleroi
Maubeuge
Wattignies
Cambrai
SAMBRE

French relief force. Three days later the Army of the North launched its first attack in Flanders. The French captured Courtrai and surrounded Menin, but on April 30 the allies fought their way out of Menin, while in the center the Austrians captured Landrecies.[37]

In the first weeks of May the allies tried and failed to recapture Menin, and on May 17 they launched a large-scale attack against the French at Tourcoing. The allies, however, advanced in six unco-ordinated echelons, and Pichegru was able to repulse individual units as they reached the battlefield. The following day the French counterattacked and forced the allies to fall back to Tournai. On the twenty-second Pichegru tried to take the city. He inflicted four thousand casualties on his enemies but lost sixty-five hundred men of his own and failed in his objective. Nevertheless, he had scored a strategic triumph; he had seized the initiative in Flanders and forced Coburg to shift reserves from the Sambre-Meuse area to the west at the very time when Jourdan was preparing to unleash his offensive.[38]

Under the watchful eye of Saint-Just, a member of the Committee, French troops had first crossed the Sambre on May 12, but had failed to secure a foothold on the Austrian side. Urged on by Saint-Just, Jourdan crossed the river again on May 20, only to have the Austrians dislodge him four days later. Renewed attacks failed on May 25, and assaults launched on the twenty-ninth, which brought the French to the walls of Charleroi, collapsed under allied counterthrusts on June 3.[39]

[37] See *Min. de la Guerre A.H., M.h., Exposé des opérations des Armées du Nord et de Sambre Meuse, 1794–1795 280.* For general secondary accounts see J. W. Fortescue, *History of the British Army* (London, 1906), IV, Part 1; H. Coutanceau, *La Campagne de 1794 à l'armée du Nord,* 4 vols. (Paris, 1903–8); L. Jouan, *La conquête de la Belgique; mai–juillet 1794* (Paris, 1914); and R. W. Phipps, *The Armies of the First French Republic; The Armées de la Moselle, du Rhin, de Sambre-et-Meuse, de Rhin-et-Moselle* (London, 1929).

[38] *Min. de la Guerre A.H., M.h., 280.*

[39] Ibid.

Defeated on one flank, the French quickly switched their efforts to the other. On June 1 Pichegru began to attack Ypres, and on June 10 and again on the thirteenth his troops repulsed allied attempts to relieve the garrison. Ypres fell to the Army of the North on June 17, while on the Sambre, Jourdan was again on the move.[40] In the previous weeks Carnot had placed Jourdan in command of the right wing of the Army of the North, the Army of the Ardennes, and his own Moselle Army. He built this force, later known as the Army of the Sambre-Meuse, to a strength of ninety-three thousand men, and ordered Jourdan to cross the river again and seek a decisive battle with Coburg's field army. On June 12 Jourdan advanced. Driven back on the sixteenth, he returned to the assault on June 18 and finally secured a permanent lodgment on the Austrian side of the river. The French then proceeded to besiege Charleroi in order to draw the Austrians into a major battle. Coburg rose to this bait and raced to the garrison's relief, but he was too late. On June 25 Charleroi had surrendered to the French.[41]

On June 26, 1794, Coburg led his 52,000-man force against Jourdan's army in an attempt to recover Charleroi and drive the French back across the Sambre. The republican forces took up positions covering Charleroi, with their line of battle passing in front of Fleurs, a small village from which the ensuing battle derived its name. The Austrians attacked at dawn and fighting raged throughout the day. Coburg broke through the French center, but Jourdan quickly sent forward reinforcements, and the new assault columns sealed the breach. The Austrians also broke through the French right, but once

[40] *Min. de la Guerre A.H., M.h., 280.*

[41] *Min. de la Guerre A.H., M.h., Mémoires militaires du Maréchal Jourdan Campagne de 1794 608*[2], and *Min. de la Guerre A.H., Correspondance Armées du Nord et de Sambre et Meuse, 1–13 juin 1794, carton B*[1]*33*. See also *Min. de la Guerre A.H., Diverses sur les armées de la République carton X*[p]*81.*

again reinforcements arrived, delivered vigorous counterattacks, and after heavy hand-to-hand fighting regained all lost ground. By nightfall Jourdan had lost seven thousand men, but he had inflicted ten thousand casualties upon the Austrians, retained control of Charleroi, and defeated their field army.[42]

The French victory was decisive. With their right flank shattered and their field army defeated, the coalition could no longer hold Belgium. All along the front the French armies surged forward. The Army of the North took Bruges on June 29, Ostend on July 1, Mons on July 2, and Brussels on July 9. The Sambre-Meuse Army also advanced, entering Namur on the sixteenth. In Paris, the Committee of Public Safety elaborated an occupation policy designed to strengthen the nation's frontiers and reduce the possibility of future invasions. The Committee ordered its generals to disarm all Belgian civilians regardless of their attitude toward France, and to levy contributions upon the rich. The Committee also told its generals that France planned to retain strategically important areas in Belgium, and Carnot suggested extending the Republic's frontiers to a line running from Antwerp to Namur. The Committee planned to annex the rest of Belgium at a later date and transform it into a satellite state closely linked to France.[43] Continued battlefield victories brought this policy ever closer to fulfillment.

After taking Brussels, Pichegru harried the English, Dutch, and Hanoverian forces as they retreated into Holland, while Jourdan turned east and pursued the Aus-

42 *Min. de la Guerre A.H., M.h., Relation de la bataille de Fleurs livrée le 8 messidor an 2 (26 juin 1794) 274; Min. de la Guerre A.H., M.h., Campagnes des armées du Nord des Ardennes et de Sambre Meuse (5 mai 1794–18 mars 1795) 293;* and *Min. de la Guerre A.H., Correspondance Armées du Nord et de Sambre et Meuse, 16 au 30 juin 1794, carton B¹34.*

43 See Carnot's orders to Pichegru of June 18 in *Min. de la Guerre A.H., carton B¹34.*

trians toward Germany. Even the political crisis in Paris, which led to the death of Robespierre and the destruction of the Committee's power and influence, did not halt the French armies. On July 27, the ninth day of Thermidor in the French republican calendar and the day that Robespierre fell from power, Pichegru's troops entered Antwerp and Jourdan's army took Liège. In August the French retook the fortresses that Coburg had captured in 1793, Pichegru prepared to invade Holland, and Jourdan crossed the Roer and advanced to the Rhine.

The French were equally successful on other fronts. After standing on the defensive in the Rhineland until July, the republican armies began to move forward. Reluctant to fight Austria's battles, the Prussians offered little resistance. They withdrew to Westphalia, and the French began to attack the Austrian garrison in Mainz. Along the Pyrenees, republican armies drove the Spanish out of France, invaded Catalonia, and took San Sebastián. Only at sea did the coalition obtain modest success. The British, after leaving Toulon, invaded and occupied Corsica, and in June 1794 defeated a French battle fleet which was escorting a grain convoy to Brest. The convoy reached port safely but the fighting ships suffered heavily. The British navy had once again forcefully demonstrated its vast superiority over its rivals. Naval triumphs, however, could not materially alter the strategic balance on the continental battlefields. In the Caribbean the British occupied the Windward Islands and Martinique, but failed to subdue Saint Domingue and Guadeloupe. Thus even in an area where the allies were the strongest, the coalition failed to win victories sufficient to offset their continental losses.

By the late summer of 1794, the Committee of Public Safety had mobilized the nation for war and, taking advantage of divisions within the allied ranks, had liberated French territory and carried the war into the lands of France's enemies. A hostile but observant Austrian diplomat described the causes of French success: "On the side of the enemy one sees only audacity, energy, celerity, resolution, redoubtable firmness, 800,000 men destined for combat. . . . On the side of the coalition powers one sees neither co-operation, nor accord, nor sufficient means. . . ."[44]

[44] Vivenot, *Quellen,* IV, p. 130.

CHAPTER 4

THE ASSAULT UPON EUROPE

The fall of Robespierre, the dismemberment of the government of the Terror, and the revival of conservative republican and royalist factions did not prevent French arms and diplomacy from winning further victories. Between July 1794 and October 1797 France conquered the United Provinces and transformed them into a satellite republic; drove Prussia and Spain from the war and then convinced Spain to re-enter the conflict as a French ally; established hegemony over most of Italy; threatened to invade Ireland and England; forced the British to seek peace; and wrested important territorial concessions from the Hapsburgs. Still, despite the triumphs, the Thermidorian Convention and the Directory failed to obtain final victory and an enduring peace.

The collapse of Robespierre's government led to a steady decline in the strength of France's armies. With the removal of economic controls, supplies and pay became sporadic, desertions increased, and the *levée* ceased to function effectively. Consequently, the army's strength shrank to 450,000 men by the end of 1795, and by the winter of the following year France had but 346,000 men under arms.[1] Nevertheless, the momentum of past triumphs enabled the republican forces to continue their offensives against the allied powers.

In the late summer of 1794 French troops invaded Holland. The Dutch army collapsed, and the British army along with its German contingents retired hastily

[1] For the problems besetting the French armies see the reports of the Minister of War in *A.N. AF III 149, 331, 332,* and *333,* and *AF III* 202.*

to Hanover, leaving the French and the Dutch democrats to settle Holland's fate between themselves.

Even before the French entered the United Provinces, many Dutchmen were preparing their own revolution. Dutch revolutionaries came from all walks of life, from apprentices to merchants and financiers. Only the very poor and the oligarchs remained aloof. Many of the democrats had participated in the radical ferment of the 1780s, while others were new recruits to the revolutionary movement. By the summer of 1794 Dutch democrats had formed numerous "reading societies." There were thirty-four such clubs in Amsterdam, twelve in Utrecht, and smaller numbers in other major cities. These "reading societies" were, of course, revolutionary cells which stored arms, exchanged delegations with each other, and maintained contact with French officials and with Dutch radicals who had gone into exile after 1787. At the end of July two delegates, representing an assembly of radical clubs from all seven provinces, proceeded secretly to the French army headquarters to learn whether the French would treat the Dutch state as a conquered region or as an ally. The French told the agents that France would regard the Dutch as allies if they first carried out their own revolution. When the French advanced into the United Provinces, the radicals went into action. Riots erupted in Amsterdam and other towns and cities; the old order collapsed, and revolutionary committees installed provisional governments. By keeping their political demands and military requisitions to a minimum the French encouraged many Dutch moderates to support or at least tolerate the revolution. In January 1795 French cavalry charged over the ice to capture the Dutch fleet and Amsterdam. The Stadtholder, William V, fled to England, and Dutch revolutionaries proclaimed the establishment of the Batavian Republic.

In their dealings with the new republic the French continued their policy of placing their national interests above those of revolutionary ideology. In May 1795, after months of tedious negotiations, France and the Batavian Republic signed a treaty whereby the Dutch agreed to declare war on England, maintain a French army on their soil at their own expense, accept French paper money, cede Flushing and the mouth of the Scheldt to France, and pay a war indemnity of 100,000 florins. The Treaty of The Hague caused many to regret their ties with France, but the actions of the Stadtholder forced them to retain their pro-French, prorepublican orientation. William, upon arriving in England, had authorized the British to occupy all Dutch overseas possessions, and by the end of 1796 the British had captured the Cape of Good Hope and Ceylon. Meanwhile, a number of Dutch moderates entered into secret correspondence with William V, suggesting that he offer extensive political reforms in return for his restoration. The exiled Stadtholder, however, refused any concessions, threw himself completely upon England's mercy, and announced that a restoration had to include the reestablishment of the old political and social order. Consequently, all but the most conservative Dutchmen realized that the recovery of their colonies and the preservation of the gains of the revolution depended upon a continuation of the French alliance. Of all the satellite republics established by France, the Batavian regime was the most closely attached to its French protector.

While paving the way for the creation of the Batavian Republic, French diplomats were also negotiating with the Hohenzollern monarchy. The Berlin court, alarmed by their exclusion from the final partition of Poland and by the development of the Austro-Russian entente, decided to undertake peace talks with France in order to free their economic and military resources for use in the east. A Prussian envoy arrived in Basel on November 24, 1794, to begin talks with Barthélemy, the French ambassador to Switzerland.

At first neither the Prussians nor the French had a clear set of objectives. The Hohenzollern councils were divided between those who sought peace at almost any price and those who opposed a peace treaty that did not include the other German princes of the Holy Roman Empire. The "peace" faction wished to devote its major efforts in the east and regarded the prospect of French aggrandizement in the Rhineland as a convenient excuse for expanding Prussian power in Germany under the guise of compensation for the loss of Rhenish provinces. Those who opposed a separate peace with the French Republic emphasized the danger of losing influence among the lesser princes who relied upon Prussia for protection from the French and the Austrians. Thus Prussia was torn between the desires to concentrate upon eastern affairs and gain new lands in Germany and the requirements of the Empire's security.

French policy was also ill defined, for the various factions in the Convention had their own special policies for the disposition of the nation's conquests and for negotiations with foreign powers. Royalist partisans and many conservative deputies advocated complete renunciation of all conquests in return for a general peace coupled with a restoration of the monarchy in France. Political moderates including Carnot and a constitutional royalist faction wanted limited strategic alterations of France's pre-1792 frontiers. They hoped to annex parts of Belgium and Luxembourg but were willing to relinquish all other territorial gains. Republicans and regicides advocated a victorious peace for a variety of reasons. A revival of royalist sentiment within the country convinced some of them that the Republic had to produce tangible gains from the war in order to retain popular support. Others saw economic benefits in a policy of territorial expansion. The abolition of price controls had led to a rapid devaluation of the assignats, and many hoped that by increasing the nation's size and population and exporting the paper currency into the new provinces they could stem the inflationary price spiral. Finally, other republicans advocated annexations in order to provide protection for the nation's northern and eastern provinces and to gain equivalent compensation to balance Austrian, Prussian, and Russian gains in eastern Europe.

At Basel, the Prussians were at first reluctant to make important concessions in the west, but events in the east soon forced their hand. In January 1795 Frederick William learned that Francis and Catherine had decided to take the lion's share of Poland, leaving to Prussia only a relatively small area around Warsaw. The Prussians thereupon concluded that if they were to redress the eastern balance they had to end hostilities in the west at all costs and on April 5, 1795, signed a treaty with the French Republic. According to the Treaty of Basel, France agreed to evacuate all conquests on the right bank of the Rhine but was to retain control of Prussian territory on the left bank until the conclusion of a final peace with the Empire. In a secret convention, France and Prussia agreed that if the Republic gained the Prussian left-bank provinces at the final peace, Prussia would take suitable compensations within Germany. Another secret article called for the indemnification of other princes with left-bank possessions if they had to sacrifice them at the general peace. A supplementary agreement signed on May 17 provided for the neutralization of Germany north of the Main River. Prussia was to guarantee this neutrality and thereby obtained a dominant position in northern Germany for the next ten years.[2]

Both sides gained from the treaties. France did not, of course, obtain complete recognition of her claims to the Rhineland, but the Republic did secure Prussia's agreement to abandon the Rhineland and to give support to the French demands at any general peace conference.

[2] Reports on the negotiations may be found in *A.A.E. Correspondance politique* 668. Terms of the treaty may be found in A. Fugier, *Histoire des relations internationales: La Révolution française et l'Empire napoléonien* (Paris, 1954), p. 93. See also *A.A.E. Correspondance politique* 364.

Prussia, although free of entanglements in the west, was unable to alter the situation in Poland. Berlin's threats and troop demonstrations failed to convince Vienna and St. Petersburg to modify the Third Partition treaty, and at the end of the year Frederick William adhered to the Austro-Russian agreement. On the other hand, by ending the war in the west, Berlin eliminated a serious drain on its treasury and enhanced its power within the Holy Roman Empire, thereby offsetting to some degree Vienna's gains in Poland. The treaties also marked a significant step in the collapse of the First Coalition. For the first time a major European power recognized the French Republic and its conquests. This power had signed a formal peace treaty with France, left the war, and shattered the precarious unity of the anti-French alliance.

Meanwhile, other powers were deserting the coalition. To the great satisfaction of Tuscan merchants and bankers, the duchy signed a peace treaty with the Republic in 1795. The Spanish Government also decided to leave the war. The growth of British economic and political influence in the Caribbean and Mediterranean alarmed Madrid. The Spanish began to worry about the possibility of British commercial and territorial penetration into South and Central America and felt that increased British influence in the Mediterranean would be detrimental to their hopes of obtaining provinces in Italy. Madrid therefore opened negotiations with the French envoy at Basel. The Spanish began the talks by proposing the creation of a kingdom for Louis XVII south of the Loire River. The French countered this incredible proposal by demanding Louisiana and other colonial concessions and by opening a military offensive that quickly reached the Ebro River and brought French troops to the outskirts of Bilbao. At this juncture the French defeated and destroyed an *émigré* expedition which a British fleet had transported to Quiberon Bay in Brittany, but despite their success the government grew alarmed at the possible increase of counterrevolutionary activity and decided to reduce the number of its enemies by securing a peace with Spain as soon as possible. The Republic therefore decided to moderate its terms, a task made easier by the fact that Louis XVII had died, thereby removing the need to deal with the original Spanish proposal. Consequently, on July 22, 1795, France and Spain signed a treaty of peace. The French evacuated Spain and kept only the Spanish portion of Santo Domingo. Spain recognized the Republic, left the war, and Madrid's defection administered still another blow to the unity of the coalition.[3]

Encouraged by its diplomatic successes and frightened at the continued prospect of expanded domestic counterrevolutionary activity, the Convention decided to settle the fate of Belgium. To increase French security and prestige and convince the populace that France was winning the war, the Convention, on October 1, 1795, incorporated Belgium into the French Republic. The French did not annex the Rhineland at this time because they felt it necessary to wait for a general peace conference, where they could solve the problem of finding compensation for dispossessed princes. On the other hand, Prussian recognition of French occupation and probable annexation of the Rhineland was incorporated into the Basel Treaty and indicated the direction of French foreign policy in western Germany.

Despite these triumphs the war continued, for England and Austria refused to recognize either the republican regime or the growth of French power. In May 1795 Pitt granted a large subsidy to Francis II in order to keep the Hapsburg armies in the field. In September Catherine of Russia joined the coalition, and although she sent almost no material aid to the allies, her adherence to the anti-French league reduced Austrian concern

[3] See *A.N. AF III 61* for the negotiations with Spain. On Quiberon Bay see G. Lefebvre, *Les Thermidoriens* (Paris, 1960), Ch. VIII.

over the balance of power in eastern Europe. In October Prussia concluded that it was impossible to alter the division of Polish spoils because England and Russia would support their ally, and Berlin therefore accepted the provisions of the Third Partition treaty. Prussia's action in turn allowed Francis to employ the bulk of his armed forces, over 150,000 men, in western campaigns.

To force the Hapsburgs to sue for peace the French decided to launch a major offensive in Germany in the late summer of 1795. The government ordered Jourdan to cross the Rhine and attack Mainz and Düsseldorf. Pichegru was to support Jourdan's army by attacking Mannheim and then advancing on Heidelberg. A third army under Moreau was to move down the Danube.[4]

The campaign itself was a disaster. Riddled by desertion and disease and lacking pay, supplies, and munitions, the French armies were ill prepared for combat. Moreover, the three generals failed to co-ordinate their offensives. Jourdan crossed the Rhine on September 6, but Pichegru delayed his advance for several weeks, thereby exposing Jourdan's right flank to Austrian counterthrusts.[5] Despite repeated directives from the War Minister, Pichegru did not cross the Rhine and take Mannheim until September 20. He then advanced toward Heidelberg but moved at such a slow pace that Archduke Charles, the most able Hapsburg commander, was able to shift troops away from Pichegru's line of advance and concentrate them against Jourdan. In early October the Archduke attacked and defeated Jourdan, forcing him to retreat hastily back to the left bank of the Rhine. Since Pichegru had not advanced, Charles moved quickly and

[4] See *Min. de la Guerre A.H., Inventaire analytique Armées du Rhin et de la Moselle, janvier–juin 1795.* This volume contains orders, troop strength, and action reports of the armies.

[5] Deeply involved with the royalists, Pichegru may well have delayed his advance purposely in order to assure Jourdan's defeat. See E. Caudrillier, *La trahison de Pichegru et les intrigues dans l'est avant. Fructidor* (Paris, 1908).

directed his forces against him. The Austrians defeated Pichegru's forces on November 15, and by November 24 the Archduke's men had retaken Mannheim and raised the siege of Mainz. These defeats exposed Moreau's army and forced it to fall back to Alsace. By December 1795 the Austrians had not only halted the French offensive but also were threatening to invade Luxembourg and the Rhineland.

Military setbacks also ruined the plans of the newly installed Directory to negotiate peace treaties with Austria and England. Having completed their task of writing a new Constitution, the Convention had adjourned in October 1795. In its place a five-man Executive Directory chosen by two legislative councils assumed control of the nation's destiny. From the start the new regime was unpopular. Social radicals, Jacobins, and royalists all regarded the Constitution of the Year III (1795) and its institutions as an interim regime that would soon be replaced. The political moderates who supported the new government felt that an end to the war on terms that brought some gains for France would bolster their popular support at home. Thus despite the failure of the 1795 campaigns the directors sought to open secret peace talks with the Hapsburgs and the English. In December 1795 the Directory sent a secret agent to Vienna to propose that France take Belgium and the Rhineland while Austria redress its losses by taking indemnities in Germany and Italy. The Austrians, however, were not interested. Encouraged by their success in the recent campaign, they assumed they could recover Belgium and expand their domains by force of arms. Negotiations with England also ended in failure. Growing popular distaste for the war plus harsh economic conditions had convinced Pitt to undertake exploratory talks with the Directory. Secret parleys began in December but immediately foundered over the question of Belgium's fate. The British refused to recognize French control of the region, the French refused to sacrifice the area, and both parties reverted to the use of force.

Carnot, having survived the Thermidorian reaction and joined the Directory, undertook the task of devising a strategy for the 1796 campaign. In Germany he decided to repeat the strategic approach he had used so successfully in Belgium: crushing the enemy's flanks. He ordered two armies to attack the Austrian flanks on the Main and Danube rivers. After driving in the Austrian wings, the French were to combine their forces and drive on Vienna. The Directory also sought to employ political subversion as part of its strategy and authorized a secret agent to support and co-ordinate revolutionary conspiracies in south Germany. Although they were unconcerned with spreading revolutionary ideology, the directors hoped that the threat of revolution would convince the south German governments and perhaps even the Hapsburgs to negotiate.[6]

The Directory also drew up plans for operations in Italy giving command of the Army of Italy to Napoleon Bonaparte, who had enjoyed a speckled career after the fall of Toulon. Arrested briefly as a Robespierrist after Thermidor, he had regained favor with the government by dispersing with cannon fire, the famous "whif of grapeshot," a royalist rising early in 1795. He then married a former mistress of one of the directors, and it was at least in part due to the influence of his wife's ex-lover that the government gave him his new command. The Directory ordered its general to attack Piedmont, force the Kingdom of Sardinia out of the war, and then conquer Lombardy.[7] The Directory felt that an Italian campaign would force the states of Italy to sue for peace,

[6] See *Min. de la Guerre A.H., M.h., Précis de la campagne de l'armée de Sambre et Meuse pendant l'an 4 298;* and S. Biro, *The German Policy of Revolutionary France* (Cambridge, Mass. 1957), II, p. 573.

[7] A. Debidour, *Recueil des Actes du Directoire exécutif* (Paris, 1910), I, pp. 717 ff.

place additional pressure on the Austrian armies, and provide France with valuable trading counters for use in any general peace talks. As in Germany, the French planned to employ political subversion as part of their over-all strategy. Charles Delacroix, the Foreign Minister, held secret talks with Italian radicals in February and March of 1796, but at the same time the minister made sure that these democrats would act in the interests of France. While the Italians sought France's assistance in creating a unified republic, Delacroix told Bonaparte to employ subversive activity against only those states that were at war with the Republic and to leave neutral powers at peace. The Directory then instructed the government commissioner to the Army of Italy to make extensive requisitions in Piedmont and Lombardy in order to support the troops and ruin Austrian resources in the area. Naturally, such a policy would make the French and their Italian allies generally unpopular and make the task of creating republican regimes immensely more difficult if not impossible, but to the French, diplomatic and strategic considerations far outweighed concern for foreign revolutionaries.[8] On July 25, 1796, Delacroix presented a memorandum concerning the fate of Italy to the Directory. He suggested that France offer Bavaria to Austria in return for Austrian recognition of the French conquest of Belgium and the Rhineland. The ruler of Bavaria would in turn receive Italian territories, including Tuscany, Modena, Ferrara, and part of the Papal States, while the Duke of Parma took Milan.[9] Some months later the Directory informed Bonaparte that he might establish provisional republican regimes in Italy to assist the Army of Italy in administrating conquered territory and procuring supplies. The government then went on to tell its general not to establish permanent regimes because France might hand

[8] *A.N. AF III 333.*

[9] See the secret deliberations of the Directory in *A.N. AF III* 20.*

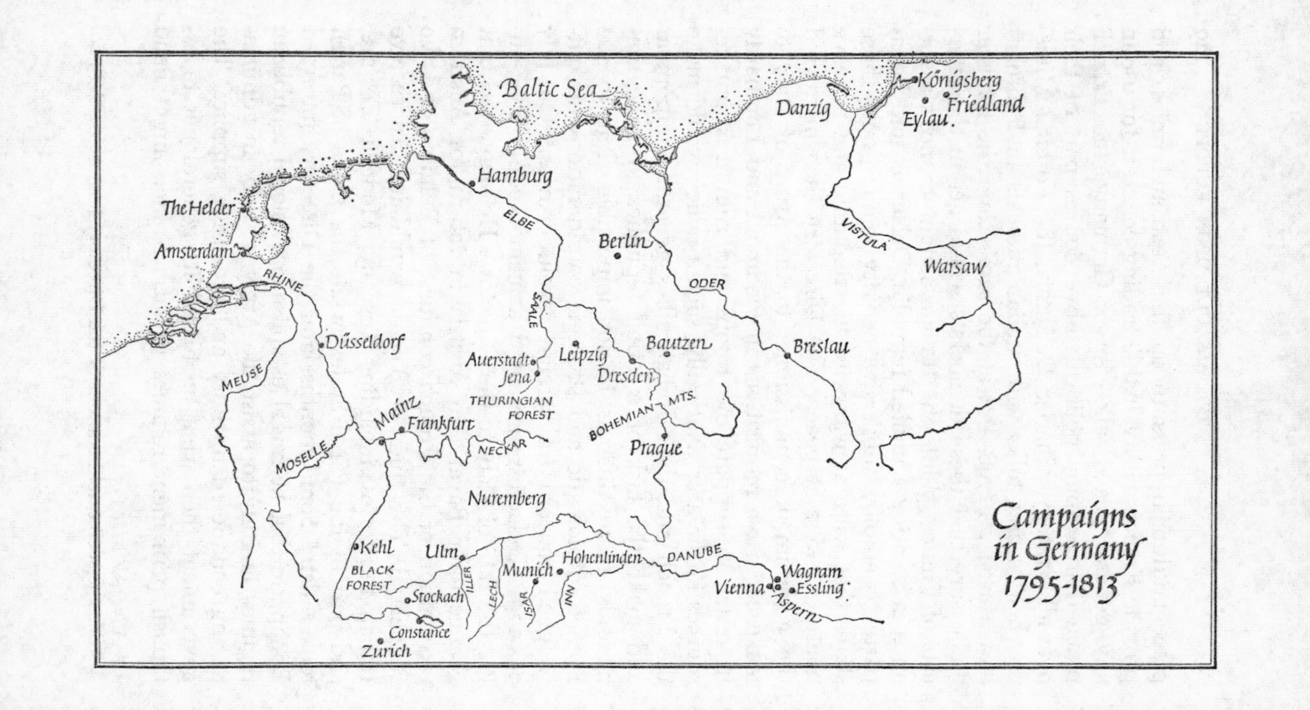
Campaigns in Germany 1795-1813
Baltic Sea
Königsberg
Friedland
Eylau
Danzig
Hamburg
The Helder
Amsterdam
ELBE
Berlin
VISTULA
Warsaw
RHINE
ODER
SAALE
Düsseldorf
Auerstadt
Jena
Leipzig
Bautzen
Dresden
Breslau
MEUSE
THURINGIAN FOREST
BOHEMIAN MTS.
Mainz
Frankfurt
NECKAR
Prague
MOSELLE
Nuremberg
Kehl
Ulm
Hohenlinden
DANUBE
BLACK FOREST
Munich
Wagram
Vienna
Essling
Aspern
Stockach
ILLER
LECH
ISAR
INN
Constance
Zurich

over her Italian conquests to other powers as part of a general peace settlement.[10] The French, then, intended to employ Italian democrats to suit their own needs and continued to subordinate republican ideology to the interests of the French state.

Military developments, however, drastically altered the Directory's plans, for in Germany, the main front, the Austrians inflicted a series of major defeats on the French armies. Jourdan with a force of about 72,000 men crossed the Rhine on May 31, but Archduke Charles with 92,000 men defeated him and forced him to fall back to the French side of the river. Meanwhile, Moreau with 77,600 men crossed the Rhine opposite Strasbourg and advanced into southern Germany. Charles sent reinforcements to check Moreau, thus enabling Jourdan to cross the river again and push to Frankfurt. After detaching troops to besiege the city, which fell on July 14, he pushed on to take Nuremberg and threaten Ratisbon. Moreau also advanced and the south German states hastened to make peace with France, whose leaders in turn abandoned their plans of stirring up a German revolutionary movement. By mid-August Moreau's forces had taken Munich and Ulm.

At this juncture Archduke Charles decided to take advantage of the fact that Jourdan and Moreau had not yet united their forces. By standing on the defensive against one of his opponents he planned to concentrate superior manpower against the other and thus defeat the French in detail. Since Moreau was not acting with great dash, Charles left thirty-eight thousand men to hold him in check and concentrated the bulk of his units for a thrust at Jourdan. With sixty-two thousand men Charles fell on Jourdan's force, which because of the necessity of conducting various sieges numbered but forty-five thousand. The Austrians defeated the French

[10] See the secret deliberations of the Directory in *A.N. AF III 20* and *A.N. AF III 442*.

and drove them back to the Rhine with heavy losses. Having defeated Jourdan, Charles then turned on Moreau, who had remained inactive in Bavaria. With his lines of communication dangerously exposed, Moreau had no choice but to retreat. He managed to avoid encirclement but had to evacuate all of Germany. By the end of October no French troops stood on the right bank of the Rhine.

Meanwhile, in Italy General Bonaparte was waging a brilliant, hard-hitting campaign and thereby transforming the secondary Italian front into the decisive theater of operations. Upon taking command of the Army of Italy, Bonaparte discovered that he had at his disposal some forty-five thousand men. His divisional commanders, including Masséna, Joubert, and Augereau, were experienced veterans, but his troops lacked supplies and equipment and had to fight forty-five thousand Piedmontese and thirty-seven thousand Austrians.[11] Since he was outnumbered, Bonaparte decided that he had to wage a campaign of rapid marches and sudden, hard-hitting attacks to allow speed and shock to offset the lack of mass. He therefore assigned seven thousand men to make demonstrations near Genoa to attract the attentions of the Austrian forces that held positions near the coast, and led the rest of his army from the Riviera north against the Piedmontese. His object was to split the allied armies, drive Piedmont out of the war, and then turn on the Austrians.

On April 12, 1796, as the main Austrian force moved to protect Genoa, Bonaparte struck north. At Montenotte his troops shattered a six-thousand-man Austrian detachment, and after detaching a division to cover his right flank against further Austrian thrusts, he continued his northward advance. On the thirteenth the Piedmontese halted the French advance and inflicted heavy losses

[11] *Min. de la Guerre A.H., M.h., Armée d'Italie campagnes de l'an IV et de l'an V 417.*

on the Army of Italy. With the Piedmontese in front of him and the Austrians concentrating against his right flank, Bonaparte realized that he had to strike quickly to avoid destruction. Since the Austrians were not yet fully concentrated, the Corsican decided to strike at them. The Army of Italy attacked and drove the Austrians from the small town of Dego on April 14. Reinforcements retook the town, but on the fifteenth renewed French assaults drove off the Austrian battalions, thereby clearing the way for renewed attacks into Piedmont.

As the French resumed their drive north the Piedmontese fell back in order to protect Turin. Despite a number of heavily contested rear-guard actions the French continued to press forward and by April 21 were threatening the city. The ruler of Piedmont-Sardinia then appealed for an armistice, which Bonaparte granted on the twenty-eighth. According to the Armistice of Cherasco the Piedmontese agreed to conclude a definitive peace with the French Republic, to allow the French to garrison several strategically located fortresses, and to grant the Army of Italy free passage into Lombardy. On May 15 the plenipotentiaries of the King of Piedmont signed a treaty of peace with France recognizing the Republic, ceding Nice and Savoy, accepting the continued presence of French garrisons in several citadels, and paying a heavy indemnity.

While the Piedmontese were negotiating with the Directory, Bonaparte was advancing into Lombardy. The Austrians after Cherasco had retreated and taken up positions behind the Ticino River, a tributary of the Po. Their left flank rested upon the northern bank of the Po. Wishing to avoid a costly frontal attack, Bonaparte decided to move rapidly along the southern bank of the river, cross to the northern side behind the Austrians, and cut them off from Milan. On May 7, after a rapid dash along the river, the Army of Italy began to cross the Po at Piacenza. The Austrians, however, had already fallen back to the Adda, another tributary of the Po. The

Austrian objective was to cover Milan, and they left a strong rear guard at Lodi to cover the main route across the Adda and halt or delay Bonaparte's advance. Anxious to take Milan and bring the Austrian army to battle, Bonaparte ordered a direct assault on the bridge. On May 10, 1796, the French swarmed onto the bridge, but Austrian artillery slaughtered the advance units and threw them back. Senior officers then rallied the disorganized troops and personally led a second charge. This time the French broke through the Austrian defenders, and although the main Austrian army made good its escape, the road to Milan lay open. On May 15 the Army of Italy, after one month and two days of campaigning, entered the city.[12]

After taking Milan, Bonaparte, following orders that the Directory had issued on May 7, detached troops for a foray into central Italy. His object was to terrorize states at war with France and produce funds for the Republic's treasury.[13] At the beginning of June the King of Naples sought an armistice, and the Republic of Venice agreed to French occupation of Verona. French troops then pushed on to Bologna, where they levied contributions of more than a million livres. The French also seized hundreds of cannons and muskets from papal arsenals. On June 23 the Pope, unable to resist the Army of Italy, signed an armistice whereby he agreed to conclude a final peace with France, close his ports to ships of any power at war with the Republic, surrender the citadel of Ancona, hand over numerous objects of art, and pay an indemnity of fifteen million livres in cash plus five and a half million livres in provisions. Other detachments forced the rulers of Parma and Modena to disgorge large indemnities, while still another unit entered Tuscany, occupied Leghorn, seized British goods, and left a garrison in the port. At Milan the Austrian

[12] Ibid.
[13] Debidour, *Recueil,* II, pp. 329–30.

garrison surrendered the citadel, and the French obtained additional war material and proceeded to extract twenty million francs from Lombardy.[14]

In addition to enriching himself and his entourage and supplying the Directory with funds from the spoils of victory, Bonaparte also began to organize an administration for the conquered regions. In this process he began to co-operate with Italian democrats, who sought to create a Lombard Republic as the first step in the development of an Italian Republic. Bonaparte was, however, not so much concerned with fostering an Italian revolution as with solving the immediate pressing problems of governing his conquests and securing his lines of communication. In the aftermath of his victories, Old Regime governments had either collapsed or shown themselves unable to keep order. Nor could the French work with local oligarchs, the Church, and Hapsburg officials, who were, of course, hostile to France. Consequently, Bonaparte sought co-operation from those who had to rely upon French backing and protection in order to secure their political objectives. In return for French support local democrats would have to keep order, help protect the Army of Italy's supply lines, and assist the French in making requisitions. Bonaparte also hoped that by assisting Italian radicals he could frighten the Austrians into negotiating in order to avoid the same fate in the Hapsburg crown lands. Never a person to underestimate his own power and ability, the Corsican general doubtless realized that his prestige would grow if he could add political accomplishments to his impressive military record.

His first step was to establish a general administration of Lombardy run by Italian democrats under French

[14] *Min. de la Guerre A.H., M.h., 417*, and *Min. de la Guerre A.H., Inventaire analytique, Armées des Alps et d'Italie, mai–juin 1796*, which contains detailed summaries of correspondence between the Directory and Bonaparte and Bonaparte's orders to his subordinates.

supervision. This agency soon organized a volunteer legion which flew the first Italian tricolor of red, white, and green. As French columns moved into central Italy rebellions broke out in many areas. Old governments collapsed, and in order to provide an effective civil authority Bonaparte at the end of 1796 brought together representatives from Bologna, Ferrara, Modena, and Reggio. Under his guidance the delegates created a league for common defense and soon afterward established a unified state known as the Cispadane Republic. Although the new republic and the Lombard administration were provisional regimes, Bonaparte had taken the first steps in establishing a permanent French presence in Italy, a policy which he was ultimately to impose upon his reluctant government.

While reorganizing Italy, Bonaparte was also pursuing his war against the Austrians. After occupying Milan, he set out to drive the Austrians back to the Tyrol. On May 30 French troops stormed across the Mincio River, forcing their foes to retreat to the Adige. The French then advanced on Mantua while the Austrians, after leaving a garrison in the city, retreated north along the shores of Lake Garda. Bonaparte in turn detached troops to watch the Alpine passes and prepared to undertake the reduction of the immensely strong fortifications around Mantua.

Determined to retain their power and possessions in Italy, the Hapsburgs prepared a counteroffensive. Vienna sent the able veteran Count Wurmser from Germany to Trent with twenty-five thousand men. After gathering up garrison units and troops that had earlier retreated to the Tyrol, Wurmser by the end of June had a force of about fifty thousand men at his disposal. He undertook to relieve Mantua by sending units down each side of Lake Garda and a third corps down the Brenta Valley. By July 29 the Austrians on the eastern shores of the lake had driven Masséna's division from Verona, and on August 1 Austrian troops on the western side arrived before Brescia. Bonaparte realized that if Wurmser broke through to Mantua he would obtain an almost unbeatable numerical superiority over the Army of Italy and concluded that he had to strike rapidly at the advancing Austrians and defeat them in detail before they could unify their separate corps. He therefore took the bold decision to abandon the siege of Mantua in order to concentrate every available man against Wurmser.

Leaving one division to check the advance of the corps on the eastern shore of Lake Garda, Bonaparte attacked the enemy forces on the western shore and defeated them at Lonato on August 3. The Army of Italy then raced back to the south, joined the division that had been guarding the eastern shores of the lake, and on August 5 attacked and defeated the Austrians at Castiglione. With two of his three corps shattered Wurmser had no choice but to retreat back in the Tyrol. He did manage to send reinforcements into Mantua, but Bonaparte's hard-driving tactics had prevented him from regaining control of the Lombard plain.

Undaunted by its defeat, the Hapsburg court directed Wurmser to mount another offensive. In his next attack the Count decided to avoid the error of moving in isolated columns by leading the bulk of his army down the Brenta Valley toward Mantua. Bonaparte's response to the renewed Austrian attack was clever and effective. Instead of meeting Wurmser head on, he maneuvered his army around the Austrian flanks and struck from behind. On September 8 the French inflicted a sharp defeat on Austrian rear guards at Bassano. Wurmser managed to avoid a decisive engagement and made good his escape to Mantua, but Bonaparte was close behind, and no sooner had the Austrian commmander entered the city than the Army of Italy re-established its siege. Thus Mantua, instead of acting as a base for Austrian offensives, became a giant trap. Short of rations, the garrison grew progressively weaker as hundreds perished from starvation.

Fearful of leaving valuable provinces in French hands, Vienna ordered a third attempt to dislodge the French from Italy. The Austrians realized that a victory in Italy coupled with their triumphs in Germany would place them in an excellent diplomatic and strategic position and consequently sent an additional forty-six thousand men into action against the Army of Italy. Baron Alvintzy was to lead twenty-eight thousand men to Bassano and from there to Verona. At Verona eighteen thousand men, having entered Italy from the Tyrol, were to join him, and the combined force was then to march to the relief of Mantua. Bonaparte responded by reviving his tactics of concentrating the greater part of his forces and striking one of the isolated enemy contingents. Leaving rear guards to hold the exits from the Tyrol, the Corsican raced to do battle with Alvintzy before Verona, but on November 12 the Austrians hurled back a French assault and inflicted over twenty-seven hundred casualties on the Army of Italy. For a moment the French position looked desperate. Alvintzy was preparing to resume his advance and the column in the Tyrol was also pushing forward. In adversity Bonaparte again chose to rely upon speed and audacity. He pulled his army back across the Adige River, abandoning Verona, and then marched against the Austrian flank, which rested on the Adige around the small village of Arcola. In three days of bitter fighting, from November 15 to 17, the French crossed the river, dislodged the Austrians from Arcola, and forced them to retreat. Bonaparte then turned to strike at the Tyrol detachment, which fled hastily north, leaving several hundred prisoners in French hands.

Alarmed at the prospect of having to sacrifice Belgium and the Rhineland to recover Italy, Vienna ordered still another attempt to relieve Mantua. Alvintzy gathered twenty-eight thousand men in the Tyrol and prepared to move on Mantua by way of Rivoli. Separate detachments in the Brenta and Adige valleys were to mount diversionary attacks, thus repeating the previous errors of dispersing combat elements and leaving them exposed to defeat in detail. Once again Bonaparte was able to throw his troops against one part of the Austrian forces, and on January 14, 1797, he halted their advance at Rivoli. The following day the French attacked and sent Alvintzy reeling back into the Tyrol with a total loss of fifteen thousand men. Rivoli also sealed the fate of Mantua. Bonaparte rushed reinforcements back to his siege lines, beat off a sortie, and captured a six-thousand-man relief column near the walls of the city. On February 2, Wurmser surrendered Mantua along with its eighteen thousand defenders.

After the capitulation of Mantua, Bonaparte, acting on orders from the Directory, sent troops against the Pope, who had tried to revive the war in central Italy at the time of the Austrian counteroffensives. The papal army collapsed, and on February 19 Pius VI signed a peace treaty with France at Tolentino. He agreed to sacrifice Ancona, Bologna, Ferrara, Romagna, and Avignon and to pay an indemnity of thirty million livres.

While crushing papal power at the behest of his government, Bonaparte was also pursuing his own political and diplomatic ambitions. The Directory had sent its own agent, General Clarke, to Italy to negotiate with the Austrians. He was to offer to return French conquests in Italy if the Austrians gave up Belgium and their possessions on the left bank of the Rhine. Bonaparte, however, had already unleashed a new offensive, driven deep into Austrian territory, and in an effort to enhance his personal fame, opened diplomatic parleys with Vienna.

In the ensuing negotiations Bonaparte drastically changed his government's diplomatic policy. He wanted to conclude a peace treaty that would allow him to pull his army back from its extended positions into Italy and at the same time allow him to win fame and glory as the individual who drove one of the Republic's most bitter foes out of the war. He also sought to enhance his prestige by a permanent retention of some of his Italian conquests. Finally, he wanted to conclude peace quickly. In April French armies had again crossed the Rhine and were moving rapidly through Germany. Not wishing to share with the other generals the glory of concluding a treaty with the Hapsburgs, Bonaparte decided to offer large inducements to the Austrian negotiators. He therefore dropped his government's long-standing demands for the Rhineland and asked only for Belgium and Milan, which he planned to transform into a French-dominated republic. In return, Austria was to obtain new territories from the Venetian Republic. Bonaparte signed the preliminary Treaty of Leoben on April 18, 1797, and the Directory reluctantly ratified the agreement because it needed the support of its most successful general against the rising tide of domestic royalism and demands for peace. Royalists had begun to establish not only an organization to win elections to the legislative corps but also a secret military branch which was to engineer a coup in the fall of 1797. Several directors concluded that they might have to resort to force to preserve the regime. Since some of their generals were proroyalist, the directors felt that they could not afford to antagonize their most successful military backer. Thus, even at the expense of altering their foreign policy, the directors sought to retain Bonaparte's support and allowed him to impose his own diplomatic solution upon both Vienna and Paris.

After Leoben, Bonaparte transformed the provisional regime in Lombardy into the Cisalpine Republic and shortly afterward merged the Cispadane regime into the new state. He reorganized the government of Genoa, transforming the city-state into the Ligurian Republic, and conquered Venice. He established a republican regime in the city of St. Mark in order to place the region completely under his control so that he would have no trouble transferring it to Austria. The general also brought peace talks with Vienna to a final conclusion, signing the Treaty of Campo Formio on October 18, 1797.

Because of the merger of the Cispadane into the Cisalpine Republic, the Campo Formio Treaty differed somewhat from the Leoben preliminaries, for instead of finding compensation for Venice, France and Austria decided to obliterate the city's independence. The final treaty gave to Austria Dalmatia, Istria, the city of Venice, and the Venetian mainland as far west as the Adige. The Cisalpine Republic received the rest of the mainland, and France took the Ionian Isles. The Hapsburgs agreed to recognize the Cisalpine Republic and gave Belgium to France. Vienna also agreed to summon an Imperial Diet to conclude peace between France and the Empire, and in a secret article Francis promised to use his good offices to secure the left bank of the Rhine for France in return for indemnities in Germany.

Once again the Directory accepted Bonaparte's foreign policy. They had relied upon his support in a coup against royalists in the Legislative Corps in September, when troops from the Army of Italy had expelled and arrested many royalist deputies from the legislature. They could not repudiate their chief supporter and most popular general. Consequently, France failed to obtain more than vague promises about the future of the Rhineland and had to bear the added burden of protecting Bonaparte's Italian conquests. Furthermore, the Hapsburgs, though willing to grab Venice, were not prepared to sacrifice their power and influence in the rest of Italy. Consequently, Bonaparte's startling military victories and diplomatic coups did nothing to bring about a lasting peace. The Austrians were ready to renew the war at the first opportunity, and the Campo Formio Treaty was little more than an armed truce.

The French Government was no more fortunate in its efforts to bring an end to its war with England. As in the case of Austria, the Directory's forces struck a number of telling blows against Britain but never succeeded in compelling Pitt's government to sign a definitive peace.

The first French triumph came in August 1796, when Spain, fearing continued isolation and the lack of allies, joined the Directory in its war against England. The Spanish declaration of war in turn altered the naval balance of power in the Mediterranean. The Cabinet had to abandon Corsica and pull fleet units stationed in the western Mediterranean back beyond the Straits of Gibraltar.

Even more alarming to the British than the setback in the Mediterranean was the growing threat to the security of Ireland, as the French sought to capitalize upon the growth of revolutionary sentiment within the country. Irish discontent with British domination had in fact been increasing for several years. The vast majority of Ireland's three million Catholics had traditionally been hostile to their foreign Protestant overlords. Middle-class Catholics objected to their exclusion from political power, while their coreligionists who made their living from the soil as tenant farmers disliked the steadily rising rents that prevailed in the last decades of the eighteenth century. Many of the 900,000 middle-class Dissenters (Protestants who did not belong to the established Church of Ireland) also objected to their virtual exclusion from public life. Even within the ranks of the 600,000 members of the established church, distaste for the landowning aristocracy that dominated the Irish Government was becoming more common.

The French Revolution demonstrated to many that political change was possible, and in 1791 thirty-six men drawn from the ranks of the middle class, including Dissenters and members of the Church of Ireland, established a reform society at Belfast. Calling themselves the United Irish Society, the reformers first advocated the enfranchisement of Roman Catholics and a liberalization of the Irish Parliament. The society grew rapidly. It soon had lodges throughout the country, and in the south members of the Catholic middle class entered the organization in large numbers. At the same time a Catholic agrarian group—the Defenders—began to call for lower rents and abolition of the tithe paid to the Church of Ireland. The Defenders also stated that they would co-operate with a French army if it ever landed in Ireland.

The British and Irish governments responded to these threats to their authority with a mixture of concessions and repression. In 1793 the rulers of Ireland granted the right to vote to Catholics possessing a forty-shilling freehold but continued to deny them access to high civil and military posts. In May 1794, after uncovering correspondence between some members of the United Irish Society and the French, the government suppressed the society's Dublin branch and began to treat other lodges as criminal subversive organizations. One immediate result of this policy was a secret meeting of United Irish Society leaders. These men decided that one of their number, Wolfe Tone, would appeal to France for armed assistance in throwing off British domination. Tone went first to the United States and from there set out for Paris. At the same time in Ireland, the United Irish Society reconstituted itself as a secret organization. Local clubs established a communications system by use of roving deputies, and the Ulster branch of the society began to function as a *de facto* national directorate. The society then began to create a military organization, and in the summer of 1796 sent two secret agents to France to assist Tone in his negotiations with the Directory.

Tone had meanwhile arrived in Paris and obtained interviews with Carnot, the Minister of War, and General Hoche, one of France's youngest and most talented generals, an ardent republican, and advocate of carrying the war with England to British shores. The French agreed to help the Irish establish their independence and as a sign of their good faith appointed Tone to the rank of brigadier general in the French army. General Hoche then went to Switzerland, where he met the two agents from Ireland and promised them that a French expedition would arrive in Ireland before the end of the year.

At this juncture the Directory was indeed planning an Irish expedition, but not because they sympathized with the aspirations of Irish republicans. Rather, the French regarded an invasion of Ireland as part of their strategy in the war against England. The directors placed Hoche in command of a 13,900-man force and ordered him to proceed to Ireland, where in co-operation with local democrats he was to drive the British from the island and establish an Irish republic. In a set of secret instructions the Directory told Hoche to retain control of any republican regime in his own hands. The French intended to use native radicals in defeating the British forces in Ireland, but they also intended to use Ireland as a pawn in peace talks with the English. Paris planned to return Ireland to the British in return for London's recognition of French continental conquests.[15] To support their Irish venture, the Directory decided to mount a secondary attack upon England itself. A "Black Legion" composed of several hundred convicts and adventurers led by an American freebooter was to land in Wales and create a republican Vendée as an additional lever against the British.[16]

Before the French could move, Pitt's government decided to undertake exploratory negotiations. The growing threat to Ireland, Spain's entrance into the war, Austrian defeats in Italy, and a mounting financial crisis caused by a steady drain of funds to pay overseas garrisons and subsidize allies convinced the majority of the Cabinet to agree to preliminary talks with the French. On October 15, 1796, Pitt sent James Harris, first Earl of Malmesbury, to Lille to discuss peace with the Directory. Harris actually had very little to offer, for British terms called for a return to the pre-1792 *status quo* or for minor frontier rectifications in favor of France, coupled with

[15] *A.N. AF III* 20.*

[16] E. H. S. Jones, *The Last Invasion of Britain* (London, 1950) gives a complete account of this aspect of the Directory's plan. See also *A.N. AF III* 20.*

English retention of the Dutch colonies seized in 1795. Since Austria still had hopes of driving Bonaparte out of Italy, Thugut refused to participate in the Anglo-French talks, while at Lille Malmesbury refused to modify his original position. Consequently, on December 19, the Directory called an end to the negotiations and resumed its military preparations in the hope that the projected invasions of Ireland and Wales would force London to adopt a more flexible attitude.

The French expeditions did not, however, succeed in seriously changing the over-all military situation. Hoche's expedition set sail from Brest in December, but storms scattered the fleet. Some units did reach the Irish coast undetected by the Royal Navy, but Hoche was not at hand, and the commander of the forces that had arrived at Bantry Bay refused to attempt a landing in the stormy seas. Nor did the Black Legion enjoy better fortunes. It did manage to land in Wales in February 1797, but capitulated almost immediately to a force of local militiamen.[17]

But although they failed to change the military balance of power, the two abortive expeditions did have an important if indirect impact upon the diplomacy and strategy of the belligerents. Hoche's expedition, despite its failure, convinced the United Irish Society that with more careful preparation they could obtain French assistance, and the members returned to their preparations for revolution with renewed vigor. In 1797, United Irishmen began to collect pikes and muskets and drill secretly. The society also gained the adherence of the Defenders by adding the economic demands of the agrarians to their own political program. The landing in Wales also had far-reaching repercussions, for when news of the forlorn raid reached London, individuals

[17] See E. H. S. Jones, *The Last Invasion*, and his work *An Invasion That Failed* (London, 1950) for an account of Hoche's expedition.

rushed to convert their paper money into gold. A major financial panic followed and on February 27 the government had to issue an order in council suspending specie payment for Bank of England notes. News of Admiral Jervis' February 14 victory over a Spanish fleet near Cape St. Vincent temporarily restored English confidence, but new problems soon beset the Cabinet.

Catherine of Russia had died in November 1796, and her successor, the half-mad Paul I, was hostile to Britain and Austria, thereby depriving the moribund coalition of still another partner. In April 1797 Vienna signed the Leoben Treaty and left the war, and England had to face the prospect of doing battle with the Republic without a single major continental ally. To make matters worse Pitt suddenly found himself deprived of his most vital strategic weapon—the fleet. Shortly after the Leoben armistice, sailors of the fleet stationed at Spithead rose in rebellion. Goaded beyond endurance by poor pay, bad food, harsh punishments, and bestial living conditions, the seamen refused to leave port until the Admiralty listened to and acted upon their complaints. After obtaining some redress of their grievances, the Spithead sailors returned to duty, but the fleet docked at the Nore suddenly followed the example of the Spithead mutineers. Ultimately the government managed to restore order, but the regime's confidence in the loyalty of the navy's rank and file was shaken severely. The cumulative effect of the defeats of 1796–97 was to convince Pitt and most of his colleagues of the necessity of resuming peace talks with France in a serious effort to end the war. Fear was not, however, the sole motive prompting the English to negotiate. The Cabinet knew of the revival of royalist sentiment in France and of the royalist victories in recent elections to the Legislative Corps. The British therefore hoped that the royalist factions would gain control of the Republic and make significant concessions in return for peace. Pitt was, in the summer of

1797, willing to sacrifice Belgium, but in order to maintain Britain's international position and justify to the King, Parliament, and the public his policy of continental concessions, he wanted France to allow England to retain Ceylon, the Cape, and Martinique. In hopes of making moderate concessions on the Continent in return for extensive colonial compensations, Malmesbury opened negotiations with the French at Lille on July 7, 1797.

The French, despite their excellent military and diplomatic position, found themselves unable to pursue a consistent and energetic policy at Lille, for the policy makers were not united. The directors themselves could not agree on a single set of demands, for they were split into a republican and a royalist faction. The Legislative Corps was similarly divided. Republicans advocated a harsh peace with minimal concessions in order to gain popular support at home by producing victory, while the royalists advocated a moderate settlement coupled with extensive concessions to England. The republicans usually set official policy, but the royalists consistently undermined them by making secret promises of their own to the British. Consequently, throughout the summer of 1797 the French were never able to devise a unified policy, and the British, awaiting a royalist victory, refused to deal seriously with the republicans' demands.

At the opening meetings the French asked Malmesbury whether or not England recognized the Republic's Constitution and treaties. An affirmative reply would have meant that the British accepted the French conquest of Belgium and the Rhineland and recognized the Batavian, Ligurian, and other satellite republics. Furthermore, since French treaties with Spain and Batavia called for mutual guarantees of territories, the British, by accepting the legality of the French Constitution and treaties, would by implication abandon possible claims for colonial indemnities. Malmesbury realized that the republican directors were trying to conclude a peace on the basis of the continental *status quo* of 1797 plus a return to the prewar colonial balance of power and replied that his government would recognize public but not secret treaties, thereby leaving open the possibility of concessions by the French. Later he pressed the French to grant extensive colonial indemnities. On July 13 the Directory, realizing that it had to give England something, modified its original position by offering to sacrifice some of France's overseas possessions, the Senegal and the Channel Islands, but the directors refused to undermine their diplomatic position by giving away their allies' colonies. The presence of Spain as a French ally kept the British out of the Mediterranean, and the Batavian fleet, army, and treasury were extremely valuable adjuncts to French strength. The republican directors, therefore, felt that they had to protect their allies' interests or risk the loss of their support. At this juncture, Portugal asked France for terms, and the Directory began to contemplate the use of Portuguese colonies as compensation for England. The directors thought of giving part of Brazil to England or giving the English several Batavian colonies and using portions of Brazil to indemnify the Dutch. Whether or not this plan was feasible will never be known, for a political crisis at Paris upset the normal course of diplomatic procedure before the Directory had a chance to pursue its new scheme.

In the Legislative Councils, royalist attacks on the government forced the directors to reshuffle the various ministers, sacrificing some republicans in order to get rid of a number of royalists. In this process Talleyrand replaced the moderate republican Delacroix at the foreign office. The ambitious and somewhat unscrupulous former aristocrat and ex-bishop, who throughout his career always managed to wind up on the winning side, was willing to work with any victorious faction in order to preserve his own power and prestige. Since the royalists seemed on the verge of gaining control of the state, he quickly adopted their diplomatic views. At Lille, Hughes Maret, a royalist, joined his entourage, and the two men secretly informed the British of the Directory's plans and assured Malmesbury that France would soon make extensive concessions. Consequently, on July 20, the British renewed their demands for overseas indemnities, and Talleyrand persuaded his government to ask the Spanish and Dutch to sacrifice some colonies as the price of peace. The Spanish and Dutch refused, but Talleyrand nevertheless continued to assure the British that the political situation in France would soon produce a government willing to sign a treaty in accordance with England's interests. The English naturally became more convinced than ever that concessions to France were not necessary to obtain peace. On August 10, Portugal signed a treaty with France and gave up some territory in Brazil, but Talleyrand, Maret, and a royalist director handed over the text of the treaty to the British, who were in turn able to put pressure on the Portuguese. The King of Portugal refused to ratify the treaty, thus rendering impossible the Directory's scheme of using Portuguese possessions as bargaining counters. Talleyrand and Maret then continued to strengthen England's resolve to obtain new colonies by reiterating their promises of eventual overseas concessions. Both parties had reached an impasse and a successful conclusion of the Lille negotiations became almost impossible.

The coup of 18 Fructidor Year V (September 4, 1797) dealt the final blow to peace talks. Republican directors supported by army elements proceeded to drive royalists from the Directory and the Legislative Corps. A new republican Directory recalled Maret from Lille and on September 11 reasserted its original position that France would make no colonial sacrifices and would retain the continental *status quo* of 1797. On September 15 the head of the British delegation announced that his country could not accept French terms and departed for London. On October 6, Pitt officially announced the failure of the Lille talks, and on the eleventh a British fleet destroyed a Batavian flotilla at the Battle of Camperdown. The naval victory reassured the British of their fleet's loyalty, provided additional security against any invasion attempts, and convinced the Cabinet that the country could continue to fight.

Once again the Directory failed to obtain a permanent peace. At Lille the secret diplomacy of the royalists had constantly undermined the government's diplomacy and convinced the British to refuse concessions in the hope that a change in the French Government would enable them to obtain better terms. The "Portuguese exchange plan" might have worked, but the royalists effectively sabotaged it. French royalists had conditioned the British to expect large gains at minimal sacrifices, and when the post-Fructidorian Directory restated its original demands, negotiations collapsed.

At the end of 1797, France had won many stunning victories and was the single most powerful state in Europe. But England continued to do battle, and Austria was anxious to recoup its losses in western Europe and Italy. France then had to defeat England before Pitt could form a new coalition, or face the prospect of perpetual war. A peace with honor and victory was no closer in 1797 than it had been four years earlier. The French nation had vastly increased its power but had to continue fighting to maintain its new position.

CHAPTER 5

WORLD WAR

By the end of 1797 the French Executive Directory understood that the Campo Formio Treaty was little more than an armed truce and that further negotiations with England were impossible. Furthermore, the Republic's leaders realized that if they were to preserve their conquests and their pre-eminent European position they had to defeat Britain before Pitt could put together a second coalition. To accomplish this objective the directors could mount an invasion of the British Isles, or they could launch attacks upon England's overseas empire, damage British commerce, and force the Cabinet to sue for peace because it could no longer subsidize allies or finance its own war effort.

Although it involved great risks, the cross-Channel assault was the most direct and decisive method of forcing England to submit. For home defense the British had but 48,000 regular troops and 135,000 ill-trained militia, who were no match for the 365,000 French veterans.[1] If a French army could land on England's shores, it would probably be victorious in combat, and the British Government would probably sue for peace to put an end to French plundering and to secure the evacuation of their territory. But moving an army across the Channel was a problem that the Directory dared not dismiss lightly. The

[1] The British also had garrisons in Ireland, the West Indies, and India, but in case of invasion the government would probably have been unable to transport these troops home in time to check a French advance on London. See J. W. Fortescue, *A History of the British Army* (London, 1906), IV, Part 2, p. 939. On the French army see P. Mahon, *Etudes sur les armées du Directoire* (Paris, 1905), and G. Lechartier, *Les soldats de la Révolution et de l'Empire* (Paris, 1902).

Royal Navy with 120 ships of the line and 382 lesser vessels, served by 100,000 sailors and 20,000 marines, was the most powerful fleet in the world. The French fleet with but 57 ships of the line and 65 lesser craft was simply no match for British naval power either in numbers or in quality of leadership.[2] Furthermore, the British victories of St. Vincent and Camperdown had so damaged the Spanish and Batavian fleets that the French could not call upon their services for any invasion scheme. Thus gaining control of the Channel even for the brief period necessary to disembark the invasion force posed an enormously difficult problem for French strategists.

A French invasion was not, however, completely out of the question. Ships of the eighteenth century were subject to the hazards of wind and tide, and given favorable circumstances a French fleet could escape the British blockaders and reach England. During the era of the Old Regime, Bourbon monarchs had not only drawn up invasion plans but also had sent men to Ireland and Scotland. Revolutionary governments had also planned invasions and had successfully sent a fleet to Ireland and landed troops in Wales. Thus in deciding whether or not to invade England, the Directory had to balance the danger of losing a fleet and an army in a single afternoon against the possibility of making a successful landing and dictating a final peace in London.

The second alternative, a blow at British commerce by means of an attack on English colonies, was also fraught with problems. The French could not be sure that colonial defeats would force the British to sue for peace, for England had suffered imperial defeats in past conflicts but had continued to fight. Furthermore, even if initially successful in an overseas venture, the French would find their expeditionary force dependent upon a long line of

[2] W. Clowes, *The Royal Navy* (London, 1899), IV, p. 153; and E. Desbrière, ed., *1793–1805 projets et tentatives de débarquement aux îles britanniques* (Paris, 1900), I, p. 287.

communications, exposed to British naval ripostes. Finally, any French overseas venture would necessitate the violation of the territory of neutral powers. These powers plus others that had an interest in the threatened area might well seek an alliance with Great Britain and form a new coalition.

On the other hand, an overseas venture had its advantages. If the French chose to attack the wealthy British holdings in India they would first have to seize the Ottoman province of Egypt as an advanced base, but the Turkish state was militarily weak, and the British had no naval squadrons in the Mediterranean. Thus a thrust toward India would enable France to seize a valuable province from a weak third power, enhance the Republic's influence in the Mediterranean, and avoid the danger of a naval confrontation with England's fleet. To strike at India from Egypt was difficult but not impossible. The French had ships and bases in the Indian Ocean; with control of the Mediterranean they could transport naval stores to the Red Sea, and they could co-operate with anti-British Indian princes. Thus with relatively small forces, Paris could realistically hope to weaken seriously British power in the East Indies. If successful, the French would also secure diplomatic advantages. They would obtain valuable territories that they could either retain for themselves or use as bargaining counters by offering to return them to England as the price of British recognition of French continental conquests.

In late 1797 there were advocates of both strategic choices. The director Jean François Reubell felt that a direct attack on England was the best means of bringing the war to a victorious conclusion. Director Barras and a number of military and naval men supported him.[3]

[3] B. Nabonne, ed., *La diplomatie du Directoire et Bonaparte d'après les papiers inédits de Reubell* (Paris, 1951), p. 156; G. Duruy, ed., *Mémoires de Barras* (Paris, 1896), III, p. 162; and

Proponents of a colonial venture were also numerous and powerful. Merchants and consular officials in Egypt had frequently called for an invasion of the Levant. The merchants wanted protection from the rapacious Mamelukes, the former slaves who had over the years become *de facto* rulers of Egypt, while the consular officials sought protection for the merchants and also regarded Egypt as an excellent base for operations against the British East India Company. Talleyrand, the Foreign Minister, also favored striking at India by way of Egypt. In July 1797 he had presented a paper to a learned society in which he argued that the Republic could reap great economic benefits by seizing Egypt and developing it as a colony. A few weeks later he sent his paper to the Directory and added that from Egypt France could strike at India. The French ambassador to The Hague suggested a French-Batavian attack on the British East Indies in conjunction with local Indian princes. A number of military figures including Bonaparte also expressed interest in a colonial venture.[4] Bonaparte even as a young officer had been interested in Egypt and the Levant, and during the Lille negotiations, when he found himself temporarily inactive, he turned again to schemes for grand campaigns in the east. He ransacked Italian libraries for works on the Near East, assembled maps of Egypt, and discussed plans for an invasion with his subordinates. He also advised Paris that France should invade Egypt in order to defeat England and reap economic gains. In addition he began to fortify Corfu and laid plans to contact malcontents in the Ottoman Empire's Balkan provinces in order to be ready to spread French influence into Albania and Greece if the Turkish state collapsed. In the second week of September, Bonaparte wrote to Talleyrand recommending the occupation

---

E. Guillon, *La France et l'Irlande pendant la Révolution* (Paris, 1888), p. 202.

[4] General Jourdan and Admiral Villaret de Joyeuse are two such men. See Duruy, *Mémoires de Barras,* III, p. 90, and Guillon, *La France et l'Irlande,* p. 202.

of Malta and Egypt, and Talleyrand showed the memorandum to the directors, who were interested in finding new ways of increasing pressure on the British at Lille. On September 23 he told Bonaparte that the government approved of his plan to take Malta and that a French army might invade Egypt if the Sultan agreed to the fiction that France was acting to restore his authority over the Mamelukes. Talleyrand concluded by stating that from Egypt the French could extend their influence into the East Indies. Thus by the end of September the Republic was on the verge of launching an eastern expedition.

In October, however, events took another turn. The Lille negotiations collapsed, and the Directory had to consider an overseas venture not only as a means of gaining limited diplomatic and strategic advantages but also as part of a general strategy for rapidly defeating England. In this new context, Reubell convinced his colleagues to abandon plans for a descent upon Egypt, a move that could no longer force London into a more conciliatory frame of mind, and to adopt the risky but possibly decisive method of a cross-Channel attack.

On October 27, 1797, the same day that they signed the Treaty of Campo Formio, the directors created the Army of England and ordered Bonaparte to command it. The government then informed the French public that the best method of obtaining permanent peace was to defeat England by landing on British shores and marching on London.[5] Meanwhile, Bonaparte attended the opening sessions of the Rastadt congress, called to arrange peace between France and the Empire, and then returned to France to supervise the invasion preparations. Troops marched to the Channel ports, and by the spring of 1798 the Army of England numbered 56,400 men.[6]

To find the necessary ships to transport them was a

[5] *Réimpression de l'Ancien Moniteur* (Paris, 1847), XXIX, p. 68.
[6] Desbrière, *Projets et tentatives,* p. 370.

much more difficult task. The Naval Minister ordered all warships in the Atlantic to concentrate at Brest to act as escorts for the transports. The minister also directed squadrons in the Mediterranean and the Adriatic to proceed to Channel ports and issued instructions to ready all ships in docks for sea duty. Bonaparte meanwhile sent orders to various ports to transform merchant vessels into armed transports and if necessary to build new ships. Still, preparations went slowly, and by the end of January Bonaparte's chief engineer officer reported that there was shipping for only ninety-eight hundred men and twelve hundred horses.[7]

Learning of French preparations, the British began to take countermeasures. In January Parliament passed a bill to permit ten thousand militiamen to join the regular army. Pitt called for vastly increased taxes, and by a vote of 183 to 5 the House of Commons, frightened at the prospect of pro-French subversive activity, supported a governmental proposal to suspend the Habeas Corpus Act. The army moved seventy-eight hundred men into the London area, and individuals contributed over two million pounds for the defense of the realm.[8]

The British need not have been so alarmed, for on February 20, 1798, the Directory learned that over half of the Army of England still lacked transport. On the following day Bonaparte returned from an inspection trip to the invasion ports and told the government that unless it vastly increased its efforts his army would be unable to put to sea in time to take advantage of the long nights necessary to blind the English blockaders and allow the French armada to make its dash to Britain's shores. The Directory responded by introducing

[7] Ibid., pp. 287–89, 295, 309–10, and 315.

[8] W. Cobbet, ed., *The Parliamentary History of England from the Earliest Period to the Year 1803* (London, 1818), XXXIII, pp. 1066 and 1432; and *The Speeches of the Right Honourable William Pitt in the House of Commons* (London, 1806), III, pp. 277–82.

emergency measures: ordering privateer crews to join the regular navy, concentrating all sloops from Bayonne to Ostend at Havre and Dunkirk, and obtaining transports for ten thousand from the Batavian Government.[9] Despite all their efforts, however, French preparations moved slowly, and as the nights grew shorter the government had little choice but to seek a possible alternative to an invasion of England.

On the first and second of March the Directory met in secret session to review its strategy. At this crucial point the Naval Minister reported that he had neither the transports nor the escort vessels to enable the Army of England to launch its cross-Channel attack. The directors then reluctantly abandoned their invasion plans and adopted the strategic alternative of attacking Britain's overseas domains. Thus the inability to procure sufficient shipping, before the advent of shorter spring nights made a Channel crossing attempt impossible, forced the French to strike at England by means of an overseas expedition.

On March 5 the Directory issued orders for troops to concentrate at Toulon, and Bonaparte traveled south to assume command of both the military and naval preparations for the eastern venture. On April 12 the Directory issued a series of decrees which gave the projected expedition its final form and defined its goals. The first decree created the Army of the East, consisting of both army and naval units with Bonaparte in command. The second decree ordered Bonaparte to conquer Egypt in preparation for securing a short sea route to India. A third called for the capture of Malta, and a final directive called for vessels berthed at Ile de France and Réunion, French island colonies in the Indian Ocean, to sail to Suez, where they would embark units of the Army of the East for an attack upon British India.

[9] *Min. de la Guerre, Correspondance militaire de Napoléon Ier* (Paris, 1876), I, pp. 464, 467–68; and Desbrière, *Projets et tentatives,* pp. 325–26.

As Bonaparte gathered his ships, men, and even a group of scientists, Talleyrand prepared the diplomatic groundwork for the expedition. On March 16 he proposed a truly grandiose scheme, suggesting that after the conquest of Egypt a special envoy from Paris should offer Sultan Selim III an alliance against Russia promising French support for Turkish efforts to retake the Crimea. Talleyrand hoped to get the Turks involved in a war with the Russians so that neither the Sultan nor the Tsar could react effectively to the French presence on the Nile. He even volunteered to carry his alliance proposal personally to Constantinople and planned to leave for the east shortly after the Toulon expedition set sail.

Meanwhile, Bonaparte's army completed its preparations, and on May 19, 1798, thirteen ships of the line, seven frigates, eighteen sloops, and three hundred transports carrying thirty thousand infantrymen, twenty-eight hundred cavalry troopers, two companies of sappers and miners, and one hundred cannon sailed out of Toulon Harbor heading east. Bonaparte assured his troops that they were acting as a wing of the Army of England and were about to spread the doctrines of liberty and equality to the non-European world.[10]

On June 9 the Army of the East sighted its first objective—Malta. The next day two demibrigades landed and began to advance on Valetta, the capital. To defend the island, the Knights of Malta had but 332 members backed by some 2000 reluctant local militia. Their position was hopeless, and after feeble resistance, the Grand Master capitulated. On June 12 he signed a formal surrender and renounced the order's sovereignty over the island. Bonaparte then organized a local government for Malta, placed a 3400-man garrison on the isle, and resumed his voyage.

The French sighted the Egyptian coast on July 1, and

[10] H. Galli, ed., *Journal d'un officier de l'armée d'Egypte* (Paris, 1883), pp. 15–16.

Bonaparte immediately sent four thousand men ashore to secure a landing place near Alexandria. On the following day grenadiers stormed Alexandria's defenses, and after several hours of house-to-house fighting, the Mameluke commander surrendered. Bonaparte then sent a division toward the Nile, and directed his fleet commander, Admiral Brueys, to anchor his warships in Aboukir Bay, a position about midway between Alexandria and Rosetta. At the same time the French commander sought to win the support of the Egyptian masses by issuing, on July 3, a proclamation in Arabic declaring that the Army of the East respected Islam and desired only to free Egypt from Mameluke tyranny.[11] Bonaparte then turned his attentions to the destruction of the Mameluke army and the capture of Cairo.

The French, meeting only sporadic resistance, marched to the Nile, and on the ninth anniversary of Bastille Day the Army of the East began to march down the western bank of the river toward Cairo. On July 20 they arrived at the Plain of the Pyramids, a scant fifteen miles north of the city. The Mameluke commanders, who had so far refused to offer battle, had little choice but to gather their forces for a desperate attempt to save their capital.

On July 21 Mameluke cavalry and native infantry levies advanced against the Army of the East's divisional squares, which held a line from the Nile to the Pyramids. The French easily drove off the wild, undisciplined cavalry assaults and then advanced and broke the infantry. By the end of the battle they had shattered their foes, killing over two thousand, at a cost of but thirty French dead. The next morning the civil governors of Cairo, wishing to avoid further useless bloodshed, surrendered, and French units crossed the Nile and entered the city.

[11] Général Berthier, *Relations des campagnes du général Bonaparte en Egypte et en Syrie* (Paris, 1800), pp. 4–9; and *Correspondance de Napoléon Ier*, pp. 191–92.

Five days later Bonaparte made a triumphal entry into the new capital of the French eastern empire.

After dispatching units up the Nile to pursue the retreating Mamelukes, Bonaparte resumed his efforts to win the support of the Egyptian people. He organized a local government for Cairo and established native-run provincial administrations. The French, of course, dominated the native governments, which had only extremely limited powers. Bonaparte also created a health commission, a postal system, a printing office, and a library. Finally, he promised to build a new mosque in Cairo and in order to offset popular hostility toward his "Christian" army, he opened discussions with Moslem leaders about the possibility of converting the entire French force to the faith of the Prophet. In all probability Bonaparte had no intention of converting his troops to Islam, but his action at least for the moment forestalled any serious outbreak of religious warfare. The policy of seeking local support, which had attained remarkable success in Italy, was less effective in Egypt. The Moslem natives persisted in regarding the French as another group of Christian invaders and soon came to regard them as exploiters as well, for to obtain funds for his army Bonaparte retained the old Mameluke taxes. He also refused to institute a policy of land reform and thereby lost an excellent opportunity to give the land-hungry peasants an economic stake in the continuation of French domination. On the other hand, resistance to the Army of the East was largely passive. Aside from isolated attacks on patrols in the countryside, the bulk of the population remained submissive. The first step in the thrust at India seemed successful, but the British were soon drastically to alter all of Bonaparte's calculations.

From journalists, diplomats, and secret agents the British had learned of the French preparations at Toulon, but they failed to discover the expedition's exact destination. In the first months of 1798 most of the Cabinet and the Admiralty believed that the French were about to strike at Ireland and gave scant consideration to the possibility of major operations in the Mediterranean. The First Lord of the Admiralty even told the Cabinet that except in the most grave emergency the fleet should stay out of the Mediterranean and concentrate its forces in the Atlantic.[12] At first only Dundas, the Secretary of State for War, who had connections with the East India Company and was a long-time advocate of the imperial school of strategy, believed that the French were planning to strike at India. It was a policy he would himself have advocated had he been French. Grenville had obtained accurate information from a secret agent divulging the true destination of the Toulon armament, but he refused to act upon the unsupported information of a single operative. Pitt, for his part, remained convinced that the French were going to strike somewhere in the west.[13]

Despite their assessment of the strategic position, however, the British Government ultimately came to the conclusion that their diplomatic situation required them to take the risk of weakening their Atlantic squadrons in order to send a fleet into the Mediterranean. Since the end of 1797 Pit had been trying to form a new coalition by convincing Prussia and Austria to review hostilities with France. A British special envoy at Berlin found that although the Prussian King was bitterly opposed to the principles of the Revolution, neither he nor his advisers would consider taking active steps against France. The Prussians were unwilling to risk their dominant position in northern Germany by resorting to arms. Moreover, the

[12] F. Charles-Roux, *L'Angleterre et l'expédition française en Egypte* (Cairo, 1925), I, p. 10; J. Corbett, ed., *Private Papers of George, Second Earl Spencer, First Lord of the Admiralty 1794–1801* (London, 1914), II, pp. 433–34; and Historical Manuscripts Commission, *Report on the Manuscripts of J. B. Fortescue, Esq., preserved at Dropmore* (London, 1905), IV, p. 166.

[13] *Dropmore Papers,* pp. 192–93, and *Spencer Papers,* p. 318. See also C. Matheson, *The Life of Henry Dundas First Viscount Melville 1742–1811* (London, 1933).

Prussians believed that a new war if successful would allow the Hapsburgs to regain many if not all of their old provinces and perhaps add new ones to their domains. Berlin was frankly unwilling to pursue a policy that in some way might benefit Vienna. Conversations with the Hapsburgs also produced no results. The Austrians informed the British that before re-entering the war they needed a guarantee of financial support, including an advance subsidy to set their war machinery in motion. The Hapsburgs also called for the appearance of a British flag in the Mediterranean. The talks, however, collapsed when the British Secretary of State for Foreign Affairs informed the Austrian ambassador that Parliament would allot no more subsidies until the Austrians repaid debts contracted in 1796 and 1797. Hopes for a quick renewal of the coalition seemed lost, and the Cabinet's one remaining hope was that by some forceful unilateral action England could convince other states to join in the war. Since their fleet was their strongest striking arm, the Cabinet decided to send a large squadron into the Mediterranean despite the lack of a formal coalition, in an effort to encourage Austria and other powers to re-enter the war.

Consequently, on April 29 Spencer ordered Admiral St. Vincent, commander of the fleet blockading Cádiz, to send a squadron into the Mediterranean. The Admiralty chose Horatio Nelson to command the Mediterranean squadron, gave him fourteen ships of the line, and directed him to protect Naples, blockade the Spanish coast, and prevent the French and Spanish fleets from uniting. Later St. Vincent, who was Nelson's immediate superior, told him to seek out and destroy the Toulon fleet and gave him a free hand in his search. Nelson set sail as soon as possible, and by May 31 his squadron was cruising off Toulon. There he discovered that the French had already left the port, and he set off in pursuit. Delayed by storms, the British did not reach Naples until June 17. Failing to find the French in Italian waters, Nelson pushed on to Sicily. He reached Messina on the twentieth, and there he learned of Bonaparte's capture of Malta. This piece of intelligence confirmed his growing suspicion that the French were heading to Egypt, and disregarding the views of most of his superiors, he gave orders to head for Alexandria. The British fleet arrived there on June 28, but to Nelson's dismay his sailors did not sight a single French ship. Nelson had in fact beaten the French to Egypt, but despite his initial failure to find the Toulon fleet he remained convinced that Bonaparte planned to take Egypt as the first step in an invasion of India. He therefore proceeded to search the eastern Mediterranean. Finding nothing, he returned to Sicily for supplies and then set out again to search the waters of the Levant. While sailing off the coast of southern Greece, he captured a French ship and learned from its crew that the French were indeed heading for Egyptian waters. He set off in pursuit, and by July 31 his ships were once again outside Alexandria. In the first light of dawn on August 1 two frigates set out to locate the French, and by afternoon Nelson had learned exactly what he had been longing to hear—the entire French battle fleet was anchored in line across Aboukir Bay.

The French position was actually quite weak, for Nelson stood between them and the open sea. Furthermore, the French line did not extend far enough to close the whole bay, and no field batteries existed to cover the gap between Brueys's lead ship and the shore. Brueys was, of course, responsible for the weak tactical disposition of the fleet, but responsibility for keeping the ships in Egyptian waters rested squarely upon Bonaparte. In order to have naval support close at hand he had told his admiral that the fleet could depart for Corfu if necessary, *but* that fleet movements were subject to the requirements of the over-all military situation. Since Bonaparte was commander in chief of both land and sea forces, Brueys could not move without a direct order.[14] Thus Bonaparte's in-

[14] A. T. Mahan, *Life of Nelson* (Boston, 1897), p. 346; G. Douin, *La flotte de Bonaparte sur les côtes d'Égypt* (Cairo, 1922), pp. 77–78; and *Correspondance inédite officielle et confidentielle de Napoléon Bonaparte, Egypte* (Paris, 1819), I, p. 201.

sistence upon keeping the fleet in Egyptian waters plus Brueys's failure to fortify properly his position gave the British an excellent opportunity to win a decisive victory.

The Battle of Aboukir was exceptionally hard-fought. Nelson initiated the action by ordering his captains to attack Brueys's van and center. Coming into the bay from the northwest, five British ships, acting on their own initiative, crossed the bows of the leading French ship and attacked from the inshore side. The two leading ships were immediately destroyed by withering British broadsides, and as more English men-of-war arrived on the scene the battle grew in intensity. Fighting raged all afternoon and on into the night. At about 9 P.M. the *Orient*, the 120-gun French flagship, caught fire and forty-five minutes later exploded with a tremendous roar. Fighting then died down due to mutual exhaustion, but dawn revealed the magnitude of Nelson's victory. The British had captured six ships, obliterated the flagship, driven three men-of-war aground and reduced another to a floating hulk. Only two French ships of the line and two frigates managed to escape the carnage. The British had suffered 895 casualties, but the French had lost 8930 men and with them their hope of rapidly defeating England.

Nelson's victory led to a rapid and drastic alteration in the balance of power between France and England. Militarily, Nelson had successfully reasserted British naval power in the Mediterranean and isolated the Army of the East midway between France and India. Furthermore, the Battle of Aboukir convinced other powers that they could strike out against France with a reasonable chance of success. Pitt was then able to find allies and to begin the process of forming a new coalition.

The Ottoman Empire and Russia were the first new powers to join in striking at the Republic. Both states had objected to the French occupation of the Ionian Islands and to Bonaparte's dealings with Balkan malcontents. The Turks feared the loss of the provinces, and the

Russians, who regarded the Balkans as their own sphere of influence, disliked the injection of French power into the region. So alarmed did the two powers become that they even worked together to disarm Denisco, a Polish revolutionary who had fled to Moldavia in 1795 and with the financial assistance of the French ambassador at Constantinople had waged guerrilla warfare in Galicia and Bukovina. The Turks were, however, unwilling to do more because they needed France as a counterweight to Austria and Russia. The Sultan therefore refused to break completely with the Directory, and even after the French landed in Egypt, the Turks refused to declare war. They did prepare an army and a fleet, but their abiding fear of Russia made them reluctant to commit their forces in Egypt and thereby leave the Balkans at the mercy of the Tsar.

Russia, however, was becoming interested in the possibility of a temporary alliance with its hereditary foe. Paul I objected to French presence in the Balkans. He also feared French subversion in Poland, and the presence of thousands of Polish *émigrés* in the Cisalpine army raised the specter of a French drive to the east. Paul first sought an alliance with Prussia, but Berlin turned down his offers. Bonaparte's occupation of Malta and Egypt posed still another threat to Russian influence in the Balkans and the Near East, and Paul ordered army and naval units to prepare for action against the French. At the same time he prepared to end at least temporarily Russia's traditional hostility toward the Ottoman Empire in order to concentrate against the more immediate problem posed by French intervention in the Levant, and he opened talks with the Sultan, who had meanwhile learned of Nelson's victory and was in a receptive mood. On August 20 the Turks and Russians signed a military convention, which included a mutual guarantee of each other's possessions, and on September 9 the Ottoman Empire, assured that Russia would not move into the Balkans, declared war on France.

In October a combined Russo-Turkish fleet and army attacked the French garrisons on the Albanian coast and the Ionian Islands. The mainland posts and smaller islands fell quickly, and by November the allies were attacking Corfu. The French managed to hold out until March 1799, but their exploit was little more than a gallant but futile gesture. While destroying French power in the Adriatic, the Turks and Russians were also strengthening their alliance, and on December 23, 1798, the two powers concluded a formal alliance treaty. The hereditary foes agreed to offer a mutual guarantee of each other's possessions, to give military assistance in case of third-power aggression, to conclude no separate peace with a common foe, and to invite other powers to adhere to their treaty. Pitt was not slow to seize this opportunity to obtain allies. Capitalizing on Paul's desire to expand hostilities into western Europe, he concluded an alliance with the Tsar at the end of December, and on January 5, 1799, the British Government acceded to the Russo-Turkish alliance. Thus Britain was no longer isolated, and the new alliances were to provide a keystone for the construction of a second continental coalition.

The ramifications of the Battle of Aboukir extended far beyond the confines of the eastern Mediterranean. In India, Syria, Ireland, Italy, Switzerland, and the New World, French power and prestige suffered repeated setbacks, and within six months after Nelson's victory the enemies of France had practically eliminated the Republic's influence outside the confines of western Europe.

Prior to August 1, 1798, the French threat to British power in India had been very real. Britain was the major colonial power on the Indian subcontinent, controlling Bengal, Madras, and Bombay. The East India Company, operating under the close supervision of a government Board of Control, defended its possessions with 57,800 Company and 22,200 government troops plus Royal Naval and Company fleet units. The British holdings on the subcontinent produced about 40 per cent of England's foreign trade revenue, and both the Cabinet and the Company were fully aware of the importance of the Indian dominions.

By contrast French holdings in the east were insignificant. They consisted of a cluster of islands in the Indian Ocean, the Ile de France, the Ile de Bourbon, and Roderigue, plus the Seychelles. With a combined population of about 19,000 whites and 103,000 slaves, plus small army and naval contingents, these isolated outposts by themselves posed no serious threat to British India. Native princes were, however, becoming progressively more hostile to British influence, and in the late 1790s several of them turned to the French for assistance, thus raising the specter of a Franco-Indian alliance.

The Mahratta Confederacy, a weak and disorganized league of princes in central India, was split into several warring factions, and in 1795 one of the feuding princes appointed a French adventurer to organize his army. Alone this action was not terribly significant, but French influence was growing in other parts of India as well. In Hyderabad, traditionally a British ally, the ruler proceeded to reorient his foreign policy. The British had remained neutral in a war between Hyderabad and the Mahrattas in 1795–96. Hyderabad lost and the ruler held the British responsible for his defeat. In revenge he dismissed all British officers from his service and began to hire Frenchmen. By mid-1798 French officers dominated Hyderabad's fourteen-thousand-man army. The French also succeeded in establishing an entente with Mysore, whose rulers had opposed British expansion in India for many decades. Tippoo Sultan had lost a major war to the British and their allies in 1792 and immediately began to seek the support of a major European power in order to renew hostilities. In May 1797 Ripaud, a French privateer shipwrecked on the coast of Mysore, arrived at Seringapatam, Tippoo's capital. Brazenly claiming to be an official of the Republic, he proceeded to organize a primary assembly and a revolutionary tribunal for a handful of French adventurers serving in the Sultan's army. On May 15 he raised a tricolor flag and swore eternal friendship with Tippoo, to whom he gave the title of Citizen Prince.

Tippoo, of course, realized that Ripaud was a fraud, but he and his advisers decided to use him as a means of gaining access to the French. On April 2 the Sultan designated five ambassadors to accompany Ripaud to the Ile de France, where they were to offer the French governor general an alliance. They were to suggest that eighty thousand troops of the Sultan join forty thousand Frenchmen in an attack on the British and Portuguese holdings in India. After the victory, Tippoo planned to take Madras and half of Bengal, leaving the rest to the French.[15]

On January 19, 1798, Tippoo's delegation reached the Ile de France, and although the governor general refused to ratify a treaty, he did send the Sultan's proposals to Paris and recruited volunteers for Mysore's army. By the time Tippoo's offer reached Paris the Directory had already decided upon an eastern expedition and was willing to undertake negotiations with Indian princes in order to add strength to Bonaparte's thrust.

The British were, of course, aware of Tippoo's hostility, and while the French were preparing their expedition at Toulon, Dundas worked to convince his colleagues that Bonaparte was going to strike at British India in conjunction with Mysore. Nelson, after entering the Mediterranean in pursuit of the French fleet, agreed with him and sent a similar appraisal to the Admiralty. The urgings of these two men plus the news of the arrival of Tippoo's agents at the Ile de France finally convinced the rest of the Cabinet that the French expedition to Egypt, com-

[15] *The Asiatic Annual Register or a View of the History of Hindustan and of the Politics, Commerce, and Literature of Asia for the Year 1799* (London, 1800), pp. 188–96. After the British conquest of Mysore the *Asiatic Annual Register* published all of the documents captured at Seringapatam.

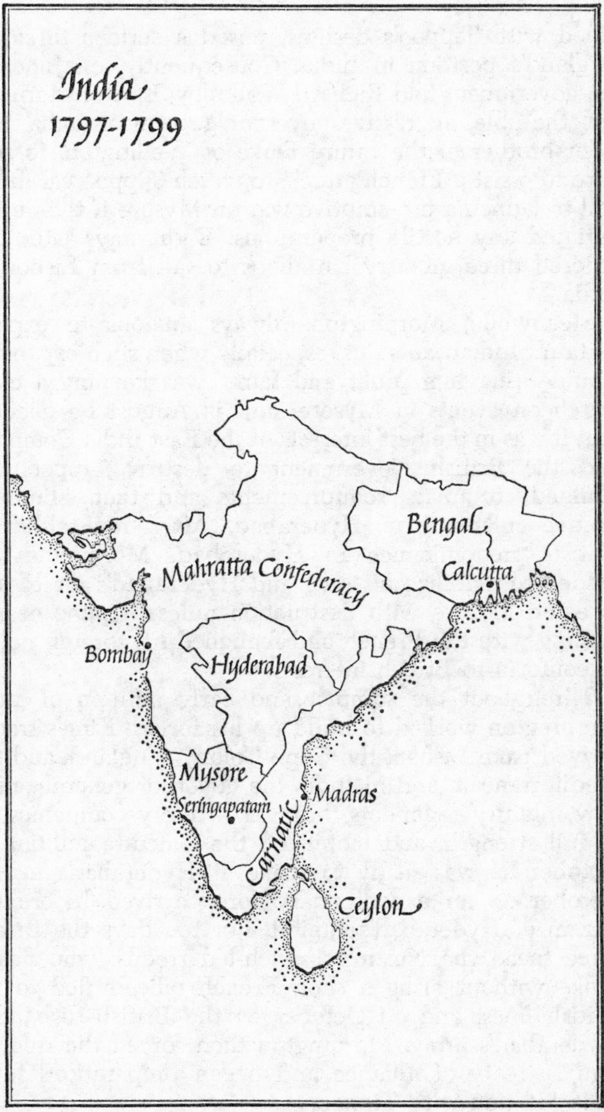

India
1797-1799

Bengal
Calcutta
Mahratta Confederacy
Bombay
Hyderabad
Mysore
Madras
Seringapatam
Carnatic
Ceylon

bined with Tippoo's designs, posed a serious threat to England's position in India. Consequently, on June 18, the government told Richard Wellesley, Earl of Mornington, the able, aggressive governor general of India, and elder brother of the future Duke of Wellington, to prepare to resist a French attack, to watch Tippoo carefully, and to launch a pre-emptive war on Mysore if the Sultan initiated any hostile preparations. Eight days later Pitt ordered three infantry battalions to sail from Lisbon to India.

Meanwhile, Mornington, always anxious to expand Britain's Indian domains, especially when such expansion would bring him profit and fame, was keeping a close watch on events in Mysore, and in August he decided that it was in the best interests of the East India Company and the British Government to destroy Tippoo. He planned to amass reinforcements and then eliminate French influence in Hyderabad. After re-establishing British predominance in Hyderabad, Mornington intended to mobilize his own and Hyderabad's forces and threaten Mysore with destruction unless Tippoo ceased dealing with the French and realigned his foreign policy to conform to British interests.

Throughout the summer and early autumn of 1798, Mornington worked to build up his forces. King's troops arrived from Lisbon, the Cape Colony, England, and the Mediterranean, and in India the governor general raised new infantry regiments, brought artillery companies up to full strength, and mobilized the Calcutta militia. By October he was ready to strike at Hyderabad, and on October 12 an expeditionary force arrived before the Nizam of Hyderabad's capital. For ten days the British force faced the Nizam's French-led troops, who finally broke without firing a shot. French officers fled to the British lines, and on October 23 the British disbanded Hyderabad's army. Mornington then forced the ruler to sign a treaty of alliance and began preparations for a confrontation with Tippoo.

On November 4 Mornington told Tippoo of Nelson's victory at Aboukir and four days later warned him to abandon his pro-French policies. In an effort to prolong negotiations until the advent of the monsoon season made campaigning impossible, Tippoo denied having any dealings with the French. On January 9, 1799, Mornington insisted that Tippoo receive a special British envoy at Seringapatam and settle all outstanding problems with him or face the consequences. Mornington, however, realized that Tippoo would try to prolong negotiations and decided to act immediately. He gathered an invasion force of thirteen thousand European and twenty-five thousand native troops, and on February 3, without awaiting a reply to his earlier note, ordered his forces to invade Mysore.[16]

The British, striking from Madras and Bombay, began to advance on Seringapatam. Tippoo's thirty-three thousand infantry and fifteen thousand cavalry were simply no match for the well-trained British troops and could do little more than delay their advance. In fact, slow-moving pack animals and poor roads did more to slow the British than the Sultan's armies, but by the second week in April Mornington's armies had reached Seringapatam and opened siege trenches. By May 3 British artillery had blown a gap in the walls of Seringapatam, and the following day three thousand English and two thousand native infantrymen launched an assault on the city. After a few moments of stiff fighting, Tippoo's forces collapsed, and the British poured into the city, slaughtering the demoralized soldiers of Mysore by the thousands. Wounded three times, Tippoo himself nevertheless kept on fighting until a British private killed him. Late that night one of the Sultan's aides, under armed guard,

[16] R. R. Pearce, ed., *Memoirs and Correspondence of the Most Noble Richard Marquess Wellesley* (London, 1846), I, pp. 213–17, 225, and 245–47; and S. J. Owen, ed., *A Selection from the Despatches, Treaties, and Other Papers of the Marquess Wellesley K.G. During His Government of India* (Oxford, 1877), p. 61.

searched through the ten thousand corpses littering the city until he found his master's body. The British allowed him to bury the Sultan the next day, and at the close of the funeral ceremony a thunderstorm of unusual violence burst over Seringapatam, marking with terror the end of a major threat to the growth of British hegemony in India. Mornington then annexed Mysore's coastline, gave his Indian allies portions of the dead Sultan's domain, restored Mysore's ancient Hindu dynasty, and forced the new ruler to agree to a binding alliance with England.

While destroying Mysore, Mornington was also expanding British influence in the Persian Gulf and southern Arabia. In October 1798 the ruler of Muscat, in return for British protection from Oman and the Turks, agreed to close his ports to French and Batavian ships, to forbid French and Dutch trading posts in his country, and to dismiss from his service citizens of states at war with England. After the fall of Seringapatam, a British agent arrived in Persia, and after many months of tedious negotiations, the Shah signed a treaty with England. Finally, in May 1799, a British regiment and six hundred native troops occupied the island of Perim near the mouth of the Red Sea. In July, British ships bombarded the Red Sea port of Kosseir, forcing the French garrison to evacuate the town. In August, the British flotilla sailed to Jidda, where its commander convinced the local ruler to forbid trade with the French. The British then transferred their garrison from Perim to Aden, thereby gaining control of the strategic passage between the sea and the Indian Ocean.

In 1798 the French threat to India appeared very real to British officials in London and Calcutta, and the Cabinet and the governor general undertook determined countermeasures. The Battle of Aboukir completely disrupted the Directory's plans, for without control of the Mediterranean, communication between France and Mysore was virtually impossible. Paris did send two agents to Mysore, but neither man ever reached India. One was arrested before his departure and the other reached Corfu but could get no farther because of the Russo-Turkish siege. In November the Directory suggested that Bonaparte might lead the Army of the East overland to India, and in December Bonaparte began to build sloops to cruise the Red Sea, and informed Tippoo that he wished to arrange for military co-operation between his army and Mysore. But in realistic terms Nelson's victory had deprived France of any real chance to influence events in India and allowed the British to regain the initiative on the subcontinent.[17] The inability of France to move men and supplies to India allowed the British to operate without interference and to score a major colonial triumph.

While expanding their power in the Indies, the British also assisted the Ottoman Empire's efforts to contain the Army of the East and render it strategically useless to the Republic. In the summer of 1798 the French position in the Near East was still strong despite the disaster of Aboukir. The Turks tried to arouse Egyptian resistance by calling for a holy war against the French, but Bonaparte's troops crushed an uprising in Cairo on October 21, 1798. Mobile columns then suppressed local risings in rural areas, and the Egyptians relapsed into their earlier attitude of passive hostility to the Army of the East. The attempt to create an insurrection having failed, the Turks began to prepare an invasion of Egypt. A field army of twenty-five thousand men moved into Syria, supported by four thousand men at Jaffa and twenty thousand at Acre. On Rhodes, eighteen thousand soldiers made ready to attack Egypt by sea, and a British flotilla of three ships of the line plus lighter craft stood ready to support the Turkish assault.[18]

Learning of his enemies' preparations, Bonaparte

[17] *A.N. Archives de la Marine carton* BB^4*129; Min. de la Guerre A.H., Indes orientales carton* B^1; and *A.N. AF III** 19.

[18] Galli, *Journal*, p. 87, and *Min. de la Guerre A.H., Ordres de bataille des armées en campagne, 1792–1815, carton* X^p3.

quickly organized a thirteen-thousand-man expedition and, on February 4, 1799, led it into Syria. Six days later he wrote to Paris explaining his reasons for the move: He claimed that he wanted to assure the security of Egypt and dislocate the planned Turkish attack by seizing the Sultan's bases in Syria. He also hoped that new French victories would convince the Sultan to negotiate, and finally he wanted to force the British to pull their ships out of the Levant by occupying the major harbors in the region. In addition to these defensive motives Bonaparte may well have had more grandiose schemes. The Directory in November had authorized him to attempt a march on Constantinople or the Indus if he thought it possible. Bonaparte was always willing to take daring steps, and on several occasions told his officers that his army could imitate Alexander's and march to India. He also contemplated mobilizing Near Eastern Christians, Druses, and other anti-Turkish minorities and using them to frighten the Turks into abandoning their English and Russian allies and joining the Army of the East in an assault upon India.[19] Obviously the difficulties of an overland march to the Indus were tremendous, if not insurmountable, but Bonaparte had attempted and frequently accomplished equally audacious operations. For the man who conquered Italy at the age of twenty-seven, forced the Hapsburgs to sue for peace at the age of twenty-eight, became the virtual dictator of France at thirty, and Emperor at thirty-six, the idea of repeating Alexander the Great's feats was not too farfetched. If Bonaparte invaded Syria to protect his base in Egypt, it is entirely possible that after his projected defeat of the Turks he contemplated an even more important, far-ranging campaign.

The initial stages of Bonaparte's Syrian campaign were

[19] *Correspondance de Bonaparte*, p. 220, and H. Bertrand, ed., *Campagnes d'Egypte et de Syrie 1798–1799 mémoires pour servir à l'histoire de Napoléon dictés par lui-même à Sainte-Hélène* (Paris, 1847), I, pp. 20–21, 123, and 173.

highly successful. After an eleven-day siege, Reynier's division forced the El Arish garrison to capitulate on February 11. On the twenty-sixth Kléber's men occupied Gaza. The Army of the East then stormed Jaffa, and by March 20 it stood before the walls of Acre, the last major Turkish stronghold in Syria, and a position that Bonaparte had to take before he could push farther, for he could not permit the existence of a large enemy force in his rear. Furthermore, if Acre remained in Ottoman hands the British fleet could use it as a base from which they could continue to blockade the Army of the East. While advancing through Palestine, Bonaparte had signed an armistice with the governor of Jerusalem, who promised to submit to French rule if Acre fell. Bonaparte also promised to liberate the Jews and Christians of Syria from Turkish domination, and to establish an independent Druse state in return for their co-operation against the Turks. But the response to his proclamations was not great, for the subject peoples of the Near East were awaiting the results of the attack on Acre before deciding whether or not to join the French.[20]

Surrounded by water on three sides and protected by a British squadron, which also supplied marines and artillerymen for the garrison, the twenty-thousand-man Turkish defense force was prepared to give a good account of itself. The British fleet struck the first blow in the siege by capturing the French transports that were bringing Bonaparte's siege guns to Acre. The French had to bring other guns overland, and it was not until March 20 that they could open their attack trenches against Acre's landward defenses. By March 28 French artillery had pounded a breach in the walls, and Bonaparte sent a picked force of grenadiers to storm the city. After heavy hand-to-hand combat, the French managed to gain a foothold in the Turkish lines, but a furious

[20] Berthier, *Relations des campagnes du général Bonaparte*, pp. 52–56, and *Min. de la Guerre A.H., M.h., Campagne de Syrie an VIII 9081*.

counterattack drove them back. Four days later Bonaparte ordered a second assault, but again the Turks hurled back their assailants. Bonaparte then tried a mining operation, but on April 7 British marines, backed by naval gunfire, attacked and destroyed the mine. At this point Bonaparte learned that the Turkish field army had crossed the Jordan and was marching toward Acre.

On April 8 a French reconnaissance force repulsed a Turkish cavalry picket near Nazareth, and the following day Bonaparte sent Kléber's division into northern Palestine. Kléber defeated a five-thousand-man Turkish detachment on the eleventh, but on April 16 he came upon the main army encamped on the slopes of Mount Tabor. Kléber attacked immediately, but overwhelming numbers of Turks soon forced his men to retreat up the mountain. The French began to run low on ammunition, but just as their position was becoming desperate Bonaparte arrived, leading an infantry division. Striking swiftly, he took the Turks by surprise and in conjunction with a renewed attack by Kléber shattered the Turkish force. After losing six thousand men, the Turks fled for the Jordan, leaving all of Syria open to French conquest if they could but first take Acre.

Upon his return from Mount Tabor, Bonaparte renewed his attacks upon Acre with increased vigor. In the last weeks of April he sent three attacks against the breach, but the Turks repulsed them all and with British support even managed to launch periodic sorties to keep the French off balance. The Army of the East kept attacking throughout the first week of May but failed to shake the Turkish defenses. On May 8, however, a massive assault carried part of the city's outer defenses. Two demibrigades captured a fortified tower and drove off a hastily organized counterattack. The Turks then sent forward units that had just arrived from Rhodes, and under the cover of British naval gunfire the new troops dislodged the French after savage fighting.

The battle of May 8 was the critical one not only for

Acre but also for all of Bonaparte's schemes for further campaigns in the Near East. Fighting continued for another week, but never again did the French seriously threaten the Turkish position. Finally, on May 21, Bonaparte admitted defeat and ordered his army to begin the long march back to Egypt. On June 3 the expeditionary force recrossed the Egyptian frontier, having left its line of march strewn with the corpses of those who had succumbed to the Black Death. During the Syrian campaign, Bonaparte had lost a quarter of his total force and had failed to alter the strategic balance of power in the Levant.[21]

On July 25 Bonaparte destroyed a fifteen-thousand-man Turkish force that had landed in Aboukir Bay earlier in the month. The victory proved that the Army of the East was still a formidable power, but the triumph did not alter the fact that the French were unable to play a major role in events outside of Egypt. The British and Turks had successfully forced Bonaparte into a defensive role. Furthermore, he realized that his loss of naval power meant that it was only a matter of time before his enemies concentrated sufficient strength to destroy his forces, and he therefore began secret preparations to desert his army and return to Europe.

In devoting its efforts to ventures in the Near East the Directory ignored an excellent chance to strike a telling blow at England in an area vital to British security. As the Army of the East sailed toward Egypt the United Irish Society launched a major uprising, but because of the commitment to the eastern venture the French Government was unable to take advantage of it.

Irish radicals had stepped up the preparations for rebellion in the months following Hoche's expedition, and at the end of 1797 Irish agents in France held several

[21] Berthier, *Relations des campagnes du général Bonaparte*, p. 98; J. Burgoyne, *A Short History of the Naval and Military Operations in Egypt* (London, 1885), p. 13; and D. Lacroix, *Bonaparte en Egypt* (Paris, 1899), p. 335.

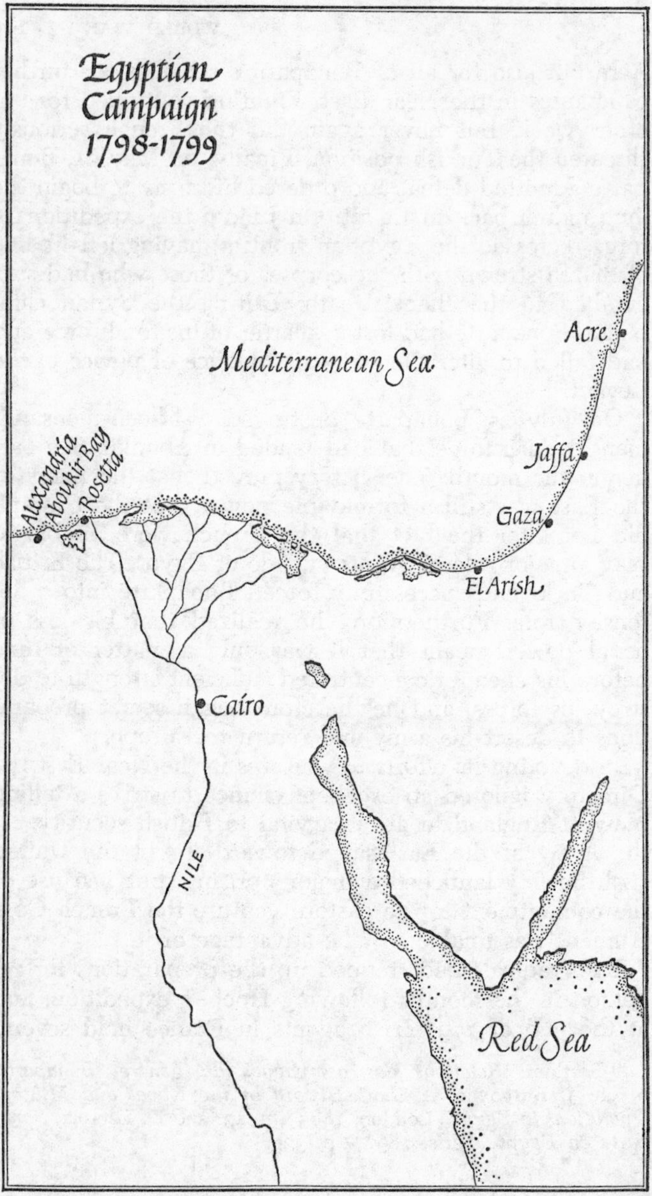

Egyptian Campaign 1798-1799

Mediterranean Sea

Acre

Jaffa

Gaza

El Arish

Alexandria

Aboukir Bay

Rosetta

Cairo

NILE

Red Sea

meetings with Bonaparte and gave him a number of memoirs describing conditions in Ireland. The delegates also met with the Foreign Minister and two directors. They obtained promises of French support but nothing more. French planners generally ignored the possibilities inherent in an Irish rebellion and concentrated exclusively on preparing a cross-Channel attack and later an eastern expedition.[22] Perhaps policy makers in Paris did not believe the claims of the Irish agents; perhaps Bonaparte felt that an Irish expedition would place undue limitations upon opportunities for independent action; or the government might have believed that an eastern venture was less dangerous than trying to transport an army to Ireland. Any, all, or none of these calculations may have influenced the French decision to ignore Ireland, but the fact remains that in the spring of 1798 the French refused to contemplate any intervention there.

Meanwhile, in Ireland, the United Irish Society was busily preparing its revolution. By the first months of 1798 the society's Military Committee reported that there were 100,000 armed men ready for action. Other figures credit the society with a total of 280,000 armed members, and some of the leaders felt that a successful rising was possible even without French support. The British became fearful for the security of Ireland, and many officials including Pitt believed that the Irish radicals and the French were planning to establish both an Irish *and* a British republic.[23] To quell the growing revolutionary sentiment the British resorted to massive force. The Cabinet increased its Irish garrison to 103,000 men, the largest

[22] W. T. Wolfe Tone, ed., *Life of Theobold Wolfe Tone* (Washington, D.C., 1826), II, pp. 454–74. See also A. de Blacam, *The Life Story of Wolfe Tone* (Dublin, 1935), and F. MacDermot, *Theobold Wolfe Tone, A Biographical Study* (London, 1939).

[23] *The Speeches of the Right Honourable William Pitt in the House of Commons* (London, 1806), III, pp. 257–58. *The Report of the Committee of Secrecy to the House of Commons* (London, 1799) also maintained that there existed a widespread conspiracy to destroy the British Government and establish republics in England and Ireland.

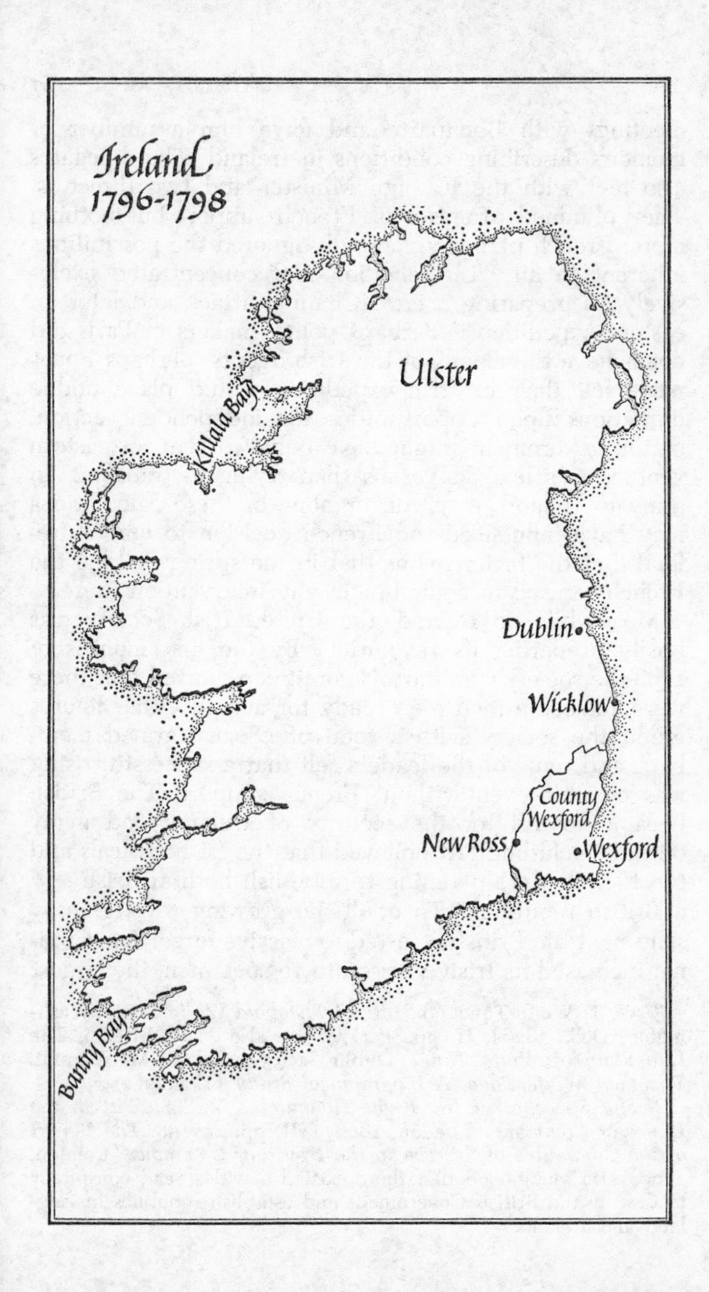
Ireland
1796-1798
Ulster
Killala Bay
Dublin
Wicklow
County
Wexford
New Ross
Wexford
Bantry Bay

single British force to take the field during the entire Revolutionary Era. Like the French in the Vendée, the British in Ireland frequently used extremely severe measures against subversives and suspects. Commanders resorted to arbitrary arrests, searches, and seizures, summary executions, torture, and the establishment of martial law throughout whole counties to combat insurrectionary elements. The results were mixed, however. The British, it is true, captured thousands of weapons and eliminated hundreds of actual or potential rebels, but the violence of their methods convinced many thousands of neutral civilians to support the revolutionary cause. Consequently, by the spring of 1798 Ireland was on the verge of open revolt.

In addition to armed repression the British also made excellent use of spies, who infiltrated the United Irish Society and enabled the government to strike directly at the rebel high command. On March 12, acting on an informer's information, British troops captured thirteen of the society's leaders. The Dublin arrests deprived the rebels of some of their most able commanders, and on May 19 the British struck again. A paid informer enabled the authorities to capture the chief of the revolutionaries' Military Committee, the only important figure who had escaped the March arrests. New men came forward and issued orders for the rebellion to begin on May 23, but two days before the date set for the rising a spy provided British authorities with the necessary information to enable them to round up the society's new leaders.[24] Consequently, when the rebellion did erupt, it lacked coordinated and effective direction.

On the evening of May 23, despite all of the repressive measures, members of the United Irish Society began to attack British posts in and around Dublin. In the days following, sporadic but bloody fighting spread to the

[24] R. Madden, *The United Irishmen, Their Lives and Times* (Dublin, 1857–60), I, p. 365, and II, pp. 57–58; and J. A. Froude, *The English in Ireland in the Eighteenth Century* (London, 1874), III, p. 345.

southern counties. Some of the clashes were quite desperate, with rebels and government forces each losing hundreds of men, but the lack of centralized leadership prevented the rebels from co-ordinating their blows, and the British managed to defeat the Irish in detail. Just as the Irish cause seemed doomed, however, thousands of peasants in the southern county of Wexford joined the revolt. Although the United Irish Society had not won many adherents in Wexford, British repression, especially the shooting of more than sixty suspects, convinced a local priest, Father John Murphy, that rebellion was his only alternative. Gathering some of his parishioners, he began to march on the town of Wexford. Others soon joined him, and on May 30 a force of thirty thousand men took the city and raised the green flag of Ireland.[25] Thus from an entirely unexpected quarter the rebellion had gained a new lease on life.

After capturing Wexford, the rebels established a Committee of Twelve to regulate the requisition and distribution of food and supplies. The Committee also transformed the predominantly peasant and Catholic rising into a political insurrection. It protected local Protestants from any acts of reprisal by the Catholic peasants, appointed Protestants and members of the United Irish Society to command the rebel forces, and on June 16 appealed to France for one thousand men and five thousand rifles to help establish an Irish republic.[26]

[25] Bishop of Bath and Wells, ed., *The Journal and Correspondence of William, Lord Auckland* (London, 1862), III, pp. 429–30; and W. Lecky, *A History of England in the Eighteenth Century* (London, 1890), VII, pp. 76–82.

[26] Lecky, *A History of England*, pp. 91–93, and Desbrière, *Projets et tentatives*, II, p. 40. Contemporary British observers also agreed that the Wexford rising, though religious and agrarian in origin, was essentially political in motivation. See C. Vane, ed., *Memoirs and Correspondence of Viscount Castlereagh, Second Marquess of Londonderry* (London, 1848), I, p. 219; and C. Ross, ed., *Correspondence of Charles First Marquess Cornwallis* (London, 1859), II, p. 355.

The French, already commmitted to the invasion of Egypt, did nothing while the British struck in overwhelming strength. London increased the Irish garrison to 130,000 men, crushed rebel bands in Ulster in a series of savage encounters, and then moved against the Wexford insurgents, whose army, though poorly armed, had grown to about 100,000 men. The Irish divided their forces into two columns. One moved against New Ross and the other along the road to Dublin, which ran through Arklow. They hoped to expand their territorial holdings and capture government arsenals before the British finished subduing the northern and central counties, but they were too late. On June 5 the British defeated the pike-armed rebels at New Ross, and four days later halted the Irish march on Dublin. Having lost some forty-four hundred men in the two battles, the Irish retreated to Vinegar Hill, a position covering the main roads into Wexford. There on June 21 the British attacked and broke the Irish forces. Government troops then pursued the rebels, killing the wounded and all who tried to surrender. By June 22 the British flag again flew in Wexford as remnants of the Irish forces fled into the country, where British patrols spent the rest of the year hunting them down. Guerrilla war continued on into 1799, but after the summer of 1798 the Irish independence movement was doomed. Thousands perished in the abortive revolution; estimates of casualties run as high as seventy thousand.[27] The revolt had a broad basis of popular support, but lacking French aid, it failed in the face of overwhelming force.

Ironically, it was only after the destruction of the main Irish forces that the French made any effort to aid the rebels. The Directory, finally realizing the magnitude of the rising, organized several expeditions, but due to

[27] Froude, *The English in Ireland*, pp. 407–11, 420–23, 436–37, and 443–44; Lecky, *A History of England*, pp. 150–51, 164–66, 175–78, and 180–82; and H. Wheeler and A. Broadly, *The War in Wexford* (London, 1910), pp. 119–20.

faulty planning and execution only one of them ever reached Ireland. In August a French battalion landed in western Ireland. Humbert, the commander, waged a skillful campaign and won several battles, but 844 men could not hold out indefinitely against 20,000 British. In early September Humbert capitulated, and the British proceeded to hunt down and hang those Irishmen who had joined him. In October another expedition arrived off the Irish coast, but the Royal Navy intercepted it and captured several ships. Among the prisoners was Wolfe Tone, who was taken ashore, tried by court martial for treason despite the fact that he was a French officer, and sentenced to die by hanging. He cheated the gallows by cutting his throat before the British could execute him. A few more feeble atttempts at invasion, none of which succeeded, complete the dreary story of the insufficient French efforts to influence events in Ireland. By going to Egypt instead of Ireland the French probably lost an opportunity to support a successful Irish revolution and thereby strike a major blow at England.

Even in areas not directly affected by the Egyptian expedition and Aboukir, the Directory was unable to improve its position. In Italy elements in the Cisalpine Republic sought to make their new state the center for a much larger Italian republic. The French opposed any efforts to draw them further into the dangers and complexities of Italian politics. The French also opposed the creation of a single Italian republic. Instead, they preferred a series of smaller republics each dependent upon France for protection rather than a unitary state which might be more independent, but despite the Directory's disapproval radicals organized a rising in Rome at the end of December 1797. It failed, but in the ensuing riots and disorder propapal mobs killed a French general serving with the embassy. The Directory, wishing to avoid the prospects of a papal alliance with Austria or England and a renewal of war in Italy, sent troops into the Papal

States early in 1798, exiled the Pope to Siena, and created a Roman Republic. The Republic, which existed only because of the presence of French troops, was generally unpopular. Peasant guerrillas, often led by their priests, began to operate in the rural areas. The court of Naples also backed them. Neapolitan officers joined the guerrillas and led them in battle and Neapolitan muskets found their way into the hands of the rebels. The French had to detach troops to fight the counterrevolutionaries while at the same time keeping a wary eye on the Italian radicals, who continued to object to Paris' refusal to unite the Roman and Cisalpine republics into a single political entity.[28]

The Directory also intervened in Switzerland. Bonaparte, before leaving for Egypt, had advocated intervention in order to dominate the strategic routes between France and Milan. He also desired to seize the treasury of several of the cantons to finance his overseas venture. In February 1798 the French invaded Switzerland, crushed initial resistance, wrested large sums of money from Berne and other cantons, and with the support of a significant minority of the urban population imposed a new constitution upon the Swiss people. The rural Catholic provinces, however, refused to accept the Helvetian Republic, and French divisions had to wage a bitter campaign to repress counterrevolutionary insurrections.[29]

Finally, France drifted into an undeclared naval war with the United States, and the two nations came perilously close to official hostilities. Ever since 1792 the American Government had refused to assist France de-

[28] See A. Dufourcq, *Régime jacobin en Italie: Etude sur la République romaine* (Paris, 1900); J. Godechot, *La contre-révolution 1789–1804* (Paris, 1961), pp. 332–33; and *Min. de la Guerre A.H., Correspondance Armée d'Italie, 1er août–30 septembre 1798, carton B³55.*

[29] See E. Chapuisat, *La Suisse et la Révolution française* (Geneva, 1946), and *Min. de la Guerre A.H., correspondance Armées de Mayence et d'Helvétie, avril–juin 1798, carton B²64.*

spite the treaty of 1778. When Edmond Genet, the French minister, had issued French military commissions to American citizens and arranged to reprovision privateers in American ports, President Washington threatened to demand his recall unless he ceased his activities. The Government of the United States also foiled a French scheme to use American freebooters to invade Spanish Florida and stopped other pro-French adventurers from attacking Louisiana. The French in turn regarded Washington's neutrality proclamation of 1793, the Jay Treaty of 1795, and the President's call for nonalignment in 1796 as pro-British acts and responded by allowing their ships to seize American vessels that carried any British cargo and by contemplating the transformation of the region west of the Alleghenies into an independent state.[30]

At the end of 1797 an American delegation went to France in an attempt to settle the problem of French attacks on American commerce. Talleyrand, however, demanded a large bribe as a precondition to any discussions. The payment of a gratuity in return for favorable consideration in a negotiation was standard procedure. The Americans' objection was not to paying the bribe but to paying it prior to the opening of talks, and in April 1798 the delegation left France. President Adams under pressure from his Federalist colleagues, who wanted to discredit the pro-French Jeffersonians, then published the documents relating to the episode—the famous XYZ papers. The result was an upsurge of anti-French sentiment, partly genuine and partly Federalist-inspired. As sea engagements continued, Adams created a Navy Department and began to build a fleet, while Congress en-

[30] *A.N. AF III carton 56;* A. De Conde, *Entangling Alliance Politics and Diplomacy Under George Washington* (Durham, N.C., 1958); A. De Conde, *The Quasi-War: The Politics and Diplomacy of the Undeclared War with France 1797–1801* (New York, 1967); and R. R. Palmer, "A Revolutionary Republican, M. A. B. Mangourit," in *William and Mary Quarterly,* (1952) IX, No. 4.

larged the army and brought Washington out of retirement to command it. Alexander Hamilton, who hoped to be the real commander of the army, began to plan for an Anglo-American assault on Spain's American colonies. He held secret talks with the British and Miranda, an early leader in the South American independence movement, and urged Adams to declare war. Thus by the end of 1798 the republics of the Old and New worlds appeared to be on the verge of open hostilities.

The months following the Campo Formio Treaty were disastrous for France. The Egyptian expedition failed, the British increased their power in India and found new allies in Europe, the Irish rebellion failed, French conquests in Italy and Switzerland produced violent counterrevolutionary reactions, and relations with the American Republic deteriorated. By the autumn of 1798 the Directory could no longer contemplate the coming defeat of Britain. Instead, the leaders of France had to fear the creation of a second coalition and the renewal of war in Europe.

CHAPTER 6

THE SECOND COALITION

French disasters in overseas ventures not only decimated the Republic's influence in the non-European world but also enabled England and Russia to find new allies and create a second coalition in Europe.

Vienna had never accepted the results of Campo Formio as permanent, and when the French diverted their resources to the Levant, Thugut slowly and cautiously began to prepare for a new round in the struggle for power in the west. As early as February 1798 the Austrian ambassador to England stated to Grenville that his government favored the re-establishment of the French monarchy, and in April the Austrians called for the creation of a coalition including Russia, Denmark, Sardinia, and Naples. At Rastadt, where French diplomats were trying to conclude a final peace with the Empire, the Austrians constantly placed obstacles in the path of peace in order to retain the option of resuming hostilities at short notice, and in Italy, Austria and Naples signed an alliance treaty in May calling for a combined attack upon the French satellite republics if a new war erupted.

Thugut was not, however, ready for war. He lacked allies because Prussia was too suspicious of Vienna to contemplate abandoning its neutrality and financial disputes prevented the establishment of an English alliance. Furthermore, Hapsburg diplomats wanted first to try to convince the French to make substantial concessions in Italy before taking recourse to arms.

An opportunity for direct talks with the French arose when a crowd in Vienna tore down and burned a huge tricolor flag that Jean Bernadotte, the ambassador, had hung from a window of his embassy. Bernadotte left Vienna on April 15, and the Directory called for negotiations to settle the incident. Austrian and French diplomats met at the Alsatian town of Selz on June 1, and the Hapsburg agent immediately demanded territorial concessions in Italy to balance out recent French gains. The French refused to show weakness and perhaps encourage other powers to assume a hostile stance. They ignored the Austrian demands and insisted upon restricting the talks to the question of rectifying the insult to the Republic's flag. Negotiations continued for a month with each side refusing to modify its original stand. Finally, the Austrians realized that they would gain nothing from the French and resumed their search for a continental ally to support them in a new war. On July 5 the Hapsburg delegate at Selz formally ended the talks and three days later set out for St. Petersburg, where Thugut had, even while dealing with France, prepared the way for an Austro-Russian entente.[1]

Early in July the Emperor's brother had journeyed to St. Petersburg and had personally told the Tsar that Francis needed the support of sixteen thousand Russian troops in order to resume the war with France. The Tsar, already contemplating war with the Republic in the Mediterranean, was quite willing to extend hostilities into western Europe and on August 8 agreed to place the required troops at Austria's disposal. By the time the Austrian delegate arrived from France the Tsar had increased the size of his military contribution to twenty-four thousand men, and Thugut had only to await the arrival of the Russian troops before renewing his attempts to strike at France.

Having committed his state to fight in western Europe, Tsar Paul then sought additional partners. Negotiations with the Prussian court failed. Frederick William III re-

[1] F. Masson, *Les diplomates de la Révolution* (Paris, 1882), pp. 188–91, 205, and 210–11; and *A.N. AF III* 59. This carton contains reports to the Directory concerning the Selz talks.

jected a Russian offer of forty-five thousand troops for a joint attack on Holland and the Rhineland and refused to abandon his policy of neutrality. Talks with England, however, had already led to more fruitful results. An Anglo-Russian treaty signed on December 29, 1798, called upon the contracting parties to work together for a restoration of the European balance of power at French expense, and England's subsequent adherence to the Russo-Ottoman treaty completed a series of alliances stretching from the Nile to the Danube. The allies still had to devise a detailed diplomatic and strategic program, but the Austro-Russian alliance, the Anglo-Russian treaty, and the Russo-Turkish-English entente provided an excellent framework within which the allies could elaborate a precise and detailed policy.

As they watched the ring of hostile alliances close inexorably around them, the directors desperately sought but ultimately failed to discover a means of preventing the formation of a new continental coalition. Their first step was to increase the size of the nation's armed forces, which had declined to 365,000 because of desertion and the failure to replace combat losses. By expanding its army the Directory sought not only to improve the nation's defense posture but also to warn other powers that France was willing to fight. On September 5 the Legislative Corps passed a new Conscription Act calling upon all male citizens between the ages of twenty and twenty-five to report for medical examination and registration. In contrast to the 1793 *levée,* an emergency measure which sought immediate mobilization of the nation's manpower, the Conscription Act more closely resembled a modern draft law in that it sought to provide an orderly yet flexible means of recruitment. On the twenty-third the government issued a decree calling two hundred thousand men to the colors, but calling for new troops and actually obtaining them were two very different things. From the first there was widespread resistance to the draft. In the former provinces of Belgium, Liège,

Brittany, Normandy, and Anjou conscripts refused to join their units and ran away to become brigands. Priests, returned *émigrés,* and former royalist rebels often assumed leadership of these bands and led them in raids against the buildings where the local authorities kept the draft and tax rolls. The deserters also attacked the homes of individuals who had purchased nationalized church and noble lands. By the end of the year only 35,000 men had reported for induction, and the government had to employ 55,500 troops to keep order and hunt down the deserters.[2]

The French also attempted unsuccessfully to divert Turkish and Russian troops from the west by creating uprisings in their rear. In November the Directory established a "commercial agency" at Ancona. The agency was in fact a blind, and its real purpose was to instigate rebellions throughout the Balkans. Lack of funds, however, prevented the agency from accomplishing its objectives. A few agents did go to Greece, but they were unable to organize any risings. The government also sent an agent to Russia with instructions to organize a coup and depose the Tsar. The agent took the Directory's money, disappeared, and was never seen again.[3] Thus Paris' ef-

[2] P. Mahon, *Etudes sur les armées du Directoire* (Paris, 1905), p. 120; *A.N. AF III* 13; A.N. AF III 150[A]*; and *Min. de la Guerre A.H., Registre de Correspondance du général Jourdan avec le Directoire et le Ministère de la Guerre du brumaire an 4 nivose an VII (23 octobre–24 decembre 1798) carton B[2*]* 260. Draft resistance need not be attributed exclusively to royalism or disaffection with the Republic. Much desertion was the result of a dislike of military service and even as late as 1907, 36 per cent of French army reservists failed to report for duty. See A. T. Horne, *The Price of Glory: Verdun 1916* (London, 1962), p. 9.

[3] *A.N. AF III* 13;* M. A. B. Mangourit, *Défense d'Ancone et des départments romains le Tronto, le Muscone et le Metauro par le général Monnier aux années VII et VIII* (Paris, 1801), I, pp. 21–22; S. Pappas, "Un point d'histoire ignoré, l'Agence de commerce français d'Ancone (1799)," in *Revue d'études historiques* (1902) LXVIII; and R. Guyot, *Le Directoire et la paix de l'Europe* (Paris, 1912), p. 876.

forts to disrupt enemy preparations ended in ludicrous failure.

The Directory also tried to conclude a final peace with the Empire. Despite the creation of an ironical legal situation wherein the Republic sought peace with Francis II in his capacity as German Emperor and prepared to fight him in his role as ruler of hereditary Hapsburg domains, the directors sought to secure the Franco-German frontier and to free units in the Rhineland for service in Italy where the Austrians were gathering their major armies. In the winter of 1797 Talleyrand had held great hopes for a diplomatic triumph at the Rastadt conference. He planned to compensate those secular princes who had to give up territory in the Rhineland at the expense of ecclesiastical rulers who were traditionally Hapsburg partisans. He would thereby create a series of medium-sized German states that would have to align themselves with the Republic in order to preserve the new *status quo* from Austrian efforts to reverse the settlement. France could then use these states as a "third Germany" to check the ambitions of either Austria or Prussia. Talleyrand also hoped to force the congress to recognize the Rhine as France's new frontier without sacrificing any of the Republic's other conquests in return. In the first months of 1798 the conference progressed favorably for France. The Hapsburg delegate who spoke for the Empire as a whole employed delaying tactics by raising numerous procedural issues, but the French, by threatening to break off talks, forced the congress to recognize the Rhine as the Republic's new boundary. As France's international position began to deteriorate, however, Talleyrand had to abandon his larger schemes and attempt instead to conclude a quick peace on the Rhine. On July 10 the Foreign Minister told his agents at Rastadt to show great moderation in order to avoid driving the German princes into the arms of Russia and Austria. The French then abandoned their claims to a number of islands in the Rhine and to several fortresses on the river's right bank, and on September 9 Talleyrand told the Directory that it should give up all plans to create a third Germany, allow the various princes of the Empire to work out their own system of compensation, and if possible conclude a peace with the Empire on the basis of the *status quo.*

In pursuit of this new goal the French delegates stated on October 3 that if the congress did not accept the Republic's concessions and proceed to settle the question of indemnities, the Directory would assume that the Empire wanted to continue the war. This threat, however, failed to move the congress; the Hapsburgs persisted in their delaying tactics, and at the month's end the delegations at Rastadt had made no progress toward peace. On December 6 Talleyrand tried again to compel the German states to conclude a definitive treaty by threatening to leave the conference. The congress accepted the French demand to settle the indemnities question, but this was an extremely complex issue involving conflicting claims of scores of princes, and the Hapsburg diplomats continued to avoid a final decision by raising numerous points of procedure and detail. Thus the Republic at the end of the year was still in a state of war with the Empire, and the Rhine frontier was not secure.

The French were also unable to halt their enemies from spreading the war to the western Mediterranean. After the Battle of Aboukir, Nelson detached units to blockade the Egyptian coast and set sail for Naples. On the way he learned that the populace of Malta, incensed at the high French taxes and the confiscation of church property, had risen against the French garrison. Nelson stopped and assisted the rebels in blockading Valetta, requested the Portuguese to take over the blockade, and when they arrived, he supplied the Maltese with arms and munitions and resumed his voyage to Naples. The French position at Valetta was strong, but the rebels held the rest of the island, and in conjunction with the blockade they rendered Malta strategically useless to the Republic. The success at Malta convinced the British to extend further their control of the western Mediterranean by seizing a permanent base off the Spanish coast, and in November three regiments landed on Minorca. In a brief and almost bloodless campaign the British conquered the island and obtained an excellent base from which to blockade the southern coasts of France and Spain.

Meanwhile, Nelson had arrived at Naples on September 22 and received a spectacular welcome from the court and crowds alike. The situation in Italy was both dangerous and unstable. Sardinia-Piedmont and Tuscany pursued a policy of cautious neutrality. The Ligurian, Cisalpine and Roman republics looked to France for protection. From Venetia the Austrians waited for an opportunity to strike, and Bourbon Naples, frightened by French power yet desirous of new provinces, stood irresolute. Nelson thereupon decided to intervene in this explosive situation. The admiral immediately after his gala reception proceeded to urge King Ferdinand and Queen Marie Caroline to attack the French. Ferdinand was already sending covert aid to rebels in the Roman Republic and concentrating troops near his northern frontier, but he was vacillating and afraid of the French army and for the moment refused to undertake open hostilities. The Austrians and English also warned him not to strike before they could prepare a co-ordinated offensive. Nelson, however, continued to urge the monarch to attack. The ambitious French-hating Queen, the British ambassador despite his government's official policy, and the ambassador's wife, who was also Nelson's mistress, seconded the admiral's efforts. Ferdinand finally succumbed to the urgings of those around him and to his desire to seize a portion of the former papal domains, and on November 24 sixty-two infantry battalions and thirty-two squadrons of cavalry began to advance on Rome.[4]

[4] H. Acton, *The Bourbons of Naples (1734–1825)* (London, 1956), pp. 303–6; A. Bonnefons, *Marie Caroline, reine des Deux-*

Lacking sufficient troops, the French withdrew and evacuated Rome on November 27, and in the first days of December, Neapolitan troops entered the Eternal City. French resistance soon began to stiffen, however. On the Adriatic coast and in the central part of the Roman Republic French demibrigades hurled back their foes. North of Rome, French and Polish battalions crushed a Neapolitan force that was attempting to drive into Tuscany and link up with five thousand men who had landed from British ships at Leghorn. On December 5 the French halted a second attack and began to prepare a counteroffensive.[5]

Meanwhile, the Army of Italy prepared to move into Piedmont. The King of Sardinia-Piedmont had been making hostile preparations for several weeks. Sardinian troops concentrated around Turin, royal agents and priests spread anti-French propaganda throughout the countryside, and the government armed over twenty thousand peasants. The Sardinians then began to demand the evacuation of the Turin citadel, and the French became fully aware of the dangers of a Sardinian attack against the rear of the Cisalpine army and the Army of Italy. When the Neapolitan army began its initial offensive, the Sardinians increased further the size of their army in order either to attack the French or to force the Directory to make concessions in order to avoid adding a new power to its growing list of enemies. The French decided to strike first, and on December 5, the Army of Italy sent troops into Piedmont. Resistance col-

Sicilies (Paris, 1905), p. 151; *Min. de la Guerre A.H., Correspondance Armée d'Italie, 1er août–3 septembre 1798, carton B³55;* J. H. Rose, *Napoleonic Studies* (London, 1904), p. 353; and A. R. von Vivenot, *Vertrauliche Briefe des Freiherren von Thugut* (Vienna, 1872), II, p. 124.

[5] *Min. de la Guerre A.H., M.h., Précis historique de la Campagne de l'armée napolitaine* 453. This document was written by General Mack, commander of the Neapolitan forces. *Min. de la Guerre A.H., Correspondance Armée d'Italie, octobre 1798, carton B³56; novembre 1798, carton B³56bis;* and 1798, *carton B³57.*

lapsed; the King fled Sardinia on the ninth, and the French quickly took control of Piedmont, thereby securing their communications between France and the Italian republics.[6]

While the Army of Italy was occupying Piedmont, French troops in the Roman Republic, on December 8, launched their own counteroffensive. On the French right General Alexandre Macdonald's troops effectively shattered the Neapolitan army, which fled south in complete disorder. The British ambassador at Vienna noted "the Neapolitan troops have begged to be excused everywhere. They have fled and deserted uniformly."[7] The French re-entered Rome on December 16 and on Christmas day began to move south while units from the Army of Italy drove Neapolitan troops from Tuscany.

After liberating the Roman Republic's territory, the French continued their advance into the Neapolitan kingdom. By January 1, 1799, the French had taken Capua and ten days later Karl Mack, the Neapolitan commander, asked for an armistice, agreed to surrender the fortified camps around the city of Naples, and then, fearing that the populace would blame him for the defeats, resigned his post and fled to the French lines. The Neapolitan royal family had already fled to Sicily, and on January 14, General Championnet, the aggressive and ambitious commander of the Army of Rome, ordered his troops to advance upon Naples. The civil authorities of the city and the bishops wished to avoid futile bloodshed and tried to surrender, but the urban masses, fanatically devoted to their cult, their priests, and their rulers, armed themselves and prepared to resist the French. After three days of bitter street fighting in which one thousand Frenchmen and three thousand Neapolitans perished, Championnet's forces, aided by a small group

[6] *Min. de la Guerre A.H., M.h., cartons* $B^3 55$, $B^3 56$, $B^3 56^{bis}$, $B^3 57$.

[7] Countess Minto, ed., *Life and Letters of Sir Gilbert Elliot, First Earl of Minto from 1751 to 1806* (London, 1874), III, p. 49.

of local republicans who seized a number of key fortifications, took the city.[8]

At this point Championnet's actions deprived the Directory of the fruits of victory. The directors wished to conclude a peace with Ferdinand, but Championnet, wishing to enhance his own fame and imitate Bonaparte, established a satellite republic in Naples without his government's consent and began to levy heavy taxes upon the hostile population. The government army commissioner protested against the taxes, which were in reality a form of authorized robbery designed to enrich the general and his fellow officers. Championnet then arrested the commissioner, and the Directory removed its general and ordered him to return to France to face a court-martial.[9] Paris, however, had moved too late to avert a major popular insurrection.

Throughout the countryside the peasantry, led by their priests, took up arms. Priests and peasants alike regarded the French not as liberators but as atheists who were attempting to destroy their Church and their way of life. Thousands of others joined the counterrevolution in search of pillage while others sought revenge against those "enlightened" noble and middle-class landowners who supported the new republic. Thus religion, avarice, and class antagonism combined to produce major counterrevolutionary movements. Early in February Cardinal Ruffo, an able organizer and tactician and Ferdinand's vicar-general for the mainland, landed in Calabria and quickly organized the separate counterrevolutionary bands into a unified army. The French had to detach men from the Army of Italy in order to maintain even the most precarious hold upon Naples. Fewer than thirty thousand men had defeated the Neapolitan army, but Paris had to employ over forty thousand men to combat

[8] *Min. de la Guerre A.H., Correspondance, Armées d'Italie et de Rome, janvier 1799, carton B³58.*

[9] Ibid., and *Min. de la Guerre A.H., Correspondance, Armées d'Italie et de Rome, février 1799, carton B³58bis.*

Ruffo's guerrillas, who nevertheless maintained such a firm control over the countryside that only large French columns could dare risk moving beyond the immediate vicinity of the city.[10] Thus the conquest of Naples was in reality a strategic defeat for France. The Directory found itself involved in a bitter guerrilla war and had to divert troops from the Adige, where the Austrians were gathering men for a major offensive.

The Directory's growing involvement in Italian affairs also prevented France from checking Austrian expansion into eastern Switzerland. When creating the Helvetian Republic, the French had not occupied the Grisons, the easternmost canton. During the summer of 1798 Paris decided to allow the Grisons to retain its independence in order to avoid alarming the German princes gathered at Rastadt. Later, the French could not act in the Grisons because of the deteriorating situation in the Levant and the growing threat of war in Italy. The initiative then passed to the Hapsburgs. In October a pro-Austrian faction in the canton crushed a republican revolt, and on the night of October 18–19 Austrian troops began to enter the province. As war flared up in Italy, Vienna continued to pour troops into the Grisons. The Directory lacked the troops to halt them, and the Austrians proceeded to transform the Grisons into a bastion from which they could launch attacks upon the Helvetian and Cisalpine republics.[11]

As the French flailed about trying to disrupt enemy preparations, the allies elaborated their political objectives and devised a military strategy for attaining them. Pitt in 1799 intended to reduce France within her former limits as they had existed before 1792. He also wished

[10] Acton, *The Bourbons of Naples,* pp. 341–42; J. Godechot, *La Contre-Révolution* (Paris, 1961), p. 353; *A.N. AF III 150^{B};* and *Min. de la Guerre A.H., carton B^{3}58bis.*

[11] *A.N. AF III* 18* and *Min. de la Guerre A.H., Correspondance Armées de Mainz et d'Helvétie, septembre 1798, cartons B^{2}66 and B^{2}67.*

to restore the Bourbon monarchy in order to avoid future threats to the balance of power and the social *status quo.* Pitt fully realized that a French monarch, restored to power by allied arms, would in the future be less likely to pursue an aggressive foreign policy than a defeated republic thirsting for revenge. George III's first minister did not, however, intend to restore completely the prerevolutionary political system and laid plans to rearrange the territories wrested from the Republic in a manner beneficial to England. Pitt decided to destroy the Batavian Republic, restore the Stadtholder, enlarge his domains by the addition of the former Hapsburg province of Belgium, and secure England's paramount interest in the Low Countries by forcing the Stadtholder to sign an offensive and defensive alliance with Britain and compelling him to renounce his rights of neutral commerce when Britain was at war with a third power. The British of course realized that sooner or later they would have to inform the Austrians of their plan to unify Hapsburg Belgium and Holland under the Stadtholder and transform the new entity into a British protectorate. To forestall possible protests from Vienna and avoid Austrian demands for the return of Belgium or the implementation of the old Belgian-Bavarian exchange plan, the British decided to offer the Austrians Italian provinces in return for sacrificing Belgium. To make sure that the Austrians would accept his plan without too many protests Pitt decided to establish a military presence in the Low Countries by sending an expedition to Holland, a move that would also aid the coalition's military effort by turning the northern end of the Rhine barrier and exposing France to invasion.[12]

[12] W. Cobbett, ed., *The Parliamentary History of England from the Earliest Period to the Year 1803* (London, 1818), XXXIV, p. 1168; *The Speeches of the Right Honourable William Pitt in the House of Commons* (London, 1806), III, pp. 418–24; *Dropmore Papers,* V, p. 423; and H. T. Colenbrander, ed., *Gedenkstukken der Algemeene Geschiedenis van Nederland van 1795 tot 1840* (The Hague, 1907), II, p. 979.

To obtain troops for his projected invasion of Holland, Pitt again appealed to Frederick William of Prussia to participate in a joint attack upon the Batavian Republic, and called upon Tsar Paul to put military pressure upon the Prussian court and force Berlin to join the coalition. Once again, however, Berlin refused to abandon the policy of neutrality even after the Tsar sent sixty thousand men into western Poland in order to threaten the Hohenzollern court. Failing to convince or force Prussia to join the alliance, Pitt then opened talks with his Russian allies in an effort to arrange an Anglo-Russian sea-borne expedition to Holland. Negotiations dragged on until the summer of 1799 when the two parties finally agreed that 17,500 Russian and 13,000 British troops would launch a sea-borne invasion of Holland. Pitt agreed to subsidize the Russians at the rate of £44,000 per month plus an initial payment of £88,000. For an additional sum of £48,927 plus £19,642 per month Tsar Paul promised to send a naval squadron to the North Sea and employ a contingent of 45,000 troops in western Europe.[13]

As he negotiated with the Russians, Pitt also disengaged England from her war with Toussaint Louverture. By 1798 the British had not only failed to defeat Toussaint but had also suffered staggering losses in combat with Toussaint's well-trained ex-slaves, plus equally heavy casualties from the ravages of yellow fever. By the fall of 1798 the British had lost over seventy-five thousand men. To free military and naval units for employment in Europe and to divert the money spent in the West Indian campaign to subsidies for continental allies, the government decided to abandon its efforts to conquer Saint Domingue. On October 3, 1798, the British

[13] H. Weil, ed., *Le général Stamford d'après sa correspondance inéditée (1793–1806)* (Paris, 1923), pp. 217 and 141. Stamford was an English agent who tried to convince Berlin to enter the war. P. Baillen, ed., *Preussen und Frankreich von 1795 bis 1807 Diplomatische Correspondenzen* (Leipzig, 1881), I, pp. 239, 270–72, 287–88, and 302–3; and *The Annual Register or a View of the History, Politics, and Literature for the Year 1799* (London, 1801), pp. 213–15.

signed an agreement with Toussaint agreeing to evacuate the island in return for his neutrality for the duration of the European war. In the summer of 1799 Toussaint promised to refrain from attacking or encouraging slave revolts in the British West Indies and the southern portions of the United States and in return obtained a commercial agreement with both states.[14]

To force the British to retain men and money in the New World the French national agent on the island, who was in theory Toussaint's superior, proceeded to support one of Toussaint's rivals, General Rigaud, an ambitious mulatto who was willing to continue the war with England and sponsor slave rebellions in the British West Indies in return for French recognition and support of his right to rule the whole island. Unwilling to become an instrument of the Directory's global strategy, Toussaint, who held the real military and political power in most of the island despite the fact that he was in theory only a general in the French army, ordered the agent to leave the country; but before his departure, the Frenchman freed the rival general from his oath of loyalty to Toussaint. The contender proceeded to send an agent to Jamaica to organize a slave insurrection, which the British uncovered and crushed before it could do any damage. Toussaint then decided to destroy his competitor, and in June 1799 with support from the United States Navy he plunged his island into a new war, from which he eventually emerged victorious.[15]

Thus British policy in the Caribbean was successful. Pitt disengaged himself from an expensive and tactically impossible campaign, provided security for England's

[14] J. W. Fortescue, *A History of the British Army* (London, 1906), IV, Part 2, p. 665. The British lost thirty-five thousand killed and forty thousand wounded and had to discharge most of the wounded as unfit for further service. See also C. Moran, *Black Triumvirate* (New York, 1957), pp. 66–67.

[15] J. Léger, *Haiti, Her History and Her Detractors* (New York, 1907), pp. 94–95; R. C. Dallas, *The History of the Maroons* (London, 1803), pp. 308–12; and Moran, *Black Triumvirate*, pp. 68–69.

West Indian domains, and obtained men and money for war in Europe. By combining units returned from the West Indies with new recruits and men from the Irish garrison, the Cabinet was able to raise the strength of the regular army in England to fifty-two thousand. Four brigades, ten thousand men, moved to embarkation ports while the Duke of York, the supreme commander of the expedition, prepared to follow with the remainder of the British troops and the Russian contingent.[16]

As they prepared to attack the Batavian Republic the British integrated this specific campaign plan into a general war strategy. The Anglo-Russian force, after conquering Holland, was to advance into Belgium and from there into northern France. Meanwhile, Austrian and Russian forces were to drive the French from Italy and advance to the Alps. A third offensive in Switzerland by Austrian and Russian troops was to turn the southern portion of the Rhine barrier. Finally, the Austro-Russian force in Switzerland, reinforced by troops moved up from the Italian front, was to advance into eastern France, and as the Anglo-Russian army drove south from Belgium the allies planned to proclaim the restoration of the Bourbon monarchy. This proclamation would be the signal to royalist units in the Vendée, Brittany, and Normandy to launch a guerrilla war, and the Royal Navy planned to aid them by raiding the French coast. The coalition armies and French royalists would then advance on Paris and destroy the Republic.[17]

Vienna accepted the basic British political objective —the destruction of the Republic—and agreed to co-

[16] Fortescue, *History of the British Army,* p. 939; Sir J. Moore, *Diary* (London, 1804), p. 339; J. Surtees, *Twenty-five Years in the Rifle Brigade* (Edinburgh, 1931), pp. 3–5; and J. Dunfermline, ed., *Lieutenant General Ralph Abercromby* (Edinburgh, 1861), p. 179. A British brigade was equivalent in size to a French demi-brigade—about three thousand men.

[17] See *Dropmore Papers,* V, p. 423, and *Arkhiv Kniazia Vorontsova* (Papers of Mikhail Larionovich Vorontsov and other members of the family) (Moscow, 1880), VIII, pp. 237–39.

ordinate its military strategy with Pitt's general war plan. Francis II therefore stationed 94,200 men in Italy. The 24,000-man Russian corps that had entered Galicia in October began to march to the Adige at the end of the month. The Austrians also placed 45,000 men in the Tyrol and 25,000 in the Grisons, and Archduke Charles, who had shown by his brilliant German campaigns in 1795 and 1796 that he was among the best of the Austrian commanders, led an 80,000-man army in southern Germany. His task was to cover the right flank of the Austro-Russian operations in Italy and Switzerland.

Like Pitt, Thugut had his own special ambitions, including the absorption of Tuscany, Milan, the Papal Legations, and Piedmont into the Hapsburg domains. Furthermore, the Austrian Foreign Minister had never relinquished his designs upon Bavaria. If circumstances permitted, he was willing to try to seize Belgium and Bavaria in order to engineer the old exchange plan. He agreed to conform to Britain's strategy because it suited Hapsburg interests, but the wily Austrian diplomat was determined to pursue the interests of his state even if they clashed with the interests of his allies.

Tsar Paul also accepted Pitt's strategy, but like his allies he had his own specific objectives. The Russian monarch, though partially mad and terribly unpopular with his court and generals, nevertheless pursued a policy rationally designed to enhance the power of the House of Romanov and the Russian state. In 1799 Paul wanted not only to restore the French monarchy but also to bring back the deposed regimes in Italy and Switzerland. By restoring prerevolutionary governments, the Tsar hoped to prevent the Hapsburgs from increasing their power in central Europe and create a balance of power in the Mediterranean in which Russia was the dominant force.

Thus, secretly, the members of the Second Coalition intended to pursue conflicting policies in many specific instances, but despite the latent conflicts the new anti-French alliance was a strong one. Their armed forces outnumbered those of France, and in addition to devis-

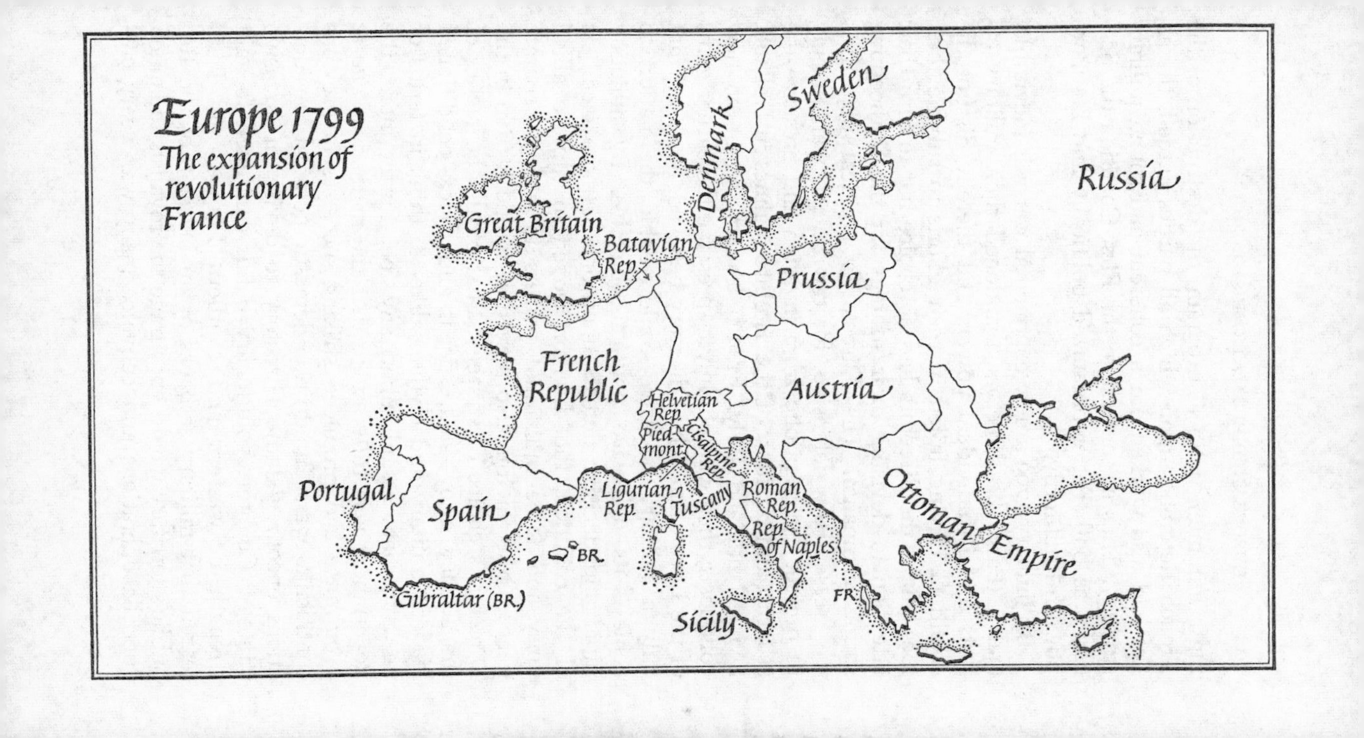
Europe 1799
The expansion of revolutionary France
Great Britain
Batavian Rep.
Denmark
Sweden
Russia
Prussia
French Republic
Austria
Helvetian Rep.
Piedmont
Cisalpine Rep.
Ligurian Rep.
Tuscany
Roman Rep.
Rep. of Naples
Portugal
Spain
BR.
Gibraltar (BR.)
Sicily
FR.
Ottoman Empire

ing a minimum political program, the destruction of the French Republic, upon which all parties agreed, the allies had also worked out a coherent and sound military strategy. Thus in contrast to the First Coalition the Second was both better organized politically and far more powerful militarily.

By January 1799 a new continental war was inevitable, and in Paris the directors abandoned their military efforts to foil individual powers and thereby disrupt the coalition. Having failed in their efforts to subdue their foes singly, the directors had no choice but to turn their attention to devising their strategy for the forthcoming spring campaign. The Directory's political objectives were essentially defensive, for the French wanted only to protect the Republic from invasion and preserve the security and territory of the satellite regimes in Holland, Switzerland, and Italy. French leaders sought no new conquests; they wanted only to preserve the earlier gains of the Revolution. The Directory believed, however, that only a military offensive could enable the nation to achieve its defensive political objective. By inflicting rapid and decisive defeats upon one or more members of the coalition, the directors hoped to rupture allied unity and force individual powers to seek a separate peace. Other factors also played a significant role in the Directory's choice of strategy. First of all, the tactics of the Frency army—*élan*, speed, and shock—conditioned leaders, military and civilian alike, to think in terms of an immediate assault upon any foe. Furthermore, the government was fully aware that the method of *guerre à outrance* had produced striking successes in previous continental wars. In addition domestic political considerations encouraged the Directory to devise an offensive strategy. Counterrevolutionary bands continued to gain strength in western and southern France, and Paris feared that military setbacks or an invasion of the Republic's territory would encourage the royalists to launch guerrilla operations and convince many war-weary citizens to support them simply to end the war.[18] Thus to bolster civilian morale and persuade the royalists to remain passive the government felt that it had to carry the war into enemy lands and achieve rapid victory. Strategic considerations, the army's tactical doctrines, and the domestic political situation combined to convince the directors to plan an immediate offensive for the spring of 1799.

After discussions with the War Minister and the Military Bureau, the Directory on January 30, 1799, issued its strategic plan, "Instructions on the Destinations and General Movements of the Armies When Hostilities Resume," to the various field army commanders.[19] The plan, however, contained a number of serious shortcomings. Instead of calling for a limited number of attacks delivered in overwhelming strength against a few vital points, the Instructions insisted on a whole series of attacks along a line stretching from Alsace to the Adriatic Sea. Furthermore, each army had to advance against a numerically superior foe.[20]

The government ordered the old veteran Jourdan to lead the 25,000-man Army of the Danube through southern Germany to the headwaters of the Danube. The army was then to continue along the river to the Inn, thereby gaining control of the Bavarian passes into the Tyrol and threatening the Hapsburg crownland. Jourdan, however,

18 On the growth of royalism in 1798–99 see Godechot, *La Contre-révolution*, and J. Lacouture, *Le Mouvement royaliste dans le sud-ouest 1797–1800* (Paris, 1932). See also the reports of the War Minister to the Directory in *A.N. AF III* 13*.

19 The Military Bureau usually gave advice on matters pertaining to supply and equipment. In 1799, however, Louis Milet-Mureau, an officer in the bureau, was to become War Minister while the incumbent took command of a field army. See *Min. de la Guerre A.H., Milet de Mureau, Louis Marie Antoine, carton* $B^{on}Y^{ld}322$; and *A.N. AF III* 152^{a}.

20 A complete copy of the Instructions is to be found in *Min. de la Guerre A.H., Correspondance, Armées de Mainz et d'Helvétie, janvier 1799, carton* $B^{2}69$.

had to move against the Archduke Charles, who led an army over three times as strong as his own. On Jourdan's right Masséna's Army of Helvetia with 26,000 troops had a double task. His left flank units were to invade the Grisons and the Tyrol, move to the Inn River, link up with the Danube Army, and then push to Innsbruck. The right flank of the Army of Helvetia was to seize the Valtellina, thereby securing one of the major routes between northern Italy and the Hapsburg domains. Masséna's task was, however, virtually impossible because more than 65,000 Austrians stood ready to dispute his progress. The Army of Italy under Barthélemy Schérer's command also received several missions. Its primary objective was to cross the Adige River, take Verona, and push up to the Piave River. In addition this 70,500-man Army of Italy was to send units to occupy Tuscany while Macdonald's 32,000-man Army of Naples was to contain guerrillas in southern Italy. Schérer, however, also faced a numerically superior enemy—over 100,000 Austrians and Russians.[21] Thus on every major battle front the Directory ordered its armies to attack against superior numbers of allied troops.

Away from the main battle zone the Directory kept thousands of men engaged in defensive tasks. On the Rhine 28,000 men protected the Army of the Danube's left flank, 15,000 troops served in the Batavian Republic; 18,000 men remained in replacement depots, and over 130,000 soldiers guarded the coasts and hunted royalist guerrillas. The failure to pare these passive forces to a bare minimum served to heighten the already glaring French numerical inferiority in the crucial combat areas.

[21] Ibid.; *Min. de la Guerre A.H., Ordres de bataille des armées en campagne, 1792–1815, carton Xp3;* and *Min. de la Guerre A.H., M.h., Campagne de l'Armée autrichienne-russe en Italie en 1799 438.* (This item is an account written by an Austrian staff officer who was later captured by the French. It gives troop strengths of the coalition armies in Italy, Switzerland, and Germany.)

Although the Directory had remarkably precise intelligence reports on the size and condition of the coalition's armed forces,[22] it nevertheless persisted in ordering simultaneous attacks along a broad front against superior forces—a policy that could lead only to disaster.

On March 12, after the Austrians ignored a French demand to send the Russian corps home and cease their own warlike preparations, the Directory asked the Legislative Corps for a declaration of war against Austria and Tuscany. The councils complied with the request on March 13, thus officially beginning the War of the Second Coalition.

The French, as a consequence of their faulty strategic planning, sustained a series of major defeats in the first months of campaigning. Jourdan had crossed the Rhine prior to the official declaration of war, and after March 13, his army moved rapidly eastward toward the Danube. The Austrians, however, were also on the move, and on March 21 advance units of the Archduke's army halted Jourdan's forward elements near the small town of Ostrach. Jourdan, stubborn as ever, then pulled back to Stockach, regrouped his forces, and lashed out again at the Austrians. On March 25 French divisions launched a furious assault on the Austrian army and achieved some striking initial success, but lacked the men necessary to achieve victory. Charles skillfully fed reinforcements into the battle and finally forced Jourdan to end his attacks and pull back toward the Rhine. The French retreat ended only when the Army of the Danube had recrossed the river and abandoned all of southern Germany to the coalition.

Jourdan's retreat exposed the left flank of the Army of Helvetia, and Masséna had no choice but to retreat. One of the best French generals, and one of the few who could command a large field army with independence, dash, and flexibility, Masséna had earned a brilliant repu-

22 See Talleyrand's report to the Directory in *A.N. AF III 59*.

tation as a leader and an unenviable name as a looter in the 1796–97 Italian campaign. Even his tactical and strategic talents, however, were not sufficient to overcome the overwhelming weight of numbers thrown against him. Prior to March 21 Masséna's troops had successfully penetrated the Grisons. After Ostrach, he had halted his advance to avoid uncovering his right flank, and after Jourdan's defeat at Stockach, he began to retreat to prevent the Archduke from driving south from Germany and encircling his army. He fell back to covering positions around Zurich while the Austrians in Switzerland plus massive reinforcements from the Archduke's army prepared an attack designed to drive him from the Helvetian Republic. Paris, meanwhile, removed Jourdan from command, merged the armies of the Danube and Helvetia, and gave Masséna command of the enlarged force. The reorganization did not, however, alter the general strategic picture, for although Masséna had some 79,400 men to hold a front stretching from Alsace to the Swiss Alps, he had to combat approximately 115,000 Austrians.[23] On June 3 and again on June 4 Archduke Charles delivered a series of attacks against French positions around Zurich. Masséna's men fought bitterly and hurled back the assaults but suffered heavy casualties in the process. Lacking the reserves necessary to halt a renewed Austrian drive, Masséna decided to abandon Zurich and take up stronger positions farther west.

On the Italian front the allies also inflicted serious reverses on the French. Schérer's Army of Italy advanced on March 26 against superior numbers, failed to gain a foothold on the Austrian side of the Adige, and lost nearly eight thousand men in a single day. Two days later Schérer, the corrupt ex-War Minister who was singularly lacking in military talent, attacked again, but the Austrians prevented his crossing the Adige and inflicted over

[23] *Mémoires de Masséna, rédigés d'après les documents qu'il a laissés,* ed. le général J. Koch (Paris, 1848–50), III, pp. 158–60.

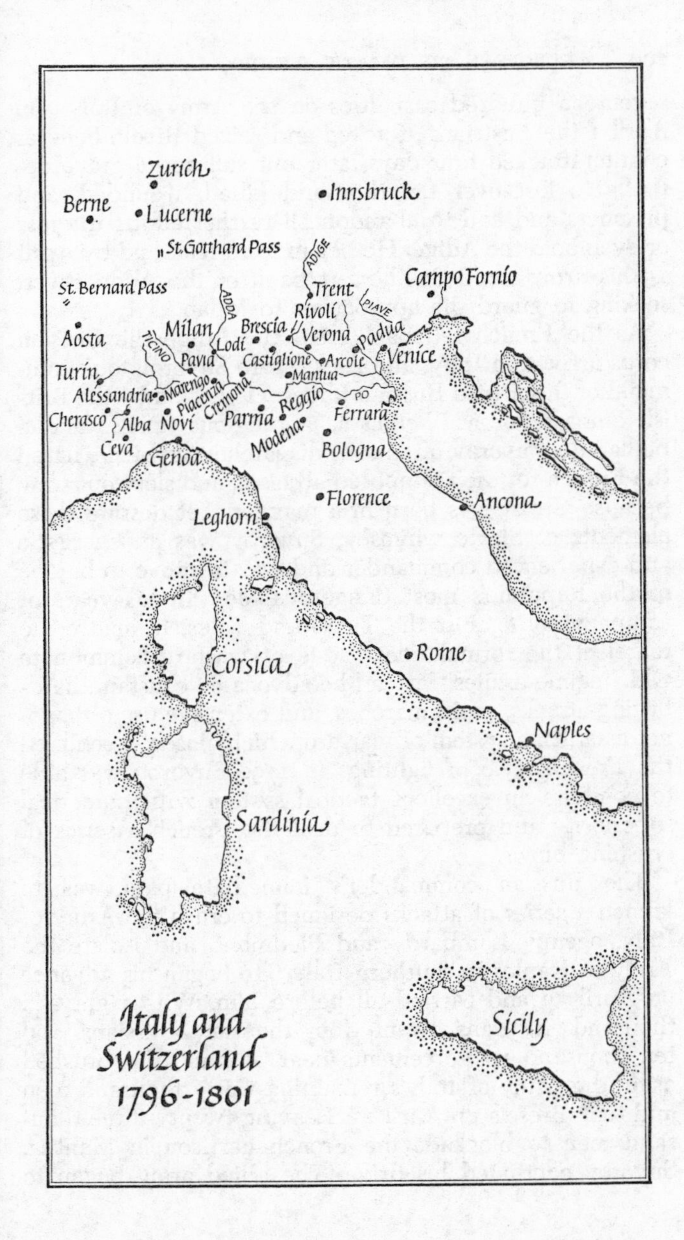

Zurich
Berne
Lucerne
Innsbruck
St. Gotthard Pass
ADIGE
St. Bernard Pass
Trent
Campo Fornio
ADDA
PIAVE
Rivoli
Aosta
Milan
Brescia
Verona
Padua
TICINO
Lodi
Pavia
Castiglione
Arcole
Venice
Turin
Mantua
Alessandria
Marengo
Piacenza
Cremona
PO
Reggio
Cherasco
Alba
Novi
Parma
Ferrara
Modena
Ceva
Bologna
Genoa
Florence
Ancona
Leghorn
Rome
Corsica
Naples
Sardinia
Sicily
Italy and Switzerland 1796-1801

seventeen hundred casualties on the Army of Italy. On April 1 the Austrians attacked and seized Rivoli. Schérer counterattacked four days later but suffered a grave defeat. He lost over ten thousand killed, wounded, and prisoners and had to abandon all further efforts to cross or even hold the Adige. He began to retreat, and by April 15 his army stood on the left bank of the Adda River, seeking to guard the approaches to Milan.

As the French fell back from the Adige the Russian corps arrived in Italy, and Aleksandre Suvorov took command of the Austro-Russian forces. Described by the British ambassador at Vienna as a religious fanatic and a bedlamite, Suvorov often sent dispatches in rhyme, hated the French for their supposed atheism, and slept on straw because Christ was born in a manger. Yet despite these elements of Slavic whimsey, Suvorov was an energetic and experienced commander and was to prove to be one of the Republic's most dangerous foes. In his years of campaigning against the Turks and Poles, he had come to reject the formal linear style of warfare common to Old Regime armies. Instead he advocated constant, hard-hitting attacks, rapid marches, and extensive use of bayonet assaults, a system of warfare which closely resembled the French style of fighting. In 1799 Suvorov was able to combine an excellent tactical system with numerical superiority and prepared to deal the French a series of crushing blows.

The Russian commander's immediate plan was to launch a series of attacks designed to crush the Army of Italy, occupy Lombardy and Piedmont, and isolate the Army of Naples in southern Italy. He began his advance on April 19 and carried all before him. With eighty-six thousand Austrians, twenty-four thousand Russians, and ten thousand reinforcements near at hand, he brushed aside the Army of Italy's remaining thirty thousand men and took Brescia on April 21. Leaving twenty-three thousand men to blockade the French garrison in Mantua, Suvorov continued his drive. The allied army began to cross the Adda River on April 26, and Moreau, the able tactician whose loyalty to the Republic was always suspect because of his constant flirting with the royalists in order to be on the safe side in case of a successful counterrevolution, replaced Schérer in the midst of the fighting but failed to halt the Austro-Russian advance. Suvorov's forces entered Milan on April 28, and almost without pause the Russian commander continued his pursuit of the depleted Army of Italy.[24] By May 7 the allied army had stormed into Pavia, Ferrara, Tortona, and Peschiera and after minor setbacks on May 10 and 11 defeated the French near Marengo on the fifteenth. On May 27 the Austro-Russian army entered Turin, and the French army, reduced to about twenty-one thousand active troops, retreated to Genoa.

The Directory, aware of the magnitude of the defeats caused by the initial strategic errors in the Instructions, began to make desperate efforts to reverse the tide of battle. By May the government realized that the Italian battle zone was the most critical area: The allies had their largest armies in Piedmont, whereas the Army of Italy had become the weakest of the French forces. Furthermore, continued allied success in northern Italy would soon enable Suvorov to threaten the Republic's southeastern departments. If Paris wished to launch a counteroffensive that would be more than a tactical diversion, it would have to strike in Italy.

The government had already begun to prepare a counterattack after the initial defeats of April. The Minister of War on April 18 recommended that Macdonald leave Naples and move north to assist Moreau. The minister believed that if Moreau and Macdonald could defeat Suvorov they could retake Naples at a later date. The Directory accepted the minister's view and on May 4 in-

[24] *Min. de la Guerre A.H., M.h., 438;* and Emmanuel Grouchy, *Précis des opérations de l'Armée d'Italie depuis l'affaire de l'Adda jusqu' à la bataille de Novi,* in *Min. de la Guerre A.H., M.h., 443.* Grouchy commanded a division in Schérer's army.

structed Moreau to recall Macdonald from Naples. The next day the War Minister promised fifteen thousand reinforcements to the Army of Italy's commanding general and called upon him to mount a counterattack in Piedmont.[25]

Expecting such an order, Macdonald, a veteran of the old Royal Army, a former noble who had sided with the Revolution, a loyal supporter of the Directory, and a competent, hard-driving commander, had already recalled his mobile columns, and on May 7 the Army of Naples began to move north to join Moreau at Genoa. In the wake of the French withdrawal, the Neapolitan Republic collapsed, and Ruffo's army, with the aid of five hundred Russian troops and Nelson's fleet, quickly occupied the city of Naples. Ruffo then signed an armistice with local republicans and the remaining French garrison, which held several vital forts. He granted them all safe-conduct to France, but the rulers of the Kingdom of the Two Sicilies rejected the terms. They gave Nelson full power to supersede Ruffo and if necessary place him under arrest and jail local republicans. British marines arrested the Neapolitan democrats, and Nelson personally arranged for the court-martial and hanging of the commander of the republican navy. Arrests continued throughout the summer until eight thousand suspects filled the Neapolitan jails, thus ending the experiment of republicanism in southern Italy.[26]

Meanwhile, Macdonald's forces continued to march north, but while en route to Genoa both he and Moreau began to contemplate a change in the Directory's original orders. On May 16 Moreau wrote to Macdonald suggest-

[25] *Min. de la Guerre A.H., Rapports du Ministre de la Guerre au Directoire exécutif 12 ventôse an 7–3 vendémiaire an 8 carton B¹²37; A.N. AF III* 19;* and *Min. de la Guerre A.H., Correspondance du Général Milet-Mureau avec les Armées d'Italie et de Naples an 7 au an 9 carton B³* 221ᵃ.*

[26] See H. Hueffer, "Fin de la République napolitaine," in *Revue Historique* (1903), LXXXIII and LXXXIV.

ing that the Army of Naples, instead of proceeding to Genoa, attack Modena and hit Suvorov's forces in the flank while the Army of Italy launched a frontal attack. Macdonald agreed to this alteration on May 19, and the War Minister gave his approval to the generals' new scheme early in June. The revised scheme exposed both French armies to defeat in detail, but on the other hand, a two-pronged offensive offered the French the advantages of surprise and a favorable position on the allied flank. If Moreau co-ordinated his moves with those of his subordinate, the armies of Italy and Naples would have the opportunity to inflict a major defeat on their most dangerous opponent.

Macdonald moved quickly, and on June 12 his men drove the Austrians from Modena and seized Parma a few days later. Moreau, however, failed to move and thereby gave Suvorov the chance to hurl his reinforcements against the Army of Naples. Gathering fifty thousand men, Suvorov met the twenty-nine-thousand-man Army of Naples at the Trebbia River. Bitter fighting raged from June 17 to June 19 when Suvorov's crushing numerical superiority forced Macdonald to break off further contact and retreat. On July 12 the Army of Naples limped into Genoa with only seventeen thousand men fit for combat.[27] Moreau's failure to support his colleague had led directly to the defeat of the Army of Naples and a further weakening of France's position on the Italian battle front.

The loss of Naples and the defeat on the Trebbia forced the directors to continue their efforts to salvage their position in Piedmont. Having failed on land, Paris next attempted to reverse the disastrous military situation by the audacious use of sea power. In March the govern-

[27] Throughout the spring and summer of 1799, although anti-French partisans harassed the armies of Italy and Naples, they did not seriously hamper the republican commanders. It was the Austro-Russian army, not the guerrillas, who drove the French from Italy.

ment had instructed Admiral Eustache Bruix to lead the twenty-four ships of the line and ten frigates of the Atlantic fleet into the Mediterranean. Bruix had orders to proceed to Toulon, take on supplies, and carry them to Bonaparte's army in Egypt. The French fleet successfully eluded the British blockade squadron at Brest and by May 20 was anchored safely in Toulon Harbor. The Directory then decided to change the scope of Bruix's mission. Instead of merely resupplying the Army of the East, he was to re-embark it and transport it back to Italy, where it would reinforce Macdonald and Moreau. To strengthen their naval forces, Paris decided to ask Madrid to contribute its fleet to the rescue venture. Leaving Toulon on June 8, Bruix arrived at the Spanish naval base of Cartagena on the twenty-second, while the British scattered their squadrons to counter possible thrusts at Ireland, Portugal, and Sicily. Despite this advantageous situation, the Spanish admiral at Cartagena refused to leave port. Although Madrid had promised to cooperate with Bruix, King Charles and Godoy were alarmed at the possibility of British naval reprisals and Austro-Russian blows against Bourbon princes in Italy. The Spanish Government, therefore, persisted in avoiding any major commitment in the Mediterranean and refused to order its fleet into action. Bruix still had the option of striking out alone at one of the scattered British squadrons, and a victory might well have weakened the blockade of Egypt and convinced the Spanish to send their fleet to sea. However, Bruix, like most French admirals, was not an aggressive warrior, and he did not act. He sat in Cartagena until July and then sailed back into the Atlantic.[28] In their haste the Directory had failed to make adequate diplomatic preparations to assure Spanish participation, and Bruix had compounded this problem by his refusal to act decisively on his own.

[28] See G. Douin, *La campagne de Bruix en Méditerranée mars–août 1799* (Paris, 1923).

Even while Bruix was waiting fruitlessly for Madrid to act, the Directory was organizing still another counter-blow in Italy. As a result of the Prairial coup (July 1799) new leaders attained power and tried to reinvigorate the war effort. The Directory, purged of its moderate members, and the Legislative Corps, dominated by men who recalled and wished to imitate the Jacobin war measures of 1793 and '94, introduced a forced loan and passed a law of hostages directed against the relatives and property of royalist guerrillas. The new Jacobins also tried to reinvigorate the army. General Jean Bernadotte, a favorite of the left, became Minister of War, Championnet obtained new employment as leader of the Army of the Alps, and Barthélemy Joubert, a young, vigorous leader, replaced Moreau as commander of the Army of Italy. The government then sent reinforcements to Joubert and brought his army up to a strength of forty-one thousand active troops. On August 3 Paris directed Joubert to advance into Piedmont before Suvorov, who had a large portion of his troops besieging Alessandria in central Piedmont, could concentrate his army and lunge into France.[29] In addition to military considerations the Directory ordered a new Italian offensive in order to check the growth of war weariness and royalism.

Joubert, however, delayed his advance until August 12, and his delay was fatal. Suvorov, having completed the reduction of Alessandria, gathered a force of about sixty-eight thousand men and raced for the small town of Novi, delighted at the prospect of another encounter with a French field army. Joubert meanwhile arrived before Novi on the night of August 14. Learning of Suvorov's overwhelming superiority, he decided to retreat the next morning but once again he delayed too long. Suvorov

[29] The purge of the Directory and the command changes in the summer of 1799 were indeed a reflection of domestic political rivalries. On the other hand the removal of defeated generals and unsuccessful ministers and politicians was and is a fairly standard procedure in many lands. See *A.N. AF III 13*.

attacked on August 15 and in desperate fighting scored another major victory. The French lost over ten thousand men; Joubert himself perished in the first moments of the battle, and the remnants of his army fled back to Genoa. Once again tactical failures led to strategic defeat, and after mid-August, the Army of Italy was too weak to engage in further offensive operations. The Directory abandoned all hopes for recovering the initiative in Italy and on September 1 ordered its armies to hold a line from Geneva to Genoa.[30]

As the French position in Italy collapsed the Republic had to face serious military and diplomatic problems in other regions. On August 27 the British navy began to disembark the first echelon of the Anglo-Russian expedition against Batavia. British troops landed successfully on the Helder peninsula, and with the aid of naval gunfire drove back Batavian counterattacks. British troops then occupied the Helder forts. The civilian population did not rally to the invaders, but sailors of the Batavian fleet, mostly non-Dutch mercenaries who had no desire to fight the Royal Navy mutinied to avoid combat, and twelve ships of the line passed into the coalition's service. By the first week of September the allies had secured a firm base on the Dutch coast from which they could mount future offensives.[31]

Allied success in turn convinced Prussia to adopt a more belligerent attitude toward France. On July 22 Haugwitz, the Prussian Foreign Minister, told the French chargé d'affaires that Holland should regain its former

[30] *Min. de la Guerre A.H., M.h.,* 438; and *Min. de la Guerre A.H., Correspondance, Armées d'Italie et de Naples, août 1799, carton B³64.*

[31] *Min. de la Guerre A.H., Correspondance, Armée de Batavie, juillet–septembre 1799, carton B¹92;* H. Bunbury, *Narratives of Some Passages in the Great War with France from 1799 to 1810* (London, 1854), p. 3; Moore, *Diary*, pp. 341–42; *The History of the Campaign of 1799 in Holland* (London, 1801), p. 56; C. D. Yonge, *The History of the British Navy* (London, 1886), II, p. 147; and Colenbrander, *Gedenkstukken,* I, p. 223.

independence and worked to convince Frederick William to attack the French in order to share in the division of the spoils. The Hohenzollern monarch hesitated, and the French sought to gain time by referring Haugwitz' demands concerning Holland to Paris, but the Directory realized that continued defeats might well bring Prussia into the war on the side of the coalition.[32]

To add to the government's problems, royalists around Toulouse rose in rebellion on the night of August 4–5. Some twenty thousand rebels took up arms, and although defeated by the Toulouse National Guard on August 7 and August 9, the counterrevolutionaries escaped destruction, and guerrilla actions flared up throughout southern France from Toulouse to the Pyrenees. Government troops did defeat and disperse the main royalist force on August 20, but small-unit actions continued throughout the rest of the year. Rebels in the Vendée and Brittany also rose in the summer of 1799. Unlike their compatriots in the south, the more experienced western guerrillas never tried to form a large army. Operating in small, flexible units, rebels in the western departments tied down fifty-five thousand government troops, who tried and failed to halt numerous small-scale ambushes and raids.[33]

Symbolic of the Republic's declining fortunes in the disastrous summer of 1799 was the report of a royalist agent in Hamburg claiming that director Barras was willing to organize a coup to restore the Bourbons in return for a large bribe and a promise of personal safety. Barras later revealed that royalists had been sending him letters,

[32] *Dropmore Papers,* V, pp. 34–35, 50, and 65–67; and Baillen, *Preussen und Frankreich,* I, pp. 319–20 and 331–32.

[33] See B. Lavigne, *Histoire de l'insurrection royaliste de l'an VII* (Paris, 1887); *Min. de la Guerre A.H., Correspondance, République Directoire, 11 an 20 août 1799, carton B13105; Min. de la Guerre A.H., Correspondance, République Directoire, 21 an 31 août 1799, carton B13106;* and P. de Bourniseaux, *Histoire des guerres de la Vendée et des Chouans* (Paris, 1819), II.

but there is no evidence that he connived at a restoration plot. It is even possible that the plot was a fabrication of the royalist agent, who wanted to get the bribe money for himself.[34] Still, the very idea that a director, even one as venal and corrupt as Barras, was ready to betray the Republic indicates the precarious position of France in the late summer of 1799. Defeated on all fronts, French armies had abandoned many of the Revolution's earlier conquests and as in 1793 were striving desperately to fend off an invasion. At this juncture the fate of the Republic hinged upon the ability of the members of the coalition to continue to co-operate effectively and upon the Directory's capacity to profit from any possible divisions within the allied camp.

Fortunately for France, allied political and military co-ordination momentarily collapsed, and the Directory quickly seized the opportunity to launch decisive counterblows and shatter the Second Coalition.

A shift in Hapsburg policy led directly to the dislocation of the coalition's strategy. Before the outbreak of hostilities Thugut had agreed to follow the British war plan. According to the final detailed plan, Suvorov after driving the French from Italy would lead the Russian corps into Switzerland, where it would join a second Russian corps of twenty-seven thousand men under General Rimski Korsakov, who had taken up positions around Zurich in August. The two Russian units plus Condé's *émigrés*, a total of sixty thousand men, would then launch a major drive westward. Austrian forces in Switzerland and southern Germany were to protect Korsakov's flanks until Suvorov reached him and then support the Russian offensive by striking at Basel and Belfort.[35] Thus the presence of an Austrian army was essential not only for the protection of the Russian right flank but also for the success of the entire offensive into eastern France. It was

[34] *Dropmore Papers,* pp. 23–28 and 178–83, and E. Daudet, *Les émigrés et la seconde coalition* (Paris, 1886), pp. 213–14.
[35] *Dropmore Papers,* pp. 251–58.

especially vital while Suvorov was in transit between Italy and Switzerland because unless protected, Korsakov's force would find itself outnumbered by Masséna's army.

Thugut had adhered to this plan because he wanted British diplomatic support for Hapsburg expansion in Italy and because he wanted to get the Russians, who opposed his plans to seize Milan and Piedmont, out of the peninsula. After the Battle of Novi, however, Thugut concluded that he no longer needed British backing, since all of northern Italy was already in his possession. He therefore began to devise a plan to regain Belgium and revive the Bavarian exchange plan. His scheme was to mount an invasion of the Rhineland and then march into Belgium from the east before the Anglo-Russian force could push south from Holland. With Belgium actually in his possession, Vienna's allies would have no other choice than to accept his policy for the distribution of the coalition's conquests. Despite British warnings that an Austrian advance toward Belgium would dislocate the entire allied strategy and the offer to return Belgium to Vienna if only he would abandon his devisive scheme, the Hapsburg Foreign Minister refused to change his plans. Most of the Austrian troops in Switzerland moved into southern Germany and joined Archduke Charles's main army. The Archduke then moved north, and by September 6 his troops were battling the French Army of Observation. On September 18 Austrian troops entered Mannheim, the first phase of their drive toward Belgium. This attack, however, left Korsakov isolated: Charles was too far north to cover his right and Suvorov too far south to protect his left.

The Directory was quick to seize its fleeting opportunity to mount a strategically decisive counteroffensive. Even before Thugut undermined the allied war effort, Paris had concluded that Switzerland had become the most vital battle zone, since it contained the only major undefeated French field army. In the weeks following the disaster at Novi the government had ordered Masséna to attack and relieve the pressure on the Army of Italy. Masséna did mount several local offensives. He failed to make any progress in central Switzerland, but one of his divisions did capture Mount Saint Gotthard. While these supporting attacks were in progress, the Directory learned of Thugut's plan to invade Belgium and Suvorov's march toward Zurich. The Minister of War then told the directors that a successful offensive on the Swiss front would do more than relieve the Army of Italy. It would, he claimed, split the allied forces, permit Masséna to threaten the coalition's armies in Germany and Italy, and regain the strategic initiative for the Republic.[36]

The directors agreed with Bernadotte's analysis and rushed reinforcements to Switzerland, bringing Masséna's strength to more than eighty-six thousand men. They urged him to attack Korsakov, and on September 5 the Minister of War told him that the government regarded a successful offensive in Switzerland as vital to the outcome of the war. The minister went on to urge Masséna to strike at the Russian corps and the Austrian units south of Zurich before Suvorov's men arrived. Finally, Bernadotte re-emphasized that a victory at Zurich would enable the Republic to triumph on other fronts.[37]

Masséna, like his superiors, was eager to profit from the opportunity presented by the Hapsburg dislocation of the coalition's strategy. As his army grew in numbers he planned not simply to defeat Korsakov's force but to annihilate it. His front resembled a letter U placed on its side with the closed end facing east. The upper part of the U followed the Rhine River; the closed portion ran along the Limmat River, a tributary of the Rhine that flows through Zurich and into the north end of Lake

[36] *Min. de la Guerre A.H., Correspondance, République Directoire, carton B12* 37.*

[37] *Min. de la Guerre A.H., Armées du Danube et du Rhin, situations 18 août–23 octobre 1799, carton B3342;* and A.N. *AF III 151a.*

Zurich, and the bottom part of the U encompassed the Saint Gotthard Pass and the Lake of the Four Cantons. Masséna intended to mount an assault across the Limmat and attack Zurich from the northwest while other units drove on the city from the south. Other divisions were to attack Austrian detachments on the Russian left.[38]

On the morning of September 25 Masséna launched his attack. Demonstrations along the Rhine convinced the Russians to remain in their positions there. Meanwhile the main attack punched its way across the Limmat, drove off several Russian counterattacks, and by late afternoon French demibrigades dominated the northern exits of the city. French troops also pushed up to Zurich's western and southern ramparts, and further south, republican forces defeated the Austrian regiments and forced them into a hasty retreat. The following morning Korsakov launched a desperate attack to open an escape route to Germany, but Masséna's men in vicious hand-to-hand fighting pushed the Russians back into Zurich. The French then broke into the city and slaughtered their foes in the narrow, crowded streets. Over two thousand Russians died and five thousand surrendered as the remnants of the corps fled north in complete disarray. To the south of the main battle the Austrians, having lost five thousand men, could offer no further resistance and fled to the east.[39] Masséna had thus split the allied front, virtually destroyed one of the coalition's armies, and reversed the course of the war.

Suvorov was the first to suffer from the allied disaster in Switzerland as Masséna shifted the bulk of his army toward the Italian-Swiss Alps in an attempt to entrap a

[38] A. Masséna, *Rapport fait par le général Masséna au Directoire exécutif sur les opérations du 3 an 18 vendémaire an VIII* (Paris, 1799), p. 4.

[39] Ibid., pp. 6–12, and *Min. de la Guerre A.H., Correspondance, Armées du Rhin et du Danube, septembre 1799, carton B²77.* For secondary accounts see L. Hennequin, *Zurich* (Paris, 1911), and J. Marshall-Cornwall, *Marshal Masséna* (Toronto, 1965).

second Russian army. Suvorov had to give up his hope of driving north to rescue Korsakov and flee from Switzerland. In a series of hard-fought encounters in the snow-covered Alps he did manage to escape Masséna's clutches but only at a cost of five thousand men, his supply train, and his artillery. By the time he led his weary men into Germany they were unfit for further combat.

Suvorov's defeat in turn influenced the Austrian campaign in Germany. Learning of the French victories over the Russians, Archduke Charles feared that Masséna would next swing north and crush his left flank and rear. He therefore halted his offensive, and on October 17 pulled out of Mannheim and marched back into central Germany. The French Rhine frontier was again secure.

Victories in Switzerland and Germany also influenced the outcome of the campaign in Holland. During the summer the tenacious, hard-fighting Brune, although giving some ground, had managed to contain the Anglo-Russian army within the confines of the Helder peninsula. In October the Directory was able to send reinforcements to the northern front, and Brune succeeded in halting further allied advances. Unable to move forward and equally unable to evacuate the army by sea because of the rapidly worsening weather, the Duke of York decided to capitulate in order to avoid complete annihilation. On October 18 the Duke signed the Convention of Alkmaar, whereby he agreed to evacuate the Batavian Republic and to return all the prisoners his forces had taken since the start of the invasion. This victory marked the end of the campaigns of 1799 and marked too the triumph of French arms on the Continent.

The Republic's military victories also had widespread diplomatic repercussions. The Prussians in the late summer of 1799 had insisted that their troops occupy Holland and the Rhineland, but the French victories of September and October convinced Berlin to abandon its aggressive policy. The Directory rejected the Prussian demands, and Frederick William quickly returned to his system of neutrality. Meanwhile, the Tsar, already annoyed by Vienna's Italian ambitions, proceeded to blame the Hapsburgs for the defeat of his armies. By mid-October the Russian ambassador at London noted that Paul was on the verge of deserting the coalition;[40] and after the capitulation of the Anglo-Russian force in Holland, the Tsar on October 22 formally withdrew from the anti-French alliance.

In the space of a month the Directory and its generals had completely reversed the course of the war. The French had shattered the coalition both militarily and diplomatically, and at the end of October, Paris began to plan an offensive designed to regain Piedmont, Milan, and Lombardy. The directors, however, never launched their Italian offensive, for on November 9, 1799, Napoleon Bonaparte, who had deserted his army in Egypt and returned to France at the height of the Republic's counteroffensive, and his temporary political allies, who were seeking to oust the radicals from office, overturned the regime. The Directory had saved France from invasion and preserved most of the nation's earlier conquests, but it was the Corsican adventurer who ultimately reaped the benefits of these triumphs.

40 *Dropmore Papers,* p. 648, and Bartenev, *Arkhiv . . . Vorontsova,* pp. 52–53.

CHAPTER 7

BONAPARTE AND EUROPE

Far from being the act that saved the French Republic from foreign invasion, civil strife, and a Bourbon restoration, the *coup d'état* of 18 Brumaire Year VIII was in reality the exploit by which Bonaparte seized control of a victorious nation. When he landed in France after deserting the Army of the East, the Directory had already turned the tide of battle in Europe. Masséna had destroyed Korsakov's army at Zurich, and Brune was successfully containing the Duke of York's army in the Helder peninsula. As Bonaparte proceeded to conspire against the republican regime, Masséna drove Suvorov out of Switzerland and forced the Archduke Charles to abandon his projected invasion of the Rhineland. At the same time, Brune obtained the capitulation of the Anglo-Russian army in Holland, and during the last days of the government's existence, the Minister of War drew up plans for an offensive against the isolated and outnumbered Austrians. The Directory was confident of its ability to regain all continental territory lost in the earlier months of the war. Thus France did not need Bonaparte to conclude successfully the War of the Second Coalition, for if the French had lost power and influence in the Near East, India, and the West Indies, they had, nevertheless, retained their position as the major power on the Continent. In the final analysis, the great powers had to struggle for supremacy in Europe, not in the colonies, and in this vital area the Directory had already laid the foundations of victory when Bonaparte came to power.

After his coup, Bonaparte had to solve two interrelated problems in order to stabilize his new and insecure dictatorial regime. He had to complete the work of the Directory by winning the war while at the same time making sure that nobody but himself would obtain the credit. By bringing peace and victory to France, Bonaparte would receive much popular support. The French, after eight years of constant warfare, wanted an end to hostilities, and a peace that protected the social gains of the Revolution and enhanced the international position of the nation would be especially popular. To prevent another popular military figure from striking at his new regime, the Corsican had also to make the successful conclusion of the war into a personal triumph.

In preparing the campaign of 1800, Bonaparte first set out to rally domestic support for the continuation of hostilities. On Christmas day, he made peace overtures to London and Vienna. Neither side took this offer seriously; the British and the Austrians rejected them out of hand, but Bonaparte gained popularity at home by posing as an advocate of peace who had no choice but to fight. He also realized that, having offered peace, he could, if victorious in the forthcoming campaign, justify harsh terms, and if defeated, avoid the reproach of having instituted hostilities. His next step was to organize his armies in a manner that would allow him to keep the strategic direction of the forthcoming campaign in his own hands and prevent other commanders who might contemplate a new coup from enhancing their reputations. He first organized an Army of Reserve, placing it under his personal direction. He intended to move this force into Switzerland, from which place he could strike into Germany or Italy. He next reinforced the Rhine Army by taking troops from French divisions in Holland, and sent Brune to subdue the Vendean rebels. At the same time, he ordered Moreau and his assistant Macdonald to proceed immediately to the Rhine.[1] His object was not only to prepare for active campaigning but also to weaken the political posi-

[1] Henri Plon and J. Dumaine, *Correspondance de Napoléon Ier* (Paris, 1859), VI, pp. 21, 23.

tion of potential rivals. Brune was a known Jacobin, and by weakening his army and transferring him to a new command, Bonaparte isolated him politically. Moreau was proroyalist and Macdonald a supporter of the old Directory. Neither man supported Bonaparte, who ordered them to the front to get them out of Paris, where they might otherwise conspire against him. The allies had defeated both of these officers in Italy and neither was very popular with the rank and file of the army; consequently, Bonaparte ran little risk in sending them to command one of his largest field armies. The First Consul next ordered Masséna to relinquish his command in Switzerland and assume control of the Army of Italy. Since Masséna was a Jacobin, the nation's most successful commander, and a popular hero, Bonaparte gave him command of the weakest of his armies. In the forthcoming campaign, Masséna would of necessity have to play a defensive role and would, therefore, be unable to win new glory and prestige that he might use to give support to a radical coup. Finally, the Consul removed the War Minister, replacing him with a devoted personal follower—Louis-Alexandre Berthier, a former engineer officer and an experienced combat commander who subordinated himself completely to Bonaparte and spent most of his career acting as the Corsican's chief of staff. Having made sure that none of his generals would be in a position to attempt to destroy his regime, Bonaparte then turned his attentions to the task of defeating the Austrians.

Because he did not want to alarm the princes of Germany and because he wished to deprive Moreau of a chance to play a major role in the forthcoming operations, Bonaparte rejected the alternative of striking north from Switzerland. Instead he decided to adopt the defunct Directory's scheme of advancing south into Piedmont while Masséna's army kept the bulk of the Austrian field army pinned down around Genoa.

On March 22, he directed Moreau to cross the Rhine between the tenth and twentieth of April and push to the Lech River. The mission of this force was essentially defensive, for it was to protect the rear and left flank of the Reserve Army as it drove into Italy. Bonaparte also instructed Masséna to hold the line of the Franco-Italian Alps with ten thousand men and concentrate another thirty thousand men in Liguria. The First Consul assumed that Masséna's army would attract the bulk of the hundred-thousand-man Hapsburg force, thereby leaving the Italian-Swiss frontier lightly defended. Meanwhile, the Reserve Army would march from Dijon to Geneva with reinforcements following from Holland and the Vendée as soon as possible. From Geneva, Berthier, after turning over his post as War Minister to Carnot, would lead the Reserve Army over the Alps and into the plains of Lombardy while Bonaparte exercised general supervision over all operations in Italy. The French would then march on Milan and seize control of the line of the Po River, thereby isolating the Austrians in Piedmont and cutting their lines of retreat back to Vienna and the Tyrol.[2] If successful, Bonaparte could destroy the bulk of the Austrian forces in Italy, re-establish French dominance in the peninsula, and repeat his campaign feat of 1797 by marching on Vienna from the south. His plan had the additional advantage of reducing the role of other generals and allowing the Consul to enhance further his glory and prestige.

On April 25, 1800, Moreau sent his army across the Rhine. Organized in four columns, the army crossed the river along a line stretching from Kehl in southern Germany to Schaffhausen on the Swiss border and began to advance through the Black Forest. On May 5, Moreau took Stockach after a sharp fight, thereby gaining revenge for the earlier French defeat. He then forced the Austrians to abandon their advanced supply depots and

[2] *Min. de la Guerre A.H., M.h., Campagne de 1800 en Italie 900 bis 2;* and Plon and Dumaine, *Correspondance de Napoléon Ier*, pp. 201 and 214–16.

fall back to Ulm. Despite the success of his initial advance, Moreau had nevertheless failed to shatter the Hapsburg army. His failure to concentrate the bulk of his army on a single decisive spot meant that the Austrians could retreat all along the line while keeping their forces intact. After the retreat to Ulm, the Austrians fought a cautious defensive campaign that succeeded in interdicting the Danube invasion route to the French Army of the Rhine. On the other hand, Moreau did succeed in pushing his opponents back far enough to offer protection to the Reserve Army, which had meanwhile started its invasion of Italy.

On April 27, Bonaparte issued orders for the Reserve Army, which he had built up to a total of some sixty thousand men, to enter Italy by way of the St. Bernard Pass. Its initial objective was to capture Milan, the main artillery depot and advanced supply base for the Austrian army. Milan was also situated astride the main Austrian route between Piedmont and Venetia. After taking Milan, Bonaparte intended to seize the small town of Stradella, located across the only other major route between the Po River and the Apennines.[3] If he could take these two places the Austrians would either have to mount a hurried and improvised counterattack or escape via the minor passes across the Apennines. In such an eventuality, the Austrian commander would have to abandon his artillery and most of his wheeled transport and in addition expose himself to a French assault against his left flank and rear.

On May 14 the Army of Reserve left Geneva. The next day the advance guard, eight thousand men, entered the St. Bernard Pass, and on the sixteenth it entered Italy and drove a small Austrian force from the village of Aosta. As the rest of the army followed the vanguard into the mountains of northern Piedmont, a small Austrian garrison at the fortress of Bard delayed

[3] *Min. de la Guerre A.H., M.h., 900^{bis2}.*

Bonaparte's advance by blocking the main road into the plains of Lombardy. The Corsican, however, soon found a side road and bypassed the fort. Leaving a division to take Bard, he continued his march, and on May 26 he ordered his troops to head for Milan.[4]

Bonaparte's advance took Melas, the Austrian commander in chief, completely by surprise because he was still concentrating his attentions and manpower on the Ligurian front. On April 19, he had succeeded in isolating Genoa from the rest of Liguria and had ordered General Ott with twenty-four thousand men to besiege the city, where Masséna with twelve thousand effectives and sixteen thousand sick and wounded personally organized and led the resistance. Melas also sent twenty-eight thousand men against the ten thousand French troops in the Italian-French Alps.[5] Consequently, when Bonaparte appeared in the north, Melas had no major force with which to oppose him, for his forty-two thousand troops not engaged in active operations were scattered all over Italy from the Swiss frontier to the Papal States.

Brushing aside small Austrian units, advance units of the Reserve Army entered Milan on June 1, and the bulk of the army arrived the next day. Bonaparte then set out to sever the Austrian lines of retreat from Piedmont. He ordered his vanguard units to hold Pavia in order to watch the west bank of the Po and sent a division to pursue any Austrians on the east bank of the river toward Lodi and Cremona. His next move was to strengthen his hold upon the upper reaches of the Po and seize Stradella, the only remaining Austrian escape route. He sent two divisions to replace the troops at Pavia, ordered the demibrigades at Pavia to push on to Stradella, and sent other units to occupy Piacenza. French troops took Stradella on June 7, thereby isolating

[4] Ibid.
[5] Ibid.

Melas in Piedmont. To finish the campaign, Bonaparte planned to push west from Stradella toward Alessandria in order to fall upon the divided Austrian army and destroy it in detail. The First Consul assigned five divisions and the cavalry to carry out his final offensive, leaving the rest of his army to hold the line of the Po.[6] He was not, however, fast enough, for by June 9, as twenty-two thousand French drove the Austrians out of Montebello, they were preparing a desperate attack of their own.

Upon learning of the French invasion of Piedmont, Melas assumed that Bonaparte would march to the relief of Genoa by way of Turin. The Austrian commander, therefore, hastened to organize Turin's defenses. When he learned that the French were in fact marching on Milan, he ordered his troops to attack the rear of the French army. Melas did not, however, have sufficient reserves to stop the French, and by the end of May, he had come to realize the full gravity of his situation. He concluded that he would have to sacrifice Genoa, Liguria, and Piedmont, concentrate his field forces, and fight his way out of Bonaparte's trap. He therefore ordered Ott, who was besieging Masséna, and units fighting in the Alps to halt their operations and proceed to Alessandria. Ott delayed his retreat for several days in order to complete the siege of Genoa. On June 5, Masséna, having run out of supplies and ammunition, agreed to surrender the city. Ott allowed the French troops to leave Genoa with their weapons and artillery, placed a strong garrison in the city, and on June 6 began his retreat to Alessandria.[7] Meanwhile, Melas with fourteen thousand men left Turin for Alessandria while Ott marched out of the city and began to move toward Stradella. The French, however, were also on the move. They encountered and defeated Ott's army on June 9. After this defeat, which cost him

[6] *Correspondance de Napoléon Ier*, p. 357.
[7] *Min. de la Guerre A.H., M.h.*, 900^{bis2}.

some three thousand men, Ott fell back in order to join Melas, and the French pursued him as far as Marengo. Despite this defeat, Melas had nevertheless managed to amass a field force of about thirty thousand men and one hundred guns, and he resolved to give battle the next day in a final effort to cut his way out of the French trap.

At this point, Bonaparte made an error so grave that he nearly suffered a serious defeat. His initial victories had convinced him that he had already crushed the Austrians and that his only remaining task was to prevent the escape of isolated and shattered units. Consequently, when he began his advance on Alessandria he left behind about two fifths of his army in order to block alternate Austrian escape routes. Worried that Melas would try to escape to Genoa, where the British fleet at Minorca would evacuate him, Bonaparte further divided his command, sending a division under Desaix, one of France's more able younger generals and a hardened fighter, to take Novi in order to cut the Austrians' escape route to Genoa.[8] The First Consul was so busy catching his enemy and cutting all of Melas' lines of retreat that he forgot that he had first to defeat his foe on the field of battle. Consequently, when Melas began to advance on the morning of June 14, he caught Bonaparte completely off guard.

Melas began his counteroffensive by striking at the two divisions in front of Marengo. Bonaparte ordered them to hold the town at all costs and rushed his limited reserves to the front. The Austrians at first failed to take Marengo, but Ott brought up reinforcements and began to turn the French right, and in the center renewed assaults finally dislodged the French, who abandoned the town and began to fall back toward Stradella. Bonaparte then committed his last reserves, eight hundred men of the Consular Guard, but as they moved forward, Austrian cavalry struck them from flank and rear and com-

[8] Ibid.

pletely shattered them. By 1 P.M., the whole of the French force was in full retreat. At first this retreat was orderly, as rear-guard units, firing from orchards and farmhouses, held back the Austrian pursuit, but as a result of continued pressure, it gradually became a rout. Had Melas kept up his attacks, he could in all probability have destroyed Bonaparte's force, but he was simply not equal to the situation. In the first place, he was convinced that he had won a great victory and saw no need for renewed and increased efforts. In addition, he was seventy years of age and was tired by the long day's fighting, during which he had been twice wounded. He therefore left the battlefield to return to his headquarters for a rest, leaving his chief of staff to finish up the destruction of the fleeing French army.

Fortunately for the French, Melas' subordinates were slow to act, and their delay gave Bonaparte precious time to obtain reinforcements and re-form a line of battle. Earlier in the day, the Consul had sent a messenger to recall Desaix, but such an action was hardly necessary, for by the time the courier reached him he had already turned his troops about and was preparing to march toward the sounds of battle. By the time the Austrians organized their forces into a massive pursuit column, Desaix had reached the battleground. His division acted as a magnet toward which Bonaparte's retreating troops gravitated. Soon the French managed to form a stable line. Desaix then flung his division against the right flank of the main Austrian column, and other units simultaneously charged the Austrian left. The effect of this combined attack was decisive. Although Desaix was killed at the start of the attack, his infantry and the cavalry pressed forward and shattered the first half of the Austrian column. The French continued their attacks and soon forced the other half of the Austrian force to flee in disorder all the way back to Alessandria. Losses were heavy on both sides when dusk finally put an end to the battle. The Austrians lost one thousand killed, fifty-five hundred wounded, and three thousand prisoners. French casualties were equally severe: eleven hundred killed, thirty-six hundred wounded, and nine hundred prisoners, but Bonaparte had achieved his objective—he had prevented Melas from retreating to Venetia, where he could continue to block the French advance toward Venice and Vienna.

Despite all of his errors, Bonaparte also managed to retain his public image as the infallible and ever victorious leader of men. That he did so was at least in part due to pure chance, for Desaix, the real victor of Marengo, had perished in battle and could not contradict Bonaparte's version of events. Bonaparte's version naturally reserved for himself full credit for the victory by claiming that overwhelming numbers of Austrians forced the French to fall back and that the Consul himself stemmed the retreat and led the final counterattack.[9] Bonaparte had won, not because of his brilliant leadership, but because of Austrian hesitation and the energy of subordinates like Desaix.

Furthermore, the Battle of Marengo was not a decisive victory. Most of the Austrians escaped to Alessandria, and the French army due to its heavy losses was in no position to exploit the tactical situation. Melas could have fortified the major cities of Piedmont and forced Bonaparte to wage long and expensive sieges, or he might still have marched to Genoa, where the British fleet could probably have evacuated his army. Had he been willing to fight, he might well have held out in Piedmont for many months, thereby strengthening Vienna's position in any peace negotiations.

Fortunately for Bonaparte, the Austrians from Melas on downward were completely demoralized by their defeat, and on June 15 Melas asked for a truce. The Truce of Alessandria, signed the same day, required the Austrians to evacuate all of Piedmont and Lombardy. The

[9] *Correspondance de Napoléon Ier*, p. 360.

Consul thereby gained control of several strategically important fortresses including Genoa, Alessandria, Turin, and Milan, and had pushed the battle front some two hundred miles farther away from France. The French success in Italy in turn endangered the position of the Austrian army in southern Germany. The Hapsburg commander there feared that Bonaparte would send reinforcements to Germany and that with this added strength Moreau would overwhelm him and march on Vienna. Consequently, he accepted Moreau's proposal for an armistice on July 15. The Parsdorf Armistice required the Austrians to evacuate most of Bavaria and retire beyond the Inn River, thereby giving up valuable military positions and moving the front closer to the Hapsburg crownlands.

As the battle fronts became quiet, Bonaparte, capitalizing on the shock caused in Vienna by the Marengo defeat, opened peace talks with the Emperor, who was so alarmed at the prospect of an invasion of his domains that he forced Thugut, who wished to carry on the war, to inaugurate preliminary talks at Paris. The Consul first suggested that France and Austria conclude a definitive peace along the lines of the earlier Campo Formio Treaty, but the Austrians were reluctant to abandon their plans of gaining a dominant position in Italy. Thugut had no intention of concluding peace with France and had already signed, on June 20, a new treaty with the British. The treaty called for England to subsidize a renewed Austrian war effort and contained a promise that neither party would sign a separate peace with France. To gain time to complete their military reorganization, the Austrians continued to negotiate with the French. Vienna asked Paris for detailed peace proposals while reinforcing their armies to a total of 280,000 men—130,000 in Germany, 120,000 in Italy, and 30,000 in depots and garrisons. To gain more time the Austrians insisted that because of their alliance with England, London should participate in the talks. Bonaparte wanted to conclude separate treaties with his foes but did not wish to appear unreasonable. He therefore agreed to consult the British, but insisted on such stiff precondition—the right to resupply his troops in Malta and Egypt even though French commanders in both places were on the verge of surrender—that the talks collapsed immediately. Alarmed by the continuing ties between London and Vienna and by the increasing strength of the Hapsburg armies, Bonaparte tried to force the Austrians to agree to an immediate separate peace. By threatening to resume hostilities, the Consul frightened the Austrian negotiators, who realized that the Hapsburg armies were not yet ready to resume hostilities, into signing an agreement much like the treaty of 1797. The Aulic Council, Francis II's chief advisory and policy-making board, immediately disavowed this preliminary treaty and even jailed the diplomat who signed it. Bonaparte thereupon ordered Moreau to lead his army up to the frontier of the Hapsburg crownlands, a move which forced Thugut to agree to the resumption of official peace talks. At Vienna, a propeace party led by Archduke Charles battled for supremacy in the Aulic Council against Thugut and his backers, including the Empress and the Queen of Naples. The advocates of peace won a momentary victory when in late September they convinced Francis to agree to an extension of the armistice. Thugut objected violently; the Emperor refused to change his mind, and Thugut demanded and received his dismissal on September 25. Louis Cobenzl, who had negotiated with the Russians the last two partitions of Poland, replaced him and proceeded to Lunéville to conduct serious peace talks with the First Consul. Thugut, however, continued to wield much influence at court, and in Cobenzl's absence, Thugut's supporters on the Aulic Council reasserted their former control over imperial policy. Vienna therefore refused to make any significant concessions in Italy and prepared to resume the war. At this point, Bonaparte was also anxious for war because he, like Thugut, hoped to gain all of his objectives by force. Consequently, by the middle of November 1800, France and Austria prepared for a final clash of arms.

Both antagonists planned to gain the initiative by launching rapid offensives. Bonaparte planned a two-pronged offensive against Vienna by sending Moreau across the Inn River with a hundred thousand men to march along the Danube toward Vienna, and by instructing Brune to lead the ninety-thousand-man Army of Italy into Venetia. Then Brune was to support Moreau's offensive by invading Carinthia and threatening the Hapsburg capital from the south. The imperial government's plan called for a single offensive. Austrian troops in Italy were to stand on the defensive while the eighteen-year-old Archduke John advanced from the Inn to the Isar River. John then planned to cross the Isar north of Munich, crush Moreau's left, and force the French to retreat into the Bavarian Alps.[10] Thus in November 1800 both sides were preparing to attack, but it was the Austrians who struck first.

Before Moreau could complete his initial concentration, John crossed the Inn, and despite the abominable weather, his right wing reached the Isar by November 29. The Austrian left had meanwhile come into contact with advanced French units and had driven them back to the village of Hohenlinden, sixteen miles east of Munich. Upon learning of the Austrian advance, Moreau ordered his right and center columns to fall back and rendezvous at Hohenlinden, and by December 2, thirty-three thousand men had reached the town and another twenty-two thousand were on their way. These moves in turn convinced John that Moreau was in full flight, and he therefore dropped his plan for a wide encircling movement around Munich in favor of a massive frontal attack on the Bavarian capital. With the hope of com-

[10] *Min. de la Guerre A.H., M.h., Situation de l'armée enemie* 386; and *Min. de la Guerre A.H., M.h., Précis des campagnes de l'an 8 et l'an 9 de l'armée du Rhin* 387.

pletely destroying what he thought was a shattered army, John ordered his left wing of thirteen thousand men plus his fifteen-thousand-man reserve force with his artillery and supply train to form a single column and advance down the main road to Munich, which ran through Hohenlinden.[11] He directed two columns, one of twelve thousand and the other of sixteen thousand men, to move by parallel roads to the right of the main force. Once through the hills, forests, and swamps around Hohenlinden, the three forces would unite on the main road, and together they would race to Munich. Thus by the morning of December 3, both the French and the Austrians were preparing for battle. Neither commander had any clear idea of what his opponent was doing, and the two armies moved forward little expecting that the small village of Hohenlinden would be the scene of a major clash of arms.

At 5 A.M. on the morning of December 3, the three Austrian columns started their advance. Since the main column was moving along the only paved road in the area, it soon left the supporting columns behind and lost contact with them. By 8 A.M., the main column was marching through a narrow defile in the forest on the eastern outskirts of Hohenlinden. As the advance guard of the column left the defile, French units after heavy fighting succeeded in preventing the Austrians from breaking out into more open terrain, where they could deploy the bulk of their infantry and artillery.[12] The French had trapped the main Austrian force, whose advance guard hemmed in the main body from the front while the supply train and artillery blocked their rear. The Austrians, however, outnumbered the French, and unless the latter received reinforcements, it was only a matter of time before the Austrians broke out of the trap.

To the south, however, a small command—two demi-

[11] *Min. de la Guerre A.H., M.h.,* 387.

[12] *Min. de la Guerre A.H., M.h., Bataille de Hohenlinden 3 décembre 1800* 384.

brigades, a chasseur regiment, and six field guns—was making its way toward Hohenlinden. In the course of the retreat the commander heard the sounds of battle and led his troops in the direction of the firing. By chance rather than by design the French units came upon the flank of the Austrian column in the defile and immediately attacked. Gun crews unlimbered their cannons and began to bombard the column, and the infantry and cavalry moved forward. Encouraged by this unexpected assistance French troops at the head of the defile renewed their assaults. Panic gradually spread through the Austrian ranks. Teamsters and artillerymen broke first and fled. Then the infantry, trapped in the defile and suffering from steady bombardment, lost heart and tried to flee. The whole column soon became a mass of demoralized individuals, each struggling desperately to escape to the rear. The French meanwhile advanced, captured entire battalions, and seized John's supply wagons and artillery. By the end of the battle, the French had killed or wounded five thousand and captured seven thousand Austrians, and the defeat of John's main column forced the rest of his army to retreat. By December 4, the Austrian army was in full flight to the east.[13]

Hohenlinden was decisive, for the French had broken the Austrian army in Germany. On December 5, Moreau began to pursue John's army, and by December 15, the French were across the Inn and advancing toward Vienna. The Austrians could do nothing to halt them, and by Christmas day Moreau was within a hundred miles of the Hapsburg capital. On the same day, Brune began his advance and pushed rapidly to the Adige River. Also on Christmas day, the Archduke Charles replaced John as commander in chief in Germany, and realizing that further resistance was useless, he asked for an armistice, which Moreau immediately granted. The Armistice of Styr called for the Austrians to evacuate the Tyrol and

[13] Ibid.

allowed the French to push to within fifty miles of Vienna. In Italy, Brune continued to advance, crossing the Adige on New Year's day 1801. The Austrians soon requested a truce on the Italian front and signed an agreement at Treviso on January 16. The Treviso armistice required the Austrians to evacuate most of their major strategic positions in northern Italy and, coupled with the Styr truce, left Austria in a hopeless military position. Vienna's diplomatic stance was no better. Paul of Russia was hostile, and England lacked the power to influence events on land. The Hapsburg Empire thus had no solution for the dual problems of military disaster and diplomatic isolation. The Emperor therefore had no choice but to conclude a separate peace with France on the best terms he could get.

France, represented by Talleyrand and Joseph Bonaparte, Napoleon's well-intentioned, enlightened, but largely ineffective elder brother, and Austria's Cobenzl quickly devised peace terms. Since Austria had relatively little bargaining power, the French virtually dictated the final treaty, signed at Lunéville on February 9, 1801. France received Belgium and the Rhineland, and Austria agreed to compensate princes who lost territory on the left bank of the Rhine by assignments of lands situated on the other side of the river. Both parties assumed that the dispossessed princes would attain their compensation at the expense of Austria's traditional allies within the Empire—the ecclesiastical princes and the free cities. An imperial congress was to implement the actual transfers of territory. France was to participate in the congress, which meant that Bonaparte would be able to extend his influence in Germany by aiding the secular princes in their scramble for new provinces. The princes in turn would have to rely upon France to maintain the new *status quo*, thereby reviving Talleyrand's plan of creating a third force in Germany to counter Austrian and Prussian power. Austria also agreed to recognize the Batavian and Helvetian republics, thus giving France two important strategic bastions on the frontiers of the Empire.

Lunéville also gave Bonaparte a dominant position in Italy. Vienna acknowledged French control of Piedmont and recognized the Ligurian and Cisalpine republics. Bonaparte also expanded the frontiers of the Cisalpine Republic to the Adige River. In March, the Consul gave Tuscany to the son of the Duke of Parma, a nephew of the Queen of Spain, and transformed the duchy into the Kingdom of Etruria. In return for fulfilling Spain's long-term ambitions in Italy, Bonaparte received the territory of Louisiana. Soon after signing the peace treaty with Vienna Bonaparte drove Naples out of the war. He sent Murat with two divisions to drive the Neapolitans out of central Italy, and the court of Naples, realizing that it could not continue the war alone, quickly sued for peace. In March 1801, the Neapolitans agreed to leave the war, to close their ports to British ships, and to allow the French to occupy the port of Taranto until the conclusion of a final peace with England. Bonaparte did allow the Pope to return to Rome and did not re-establish the Roman Republic, but the Pope, surrounded by French armies and French-dominated satellites, dared not do anything to antagonize the First Consul. In July the Consul and the Pontiff signed a concordat which ended, momentarily, the conflict between the Church and the Revolution. Bonaparte recognized the Catholic faith as the religion of most Frenchmen and agreed to pay the salaries of bishops and curés. In return the Pope accepted the confiscation and sale of church property and agreed that French clerics should take a loyalty oath to the state. The Pope in effect gave his seal of approval to Bonaparte's regime. Thus by the spring of 1801, France once again dominated the Italian peninsula.

Still Bonaparte's victory was incomplete, for England refused to recognize French continental hegemony and continued to fight on alone. As in 1797, the Royal Navy denied France her final triumph and foiled all of the First Consul's projects outside of Europe.

In the Mediterranean the British liquidated the remnants of Bonaparte's earlier eastern venture. The Malta garrison capitulated on September 5, 1800, and England gained a strategically located naval base which she was to retain for more than a century and a half. Against Egypt the British mounted two expeditions: one from England, the other from India. The Army of the East was demoralized while the British troops were well trained and far superior to the specimens who had done so badly in previous continental conflicts. After a brief campaign marked by several vicious encounters, the French commander capitulated in September 1801. The remnants of the Army of the East returned to France, and the Ottomans regained nominal sovereignty over Egypt. Bonaparte had contemplated sending a naval expedition to succor his forces in Egypt, but British naval superiority frustrated his efforts. He gathered a small squadron, but it never left Toulon. Away from dry land England ruled supreme, and French efforts to apply their power directly outside of Europe were doomed.

Recognizing this fact, Bonaparte next tried a less direct approach to the problem of effectively striking at England. He decided to gain new continental allies and lead them in an attack against his chief rival's commercial prosperity. A change in Russian policy gave Bonaparte his chance to gain the first of his new partners. Tsar Paul had left the Second Coalition in 1799 because he felt that Austria had betrayed his armies and pursued political objectives antithetical to Russia's interests. In the following months the Tsar began to develop a manifest hostility toward England. He objected to the British occupation of Malta because he was the Grand Master of the Order of the Knights of Malta and because he had nurtured hopes of transforming the island into a Russian Mediterranean naval station. Britain's expeditions to Egypt also angered and alarmed the Russian ruler. Paul, his temporary alliance with the Turks notwithstanding, regarded the Ottoman Empire as a Russian sphere of influence and a potential area of outright territorial expansion. Naturally, he did not view with favor the armed presence of another major power in a region which he looked upon as his own private preserve. Paul had gone to war with France primarily because the Directory had openly intervened in the eastern Mediterranean, and he was equally willing to counter British expansion by force.

Bonaparte actively encouraged the Tsar's anti-British sentiments. He returned thousands of Russian war prisoners, asking nothing in return, and began to point out the advantages of a policy of Asiatic expansion, especially expansion toward India, to the Tsar. Irritated by British Mediterranean ventures, Paul also disliked the Royal Navy's blockade of the French-dominated European ports, which involved rather arbitrary searches of neutral vessels by British cruisers and hindered Russia's Baltic commerce. He therefore organized a League of Armed Neutrality to protect neutral commerce, exclude English ships from the Baltic, and break the British blockade. Sweden, Denmark, and Prussia joined the league, and the Prussians occupied Hanover. He then began to contemplate an alliance with France and even ordered a Cossack expedition to march on India.

Bonaparte had thus scored another major diplomatic triumph, but events in Russia and the application of Britain's sea power suddenly undid his ambitious policy. In March 1801 a clique of aristocrats who objected to the Tsar's efforts to strengthen the throne, to his mental instability, and to his drastic shifts of foreign policy, murdered him. His son, who had connived at his deposition, while regretting the assassination, immediately modified Russia's pro-French diplomatic orientation. Upon ascending the throne Alexander I promptly abandoned the expedition to India and assumed a stance of cautious neutrality in international affairs. He even began to listen with interest to British overtures, and Russian court circles, encouraged by the judicious distribution of British money, grew progressively more cordial toward the English. Paul's murder not only cost Bonaparte a potential ally but it also ended the possibility that the League of Armed Neutrality would pose a serious challenge to Britain. Without wholehearted co-operation from Russia the northern league lost much of its importance, and in April the British moved decisively to shatter the remnants of the alliance. London sent a fleet to the Baltic, and in April admirals Parker and Nelson destroyed the Danish fleet at Copenhagen, thereby putting an end to Bonaparte's plans to turn neutral powers against the British. The league dissolved and France could find no other effective means to defeat the English.

France remained the single most powerful state in Europe, and in co-operation with Spain even forced Portugal, England's last continental ally, to conclude a peace treaty in September 1801. Portugal had to cede a province to Spain, pay an indemnity to France, and close her ports to the English. Britain, however, continued to dominate the high seas, and the English fleet protected the island kingdom from any threat of direct invasion. The strategic stalemate in turn convinced both antagonists to contemplate the possibilities and benefits of a pause in the fighting.

Alarmed by the lack of allies, the growth of the national debt, high prices, poor harvests, growing popular discontent with the economic hardships caused by the perpetual war, and a decline in trade, many Englishmen came to desire peace with France. In February 1801 Pitt retired from office, using the issue of Catholic emancipation—to which George III was adamantly opposed—as a convenient excuse to withdraw. Pitt evidently realized that peace was necessary and gave way to a Cabinet not traditionally hostile to France in order to facilitate negotiations. By leaving office Pitt also disassociated himself from the peace policy, thereby leaving himself free to return to power if that policy failed. Henry Addington, former Speaker of the House and an advocate of peace, replaced him and in March 1801 opened negotiations in London toward that end. Unable to grapple effectively with England, wishing to gain an interval in which to reorganize his state's government and finances, desiring an end to the blockade in order to restore the nation's overseas trade and exploit its newly won colonial possession in North America, and realizing the necessity of fulfilling his promise of peace to the French people, the First Consul also decided to negotiate.

Negotiations began on March 22 and continued for more than six months. Bonaparte's delegate in London first suggested that in return for the evacuation of Egypt by the Army of the East the British give up all of their colonial conquests except Ceylon. Bonaparte also expected the British to recognize all French continental conquests and made no offer to negotiate an Anglo-French commercial agreement. Addington's government did not know that the Army of the East was nearing collapse. Consequently, the Cabinet in its desire to get the French out of the Near East and conclude a final peace was willing to make significant concessions. The British therefore demanded only that the Dutch Stadtholder receive compensation and that to guarantee Malta's neutrality, troops from a major third power replace the British garrison. In September Bonaparte learned that the Army of the East was on the verge of capitulation. He realized that he could no longer use the promise to evacuate Egypt as a bargaining point once word of his army's situation reached London. He thereupon offered the British Trinidad as well as Ceylon and agreed to pull his forces out of Naples if Addington's Cabinet withdrew from Malta, restoring the Knights to the isle under great power guarantees, and evacuated Elba. To get the British to agree before they learned of their victory in Egypt and stiffened their terms Bonaparte asserted that he would resume hostilities if England did not sign by October 2. Although Addington and his colleagues regretted the lack of treaty provisions concerning continental and commercial affairs, they were anxious for peace and, on October 1, signed a preliminary treaty.

Addington then sent Lord Cornwallis, a man with a great deal of military and administrative experience but no particular aptitude for diplomacy, to France to conclude a final treaty. Cornwallis had instructions to secure a number of modifications of the preliminary London agreement. He sought to obtain an indemnity for the Stadtholder and French evacuation of Piedmont. The French, represented by Joseph Bonaparte, were determined to grant as little as possible. Negotiations dragged on for six months with the British making their demands for changes and the French making enormous counterclaims, including a demand for freedom of French commerce in India, in order to force Cornwallis to withdraw his proposals. Since peace and financial retrenchment remained the Addington government's cardinal policies, Cornwallis generally refrained from pushing his proposals too strongly and gave up most of his demands for the alterations of the London treaty. Aside from securing agreement to allow a Neapolitan force to replace the British garrison on Malta until the Knights could defend themselves the preliminary treaty remained virtually unchanged. On March 25, 1802, England and France signed a final treaty at Amiens incorporating the extensive concessions granted by the Addington Cabinet in return for an end to hostilities.

According to the terms of the Treaty of Amiens, Great Britain recognized the French Republic and the annexation of Belgium and the Rhineland. England also recognized the Batavian, Ligurian, Cisalpine, and Helvetian republics and made no protest against the continued French occupation of Piedmont. The Cabinet even neglected to secure a commercial treaty with the Republic, and Bonaparte was under no obligation to remove restrictions against British trade introduced by previous regimes. The British also made extensive colonial concessions, agreeing to return Malta, Minorca, Elba, Egypt, the French Caribbean islands, and South Africa to their original owners. Britain retained only Ceylon and Trinidad. Bonaparte for his part made relatively few concessions. He agreed to withdraw his garrisons from the Neapolitan kingdom and the Papal States and to recognize the Republic of the Ionian Islands organized in 1799 under Russian and Ottoman protection.

Thus after a decade of war Europe was once again at peace. France had survived revolution, civil war, and invasion and had become the Continent's single most powerful state. England had avoided defeat, made minor colonial conquests, and enhanced her position as the world's leading maritime power.

The peace of Amiens did not, however, provide a firm basis for tranquillity. Bonaparte was ambitious to expand his power further, and the other powers feared exactly this possibility. The threat of French hegemony made the renewal of hostilities virtually inevitable. The Amiens peace was little more than a truce—a breathing space for France and her rivals to gather their strength for new conflicts.

[illegible] Egypt,

sions. [illegible]
[illegible]
[illegible]
[illegible]
[illegible]
[illegible]
[illegible]
[illegible]
[illegible]

basis for [illegible] Bonaparte [illegible]
[illegible]
[illegible]
[illegible]
[illegible]
[illegible]
[illegible]

CHAPTER 8

NAPOLEONIC HEGEMONY

In the months following the Amiens Peace, Bonaparte continued to expand his power both at home and abroad. In May 1802 a subservient Senate extended the consulship to a ten-year term, and in August the Corsican became Consul for life with the right to name his successor. The Government of France thus reverted to the old system of hereditary rule and became a monarchy in all but name.

Bonaparte also extended his power beyond France's frontiers. He justified his actions as defensive moves designed to protect France and the peace of Europe, but the result of his activities in 1802 and 1803 was to increase further his state's power and influence. Bonaparte's inherent affinity for action and glory and his unwillingness to accept limitations doubtless influenced him to pursue an activist foreign policy. Furthermore, the realization that the other great powers were fundamentally opposed to France's paramount position forced him to conclude that he had either to make significant concessions to assure other rulers of his pacific intentions or else to consolidate and expand French power to a point where no rival would dare challenge him. The First Consul preferred to risk complete defeat in order to obtain complete hegemony.

After signing the peace treaty with England, Bonaparte moved quickly to increase his control over northern Italy. In September 1802 he annexed Piedmont, and by revising the Ligurian Republic's constitution he transformed the region around Genoa into a *de facto* French military department. The Consul also rewrote the Cisalpine Republic's constitution. He changed the name of the regime to the Italian Republic and proclaimed himself president. After the Duke of Parma's death, French troops occupied the duchy, thereby placing all of northern Italy save Venetia under Bonaparte's control.

To secure the line of communication between France and Italy, Bonaparte forced the Helvetian Republic to relinquish Valais, which he proceeded to transform into a new satellite state. He then proceeded to reorganize the rest of Switzerland in February 1803. He abolished the Helvetian Republic and brought into being the Swiss Confederation, which signed a fifty-year offensive and defensive alliance with the French Republic.

Napoleon forced his Batavian allies to continue to maintain an eleven-thousand-man French force at their own expense and intervened decisively in the reorganization of Germany. According to the Lunéville treaty, an Imperial Diet was to convene and with the French in attendance arrange the complex territorial exchanges necessary to compensate those princes who abandoned Rhenish provinces to France. Individual rulers, however, began to negotiate secretly with France prior to the opening of the Congress. The avarice of the princes allowed Talleyrand to pocket a fortune in bribes and enabled Bonaparte and his Foreign Minister to revive and elaborate the Directory's 1797 plan of creating a "third Germany" composed of medium-sized states which France could employ against either Prussia or Austria.

To achieve this goal the First Consul conducted three sets of talks: the first with the rulers of the secular principalities of southwestern Germany, the second with Berlin, and the third with the Russian Tsar. Bonaparte promised the princes and the Prussians extensive indemnities. He also convinced Alexander to associate himself with French plans by promising extensive concessions to German princes related to the Romanov family and by convincing the Tsar that Russia was playing a major role in German affairs. Thus by the time the Imperial Diet convened in the spring of 1802 Bonaparte had succeeded in winning widespread international support for his plan to impose a territorial revolution upon Germany. The Hapsburgs and the ecclesiastic princes naturally opposed the French plan but without international backing they could not influence the Diet, and on February 25, 1803, accepted the French-designed reorganization of Germany.

The Imperial Recess of 1803 sanctioned the destruction of 112 states of the Holy Roman Empire. Most of the free cities lost their independent status, and all but one ecclesiastical state disappeared from the map. Prussia obtained some 375,000 new subjects and about five times as much territory as the Hohenzollern monarch abandoned in the Rhineland. Bavaria increased its population by 200,000 souls and its territory by about 5000 square miles. Baden and Württemberg made smaller but still significant acquisitions. Furthermore, Baden, Württemberg, Hesse-Cassel, and Salzburg were given electoral status. Since the first three states were pro-French and depended upon France to maintain the new *status quo,* Vienna's influence within the Empire declined accordingly. It remained only for France to conclude a formal alliance with the secular German princes who had received new lands to complete the policy of creating a third force in Germany. The Hapsburgs did obtain the bishoprics of Brixen and Trent, and were able to provide the deposed Grand Duke of Tuscany with Salzburg, but these gains could not disguise the fact that France had scored a major triumph. Bonaparte had obtained the Rhineland, laid the foundations for a "third Germany," established close ties with Prussia and Russia, and dealt a mortal blow to the ancient and venerable Holy Roman Empire.

Nor did the energetic Corsican neglect the non-European world. He decided to re-establish French influence in the Western Hemisphere by restoring his authority in Haiti, resuming the old and profitable colonial trade, and using Haiti as a base from which to exploit the vast Louisiana territory. Bonaparte had, however, failed to reckon with Toussaint Louverture, who had established peace and developed commercial relations with the British and Americans and had no desire to revert to the position of a simple functionary in the French colonial empire. Toussaint had created an effective army and an able corps of subordinate leaders, and in 1802 he was prepared to fight against French intrusion just as he had resisted the British invasion of 1794.

Bonaparte did manage to land a 33,000-man force in Haiti by a ruse—he informed Toussaint that the expedition, commanded by his brother-in-law, Charles Leclerc, was to reinforce, not to fight, the Haitian garrison. Once ashore the French began to occupy strategic areas. Toussaint began to resist and within two months the army of former slaves inflicted 13,000 casualties upon some of the finest troops of Europe.

To avoid further destruction and bloodshed Toussaint agreed to negotiate with the French, but when he appeared for the talks Leclerc's men seized him and sent him to a French prison, where he died in 1803. Toussaint's generals, however, resumed the war and, aided by an outbreak of yellow fever, inflicted twenty-four thousand casualties on their foes. Bonaparte finally concluded that he could never reconquer Haiti at an acceptable price in men and treasure, withdrew from the island, and abandoned his plans to revive a French domain in the Americas.

Bonaparte also decided to divest himself of Louisiana, which he could not defend, and to avoid the possibility of the region falling into British hands, he arranged for a neutral power to take possession of the midcontinent area. The American President, Jefferson, had already expressed an interest in gaining control of New Orleans in order to secure an outlet for America's western trade, and when the First Consul offered all of Louisiana for the paltry sum of fifteen million dollars, Jefferson seized the chance to expand his nation's frontiers beyond the Mississippi.[1] Bonaparte thus won some sympathy in the United States and avoided the possibility of further British imperial expansion, although his more grandiose policy of reasserting French influence in the New World was a costly failure.

Despite his fiasco in the west the ruler of France did not abandon all imperial designs outside Europe. He intimated to the Tsar that he was interested in coordinating the partition of the Ottoman Empire with Russia. French agents again sought contact with discontented groups in Greece, and Bonaparte sent Sebastiani, an engineer colonel, on an intelligence mission to Egypt. Upon his return Sebastiani reported that the Turks were so weak that a small French expedition could easily repeat the feats of 1798. In the winter of 1803 the Consul published the report in the semiofficial journal, *Le Moniteur*. His motives for making public the contents of the intelligence summary were first to distract public attention from the collapse of the West Indian and American venture; secondly, to strike back at the British press, which was engaged in a campaign of vituperation against him; and finally, to place the other powers on notice that France was going to play a major role in deciding the future of the Levant.

In economic affairs too, the Corsican worked to expand French power. He forced the various satellite states to sign commercial treaties favorable to France and refused to open the Republic's markets to British competition. A tariff law of April 28, 1803, established complete protection of the home market for French businessmen and destroyed English hopes for revived and expanded European trade.[2]

1 See A. S. de la Faverie, *Napoléon et l'amérique* (Paris, 1917); G. Labouchere, "L'annexion de la Louisiane aux Etats-Unis," in *Revue d'histoire diplomatique* (1916), XXX; and E. Lyon, *Louisiana in French Diplomacy* (Norman, 1935).

2 B. de Jouvenal, *Napoléon et l'économie dirigée* (Paris, 1942), and A. Chabert, *Essai sur les mouvements des revenus et de l'activité économique en France de 1798 à 1820* (Paris, 1949).

The result of Bonaparte's flurry of activity was to convince some of the great powers of the necessity of resisting French expansion before it was too late. The British, who had not yet evacuated Malta, decided to extend their occupation, and they resumed their search for a continental sword and made overtures to the Russians, who had become alarmed by the renewal of French interest in the Balkans and Near East. Alexander was not, however, willing to go to war at this time, but he did advise London to refuse to honor the provision of the Amiens Treaty that called for the withdrawal of British troops from Malta and retain control of the isle. In April 1803 he agreed to join England in a guarantee of Turkish integrity.

Addington next began to re-equip the fleet and recommission vessels taken out of service after the Amiens truce. The British continued in their refusal to evacuate Malta and insisted that Bonaparte pull his troops out of Italy and Switzerland. Bonaparte offered to permit the British to garrison Malta for three or four years but said nothing about the expansion of French power into Italy and the Low Countries. Addington therefore concluded that war was England's only alternative to abandoning her status as a major force in continental affairs. Consequently, in May 1803 Europe's greatest land and maritime power—the Behemoth and the Leviathan—resumed their struggle.

Bonaparte realized that the rapid defeat of England was a function of his ability to transport an army safely across the Channel. If he could land in the British Isles he could probably force the English to capitulate, dictate a final peace, and eliminate his most persistent and dangerous adversary. But, as in 1797, he had to solve the problem of crossing the Channel in the face of the world's best navy.

Never afraid of undertaking a major project, Bonaparte proceeded to gather 150,000 veteran troops—the Grand Army—around Boulogne. While the army held massive reviews, received its regimental organization and eagles, which replaced the old demibrigade system, and eighteen of France's leading generals obtained the title Marshal of France, Bonaparte had his engineers hard at work constructing hundreds of transports. The Consul also forced and cajoled his allies into assisting the projected invasion. Batavia supplied sixteen thousand men, and Spain contributed six million livres per month to the French treasury. Not satisfied with monetary aid, the Corsican wanted to deploy the Spanish navy against the British and sought to convince Madrid to enter the war as an active partner. Fearing a renewal of the British blockade and the consequent loss of colonial trade, Charles IV of Spain was reluctant to become a belligerent. Godoy, the Queen's lover and *de facto* ruler of Spain (he was also the King's most trusted adviser), wanted Bonaparte's support to retain power at court and to carve out a principality for himself in Portugal, and he therefore advocated Spain's joining the French as a belligerent. When the British fleet seized several Spanish galleons in October 1804, Godoy was able to convince Charles to declare war.[3]

Despite his diplomatic triumph and the addition of the Spanish fleet to his naval ranks, Bonaparte still did not have sufficient strength to gain control of the Channel long enough to ship his army to England's shores. He therefore decided upon a massive diversion—ordering his Atlantic squadron to proceed to the West Indies and directing the Toulon fleet under Admiral Villeneuve to sail to Cádiz, pick up the Spanish fleet, and join the Atlantic flotilla at Martinique. The combined force would then threaten the British Caribbean colonies and force the Cabinet to detach ships from European waters for service in the Indies. Finally, the French and Spanish vessels

[3] H. Deutsch, "Napoleonic Policy and the Project of a Descent upon England," in *Journal of Modern History* (1930), VII; and H. Madol, "De Bâle á Bayonne: Napoléon et Godoy," in *Revue d'histoire diplomatique* (1935), XLIX.

would return to European waters, wrest control of the Channel from the weakened British home squadrons, and escort the army to England.

In the late spring of 1805 Villeneuve successfully escaped from Toulon and made sail for the West Indies. Nelson pursued him and failed to bring him to battle in the Caribbean. The rest of Bonaparte's overcomplicated naval strategy collapsed, however. A "land animal," the Emperor never really understood the complexities of naval strategy and, ignoring such problems as weather morale, and lack of good officers, ordered his ships about as if they were infantry battalions. Because of the immense problems involved in co-ordinating the actions of several fleets stretched over thousands of miles of ocean, the Atlantic fleet failed to join Villeneuve, and Nelson, divining the French admiral's next moves, sent a fast brig to warn the Admiralty that the Toulon squadron was heading for the French Atlantic coastal ports. Nelson then beat his way back across the ocean while the Admiralty reinforced its squadrons cruising near Brest and the northern coast of Spain. Consequently, when Villeneuve reached European waters a British force was there to meet him. After an indecisive clash in Spanish waters, instead of trying to break through to Brest, he elected to put in to Vigo to repair and resupply his ships. In mid-August the French admiral decided not to risk a clash with the British and made for Cádiz, thereby destroying all hopes of concentrating a major battle force at Brest.

Although he had given his admiral discretionary authority to withdraw to Cádiz, Bonaparte was angered and dismayed by Villeneuve's timorous conduct, which had ruined any chance of a cross-Channel thrust at England. In messages full of contempt Bonaparte ordered the Franco-Spanish fleet to put out into the Mediterranean and attack Naples. Stung by the harsh and largely unjustified reprimands, Villeneuve ordered his thirty-three ships of the line to set sail before they were fully ready, and on October 21, 1805, Nelson, whose squadron had been blockading Cádiz, sighted Villeneuve's fleet near Gibraltar off Cape Trafalgar.[4]

Stretched out in a single line some five miles long, the French and Spanish were unprepared for Nelson's unorthodox tactics. The British admiral disposed his twenty-seven vessels in two parallel columns and, rather than fight line against line, ordered them to split the enemy formation and engage in a general melee where superior British fire discipline could prove decisive. Although absorbing very heavy punishment on their approach, the British fleet finally broke Villeneuve's line and began to engage French and Spanish ships at point-blank range. Nelson, felled by a sniper, perished early in the battle, but his captains continued to execute his tactics with near perfection. Amid terrible carnage, Spanish and French ships began to sink or surrender. Only one third of Villeneuve's ships returned to port, while the British lost not a single vessel.

Nelson's total victory at Trafalgar was a major strategic triumph for England. The British had not only inflicted a heavy tactical setback upon the French but also convinced Bonaparte that he could never successfully challenge the British for control of the high seas. Despite the fact that the French, even after Trafalgar, possessed numerous vessels and built new ones, many of them superior in design and armament to equivalent British ships, Bonaparte never again tried to mount a major naval operation in the Mediterranean or directly against England. The outcome of Trafalgar, then, convinced the Corsican to relegate naval strategy to a distinctly subordinate role and confirmed Britain's domination of the oceans.

The immediate results of the battle were not nearly so critical as the long-term implications. Once Villeneuve

[4] *Correspondance de Napoléon* (Paris, 1862), XI, pp. 102–3, 138–39, 236–37, 247, and 262–63 contains Napoleon's instructions to his admirals.

entered Cádiz, chances for a cross-Channel attack were virtually nil, and by the time the French admiral sailed forth to destruction, Bonaparte had already given up all invasion schemes and was leading his Grand Army into central Europe.

While preparing to invade England, Bonaparte had not been inactive in other areas, and his policies ultimately convinced Russia and Austria to seek an alliance with England in order to check the Corsican's seemingly unbounded ambitions.

On December 2, 1804, Bonaparte, bedecked with the insignia and sword of Charlemagne, appeared before the altar of the Notre Dame Cathedral. There, with the Pope in attendance, he crowned himself Emperor of the French and assumed the appellation Napoleon I. His reestablishment of a hereditary regime also raised the possibility that he would seek to revive the old Carolingian Empire, destroy the Holy Roman Empire, and become the ruler of a continent composed of a French imperial domain surrounded by satellite kingdoms. In expectation of such a move, Francis II proclaimed himself Emperor of Austria, taking the title Francis I. Although he also retained the German imperial dignity, his actions indicated that he had little faith in the future of the Holy Roman Empire and that only an Austrian Hapsburg state could pose a barrier to French imperial ambitions.

In the spring of 1805 the French Emperor gave further indications of the extent of his ambitions by annexing Genoa to France and by transforming the Italian Republic into the Kingdom of Italy and, following the venerable Carolingian precedent, crowning himself with the iron crown of the old Lombard rulers.

Despite promises that he would not permanently unify the French and Italian crowns, Napoleon's overtly expansionist actions stung the Romanov ruler into action. On April 11, 1805, Alexander signed a formal alliance with the English Government, which was once again guided by William Pitt, thus forming the Third Coalition. The treaty called for a British subsidy to enable Russia to send 115,000 troops into action in western Europe. The two powers also agreed that in case of victory they would reduce France to her pre-1792 frontiers and erect a series of barrier states—an independent Holland enlarged by Belgium and a free Sardinia including Piedmont, Genoa, and Savoy—to guard against a revival of French expansionism, a policy almost identical to the aims of the Second Coalition and one that future British governments would pursue until 1815. Alexander also proposed a system of collective security based upon what he termed the rights of humanity, but, not forgetting the rights of Russia, he also asked Pitt to evacuate Malta, demanded permanent Russian occupation of Corfu, and called for a maritime code that would protect the rights of neutral commerce in wartime and, incidentally, severely limit the effectiveness of any British blockade. Naturally, Pitt rejected the romantic and expansionist Russian demands, and, after further negotiations, the two powers agreed to a minimum program—an alliance, a subsidy, and a reduction of French influence.

In September 1805 Alexander further enlarged the Third Coalition by signing a treaty with Naples whereby the Tsar agreed to guarantee the integrity of the Kingdom of the Two Sicilies in return for permission to land Russian troops in Neapolitan ports. Alexander thus opened another front against Napoleon, and by driving the French from the shores of the Adriatic he hoped to enhance his own influence in the Balkans. Sweden and Austria also joined the coalition in the summer of 1805, but Prussia, as suspicious of the Hapsburgs as ever, refused to abandon the system of neutrality. Frederick William III, a timorous, vacillating ruler who hated the principles of the French Revolution yet lived in dread of Napoleon's power, had signed in the spring of 1804 an agreement with Alexander to resist French aggression in northern Germany, but in 1805 he preferred tacit cooperation with Napoleon to fighting for an increase of

Hapsburg and Romanov power. Nor did the smaller Germai princes join the coalition. Fear of French arms plus promises of territorial aggrandizement convinced most of them to remain neutral while several, including Bavaria, Baden, and Württemberg, actually joined the French. Thus, like earlier anti-French alliances, the Third Coalition did not include all the major powers; members of the alliance, had conflicting ambitions, and many of the lesser powers refused to side with the coalition. Still, the allies had a minimal political program and sizable land and naval forces with which to attempt to impose it.

If national policy supplies the logic of war, military operations must still have their own grammar. But allied strategy in September 1805 resembled a tower of Babel. Anxious to reconquer Italy, Vienna sent its largest army, 94,000 men, to the Adige with orders to march on Milan. A 22,000-man detachment guarded the Tyrol, and 72,000 men with General Mack, the ill-fated commander of the Neapolitan army in the 1798 campaign, as chief of staff, moved into Bavaria with orders to halt at the Iller River to await the arrival of a Russian army before striking at Alsace. The allies also mounted two diversionary attacks: an English, Russian, and Neapolitan invasion of the Kingdom of Italy and a Swedish, English, and Russian descent upon Hanover.

The wide dispersal of effort was in itself dangerous, and the failure of the Russians to move quickly into Bavaria transformed danger into disaster when the Emperor of the French moved to defeat his foes in detail. Napoleon, after ordering Masséna with 50,000 men to hold the Adige, placing 18,000 men in southern Italy to protect Rome, and assigning 30,000 troops to guard the Channel coasts, prepared to lead the Grand Army's seven corps, 207,000 men, into Germany. He planned to advance toward Vienna, striking the separate coalition armies on the way. Thus while the allies scattered their strength from the Baltic to the Adriatic, the French Emperor concentrated his forces for a single decisive campaign.

As the Grand Army moved to the upper Rhine, cavalry units crossed the river and made demonstrations in front of the Black Forest to convince the Austrians that the main French force was going to move through southern Germany. Taken in by this ruse, Mack concentrated the bulk of his army around Ulm, while the Grand Army drove southeast, crossed the Danube, and cut Mack's communication line with Vienna. Napoleon's Marengo-type maneuver was highly successful and the French corps pushed the Austrians into Ulm. There on October 20 Mack surrendered the bulk of his army, about twenty-three thousand men.[5] A few units did manage to escape the French trap, but the Emperor had, nevertheless, completely dislocated the allied war plans.

Napoleon next set off in pursuit of the forty-thousand-man Russian army. General Michael Kutusov, once an active, bold, and ruthless leader and a favorite of Suvorov in the campaigns of the 1770s and 1780s who had become fat and slothful with advancing years, immediately fled Bavaria and fell back into Moravia to await Austrian reinforcements. The French, following, pushed their way into Vienna on November 13 and then marched into Bohemia. Kutusov meanwhile halted at Olmütz, where additional units joined him. Alexander also joined the eighty-thousand-man allied army and agreed with the Austrian proposal for an immediate counterattack. Francis wanted to liberate his territory and encourage the Prussians to join the coalition, and Alexander felt that he could defeat Napoleon, whose field army, because of straggling and the detachment of garrison forces, numbered only forty thousand men. Consequently, in the last days of November the Austro-Russian army began to move against the French positions at Brünn. The allies intended to strike at Napoleon's right, cut him off from

[5] *Min. de la Guerre A.H., M.h., Extrait de la relation de la prise d'Ulm 632.* This is a captured Austrian account. For French accounts see *Min. de la Guerre A.H., Grande Armée ordres du jour 1805 à 1807 carton C²11.*

Vienna, and compel him to retreat or fight at a disadvantage.[6]

Far from being reluctant to fight, the French Emperor was anxious to engage the allied forces and crush them before the Prussians decided to act. When the Grand Army had moved on Ulm, French troops had passed through Prussian territory, an act that convinced the Hohenzollern monarch that France had no real intention of treating Prussia as an equal and would violate Prussian sovereignty at will. Frederick William thereupon allowed Alexander's forces to move through his lands and promised the Tsar that he would offer armed mediation to Napoleon. If Bonaparte did not accept Prussian mediation by December 15, Frederick William intended to join the coalition. Napoleon realized that he had to resolve the war quickly and while fending off a Prussian envoy laid plans to lure the allied army into a battle of annihilation.

He began by convincing Alexander that his position was weak by retreating from a good defensive position on the Pratzen plateau, south of Brünn. He then placed his right flank behind a small brook. Moreover, he purposely placed weak units on his right in order to attract the main allied thrust. At the same time he ordered Davout's crack IIIrd Corps, located seventy miles south of the main army, to move up and secure the Grand Army's right flank. In a grueling forty-four-hour march, Davout brought his men to the battlefield, thereby giving his Emperor a total of seventy thousand men and sufficient strength to hold off allied attacks against his right while Soult and Lannes launched their corps against the Austro-Russian center.

Named after a small town behind the allied lines, the Battle of Austerlitz ranks as one of Bonaparte's most com-

[6] *Min. de la Guerre A.H., M.h., Relation de la Bataille d'Austerlitz 633.* This is Berthier's report and covers the movement of French corps from Ulm to Austerlitz. Also, Count Yorck von Wartenburg, *Napoleon as a General* (London, 1897), I, Ch. X.

plete and brilliant victories. On December 2, 1805, the first anniversary of Napoleon's coronation, the allies fell into the French trap. They took troops from their center on the Pratzen plateau and attacked the Grand Army's right flank. Davout's 10,000 men held off 40,000 Russians while Soult's 23,000-man corps awaited the imperial command to advance. Waiting until the allies had fully committed themselves to the attack against his right, Napoleon ordered Soult's divisions to take the Pratzen and shatter the coalition's center. French infantry seized the plateau and held it against desperate Russian counterattacks while on the left Lannes's troops moved forward and prevented Kutusov from reinforcing his shattered position. Soult, meanwhile, swung his corps south, driving thousands of allied troops into the frozen marshes and ponds in front of Davout's corps. Hundreds fell through the ice and drowned. Hundreds more fell before French bullets and bayonets and when dusk put an end to the conflict 9000 French and 26,000 allied casualties littered the battlefield. Napoleon had completely shattered the allied army, and with it the Third Coalition.

In the aftermath of their defeat the Austrians requested, and the French granted, an armistice that called for the Hapsburgs to remove Russian troops from their domains and to deny entry to the Prussian army. Napoleon then had to choose between imposing mild or harsh terms on Vienna. Talleyrand favored a "soft" peace in order to influence Austria to turn her attentions toward the Balkans, which would bring on a clash between the Hapsburgs and the Romanovs and leave the French a free hand in Germany. The Emperor, however, believed that the Hapsburgs would never give up the desire to regain their influence in Italy and Germany and decided to rob them of the means of resuming hostilities in the near future. Consequently, on December 26, 1805, Napoleon forced the Austrians to sign the Treaty of Pressburg, which compelled Vienna to relinquish Venetia, Istria, and Dalmatia to the Kingdom of Italy, and the Tyrol and Vorarlberg to Bavaria and Württemberg. Vienna also agreed to pay an indemnity of forty million francs and recognize the rulers of Bavaria and Württemberg as kings. Francis also ceded the Adriatic port of Cattaro to France, but Russian troops seized it first. Despite this minor setback, Napoleon had succeeded in driving the Hapsburgs from Italy and in further weakening their influence in Germany.

The victor of Austerlitz next used his enhanced power and prestige to compel the Hohenzollern King to abandon both his policy of armed mediation and his ten-year-old position of neutrality and become a French ally. After defeating the allied army, Napoleon, by a combination of threats and bribes, forced the Prussian envoy to sign a preliminary treaty on December 15, whereby Prussia agreed to occupy Hanover, still an appendage of the British crown, recognize all changes wrought in Germany and Italy, and conclude a formal alliance with the French Empire. Frederick William was reluctant to ratify the treaty but even more reluctant to face the Grand Army. He agreed to sign if Napoleon agreed to slight modifications. The Corsican refused, threatened violent retaliation, and the King of Prussia's resistance collapsed. On February 15, 1806, the two powers signed the Treaty of Paris, whereby Frederick William agreed not only to occupy but also to annex Hanover, and to close his entire coastline to British commerce. Despite Pitt's death in January, the new ministry in London, known as the ministry of All the Talents, a narrow-based grouping of factions dominated by Charles James Fox, quickly declared war on Prussia, and the Royal Navy began to force Prussian commerce off the seas. By acting too slowly and hesitantly, Frederick William left himself exposed to Bonaparte's wrath and then found himself forced to become a junior partner in a French alliance.

Having dealt with Prussia, Napoleon, in the spring of 1806, decided to punish Naples for its participation in the coalition. French troops marched into the Kingdom of the Two Sicilies. A small British force inflicted several reverses on the overconfident invaders but lacked the strength to do more than delay the French. By May 11, 1806, the British fleet had evacuated the Bourbons to the island of Sicily, and Napoleon's brother Joseph occupied the royal palace in the city of Naples. A vicious guerrilla war, reminiscent of the campaigns of 1799, erupted in the provinces, and the English seized the island of Capri, but neither the partisans nor the British could shake French control of the major cities and strategic points in southern Italy.

Napoleon also inaugurated a series of political measures designed to strengthen further his influence outside the French Empire's borders. Although Joseph became King of Naples, he nevertheless retained his rank as a grand dignitary of the French Empire, and therefore remained legally subject to the Emperor's authority. Napoleon's personal domination of his elder brother transformed the legal situation into a political reality. Napoleon gave to Bernadotte and Talleyrand papal enclaves in Naples, but they too retained their status as French subjects. In northern Europe the ambitious Corsican abolished the Batavian Republic and in June 1806 replaced it with a Kingdom of Holland. His brother Louis became the new Dutch King. Joachim Murat, Bonaparte's brother-in-law, received a Rhine duchy, Berg, created from the former Prussian province of Cleves, which Berlin had surrendered in return for Hanover. Napoleon's chief of staff, Louis-Alexandre Berthier, obtained still another Prussian territory, Neuchâtel.

In addition to rewarding some of his closest collaborators and finding employment for his relatives, whom he could easily dominate, Bonaparte had also begun to create a new European nobility tied directly to the French Empire. Nor did the Emperor neglect the more traditional means of enhancing his influence. He contracted marriage alliances between his stepson Eugene, the viceroy of Italy, and a Bavarian princess, and between his wife's niece and a prince from Baden. And finally, Napoleon brought to fruition the policy of creating a "third Germany." Previous regimes, monarchical and republican alike, had sought to conclude alliances with some of the lesser German states. Napoleon, however, went further by seeking to create a permanent league with himself as its leader. The princes opposed a perpetual union and wished to limit their commitment to a temporary alliance, but Napoleon insisted upon establishing a formal league. In the summer of 1806 Bavaria, Baden, Württemberg, Hesse-Darmstadt, and a number of lesser principalities bowed to the Emperor's desires and created a Confederation of the Rhine. The member states absorbed nearly seventy smaller entities plus the estates of the imperial knights, recognized Napoleon as the protector of the confederation, and agreed to furnish him sixty thousand troops in wartime. In addition to vastly expanding French dominance in Germany, the creation of the Rhine Confederation spelled the end of the Holy Roman Empire, for the confederation declared that it did not recognize Hapsburg imperial authority. On August 6, 1806, Francis, recognizing the futility of hanging on to an empty honor, formally announced the demise of the venerable *Reich.*

While redrawing the map of central Europe, the French Emperor also carried on negotiations with Russia and England in an attempt to split his two remaining foes and perhaps arrange a favorable peace with one or both of them. At Paris Napoleon succeeded in concluding a treaty with the Russian envoy. He promised to accept permanent Russian occupation of the Ionian Islands if the Tsar abandoned Cattaro. He also promised to pull his troops out of Germany, although he insisted upon remaining the Rhine Confederation's protector, and agreed to a joint Russo-French guarantee of the Ottoman Empire's integrity. Finally, the Russian envoy acceded to a French proposal to give Ferdinand of Naples the

Balearic Islands, while Joseph obtained Sicily. In his talks with England, Napoleon offered to allow the British to retain permanent control of Malta and the Cape and agreed to return Hanover if the British in return gave him Sicily. Since Bonaparte was willing to sacrifice nothing that would seriously reduce his power in Italy or Germany and offered but small compensation to the Russians and the English in return for their acceptance of French hegemony in western Europe, the negotiations failed. Alexander disavowed his envoy and refused to ratify the treaty, and Fox, long an advocate of peace with France, realized that Napoleon was unwilling to make any serious concessions. The British Government, therefore, allowed the talks to languish. The most significant result of the abortive diplomatic efforts was to frighten Berlin into resisting French expansion.

The Prussians had objected to Bonaparte's cavalier treatment of their sovereignty in 1805, regarded the French-dominated Rhine Confederation as a threat to their own influence in northern Germany, and were dismayed by Napoleon's offer to return Hanover to Britain after virtually forcing them to appropriate the region. Concluding that Prussia's independence and great power status were in danger of eclipse, Frederick William decided to fight. In July he concluded with Alexander a defensive alliance, and the next month he mobilized his army and summoned the French to pull their troops back across the Rhine by October 1. Thus, after ten years of neutrality, the Prussians decided to act at the worst possible moment. Austria was unable to renew hostilities, the Russians were too far distant to send immediate aid, and the British lacked the troops for an expedition to Europe. Furthermore, the Prussian army was in no condition to face the Grand Army of France unaided, for it had declined in quality even from the sad days of the 1790s. In 1806 the Prussian general officers were superannuated, while their battalion and company grade commanders were old by French standards. With advanced age came intellectual ossification, and the Prussian high command had not by 1806 undertaken any significant military reforms to cope with French tactical innovations. Finally, the monarch and his chief advisers lacked confidence in their ability to beat the French, and seemed incapable of flexible, rapid, and effective responses to Napoleon's strategy. As the Prussian army slowly gathered about Weimar and the King and his staff debated their next moves, the French Emperor was preparing another of his swift, devastating campaigns.

Napoleon gathered six army corps in southern Germany and ordered them to execute a flank march through the Thuringian Forest. His object was to gain a position between the Prussian army and Berlin and force Frederick William to fight a defensive battle on his own territory. As usual the Emperor's marshals moved swiftly, and by October 11 their soldiers stood behind the Prussian army ready to fight a major battle. Napoleon then ordered his forces to wheel left. Two corps moved on Weimar, two others supported them on the right, and the remaining two formations executed a wider sweep to the right to take the Prussians from the rear.

Realizing their plight, the Prussians began to retreat on October 13. Leaving a 38,000-man rear guard at Jena, the main army marched north toward Auerstädt, a village on the route to Berlin. The Prussians did not move fast enough, however, for on the morning of October 14, Napoleon threw four corps, 96,000 men, against the rear guard at Jena. French light infantry and field artillery reaped havoc among the enemy battalions and the main forces then swept the Prussian troops into a rout. Meanwhile, at Auerstädt, Davout's corps fought a much more difficult and decisive battle. As the Emperor fought the Prussian rear guard, Davout's 27,000 men met Frederick William's 63,000-man main force. By moving his wings forward, Davout was able to establish an effective artillery crossfire pattern that succeeded in shaking the Prussian advance. The Hohenzollern monarch then failed to send forward his reserves and instead ordered his men to retreat to Jena. On the way back Frederick William's force encountered fugitives from the clash with Napoleon, and in short order discipline collapsed throughout the entire Prussian army, leaving the kingdom helpless before the Grand Army.

Hardly pausing to regroup, Napoleon launched his army in a vigorous pursuit of his demoralized foes. Fortress after fortress capitulated without resistance, and by October 25 Davout's men had entered Berlin. The Prussian court fled to the east with the remnants of its army to await the arrival of Russian forces, while the French Emperor further consolidated his hold upon Germany. His troops occupied Hesse-Cassel and the Duke of Brunswick's lands, and Saxony, with its Elector raised to the rank of King, joined the Rhine Confederation. Thus, by the end of 1806 it appeared as though Napoleon had but to defeat the Russians to consolidate his dominant position in central Europe.

Pushing into Prussian Poland, the Grand Army, despite poor roads and supply shortages, took Warsaw and went into winter quarters. The Russians, however, launched an offensive in January 1807. As the Tsar's army moved across northern Poland, the French concentrated quickly and threw themselves across the Russian communications lines. The Russians fell back; the French pursued, and the two armies clashed at the small town of Eylau on February 8, 1807.

In the midst of a driving snowstorm French troops hurled themselves against the Russian lines but failed to break the Muscovite ranks. Once again, however, Davout turned the tide of battle as his corps, having lost direction in the blizzard, finally appeared on the Russian left and began to roll up their line. Only the opportune arrival of a Prussian force allowed the Russian commander to extricate himself from a disastrous situation. The antagonists each lost about twenty thousand men. Napoleon claimed a victory because he remained in possession of the battlefield, but in fact he had failed to destroy the Russian army and shatter the Russo-Prussian alliance.

The continued existence of the alliance not only posed a military problem for the Emperor but also produced dangerous diplomatic complications outside of the immediate battle zone. When in the spring of 1807 the Hohenzollern and Romanov rulers formally created the Fourth Coalition, invited other powers to join them against France, and pledged themselves to liberate Germany and Italy in the next campaign, Bonaparte had to face the unpleasant possibility that Austria might join them to gain a share of the spoils. Spain, too, was growing restive and Godoy began to have second thoughts about continuing his pro-French policy. Napoleon's refusal to attack Portugal and carve out a principality for Spain's chief minister angered Godoy. Britain's actions also alarmed him. In the summer of 1806 a British fleet and expeditionary force had appeared in the Río de la Plata and captured Buenos Aires. Although the Spanish recaptured the city, they learned again that the English could wreak havoc in their colonial domains. Consequently in the fall of 1806 Godoy began serious talks with the Russian ambassador at Madrid and undertook military preparations to place his army on a war footing. The Prussian collapse put an end to Godoy's maneuvering, but the French Emperor had reason to fear that continued lack of success in the east might convince Madrid to renew dealings with France's enemies.

The failure to crush the Russians at Eylau also undermined a growing French influence in the Balkans. In 1805 Sultan Selim III had renewed his alliance with the Tsar, but Napoleon's triumphs of that year convinced him that he could with safety remove himself from the Russian embrace. In February 1806 he recognized the Corsican dictator's imperial pretensions, assured Napoleon of his pro-French sentiments, and removed the anti-French hospodars (governors) of the Danubian principalities. He also closed the Straits to warships of all belligerent powers, a move that affected the Russians adversely because they needed access into the Mediterranean to maintain themselves on the Ionian Islands. The Turks also refused to renew their alliance with Great Britain. The Russians, of course, protested, and England sent a fleet to the Dardanelles. Just as the Sultan was ready to capitulate, the Battle of Jena strengthened his resolve to break free of English and Russian domination, and he began to enlarge his army and improve the fortifications around the Straits. To check the growth of French influence in the Balkans and support the Serbian rebellion, which had erupted in 1804, Alexander sent troops into Moldavia, and the Sultan replied with a declaration of war in December 1806, thereby becoming a *de facto* French ally. However, Napoleon's inability to force Russia to sue for peace enabled the Tsar to continue his advance into the Balkans. Furthermore, a British fleet was preparing to enter the Straits, and London began to contemplate a new expedition to Egypt. Unless the Emperor could achieve a rapid victory in 1807, his foes might defeat the Turks, gain new lands, and shut France out of the Balkans and the east.

In the months following Eylau, however, England and Russia failed to co-ordinate their strategy and diplomacy, thereby giving Napoleon an opportunity to gain still another dramatic series of victories. To force the Sultan to reverse his pro-French policy, a British squadron led by Admiral Duckworth entered the Straits on February 19, fought its way past the Turkish fortification, and by evening was anchored in the Sea of Marmora. Duckworth then decided to wait until his scattered ships reconcentrated before sailing to Constantinople, a decision which gave the Turks, encouraged by the French ambassador, time to prepare their defenses. Unfavorable weather imposed further delay on the British squadron, and when the wind changed on March 2, Duckworth concluded that the Turkish bastions were too strong to send his ships against them. He then left the Straits, and with his vessels went the opportunity to force the Turks out of the French camp.

Having failed at Constantinople, the British decided to exert pressure on the Turks by seizing Egypt, a move that would also enhance English influence in the Levant while blocking that of the French. The expedition was, however, a fiasco. A six-thousand-man force took Alexandria but suffered a heavy reversal when it marched on Rosetta. A second attempt in the spring also failed, and the Cabinet, admitting defeat, pulled its battered force back to Sicily.

Efforts by England to enhance her influence in South America also foundered. The government mounted a second expedition to take Buenos Aires and then conquer Valparaiso, thereby detaching a large portion of South America from the Spanish crown. The British landed in June, but failed to carry the city when they stormed it on July 5 and had to give up their plans of carving out new conquests in the Americas.

In 1807 the British had not only dispersed their forces in peripheral areas but had also failed to make even limited gains. Furthermore, London's excessive concentration upon colonial projects antagonized Alexander, who began to feel that the English were letting him bear the brunt of the anti-French war while they profited from Franco-Russian involvement in Europe by expanding their overseas empire. Consequently, when fighting resumed in Poland, Alexander lacked direct British assistance and was growing ever more suspicious of his only ally.

With the coming of spring the French Emperor inaugurated another campaign to force the Russians to sue for peace. In April his army took Danzig, and eighty thousand men moved into East Prussia. On June 14, the anniversary of Marengo, advance units of the Grand Army encountered the Russian hosts in the process of crossing a small river, the Alle, near the village of Friedland. Seizing his opportunity, Napoleon gathered his reserves, while skirmishers pinned the Russians to the riverbank. The Emperor then ordered Michel Ney, one of his more dashing marshals, to assail the Russian left and drive it into the village. Without pausing to deploy, Ney ordered his divisions, which were just reaching the front, to move directly on the town. Despite heavy losses Ney led his men forward and accomplished his mission. A battery of thirty field guns raced forward and poured volley after volley of canister into the Russian regiments crowded into Friedland. After enduring the slaughter for nearly half an hour, the Russians broke and French infantry stormed into the town. Leaving eleven thousand dead and seven thousand wounded behind, the Russian army fled back across the Alle, and the whole force, once more united, retreated toward Tilsit. Having suffered still another military reverse, Alexander, always a man of mercurial temperament, began to contemplate a drastic revision of his foreign policy.

The Tsar was extremely reluctant to continue the war. His generals had already told him that militarily an armistice was indispensable. Furthermore, he feared that more fighting and new defeats might lead to a French invasion of Russia, which in turn might spark a Polish uprising, peasant rebellions in Russia itself, and a military-noble coup that would depose him and establish a regime that would make peace with France. In addition, Alexander was discontent with English policy. London had failed to send him military or naval assistance, and Britain's policy of mounting peripheral expeditions to South America and Egypt convinced him that he could not rely upon England. Consequently, he requested an armistice on June 19. Napoleon granted it on June 21, since he too desired peace, realizing that despite his recent victory he had not destroyed Russia's capacity to wage war. If the Tsar decided to continue fighting, French armies would have to invade Russia. An invasion would involve extensive and expensive preparations and would produce heavy losses in men, material, and money. A Russian campaign would also prevent the Emperor from concentrating his resources against his chief enemy, England, and the diversion of the French armies to the east might encourage Austria to strike in central Europe and Italy. Finally, Napoleon hoped that the truce and the ensuing peace talks would not only give him an opportunity to conclude a favorable peace treaty but also enable him to convince Alexander to join France in an alliance.

At this juncture a Prussian proposal inadvertently opened the way for serious talks between the two powers. Anxious to salvage something from their recent catastrophe, the Prussians on June 23 presented the Tsar with a plan calling for a new realignment of the powers and a massive reshuffling of provinces. The proposal called for a three-power alliance—Prussia, Russia, and France—to wage war upon England. It also called for a partition of the Ottoman Empire between Russia and Austria. In return Austria and Russia would relinquish the Polish provinces they had taken in 1793 and 1795. Prussia would also give up its share of the Second and Third partitions. The allies would then reconstitute a Polish state and grant its throne to the ruler of Saxony, a French ally. The Prussians as compensation would take Saxony.

Alexander was impressed with this scheme and decided to act upon it. He sought an interview with Bonaparte and on June 25 met the French Emperor on a raft anchored on the Niemen River. Day after day each of the rulers tried to impose his personality and policy on the other. Alexander at first tried to convince Napoleon to accept the Prussian proposal in its entirety. The French Emperor, however, had no intention of including Prussia as an equal partner in any diplomatic combination. By holding out the glittering prizes of a Franco-

Russian entente that would dominate Europe and a dual partition of the Turkish state, Bonaparte convinced the Tsar to abandon his Prussian ally. Finally, between July 7 and July 9, the emperors concluded and signed the open and secret treaties of Tilsit. In the public treaty Alexander recognized the changes that Napoleon had wrought in Holland, Italy, and Germany and agreed to abandon Prussia to the mercies of France. Napoleon then took all Prussian territory west of the Elbe, combined it with Brunswick, Hanoverian, and Hessian lands into the Kingdom of Westphalia, and placed his brother Jerome upon the new throne. Napoleon also detached the Polish territory acquired by Prussia in the eighteenth-century partitions from the Hohenzollern domains and created the duchy of Warsaw. He made the King of Saxony, his ally and a member of the Rhine Confederation, ruler of the new Polish state and compelled Frederick William to grant the use of a military road through Silesia to Napoleon's French and allied troops. Moreover, the hapless Prussian King had to accept French occupation of several important fortresses until Prussia paid an indemnity, the amount of which the French would set at a later date. In addition, French troops were to occupy a number of Prussia's ports until the conclusion of a final peace with England, and Frederick William agreed to co-operate with France and Russia to compel the British to negotiate. Napoleon had thus deprived Frederick William of about one third of his territory and nearly half of his subjects, reducing mighty Prussia to a vassal state of second-rate importance.

In the secret treaty, Alexander agreed to call upon England to return all post-1805 conquests and recognize freedom of neutral commerce on the high seas. If the British refused to accede to these demands by November 1, 1807, Alexander promised to declare war, close his ports to England's commerce, and join France in forcing Sweden, Denmark, and Portugal into the Franco-Russian alliance system. The Tsar also agreed to evacuate the Ionian Islands and Cattaro and to pull his naval units out of the Mediterranean. In return Napoleon agreed to let Russia retain Moldavia and Wallachia and to offer his mediation to end the Russo-Ottoman conflict. If the Sultan refused to negotiate, the French Emperor agreed to make common cause with the Russian Tsar and partition the Balkans except for Roumelia and Constantinople.

Both rulers were satisfied with the Tilsit agreements. Alexander had escaped from a dangerous war and secured Napoleon's promise to assist him in the destruction of Ottoman power. Although the Corsican had made no specific promises, Alexander was sure that he would receive the lion's share of any Balkan partition. Furthermore, Napoleon by implication gave the Russians a free hand in Finland. Thus for the moment Alexander pictured himself as the Ruler of the East working with the Ruler of the West to impose their collective will upon the civilized world.

For the Corsican, Tilsit was equally satisfying. Russia became a French ally, and Alexander accepted the French imperium as legitimate. No major continental power challenged France; only England and Portugal remained at war, and the French Emperor had high hopes that with Russian co-operation he could bring his remaining foes to their knees.

Since 1802 the territory that Napoleon controlled, directly or indirectly, had doubled. He had annexed large parts of the Italian peninsula and placed the remaining portions under the control of his relatives. A brother reigned in Holland and still another in Westphalia. He had also destroyed the Holy Roman Empire, driven the Hapsburgs from Germany, and organized the middle-sized German states into a league dominated by France. He had shattered Prussian power, restored a semblance of Polish independence, tied the new Polish state to his own fortunes, and established his presence on the Adriatic. The Corsican upstart had thus created an empire larger than Charlemagne's and raised France to a position of power and influence that surpassed even the glories and prestige of the Sun King.

CHAPTER 9

THE GRAND EMPIRE

Despite his amazing military and diplomatic triumphs, Napoleon in 1807 still had to find a way to compel England to accept peace on his terms or face the prospect of perpetual war. The Royal Navy could effectively stifle French trade and influence in the non-European world and encourage and finance any power or coalition wishing to challenge French hegemony. Therefore, to make his accomplishments permanent Bonaparte had above all things to crush England.

Recalling Aboukir and Trafalgar, the French Emperor never seriously considered challenging England in her chosen element. Nor did he contemplate another invasion attempt. Since Great Britain would never accept Napoleonic hegemony, meaningful negotiations were also out of the question. The Emperor therefore decided to resort to economic warfare. His object was to drain wealth from England, make it impossible for the Cabinet to finance new wars, convince the mercantile classes to demand an end to the war at almost any price, and force the government to recognize the necessity for peace even on French terms.

Napoleon's economic strategy was to organize the European states into a continental system that would refuse goods *from* Britain while continuing to export items *to* the British Isles. England would then suffer an unfavorable balance of payments and lose the ability to use her financial power in foreign affairs.[1]

In 1807 Britain's industrial production was worth about

[1] For a standard study and interpretation of the continental system see E. F. Heckscher, *The Continental System; an Economic Interpretation* (Oxford, 1922).

£100,000,000 per annum, and merchants exported about 40 per cent of this total. More than 35 per cent of England's exports went to the Continent,[2] and if the Emperor could indeed exclude British products from Europe, he could reasonably expect to wreak havoc upon his foe's economy. Bonaparte hoped further that as British trade collapsed French trade would expand, and he expected French entrepreneurs to increase production to fill the gap created by the destruction of the British export market. France's economic position would thus improve, economic supremacy would bolster French military and diplomatic dominance, and the business classes would support his regime with ever increasing fervor.

Bonaparte based his policy of economic—or, more accurately, financial—strangulation upon a long series of precedents. During the prerevolutionary era European states had waged financial war, sought favorable trade balances, and devised tariffs designed to protect domestic commerce and industry. A movement for less commercial restriction developed in the last decades of the eighteenth century, but the advent of war witnessed a rapid return to more traditional policies. In 1793 the Committee of Public Safety introduced an exclusion act directed against British goods and a navigation act hopefully designed to hamper British shipping. The exigencies of war, however, forced the Committee to suspend the acts and encourage neutral ships to engage in the carrying trade. The twelve also adopted the policy of expanding governmental economic power in order to pursue effectively the goal of general mobilization. After Robespierre's overthrow in July 1794, the Convention and its successor, the Directory, reverted to the policy of

[2] For an important new study of England's economy see F. Crouzet, *L'économie britannique et le Blocus Continental* (1806–1813), 2 vols. (Paris, 1958). See also A. Gayer, W. Rostow, and A. Schwartz, *The Growth and Fluctuation of the British Economy 1790–1850*, 2 vols. (London, 1953).

protection without regulation. Monopolies, guilds, unions, and internal tariffs remained outlawed, and post-Thermidorian regimes also dismantled the Committee's system of economic controls. In addition, the Directory ended the experiment of paper currency. Due to the abolition of price controls the assignat had lost most of its value. After a brief, unsuccessful experiment with a new paper currency, the mandat, the government returned to a metallic currency, which, if it did restrict the amount of available risk capital, also stabilized the monetary system, ended the inflationary price spiral, and restored business confidence. The Directory also sought to stimulate business by holding industrial fairs to publicize new production techniques, bringing machinery and skilled workers to France from conquered areas, forcing satellite regimes to sign commercial treaties with the Republic, and maintaining a high protective tariff. The Directory also continued the commercial war against England, excluding British goods from the Republic's territory, and this exclusion encompassed not only areas annexed by France but also by the satellite states.

In 1798 the Directory enlarged its commercial war with England by declaring that neutral ships laden in whole or in part with British goods were lawful prizes. An undeclared naval war with the United States, in which France lost over eighty vessels, ensued. Bonaparte in 1800 ended the hostilities, renewed commercial relations with America on the most-favored nation basis, and incorporated into the treaty articles a provision that called for liberal neutral trading rights in time of war, a thrust at England's blockade techniques.[3]

[3] For discussions of French economic policy before Napoleon see S. Clough, *France, A History of National Economics, 1789–1939* (New York, 1939); R. G. Hawtrey, *Currency and Credit* (London, 1919); S. E. Harris, *The Assignats* (Cambridge, 1935); G. Dejoint, *La politique économique du Directoire* (Paris, 1951); and F. L. Nussbaum, *Commercial Policy in the French Revolution* (New York, 1923).

Thus Bonaparte adopted most of the basic economic objectives of previous regimes—assistance for French businessmen and commercial war on England. Where he differed from his predecessors was in the scope of his plans, for as his armies bestrode the Continent, the Corsican undertook to organize all Europe into a single economic system dedicated to enhancing French, and ruining English, prosperity.

In 1803 Bonaparte introduced a protective tariff designed to secure the home market for French entrepreneurs. After defeating Austria and breaking the Third Coalition, the Emperor in April 1806 introduced a new tariff subjecting colonial products to heavy duties and excluding virtually all cotton goods. This tariff was of course a thrust at England, whose merchants dominated the colonial trade and the cotton industry. He also added some of the north German ports to the list of areas closed to British exports. The British responded in May with an Order in Council proclaiming the existence of a blockade from Brest to the Elbe. After defeating the Prussians, Napoleon struck again at British commerce by directing his forces in northern Germany to seal the mouth of the Elbe, occupy Hamburg, Bremen, and Lübeck, and confiscate all British products found in occupied regions. Since English merchants had used the Hanseatic towns as entrepôts, the Emperor's generals managed to commandeer thousands of pounds' worth of British goods.[4]

On November 21, 1806, Napoleon issued the Berlin Decree, an attempt to organize all of western Europe for economic hostilities against England. The decree placed the British Isles in a state of blockade, forbade all trade between the Continent and England, ordered the arrest of all Englishmen residing in Europe and the confiscation of their goods, refused entry to any vessel coming

[4] See J. H. Rose, "Napoleon and English Commerce," in *English Historical Review* (October 1893), and Crouzet, *L'économie britannique*, I.

to the Continent from England or her colonies, and refused access to European ports to ships calling at British ports after the publication of the decree. The Emperor could not, of course, establish a physical blockade of the British Isles, nor was this his intention. His objectives were to close the ports of Europe from Hamburg to Naples to English exports, and hamper neutral trade with Great Britain by threatening non-belligerents with the possibility of seizure by French privateers and denying them access to continental markets if they persisted in dealing with England.

The Berlin Decree did not, however, produce the anticipated effect. Several of the Emperor's satellites continued to do business with England. The British put effective counterpressure upon neutral states, and neither they nor Russia adhered to the decree's provisions. In January 1807 an Order in Council forbade neutral trade between French ports and between French ports and the ports of Napoleon's allies. Napoleon, meanwhile, proceeded to win Russia as an ally, and the two rulers agreed to force other powers into the continental system. Aware of the import of the Franco-Russian alliance, the British undertook to neutralize Denmark, for if Napoleon drew Denmark with its large fleet and strategic location into his system, he could isolate Sweden and close the entire Baltic to British ships and goods.

The Duke of Portland's Cabinet, another unstable coalition of factions which had replaced the Talents in the spring of 1807, first offered the Danes a secret alliance, the terms of which called for Denmark to turn her fleet over to the British for the war's duration. The Danes refused the offer, and the British Government thereupon decided to attack Copenhagen and seize or destroy neutral Denmark's fleet. In September 1807 an English expedition bombarded Copenhagen, compelled the Danes to capitulate and give up eighteen line-of-battle ships and fifteen frigates. Angered and humiliated by the violation of his neutrality, the Danish King Frederick VI retaliated by concluding a military alliance with Napoleon and joining the continental system. Still the British had scored a victory, for they had the Danish fleet, and had avoided the possibility of the Emperor's supplementing his blockade of exclusion with real naval action.

Undaunted by England's victory, Napoleon began to issue orders for the subjugation of Portugal, while Alexander on November 7, 1807, carried out his Tilsit Treaty commitments by declaring war on Great Britain and closing his ports to English vessels. Since Sweden refused to join the continental system because the preservation of exports to England was vital to her economy and because Gustavus feared a Franco-Russian Baltic hegemony, Russia invaded the Swedish province of Finland in February 1808, and Denmark joined her by declaring war in March.

To counter Bonaparte's economic offensive the British issued another series of Orders in Council in November 1807, declaring that all enemy countries and their colonies would henceforth be considered to be under a strict blockade. All goods coming from enemy harbors and any vessel trading to them without a special British license, along with its cargo, were to be fair prizes. Since British merchants did not have to obtain licenses, they received an important economic advantage because the charges for a re-export license amounted to an extra import duty. The British Government thus sought to make their products cheaper, seize neutral trade for their own profit, and use neutral ships to transport their own products to Europe.

Lashing back at the British, Napoleon, in the Milan Decree dated December 17, 1807, declared that all neutral ships submitting to British search on the high seas would lose their neutral character, and French privateers could seize them as legal war prizes. The decree also allowed privateers to take neutral ships that had called at

English ports and obtained licenses.[5] The Milan Decree then was not only an effort to strengthen the policy of economic strangulation but also an attempt to compel neutrals to resist British maritime domination.

To enforce his system effectively the Emperor had to tighten further his political hold on Europe. He could not mount a naval blockade of England's shores, nor, despite a continual effort to restore and expand his fleet, could he prevent the British from isolating Europe from the outside world. Therefore, it became vital for Napoleon to seal hermetically the European coasts and thereby prevent the British from flooding goods into uncontrolled areas. The necessities of the Corsican's economic policy in turn gave added impetus to his natural aggressiveness and virtually limitless ambitions, and as governments hurled decrees and Orders in Council at one another, French armies marched.

Leaving the Tsar to deal with Sweden, Napoleon decided to conquer Portugal, bring that state into his economic sphere of influence, deprive the English of their last continental ally, and threaten Britain's position in the Mediterranean. On October 27, 1807, the Emperor concluded the secret Treaty of Fontainebleau with Charles IV of Spain. The two rulers agreed to conquer and partition the Portuguese kingdom. The Bourbon ruler of Etruria was to obtain northern Portugal while France annexed Etruria. French troops were to occupy Lisbon and central Portugal, and Godoy was to have southern Portugal as his own principality. General Andoche Junot, a former law student who had served in the army since 1792 and was destined to go mad and kill himself in 1813, led his corps of twenty-three thousand men, plus sixteen thousand Spaniards, on Lisbon in November. The Portuguese offered no resistance, and at the end of the month the royal family and fleet fled to Brazil as Junot's

[5] See F. E. Melvin, *Napoleon's Navigation System* (New York, 1956) for an extended discussion of the Milan Decree. See also B. de Jouvenal, *Napoléon et l'économie dirigée* (Paris, 1942).

troops, after a grueling march, entered the Portuguese capital.

The conquest of Portugal in turn enabled the French Emperor to extend his continental system from Gibraltar to the North Cape, and increase the economic pressure upon Britain. English merchants in the year after 1807 suffered a £2,000,000 decline in exports and a 5 per cent reduction in industrial productivity. Bank failures increased and trade suffered a further blow as a result of the American Non-Importation Act of April 1806, and the embargo of December 1807. The latter prohibited American trade with Europe in an effort to force the belligerents to modify their blockade decrees and to compel the British to cease impressing American seamen into the Royal Navy. Agitation among English workers for peace and higher wages increased, and on several occasions the government had to use troops to disperse worker demonstrations.[6]

Cheered by the apparent success of his economic war and by the easy conquest of Portugal, Napoleon next decided to gain greater influence at Madrid in order to co-ordinate more fully Spain's fiscal, diplomatic, and military activities with those of his Grand Empire. Napoleon realized that Charles IV, "whose talent for hunting was in inverse proportion to his knowledge of world affairs,"[7] was a figurehead and that Godoy, the Queen's lover and the King's chief minister, had been willing to betray France in 1806 and in suitable circumstances would probably try again to join the Emperor's foes. The alternative to Charles and Godoy, the Crown Prince Ferdinand, was equally depressing, for the Prince was among the least able of a long line of ineffective rulers.

[6] See Crouzet, *L'économie britannique*, II, and M. Dunan, "Napoléon et le systeme continental en 1810," in *Revue d'histoire diplomatique* (1946), LX, which has background material on the earlier years.

[7] G. H. Lovett, *Napoleon and the Birth of Modern Spain* (New York, 1965), I, p. 5.

Bonaparte knew of the prevailing chaos in the Spanish bureaucracy and the stagnation of the economy. He saw, too, that the army with most of its effective units serving with the French on the Baltic was understrength and poorly led, and that the navy with but twenty ships of the line ready for combat and only a third of its sailors present for duty was steadily deteriorating in size and quality. The Spanish pupulace was on the whole courageous, proud, and loyal to the throne and altar. Spain's millions of inhabitants in fact represented an enormous potential, but the Corsican saw that the Bourbon regime had failed to organize and direct the energies of its subjects.[8]

Assuming that a new regime guided by Frenchmen would produce more arms, men, and money for the imperial cause, and enhance the effectiveness of the continental system, Napoleon began to search for a means to increase his influence in Spanish domestic affairs. He and his advisers devised three alternatives: a marriage between Ferdinand and a Bonaparte princess; annexation of Spanish territory between the Pyrenees and the Ebro River while Madrid in turn took Lisbon; or the elimination of the Bourbon monarchy and the substitution of a Bonaparte upon the Spanish throne. The Emperor's agents in Spain informed him that the Spanish populace would in all probability react violently against any foreign intervention, but developments at Madrid convinced Napoleon that direct intervention was the only way to gain effective control of Spain's government.

In the winter of 1807, the Crown Prince had organized a conspiracy to depose Godoy, but his scheme was uncovered, and after giving away his fellow plotters, Ferdinand appealed to Napoleon to save him from the consequences of his treason. Napoleon did intervene to save

[8] Ibid., pp. 24 and 28–30. For additional studies on Spanish conditions see M. Artola, *Los Origenes de la España Contemporánea* (Madrid, 1959), I, and G. Desdevises du Dezert, *L'Espagne de l'Ancien Régime* (Paris, 1899), II, Chs. VI, VII, VIII.

the Prince, but the political situation at court remained explosive. The royal couple and Godoy were unpopular because of the hardships wrought by the unsuccessful war with England, and Ferdinand remained a symbol for those who sought progressive change. On March 17, 1808, a popular manifestation against Godoy frightened Charles into dismissing him. Rioting continued throughout the following day, and Ferdinand, urged on by his advisers, told his father that he would save Godoy's life and disperse the mob. In return he insisted that his father abdicate in his favor. Fearing for his own safety, Charles accepted his son's proposal with alacrity and abandoned the crown.

The "revolution" of March 17–18 in turn convinced the Emperor that he had to take personal control of Spanish affairs. Although he never trusted Charles or Godoy, he had been able in the final analysis to dominate them; but Ferdinand, in addition to being as unreliable as his father and Godoy, did not owe his position to French support, and because of his extensive popularity he was less subject to French pressure than the deposed rulers. Napoleon therefore decided to avoid further embroilment in the Byzantine labyrinth of Bourbon court politics by totally altering the *status quo*, eliminating the ruling family and placing one of his own relatives upon the Spanish throne.

Prior to making his final decision, the Emperor had sent thousands of troops into Spain under the guise of reinforcing his army in Portugal. By the end of March, over one hundred thousand French troops had entered Spain and were ready to give added weight to whatever policy Napoleon might adopt. Engineer officers had busied themselves mapping Spain's most important fortresses, and the invaders by ruse had already seized several important forts along the northern frontier.

On March 23 Joachim Murat, Napoleon's brother-in-law and a dashing if not overly intelligent cavalryman, entered Madrid with over twenty thousand men and quickly reinforced his garrison to thirty-five thousand. Napoleon's emissaries then lured Ferdinand out of Spain by dangling before him the promises of French recognition and marriage to a Bonapartist princess. In April Ferdinand departed for Bayonne to discuss the details of the offers with the Emperor, but once the Prince was in France, Napoleon bluntly informed him that the House of Bourbon should cease to govern. The Emperor then produced Ferdinand's parents, who had gone to France after their abdication and claimed that the Crown Prince had obtained their abdication by force. Charles, supported by Napoleon, asserted that his abdication was invalid, that he regarded his son as a traitor, and that if Ferdinand did not abandon his illegally won crown he would be treated as a rebel. Recalling the execution of another Bourbon prince, the Duke of Enghien, whom Bonaparte had kidnapped from neutral Germany in 1804, Ferdinand abdicated on May 6. The following day Napoleon manufactured a treaty between himself and Charles, wherein the Spanish King renounced his rights to his throne in favor of the French Emperor's nominee. Napoleon then sent the Spanish Bourbons into a luxurious captivity, induced a group of supine Spanish notables to ask Joseph Bonaparte to become their ruler, ordered Joseph to proceed to Madrid, and gave the Kingdom of Naples to Murat.

Napoleon's triumph was, however, deceptive, for the Spanish people were far less malleable than their rulers. As reasonably accurate rumors of Napoleon's intrigues spread through Madrid, tensions between the inhabitants and the French garrison mounted. Leaflets describing the fate of the royal family circulated freely, and Murat made matters worse by rounding up the remaining members of the Bourbon family. On May 2, 1808, a crowd tried to prevent the French from sending Ferdinand's younger brother out of the country, and one of Murat's battalions fired into the mob. Noise of the musketry roused more people, who took to the streets and began to assault French troopers. Murat in turn called in reinforcements from the suburbs and cleared the streets. The insurgents then took cover in houses and began to snipe at the French, but Murat's men went after them and in four hours quelled all further resistance. About one thousand people, mostly Spanish, died on May 2. Bonaparte assumed that the rising was merely an isolated incident and that Murat's harsh and rapid countermeasures had taught the Spanish a salutary lesson. The May 2 revolt was not, however, the end of popular resistance. Rather, it marked the opening of an insurrectionary movement surpassing in intensity any of the earlier counterrevolutionary risings in the Vendée and Italy.

As word of the Madrid rising spread throughout Spain, antagonism between the populace and the French occupation army grew more bitter, and news of the Bayonne abdications acted as the catalyst for rebellion in the provinces. Between May 23 and June 5, word of Napoleon's coup spread throughout the peninsula, and in areas not directly controlled by French troops the populace took up arms against foreign domination. The revolts were both popular and spontaneous: Crowds murdered pro-French officials, and, not infrequently, individuals who failed to show sufficient enthusiasm for the rebellions, even if they were anti-French, also perished. The rebels then elected juntas to organize and direct the resistance. Although the church hierarchy, the aristocracy, the army, and the government did not support the rising, individual nobles, priests, army officers, and bureaucrats joined the rebellion and dominated the juntas that began to function in Andalusia, Galicia, Aragon, Valencia, and Catalonia. The juntas began to raise troops, and on June 15 the Seville junta, which controlled Andalusia, struck the first blow against Napoleon by bombarding and capturing the French men-of-war, survivors of Trafalgar, lying at Cádiz.[9]

[9] O. Connelly, *Napoleon's Satellite Kingdoms* (New York, 1965), pp. 224–25.

The French reacted by forming large mobile columns and moving against centers of organized resistance. The French army in Spain was, however, not well suited to the tasks before it. Units were filled with half-trained conscripts, while veterans of the Grand Army remained encamped in Germany. Furthermore, regiments in Spain lacked logistical support. In Germany and Italy, imperial forces had obtained supplies by the time-honored method of levying requisitions upon conquered areas, and Napoleon had never bothered to create a well-organized commissary corps. Spain, however, was a relatively poor country with little surplus food. Consequently, French commanders often found themselves in the dilemma of having to choose between risking defeat in detail by scattering their troops in order to find sufficient food or remaining concentrated and starving. Thus in the summer of 1808 French forces in Spain, despite their reputation of invincibility, were in fact singularly unprepared to cope with the tasks of counterinsurgency.[10]

At Valencia and Saragossa Spanish regulars and volunteers repulsed French columns, while in Andalusia the Spanish army waged a successful campaign against General Dupont's force of twenty thousand men, whose orders were to capture Cádiz. Dupont's troops had sacked Cordova, and in reprisal local guerrillas began to attack French foraging parties, which soon found it impossible to operate at any distance from the main body. Unable to find food and worried by the growing numbers of regular and irregular troops gathering against him, Dupont decided to retreat to Madrid. But he failed to move fast enough and Spanish forces seized Bailén, a town directly astride his line of march. The French conscript soldiers rushed the Spanish positions but failed to dislodge their foes. Suffering from the grim summer heat and lack of food and water, Dupont's force became completely demoralized, and to save his corps from total destruction

[10] C. Oman, *A History of the Peninsular War* (London, 1902), I.

the French general surrendered his entire command on July 20. More than seventeen thousand Frenchmen laid down their arms, the first major capitulation of a French army since Bonaparte had come to power.[11] Dupont's troops were not, of course, among the best of Napoleon's legions; but nevertheless, the loss of imperial eagles to some of the worst-trained troops in Europe was a major political disaster for the Emperor.

The Bailén victory naturally encouraged the insurgents to greater efforts, and in August the junta of Galicia sent invitations to other juntas to form a nationwide governmental body. On August 10 three juntas, Galicia, León, and Castile, established a union dedicated to improving the co-ordination of the war effort. Provincial juntas then sent two deputies to a Supreme Central Government Junta of Spain and the Indies, a body which met for the first time in late September at Seville. All parts of Spain not occupied by French armies recognized and obeyed the instructions of the new national directorate.

On the battlefields the Spanish armed forces began to advance on Madrid. On August 1 Joseph, "the intrusive king," fled his capital, while on the same day a thirteen-thousand-man British expedition landed in Portugal to aid the Spanish, harass the French, and open Iberia to English merchants.

Led by Sir Arthur Wellesley, the future Duke of Wellington, who had served in Flanders, India, and in the Copenhagen expedition of 1807, the English troops were well trained and led by officers who had learned how to counter the French tactical system of combining light infantry with massed attacks. Guided by Sir John Moore, who in 1803 had assumed command of the Light Brigade, an elite infantry unit originally designed to perform scouting missions and to harass an enemy line of battle, British officers had improved and modified the linear style

[11] Lovett, *Birth of Modern Spain,* I, pp. 197–222, and *Min. de la Guerre A.H., les armées françaises de 1791 à 1870, Espagne 1807–10 carton Xp33.*

of tactics. Moore had increased the number of light troops and improved their individual training and marksmanship until they were the equal of the French *tirailleur.* In combat their mission was to hold back or drive off the French skirmishers. Moore also thinned his main battle line from three ranks to two, thereby enabling commanders to lengthen their lines, obtain positions from which to deliver enfilading fire, and increase their available firepower. In combat the light troops, after engaging their French counterparts, would fall back to cover the flanks of the line infantry, who would fire aimed volleys and if successful, follow them with a bayonet charge.[12] Moore believed that firepower was superior to shock tactics, and the first battle in Portugal proved the accuracy of his assumptions.

Junot raced forward from Lisbon to throw the British back into the sea, and on August 21, after two minor, indecisive clashes, thirteen thousand French troops assaulted the British force near Vimeiro. Three times the French advanced and on each occasion Wellington's troops hurled them back with heavy losses. Junot was beaten, but at the point of victory a more senior general superseded Wellesley in command of the expedition. Overly cautious and timid, the new commander signed the Convention of Cintra with Junot, agreeing to transport the general's troops back to France with all their arms and equipment. The British thus lost an opportunity to destroy another French force and diminished the political impact of their victory. Still, despite the outcry in London, the expedition had dealt a blow to Bonaparte's prestige and cleared his forces out of Portugal. Furthermore, the Vimeiro triumph, the successful evacuation by the Royal Navy of the Spanish units that Napoleon had

[12] For Wellington's early career and British army reforms see J. Fortescue, *Wellington* (New York, 1925); C. Petrie, *Wellington, a Reassessment* (London, 1956); and M. Glover, *Wellington as Military Commander* (London, 1968). For an older but still useful account see C. Oman, *Wellington's Army* (London, 1913).

earlier transferred to northern Germany, and continued Spanish resistance forced the Emperor to mount a major campaign in Iberia, an area he thought he could conquer by a *coup de main.*

Before crossing the Pyrenees, Napoleon first tried to secure his position in central Europe. In September 1808 he imposed a new treaty upon Prussia forcing Frederick William to pay a huge war indemnity, reduce his army to forty-two thousand men, and agree to continued French occupation of many of his important fortresses. The Emperor then met with Alexander at Erfurt in an effort to secure the latter's continued support. Realizing Napoleon's predicament, Alexander was anxious to profit from the imminent diversion of French strength to Spain. His nobles had expressed their discontent with Russian participation in the continental system, a participation that was producing dolorous effects upon the sale of agricultural products to England. Alexander's diplomats were anti-French. They maintained that if Napoleon continued to expand his power he would be able to block Russian expansion into the Balkans and exclude the Tsar from any real influence in continental affairs. They advocated an alliance with Prussia and Austria as a counterweight to France. Furthermore, the refusal of French and Danish troops to assist his army had limited his progress against the Swedes, and after Tilsit the Emperor had persistently refused to conclude with him a definitive treaty for the partition of the Ottoman Empire. Frustrated by the Corsican's refusal to treat the Tilsit alliance as a league between equals, Alexander was determined to exact a high price for his continued friendship.

The glorious military reviews, the operas, and the gala theatrical performances staged by the Emperor at Erfurt failed to impress the Tsar. Nor did Napoleon's glittering court of sycophant princes alter Alexander's determination to secure the interests of his state. Throughout the interviews between the two rulers, he sought to strengthen Austria and Prussia to balance French influence in eastern Europe, and carefully avoided any further entanglement with the Emperor. In a series of private interviews Talleyrand, believing that his master had overextended himself and was ultimately doomed, secretly encouraged the Tsar in his determination to pursue an independent course. Just before the conclusion of the talks on October 12, the Tsar did agree, however, to renew the Tilsit alliance and to assist France if Austria renewed hostilities. But henceforth, Russia's commitment to the French alliance was to be primarily defensive, a fact that gave Vienna greater initiative in selecting foreign policy alternatives. For his part, Napoleon agreed to withdraw his offer to mediate the Russo-Turkish conflict, which meant that at least for the moment he was abandoning Turkey to Russia's mercy and would pose no further obstacle in the way of Russian expansion in the Balkans, and recognized Alexander's right to annex Moldavia and Wallachia upon the termination of the Anglo-French war. Also, the Emperor agreed to scale down the total contributions due from Prussia and remove his occupation forces. These concessions restored to some degree Prussia's independence and also bolstered Russia's strategic position. The withdrawal of the French army behind the Elbe left Russia as the strongest power in eastern Europe. Thus, in return for Russia's merely passive support, Alexander had wrested several important concessions from Napoleon, lightened Prussia's burdens, and strengthened Austria's position as a useful balance to French influence in eastern Europe. Taken together, events in Spain and at Erfurt indicated to many statesmen that the Emperor of the French was no longer the absolute master of events and that he was not, in fact, invincible.

On the other hand, Napoleon had obtained the security necessary to remove the Grand Army from Germany and throw massive reinforcements into the Iberian peninsula in order to win a rapid and complete victory that would restore his power and prestige throughout Europe.

By November, over two hundred thousand veteran troops led personally by the Emperor were ready to overwhelm all Spanish resistance. Spanish regular forces numbered about the same. But they were poorly trained and equipped and, as usual, badly led. Stretched along the line of the Ebro River, they were ill prepared to meet the Emperor's concentrated assaults. On November 7 two corps led by marshals Victor and Lefebvre struck the Spanish left, and by the eleventh the Spanish were in full flight toward the hills of Galicia. Meanwhile, Soult had struck for Burgos, entering the city on November 10. He then swung north to assist his colleagues in the destruction of the Spanish left, and on the fourteenth his forces captured part of the retreating Spanish army at Reinosa. Napoleon then sent detachments to pursue the remnants of the Spanish left wing and launched another massive blow against his feeble opponents—this time against their center and right. On November 23 Marshal Lannes defeated a force that outnumbered his two to one and trapped forty-five thousand troops in Saragossa. This attack in turn forced the Spanish armies in Catalonia and Aragon to retreat from the Ebro in a desperate effort to avoid encirclement. Napoleon then ordered Victor's corps to take Madrid. Brushing aside all opposition, the French reached the outskirts of the city by December 2. The junta government fled south; the Emperor's artillery opened fire upon the city on the third, the garrison fled that night, and French troops entered the capital the next morning.

Thinking the campaign almost concluded, the Emperor prepared to complete the destruction of the Spanish field armies and crush a British force that had entered Spain in a desperate attempt to bolster the decimated Spanish ranks. Led by Sir John Moore, the British had advanced from Portugal into northern Spain, where reinforcements, landed at the port of Corunna, brought the army's strength to about twenty-eight thousand. After the fall of Madrid, Moore contemplated a retreat to Portugal, but British diplomats, Spanish officials, and many of his own officers advocated continuing the march in the hope of revitalizing resistance. Moore agreed, and ordered his force to move on Burgos in order to threaten Napoleon's communications with France.

Surprised by Moore's audacity, the Emperor quickly recovered his composure and hurled thousands of troops against the British in a vast enveloping movement. Moore had no choice but to retreat and led his army back toward Corunna and the safety of the British fleet, which had sailed to the northern Spanish coast to render logistical support to the army. From there he could, if necessary, evacuate his force. Convinced that the Peninsular War was all but over, Bonaparte departed for Paris on January 1, 1809, leaving the pursuit of the English to Marshal Soult. Moore, however, managed to elude his foes. Despite harsh conditions and a rapid decline of discipline and morale, the British outmarched the French veterans. In the hills around the port Moore's men again proved the superiority of their new tactics by beating off all of Soult's attacks. Moore perished in the fighting of January 14, but his subordinates completed the embarkation, and the expedition reached England safely. By these maneuvers, the British proved they had profited from the victories of Trafalgar and Copenhagen. They had shown themselves able to send large forces to foreign shores, supply them, and evacuate them in the face of overwhelming odds, and in 1809 the Royal Navy was ready to mount similar operations whenever an opportunity presented itself.

In a more immediate sense, the British expedition, though a tactical failure, produced a number of strategic benefits for the English and their Iberian allies. Even after the Corunna evacuation, a British garrison continued to hold Lisbon, thus keeping Portugal in the war. If the Cabinet desired it could use its navy and its foothold on the Continent to mount another military expedition against the French. Furthermore, the pursuit of

Moore's troops had seriously dislocated the Emperor's plans for the rapid subjugation of Spanish resistance. The weeks devoted to chasing Moore gave the insurrection time to take a deeper hold upon the will of the populace, with the result that military victories did not bring political triumphs in their wake. After Corunna, Soult marched into Galicia and northern Portugal; other units routed a Spanish army attempting to liberate Madrid, and two more corps conquered Saragossa by February 20, but none of these victories broke the Spaniards' will to resist.

Defeated in the field, the Spanish reverted to a far more effective style of combat—guerrilla warfare. The very term *guerrilla*, used to describe irregular partisan bands waging a war of attrition and harassment against regular forces, is of Spanish origin, for partisan activity was the military response that best suited Spanish abilities and minimized their shortcomings. Guerrilla warfare enabled the populace as a whole to join in the resistance to the intrusive King and his French armies, either as members of partisan bands or as active sympathizers supplying intelligence and logistical support to the fighting cadres. Talented individuals could rise rapidly and act effectively in irregular units and were not hampered by the poor leadership, faulty tactics, and stifling limitations of the Spanish standing army. Furthermore, the terrain in much of the peninsula, plus the shortage of food, favored the activities of flexible, mobile, partisan units.

Guerrillas had taken up arms as early as the spring of 1808, but the juntas had devoted their major efforts to raising regular armies. In the wake of Moore's retreat and the defeat of the conventional armed forces, the Spanish resorted in ever growing numbers to partisan tactics. During the course of the Peninsular War, between thirty-five-to fifty thousand people joined the guerrilla bands. Partisans came from all walks of life, although most were of peasant origin. The bulk of the populace sympathized with and supported the guerrillas, and the Supreme Junta recognized their importance by issuing in 1809 a decree authorizing privateering on land. But the Spanish Government never really controlled the formation and activities of the partisans, who were a reflection of a more general resistance to foreign intervention.

Guerrillas operated in all regions of Spain. In Navarre a young man known simply as Mina led attacks on French couriers and convoys. When he was captured in 1810, his uncle, also known as Mina, took his place and ruthlessly extended his control over other partisan bands, welding them into a highly effective force. He waged a bitter war with the French, giving no quarter and taking no prisoners. The French responded with equal viciousness but without success. By 1812, thirty-seven thousand French troops badly needed in combat zones proved unable to halt Mina's raids and ambushes.

In León and Castile partisans waged an effective campaign against French communications with Portugal, while in Catalonia guerrillas operating in small bands constantly harassed French convoys.[13] Even the region around Madrid was unsafe, for a certain El Empecinado, with a band of twenty-five hundred men, harassed the armies of King Joseph and supplied the British in Portugal with valuable intelligence seized from ambushed messengers. In Galicia partisans attacked French coastal garrisons, frequently in co-operation with the Royal Navy. Guerrillas in the Pyrenees made forays into France, carrying away livestock and money, and in Andalusia partisans fought a vicious round of small-unit actions, blinding prisoners with spikes, burning wounded Frenchmen alive, and even lowering a captured general slowly into a vat of boiling water so that his screams provided a gruesome afternoon's entertainment for the insurgents.

[13] *Min. de la Guerre A.H., M.h., Retraite des armées françaises d'Espagne 774.* This is a staff report written in 1813 dealing in part with the problem of maintaining communications in the face of constant guerrilla attacks.

Led by students, noblemen, clerics, soldiers, and members of the bourgeoisie—a cross section of Spain's elites—the guerrillas fought in defense of their old monarchy, their Church, and their local dwelling places. They fought against a foreign King, imposed by foreign bayonets. Joseph's well-intentioned reforms—a new constitution and court system, suppression of church courts, guilds, and the feudal system, and the funding of the Bourbon debt—failed to produce a surge of popular support for his regime, for he could never remove the stigma of Napoleonic domination nor assuage outraged local, provincial, and national loyalties.

Nor did the presence of as many as 360,000 French troops solve the problem of defeating the insurgents, although French tactics were both clever and resourceful. Garrisons and patrols held the major towns and communication routes; commanders employed baited columns to lure the partisans into ambushes, and mobile units, rotated frequently to keep the troops fresh, constantly pursued the insurgent bands to prevent them from establishing base camps and wear them down by forcing them into perpetual action. The French also employed the device of passing false information to the Spanish to lure them into traps or cause disunity among the paramilitary groups. But tactical victories, and there were many, did not suffice to overcome the political failure to win popular acceptance for the Josephist regime. French generals with rare exceptions did little to assist the Spanish civil authorities. Napoleon in fact placed most of Spain under military governments commanded by generals who answered not to Joseph at Madrid but to the imperial government at Paris. The generals naturally sought a military solution to the guerrilla problem, but massive reprisals plus organized plundering, far from terrorizing the Spanish into submission, only produced equally brutal counterreprisals. Consequently, Joseph, his advisers, and a small coterie of pro-French Spaniards remained isolated in Madrid while a rising tide of violence swept the provinces.[14]

The political failure to win popular support and popular insurrection against French control had sweeping strategic consequences. The guerrilla war, in addition to forcing the French to employ tens of thousands of troops in counterinsurgency operations, also produced a steady drain on their manpower. Some estimates claim that Bonaparte's armies lost a hundred men a day for six years in small, bitter clashes. Even if this claim is exaggerated, it is nevertheless true that French losses were severe.[15] Consequently, the French were unable to throw the full weight of their human and material resources against the British, who capitalized upon Spanish insurgency to renew their campaign in Portugal.

In the first months of 1809 the Cabinet had to decide whether to reinforce or evacuate the garrison that had remained in Lisbon during Moore's campaign. Wellesley assured the government that he could hold Lisbon with relatively small forces against vastly superior numbers of Frenchmen, and the Cabinet decided to take the risk of maintaining a field army on the Continent. Absolved of all blame for signing the Cintra Convention,[16] Wellesley returned to Portugal on April 22 and assumed control of the British and Portuguese forces.

After organizing his commissariat department and re-

[14] See Lovett, *Birth of Modern Spain*, II, pp. 507–8; *Min. de la Guerre A.H., Les armées françaises de 1791 à 1870 Espagne 1810–1812, carton Xp34;* and P. Paret and J. W. Shy, *Guerrillas in the 1960's* (New York, 1962), pp. 6–9, which deal with the Spanish insurrection in the context of partisan warfare. See also O. Connelly, *The Gentle Bonaparte: A Biography of Joseph, Napoleon's Elder Brother* (New York, 1968), p. 168.

[15] Lovett, *Birth of Modern Spain*, II, p. 683, states that the French between 1808 and 1813 lost 180,000 men to the guerrillas while killing about 25,000 partisans.

[16] There had been a tremendous outcry in Parliament against the convention and all of the generals involved, but it had soon become clear that it was not Wellesley but his superiors who were responsible. The government therefore gave him a new command.

ceiving reinforcements, Wellesley at the head of eighteen thousand men moved out of Lisbon heading north. His objective was to defeat Soult's thirteen-thousand-man force, which had taken up positions behind the Douro River in northern Portugal. On May 12 British troops reached the river and a small force managed to find some barges in which to make a surprise crossing. After securing a foothold on the French side, the advance force held off French counterattacks while Wellesley rushed more men to their assistance. Soult's hasty attacks failed, and having insufficient strength to continue the battle, he retreated toward Spain. By May 19 the French, having lost some four thousand men, crossed the Spanish frontier, leaving Wellesley in full control of Portugal.[17]

Wellesley then marched against Marshal Victor, who was massing twenty thousand men on Portugal's eastern frontier for a march on Lisbon. To dislocate the impending attack, Wellesley decided to drive on Madrid in conjunction with a thirty-thousand-man Spanish army. The English and Spanish forces concentrated at Talavera, some eighty miles southeast of Madrid, but before they could commence their advance, fifty-five thousand French troops attacked. British units bore the brunt of the attack, as the Spanish forces remained virtually stationary throughout the battle. During the fighting of July 27 the French charged and failed to break the English lines. A British division tried to pursue the French, but were turned upon and driven back in disorder. Wellesley rushed reinforcements to the threatened portion of the line, however, and soon restored the situation. Having lost seven thousand men, the French did not mount a new attack. The British for their part remained at Talavera for six days, and then fell back to Portugal

[17] On the organization of the British army see S. G. P. Ward, *Wellington's Headquarters* (London, 1957), and G. Davies, *Wellington and His Army* (Oxford, 1954). On the campaign in northern Portugal see N. J. Soult, *Mémoires du Maréchal-Général Soult Duc de Dalmatie,* 3 vols. (Paris, 1854), II, Ch. IV, and M. Glover, *Wellington's Peninsular Victories* (London, 1963), p. 16.

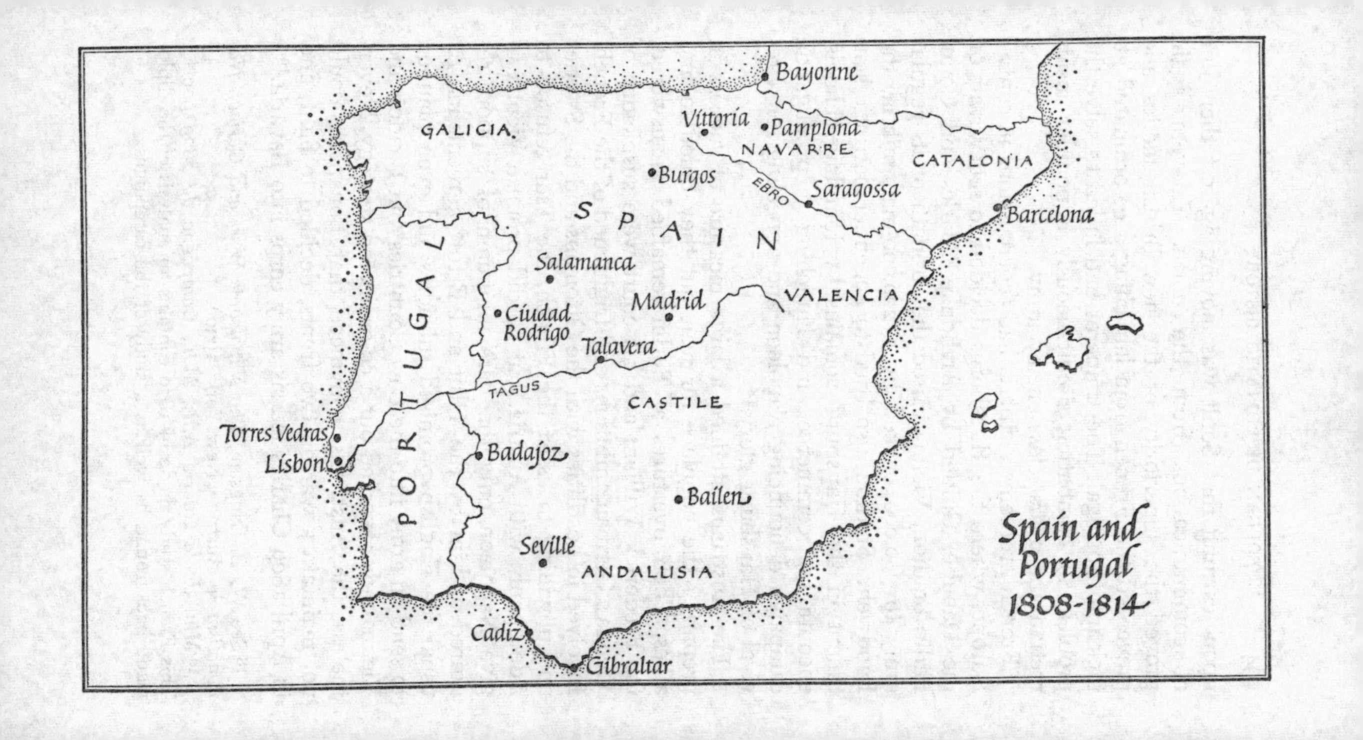
Bayonne
Vittoria
Pamplona
GALICIA
NAVARRE
CATALONIA
Burgos
EBRO
Saragossa
Barcelona
SPAIN
PORTUGAL
Salamanca
Madrid
VALENCIA
Ciudad Rodrigo
Talavera
TAGUS
CASTILE
Torres Vedras
Lisbon
Badajoz
Bailen
Seville
ANDALUSIA
Cadiz
Gibraltar
Spain and Portugal 1808-1814

upon learning that Soult was moving against their line of communications from the north. Talavera again proved the superiority of the new British tactics and prevented the French from launching a co-ordinated attack into Portugal. The Emperor had failed to solve the problem of combating simultaneously a popular insurrection and a first-class enemy army.

French problems in Iberia had repercussions in central Europe, where the Hapsburgs decided to renew war on the Danube. Guided by Archduke Charles and Count Philip Stadion, Vienna raised the strength of its regular army to 300,000 backed by a 200,000-man militia, the Landwehr. Stadion also tried to engender patriotic sentiment in the Hapsburg domains by founding schools, encouraging commerce, and launching a propaganda campaign denouncing Napoleon and appealing for a revival of Hapsburg glory.[18]

The Austrians attained a large measure of success in preparing the populace for war, but they failed to find allies. Their overtures at Berlin remained unanswered, for Frederick William and his court were suspicious of Vienna's German ambitions and frightened of the French. Involved in hostilities with the Ottomans and the Swedes and unwilling to assist the French, the Tsar refused to side openly with Austria, but he did promise Vienna to give Napoleon only the bare minimum of support required of him by the Tilsit and Erfurt agreements. As usual the English promised subsidies and even planned to send an army into the Low Countries, but London and Vienna never worked out a co-ordinated strategy. Nevertheless, the Austrians, convinced that Bonaparte could not maintain a war on two fronts, decided to fight, and in April 1809 Charles led six army corps into Bavaria.[19]

[18] See W. C. Langsam, *The Napoleonic Wars and German Nationalism in Austria* (New York, 1930).

[19] *Min. de la Guerre A.H., M.h., Campagne de 1809* 900^{bis2}. This French study made in 1870 contains an analysis of the diplomatic background as well as a study of the campaigns.

Napoleon as usual responded quickly. He called conscripts to the colors, brought units back from Spain, and gathered a striking force of some two hundred thousand men in southern Germany. Although his army was below the quality of the men of 1805–7 due to the admixture of recruits and foreign troops, the Emperor nonetheless decided to follow his typical strategy of attempting to shatter his opponent's will to resist by inflicting sharp military defeats upon him at the outset of the war.

Gathering his divisions along the southern Danube, Bonaparte launched a series of attacks against isolated Austrian corps, and by April 20 he had halted Charles's offensive and was pursuing the Archduke through Bavaria. By May 12, French troops entered Vienna while Napoleon's generals in Italy marched on Austria from the south. Stirrings of German nationalism and popular resistance to foreign domination did little to alter the course of the campaign. Baron von Dornberg's rising in the Kingdom of Westphalia failed to rouse mass support and collapsed. A Prussian major, Frederick Schill, also invaded Westphalia in an attempt to raise a popular insurrection and force his government to take up arms against Napoleon. Once again the masses remained passive, the Prussian Government disavowed Schill's actions, and the French ultimately ran down and killed the rebel major. Duke Frederick William of Brunswick formed a Black Legion, seventeen hundred men strong, and even managed to seize Dresden for a short time, but this successful coup led to no popular movement. The Duke had to flee to the North Sea coast, where the British rescued him and his followers. A peasant insurrection in the Tyrol led by Andreas Hofer enjoyed momentary triumphs since the French were content to contain the Tyrolese partisans until they dealt with the Austrians. After the fall of Vienna, however, Hofer was unable to obtain aid from the Hapsburgs and his rising was doomed. Thus, if the German partisans of 1809 contributed to the legend of national resistance to Napoleonic imperialism, their real military and political contribution was minimal. Unlike the Spanish, the Germans did not offer massive popular resistance to the French armies and the outcome of the war hinged upon the actions of the regular armies on the banks of the Danube.

On May 19 Napoleon's troops seized Lobau Island and on the twentieth began to cross to the Austrian side of the river. The French occupied the villages of Aspern and Essling to cover their left and right flanks, but on May 21 Charles launched a massive attack in an effort to destroy part of the Emperor's army before reinforcements could follow the advanced units across the river. The French repulsed all attacks upon Essling while at Aspern the Austrians took the village and then abandoned most of it when Masséna organized a counterattack.

Fighting resumed on the twenty-second with a French thrust against the Austrian center. The advance made good progress until the Austrians floated barges down the river and broke the French bridges. Lacking the reinforcements and extra ammunition necessary to complete their breakthrough, the French had to halt their advance and fight desperately to stave off new Austrian attacks. Aspern changed hands four times until Masséna finally secured it. On the other flank six Austrian columns penetrated Essling, but the Young Guard, formed in 1809 and consisting of light infantry battalions recruited from the best physical specimens among new conscripts, recovered the town after bitter fighting. In the center the French repulsed all Charles's attacks. Austrian artillery then began to pound the French lines. Due to ammunition shortages the Emperor's field guns could not reply, and his infantry absorbed severe punishment, although it did not break. In the afternoon Charles broke off the battle, having lost some twenty-three thousand men while inflicting twenty thousand casualties on Napoleon's army.

Although he remained in possession of the battlefield and caused heavier losses than he absorbed, Bonaparte for the first time since 1799 had failed to win decisively a major battle. He had sent part of his army across a river without adequate preparations, repeating the Russian blunder at Friedland, and nearly suffered a major defeat. After the battle, he evacuated his bridgehead and withdrew to Lobau Island, thus giving credence to Vienna's victory proclamations.

Still, it would take more than a single setback to stop Napoleon, and he immediately took steps to renew his offensive before other powers could take the results of Aspern-Essling as a sign to intervene. On his side of the river he gathered 180,000 men and collected pontoons, rafts, small boats, and portable bridges to guarantee the safety of his next river crossing. In less than two weeks he was ready to strike again.

On July 5 under cover of a heavy artillery bombardment three corps crossed the Danube several miles to the east of the old battleground and moved against Charles, who had pulled his forces back to high ground around the village of Wagram. Both sides deployed their men and prepared themselves for a decisive battle on the following morning.

Both Napoleon and Charles attacked on July 6. Bonaparte ordered the bulk of his army to move directly on Wagram while Davout's corps crumpled the Austrian left. Charles threw his main assault against the French left with orders to take Aspern and Essling and cut the imperial army off from the Danube. Bitter but indecisive fighting soon raged around Wagram, while the Austrian right began to threaten the Emperor's left. Bonaparte then sent a battery of 102 field guns to check the Austrian advance and ordered Macdonald to launch a counterattack. The marshal drew up three divisions in a single mass formation and, covered by the artillery, sent it forward. The French checked Charles's advance, and along the rest of the battle front Napoleon's troops moved forward. Wagram fell. Davout began to push in the Austrian left, and Charles finally gave orders to retreat. He made his withdrawal in good order but left forty-three thousand casualties behind. Bonaparte had lost thirty-four thousand men, and his army was too tired to pursue, but Wagram was nevertheless a decisive victory, for it broke the Austrian will to continue the war.

Despairing of further resistance, Charles requested an armistice, and Francis sued for peace. Meanwhile, a British expedition had landed in Flanders, but it arrived too late to influence the Austrian decision. The British took Flushing as a preliminary step in an advance on Antwerp, but instead of continuing their advance they took up defensive positions on Walcheren Island. Contained by second-line troops and decimated by disease, the English clung to their foothold until late September, when the navy evacuated the shattered remnants of the 35,000-man force. With this defeat the Portland government collapsed. George Canning, the ambitious, clever, and aggressive Foreign Secretary who had opposed the expedition, fought a duel with Viscount Castlereagh, who as Secretary for War had supported the attack. Both then resigned. Portland died of a stroke before the end of the year, and a new fragile coalition headed by Spencer Perceval took office.

The Austrians meanwhile continued negotiations with the French and signed a peace treaty on October 14, 1809. The peace of Schönbrunn imposed heavy sacrifices on the Hapsburgs. Francis had to relinquish Salzburg and Engadine to Bavaria, Galicia to the Grand Duchy of Warsaw, and Trieste to France, with a total loss of 3,500,000 subjects. Francis also had to agree to reduce his army to 150,000 men, pay a huge war indemnity, break with England, and join the continental system. At the end of the year the French Emperor divorced his wife, and in the spring of 1810 concluded a marriage with a Hapsburg princess. The marriage alarmed the Tsar, but Bonaparte was willing to pay this price, for his Hapsburg bride could bear children and secure the Bonaparte dynasty's succession, and the new Empress graphically symbolized Austria's dependent status.

Central Europe was not the only area of French expansion in 1809. In Italy the Corsican annexed the Papal States to the French Empire and made a virtual prisoner of the Pope. In the Baltic the Swedes had lost Finland to Alexander's armies, and the Danes had frustrated a Swedish attempt to invade Norway. The British had sent an expedition to the Baltic in 1808, but the English and Swedes could not agree on a common policy, and London had finally withdrawn its forces. As Sweden's position worsened, cliques of nobles, civil servants, and military men conspired to rid themselves of King Gustavus IV. In March the conspirators deposed their monarch, placed his uncle upon the throne as Charles XIII, and made peace with Russia by sacrificing Finland and the Åland Islands and joining the continental system. Diplomatically isolated, the Swedes sought to win French support by nominating one of Napoleon's marshals to succeed the childless Charles XIII. In August 1810 the Swedes proclaimed Marshal Bernadotte, the ex-Jacobin who bore an antimonarchical tatoo on his arm, ex-War Minister of the Directory, and member of the Napoleonic nobility, as heir apparent. Charles later adopted the Gascon general, giving him the title of Crown Prince and the name Charles John.[20] Bernadotte held personal and political grievances against the Corsican, for as a political Jacobin and the darling of the left in 1799, he had been levered out of office by Bonaparte's allies at the time of the latter's coup, which he had opposed. Afterward, he never obtained any position of real power or influence and he naturally objected to his relegation to the rank of a mere servant of the Emperor. In his new position, although he had no intention of remaining forever a satellite of the French Empire, Bernadotte nevertheless at first aligned

[20] F. D. Scott, "Bernadotte and the Throne of France, 1814," in *Journal of Modern History* (1933), V. This article contains a discussion of Bernadotte's accession and his early policy.

himself with France, thereby increasing Napoleonic influence in the Baltic and the effectiveness of the economic war against England.

While fighting in Spain and in central Europe, the Emperor had been unable to conduct his economic policy with full vigor. The British had maintained their commerce by exploiting Brazilian and South American markets and by conducting a lucrative smuggling trade with Dutch and north German merchants. To reduce illicit trade the Emperor in January 1810 authorized the sale of prize cargoes subject to a substantial duty that would go to enrich the French treasury. In August he legalized the importation of colonial products and began to sell licenses to French merchants, permitting them to import goods from Britain provided they exported products of equivalent value. At the end of the year Napoleon ordered the confiscation of all English products in Europe save those granted immunity under the license system. To enforce these and his other economic decrees, Napoleon proceeded to incorporate the Kingdom of Holland and northwestern Germany into the French Empire.

French officials and soldiers began to enforce the imperial edicts, which contributed to a sharp decline in England's commercial prosperity. Britain's trade with Europe fell sharply and, coupled with overinvestment in South America, the revival of the Non-Intercourse Act by the American Government, and continued high imports, this produced for her an unfavorable trade balance and a severe economic crisis. Unemployment grew along with labor unrest, thousands of banks and businesses failed in 1810–11, and the pound suffered a heavy depreciation. Thus rigorous application of the continental system placed a severe strain upon Britain's ability to wage war.

The territorial expansion of France in 1810 may have had more than economic implications, for many believe that Napoleon was intent upon transforming his federative imperial system into a unitary Roman-style regime governed from Paris. The annexations of 1809 and 1810 may have been the first steps in the abolition of all territorial sovereignties except that wielded by the Emperor.[21] Since Napoleon was constantly evolving plans ranging from temporary expedients to grand strategy, it is difficult if not impossible to fathom his ultimate designs upon the Continent he dominated. Furthermore, the Corsican realized that before he could implement any far-reaching, grandiose scheme he first had to solve a series of interconnected and immediate strategic and diplomatic problems. He had to establish his authority in Spain and Portugal, drive the British army into the sea, and at the same time keep his satellites and reluctant allies tied to his economic and political system. Upon his ability to accomplish these awe-inspiring tasks rested the future of French hegemony.

[21] E. Driault, "La politique extérieure de Napoléon Ier," in *Revue des études napoléoniennes* (1915), VII, pp. 12, 27, and 37.

CHAPTER 10

COLLAPSE

For the reduction of Spain and Portugal the Emperor sent tens of thousands of reinforcements south of the Pyrenees, bringing his troop strength there to more than 350,000 men. The Spanish guerrillas, however, were so effective that he could spare but 65,000 men for a campaign in Portugal. Reluctantly, Masséna accepted command of the Army of Portugal and in the summer of 1810 the marshal, suffering from advancing years, ill health, and the exertions of the previous year's battles, set about implementing his Emperor's orders for the methodical conquest of Portugal and the expulsion of the British army from Europe.[1]

Masséna first captured the Spanish frontier fortress of Ciudad Rodrigo, thereby opening an invasion route into Portugal, and then in August reduced the Portuguese fortifications at Almeida and prepared to march on Lisbon. To his dismay, however, the marshal discovered that Portugal's terrain was incredibly rugged, that his maps were inaccurate, and that his Portuguese guides were actually quite ignorant about local road systems. Furthermore, the British and Portuguese had worked hard and effectively to make conditions even more treacherous. Local guerrillas stood ready to harass the French army, and units of the allied regular forces had evacuated or destroyed pack animals, food, and fodder.

[1] For the campaign in Portugal see *Min. de la Guerre A.H., M.h., Campagne de Portugal 918[1]; Min. de la Guerre A.H., M.h., Armée du Portugal 919;* J. Marshall-Cornwall, *Marshal Massena* (London, 1965), pp. 185–87; A. Augustin-Thierry, *Masséna* (Paris, 1947), pp. 300–1; and C. Oman, *A History of the Peninsular War* (London, 1908).

Thus when the French moved forward in September, they moved into a desert.[2]

Guerrilla attacks and Masséna's own declining vigor slowed the Army of Portugal's advance while Wellesley, by now elevated to the peerage as the Duke of Wellington, concentrated some fifty thousand men on Bussaco ridge, about fifty miles northeast of Lisbon. His object was to delay further Masséna's progress while his engineers completed the construction of a series of fortified lines around Lisbon. Hoping to crush the British before they could get into their defensive positions, Masséna rejected his subordinates' suggestions for further reconnaissance and flanking maneuvers and on September 27 ordered a frontal assault on the ridge line. French divisions moved forward but could not break through the English line. Wellesley lost twelve hundred men but inflicted over forty-four hundred casualties on Masséna and then withdrew to his fortifications.

During the summer Wellesley had transformed the area around Lisbon into a vast entrenched camp stretching from the Atlantic coast to the banks of the Tagus. The defense works consisted of a series of fortified lines, and each line was composed of mutually supporting strong points held by second-line troops. The first series of fortified posts ran through the village of Torres Vedras, from which the whole complex derived its name. Behind the fixed defensive works thirty-five thousand British and twenty-five thousand Portuguese regulars stood ready to fall upon any French column that managed to fight its way into open terrain. With the Royal Navy providing all necessary logistical support, Wellesley intended to remain on the defensive until fruitless attacks and supply shortages weakened his opponent, and then spring forward and destroy him.

At the end of the year the Army of Portugal arrived

[2] *Min. de la Guerre A.H., M.h., Notice sur la campagne de Portugal en 1810 et 1811 748.* This account was written by one of Masséna's aides, General Pelet.

before the Torres Vedras positions, and Masséna immediately realized the impossibility of taking them by direct frontal assault. He therefore encamped his army before the Anglo-Portuguese lines and watched it waste away from desertion, disease, starvation, and guerrilla ambushes. By January 1811 he had lost about eighteen thousand men, and because of the continual pressure of partisan warfare in Spain, the Emperor was unable to do more than replace his losses. Consequently, Masséna was never able to gather sufficient troops for a full-scale attack upon the Anglo-Portuguese army. The Army of Portugal maintained itself opposite the Torres Vedras lines until March, when Masséna finally had to admit failure and pull his depleted forces back to central Portugal. The British launched a rapid if unco-ordinated pursuit, forcing the marshal to retreat all the way back to the Spanish frontier save for a garrison at Almeida. Farther south, Soult had managed to take Badajoz, an important frontier fortress, but Masséna's retreat and the continued Spanish resistance at Cádiz minimized the strategic impact of his success.

Having cleared Portugal of French troops, Wellington next laid siege to Almeida, and Masséna prepared to march to the garrison's relief. On May 3 the two armies met midway between Almeida and the Spanish stronghold of Ciudad Rodrigo. Once again Wellington positioned his forces along a ridge line, and anchored his right flank upon the village of Fuentes de Oñoro. Masséna launched frontal attacks, and the British, after driving back the French light infantry, repulsed the rushing columns with rapid musket volleys. On May 5 Masséna attacked again, thrusting at Wellington's right. The British quickly swung their line through a right angle and inflicted another bloody repulse upon the Army of Portugal. Shortly after the battle, Napoleon relieved Masséna and sent him into permanent retirement, a poor end to a glorious military career.

Meanwhile, a detached British force laid siege to Badajoz. Marshal Soult led twenty-five thousand men against the English, but on May 16, at Albuera, he failed to dislodge his opponents and suffered heavy losses. Wellington then moved his main force south and renewed attacks upon Badajoz. Lacking heavy artillery, he could not take the fortress, and when the French concentrated sixty thousand men near the town Wellington abandoned his siege. The French, however, did not attack, and after a few weeks, Soult led part of the army back into Andalusia to deal with renewed partisan activity, and Auguste Marmont, a vain, ambitious officer who had served in the artillery corps as Bonaparte's aide-de-camp, and later became the governor in Dalmatia, took the remainder into Castile to find supplies.[3] Thus, despite his inability to take Badajoz, Wellington had achieved a strategic success. He had forced Masséna out of Portugal, beaten off a major counterattack at Fuentes de Oñoro, and prevented Soult and Marmont from launching a new invasion. By the fall of 1811, the French were no longer contemplating attacks upon Portugal. Rather, they were seeking to prevent a British thrust into Spain.

After leaving Badajoz, Wellington moved north to blockade Ciudad Rodrigo until the arrival of heavy guns from England enabled him to mount a full-scale siege. Marmont brought fifty-eight thousand troops to the frontier, but since the British moved into strong defensive positions, he did not attack. Supply shortages and constant partisan harassment ultimately forced Marmont to retreat, and Wellington, having received his siege artillery, closed in on Ciudad Rodrigo. Early in January 1812 his large-caliber cannon began to bombard the fortress, and on January 19, storming parties entered the fort and compelled the garrison to surrender.[4]

Wellington then shifted his line of operations to the

[3] *Min. de la Guerre A.H., M.h., Bataille de Albuera 768.*

[4] M. Glover, *Wellington's Peninsular Victories* (London, 1963), pp. 57–59; and *Min. de la Guerre A.H., M.h., Commencement de la Campagne de 1812 en Espagne 918[1].*

south in a new effort to take Badajoz. Early in April the English stormed, captured, and plundered the fortress and town. They lost five thousand men but had captured the last major bastion guarding the routes to the interior of Spain. By the summer of 1812 Wellington was ready to march on Madrid, but at the same time Napoleon was preparing to launch a larger campaign of his own by marching on Moscow.

Despite their formal ties, Alexander and Napoleon were suspicious of each other, and in the months following the defeat of Austria their relations steadily worsened. The addition of Galicia—the Polish province taken by Austria in the First Partition of 1772—to the Grand Duchy of Warsaw alarmed the Tsar. The latter felt that despite the Emperor's promises never to re-establish a Polish kingdom and to keep the duchy limited in both size and independence, the duchy could well become a focal point for a revived Polish state and renewed French and Polish ambitions to expand its frontiers all the way to the borders of the old prepartition kingdom, i.e., all the way to the Dnieper River. With millions of restive Polish and Lithuanian subjects under his sway, Alexander naturally regarded the pro-French Warsaw regime as a threat to his security and his position as a major power.

The French Emperor's Balkan policy also alarmed and angered the Tsar. At Tilsit Napoleon had discussed the probable partition of the moribund Ottoman Empire, but by 1810 he was avoiding talks about specific plans for the division of the spoils. Alexander soon realized that his nominal ally had no immediate intention of allowing Russia to obtain Constantinople and the Straits.[5]

Russian adherence to the continental system provided still another irritant in the relations between Paris and St.

[5] A. de Nesselrode, ed., *Lettres et papiers du Chancelier Comte de Nesselrode* (Paris, 1905), III, pp. 258–59 and 417–18 indicates that the Tsar was also alarmed by the French-Austrian marriage and by French expansion in northern Germany.

Petersburg. Trade with England declined, and Russian merchants and noblemen engaged in commercial agriculture protested vigorously the loss of their best customer. Napoleon's refusal to lower French tariffs and absorb some of Russia's surplus indicated that the Corsican would at least have no objection to transforming Russia into a French commercial satellite. Alexander, recalling the fate of Paul I, realized that he had to retain the support of the aristocracy or face the possibility of a *coup d'état*. Thus power rivalries, economic considerations, and the domestic political balance combined to influence the Tsar to reorient his foreign policy.

Consequently, in 1810, when Napoleon insisted that Alexander confiscate neutral ships in Russian ports on the grounds that they were carrying English products, the Tsar refused. By opening his state to British goods conveyed in neutral vessels the Romanov ruler ruptured not only the continental system but also the Tilsit alliance. Finally, on December 31, 1810, Alexander made the break with France definitive, on this day issuing a decree explicitly favoring the entry of neutral shipping into his ports and simultaneously placing a prohibitive tariff upon the chief French exports to Russia.

Both Alexander and Napoleon then undertook diplomatic and military measures to prepare for what both had come to regard as an inevitable clash. Alexander was determined to resist French domination and if possible extend his influence into Poland and Germany; Napoleon hoped to subdue Russia, reduce Alexander's power, and force him to conform to his own policies.

Alexander first tried to win the support of the Warsaw Poles by promising to establish an autonomous Polish state within the Russian Empire. The Poles, however, remained unmoved by promises from a power that had so often despoiled them in the not so distant past. The Tsar's manifest interest in expanding his influence westward alarmed the Prussian and Austrian rulers as well. The idea of a Russian-dominated Poland was no more pleasing to Berlin and Vienna than the existence of the French-oriented duchy of Warsaw. Neither the Hapsburg nor the Hohenzollern monarch was willing to risk another war with Napoleon simply to pass Polish territory from France to Russia. Thus, despite their desire to throw off Napoleonic domination, neither Prussia nor Austria could see any possible military or diplomatic advantages in joining Russia, and both courts decided to retain their ties with France while doing as little as possible to aid either antagonist. On February 24, 1812, Frederick William agreed to furnish Napoleon twenty thousand troops for use in a campaign against Russia and to permit French troops to march through his domains and make requisitions whose value would be deducted from unpaid war indemnities. On March 14, Francis promised to provide a thirty-thousand-man corps to Napoleon's army. Alexander thus failed to gain allies in central Europe, and consequently had to abandon plans to carry hostilities west of the Vistula and was forced to prepare instead a defensive campaign.

Better fortune crowned the Tsar's efforts to eliminate threats to Finland and the Ukraine by coming to terms with Sweden and the Ottoman Empire. The Crown Prince, Bernadotte, had never intended to follow blindly Napoleon's directives, and although he had in the name of the senile Charles XIII declared war upon England, he did not prosecute it vigorously and connived at promoting the flourishing contraband trade between Swedish and English merchants. The French Emperor retaliated by seizing Swedish Pomerania early in 1812, but even the loss of a province failed to force the Swedish Crown Prince to enforce rigorously the continental system and remain in the status of humble satellite. In April 1812, having negotiated with the Tsar and the Emperor, Bernadotte decided to side with the Russians, who promised to deliver Norway, part of the Danish kingdom, into his hands. The French on the other hand, allied to Denmark, could not make such an attractive offer. Sweden and Russia concluded an alliance that freed the former from French dominance and secured the latter's northern and Baltic provinces from the threat of a Swedish attack. In May the Tsar ended his long war with the Turks by abandoning Moldavia and Wallachia and his support of the Serb rebellion and keeping only Bessarabia. By agreeing to a moderate peace, Alexander neutralized the Ottoman armies and freed his own southern army for employment against Napoleon's forces.

Napoleon, meanwhile, was gathering a gigantic invasion army from every corner of Europe. French, Italian, Austrian, Prussian, Rhine Confederation, Swiss, Dutch, Croat, Spanish, Portuguese, and Polish units began to march east until by the beginning of June 1812 some 674,000 men awaited their Emperor's order to march against the Tsar.

Under his personal command Napoleon gathered the Imperial Guards, two cavalry, and three infantry corps, a total of about 250,000 men, mainly French. Two auxiliary armies, one of 80,000 Italians and Germans and the other of 70,000 Germans and Poles, operated in close support of the imperial striking force. On the Baltic coast 32,500 men prepared to invade Lithuania while 34,000 Austrians guarded Napoleon's right. An additional 165,000 men stood ready to act as replacements for the main force; 60,000 troops garrisoned forts along the Vistula, and thousands more served in land transport battalions and naval supply columns. The Emperor had carefully studied his opponent's domain and the disasters that had befallen the Swedish invasion of 1709. He concluded that his army could not live off the country (a conclusion he might equally have drawn about conditions in Spain) and his supply troops formed but a part of a huge logistical system. He also gathered vast herds of cattle, constructed huge forward depots holding tons of food and fodder, and each man entering Russia carried enough provisions for several weeks of campaigning.

The Tsar had about 420,000 men scattered from the

Baltic to the Black Sea, and the Emperor concluded that the Russians would probably fight a defensive campaign, sacrificing space for time in order to wear down the French and concentrate their own forces. Napoleon therefore planned to defeat the main Russian armies in the western borderlands before they could retreat to the interior. He intended to lead his main armies north of the Pripet marshes, threaten to move against either St. Petersburg or Moscow, and defeat the Russian First Army of 127,000 men holding positions along the Niemen River from Courland to southern Lithuania before the 48,000-man Second Army could link up with it. If he was successful, Russian forces south of the marshes, along the Danube, and in scattered depots would be helpless against the concentrated and victorious Grand Army. Napoleon could then move to Smolensk, spend the winter there, and resume his advance in the spring; alternatively, he could lunge at one of Russia's major cities in the autumn. In either eventuality he assumed that if he could shatter the Russian main armies, the Tsar would have to seek peace on French terms.

Careful planning and extensive preparations notwithstanding, the Emperor's Russian venture was fraught with many grave problems. In the first place the multinational Grand Army was not of the same high quality as the forces that had performed so brilliantly in 1805 and 1806. Many of Napoleon's best troops were engaged in the bitter, futile Spanish campaign; the French units in the east contained a high percentage of new conscripts, and the foreign troops were of uneven quality. The Polish soldiers, for example, were well trained and highly motivated, but many German units were indifferent to the Emperor's designs and wanted only to survive their forthcoming ordeal, while the Spanish and Portuguese battalions had no desire at all to fight Russians at the behest of the French. Furthermore, the army was so large that it tended to be unwieldy. The Corsican's earlier victories in Italy and Germany were equally a function of mass and mobility. Wagram was an exception; there Bonaparte relied primarily upon the weight of numbers, and Wagram was not one of his more notable triumphs. In 1812 the very size of his army coupled with the state of communications made it difficult for the Emperor to move forces rapidly and flexibly. To defeat the Russian field armies before they could escape eastward required hard-hitting attacks followed by quick exploitation, but these were the tasks that the imperial army was least suited to fulfill.

Napoleon also neglected to supplement his military preparations with a political program designed to undermine the Tsar's regime from within. The Russian serf, existing in conditions akin to slavery, was traditionally discontented with his lot. Throughout the seventeenth and eighteenth centuries this discontent had boiled over in massive regional rebellions and numerous local risings. In the past, the Emperor had made good use of popular hostility to existing regimes, but in 1812 Napoleon was no longer Bonaparte, the general of the Revolution. He was an emperor, married to a princess of one of the oldest ruling houses of Europe. He had made his relatives kings and his marshals and advisers noblemen and was doing his best to forget his revolutionary heritage. He was willing to redraw the map of Europe but employed the traditional methods of arms and diplomacy. He did of course try to win popular support in newly conquered regions by inaugurating extensive reforms, but as in the days of the "enlightened despots" before him, reforms emanated from above; they did not arise from the articulate demands of the local populace. As hereditary Emperor of the French, Bonaparte preferred to deal with other established monarchs and no longer attempted to employ revolutionary sentiment in his state's national interest. Consequently, he made no plans to incite the peasantry of Russia against the Romanov regime and prepared to enter Alexander's domains not as a liberator but as an invader.

Finally, by attacking Russia before he had conquered Spain, Napoleon created for himself the additional problem of waging war on two widely separated fronts. Moreover, he had transferred units from Spain to the eastern front, thereby weakening the forces facing Wellington while not decisively strengthening the Grand Army. The attempt to fight two major campaigns at the same time only doubled the chances of defeat while not materially enhancing the Emperor's chance of victory.

Nor did developments across the Atlantic, even though they posed something of a threat to the British, materially improve his strategic situation. For years the United States Government had been trying by application of economic pressure to force the European belligerents to ease their rules of blockade and commercial warfare. In 1810 Napoleon scored a diplomatic advantage with the Americans by assuring them that he had suspended the Berlin and Milan decrees as they affected American shipping, and Madison then invoked the Non-Importation Act against England. Neither England nor France, however, had at that time any intention of relaxing their efforts to deprive the other of foreign trade, and both powers continued their depredations upon American shipping. Because she was the world's leading naval power, England's actions had the most immediate and extensive impact upon the United States. The license system gave special advantages to British merchants exporting goods to the Continent, the Orders in Council hindered American commerce, and impressment, regarded by the Cabinet as essential to the maintenance of the navy, fell heavily upon Americans. British warships would frequently intercept American vessels on the high seas and seize individuals, designated by English officers as subjects of the King, for service in the Royal Navy. Many hijacked seamen were deserters from the British fleet, but many others were legitimate citizens of the United States. The whole system of impressment was a threat to American sovereignty and their independence was rendered meaningless if the nation's flag could not protect citizens from the arbitrary actions of a foreign power.

By the autumn of 1811 many congressmen were openly calling for war. It was believed that British officials in Canada were inciting Indians in the Northwest to harass American settlements, and the existence of an agricultural depression caused by a combination of overproduction, American embargo acts, and continental harassment was also attributed to British scheming. England's economic policy—designed to benefit British merchants at the expense of neutrals—gave some credence to this view and gave added impetus to the bellicose policies of the war hawks. President Madison called for expansion of the army's strength by ten thousand men, and the Congress went even further by increasing the regular army to twenty-five thousand. In the spring of 1812 Napoleon encouraged prowar sentiment in America by publicly announcing his revocation of the Berlin and Milan decrees. The British, meanwhile, began to contemplate lifting their Orders in Council in order to avoid hostilities in the New World while the bulk of their human and material resources was engaged in the European war. Bureaucratic delay and the confusion caused by the assassination of England's Prime Minister Spencer Perceval, and the ensuing delay while Lord Liverpool—Perceval's principal ally between 1809 and 1812—reconstituted a ministry, prevented London from revoking the Orders in Council until June 23. But it was too late, for the United States had declared war on England on June 18.

The Americans planned to invade Canada and use it as a pawn to force the British to abandon their affronts to United States sovereignty. A number of congressmen contemplated retaining part of this projected conquest as well. Had the nation's preparations been as extensive as the ambitions of some of its politicians, the forces of the United States might have inflicted a severe defeat upon the British and in so doing given significant if accidental assistance to the French. The regular army, however, was small, poorly trained, and badly led, and the state militias were even worse. The American navy, aside from a few excellent frigates, was almost non-existent and the populace as a whole was deeply divided over whether or not to fight. The Federalists and even some elements within Madison's republican party opposed the war and called for a rapid end to hostilities. As a result of ill-preparedness and internal divisions, the nation was unable to put any serious pressure upon the British.

In the summer of 1812 a series of ill-co-ordinated offensives against Canada collapsed, and the Americans were similarly unable to harm the British on the oceans. The English were able to contain the forces of the United States with local garrisons and naval squadrons and did not have to divert large military or naval units from the major conflict in Europe. The outbreak of Anglo-American hostilities, encouraged in part by Napoleon's diplomacy, gave little aid or comfort to the Emperor. Madison's inability to back his diplomatic policies with effective force meant that Napoleon still had to face the full might of his foes in both Spain and Russia.

In the darkness of the morning of June 24 the Emperor's armies streamed into Russia. Napoleon once again was waging a desperate game for high stakes. If victorious, he would not only drive the Russians away from central Europe, but he would also gain *de facto* control of the Balkans, and might be able to force a subservient Alexander to attack British India while hundreds of thousands of men marched into Spain to overwhelm all resistance in Iberia by sheer weight of numbers. Defeat, on the other hand, could lead to catastrophe, since a Russian triumph might well convince other powers to unite in an effort to destroy French hegemony.

As the Grand Army advanced the Russian First Army fell back to its fortified camp at Drissa, where the Tsar hoped to fight a major defensive battle. Napoleon entered Vilna, devised a plan to create a Lithuanian state,

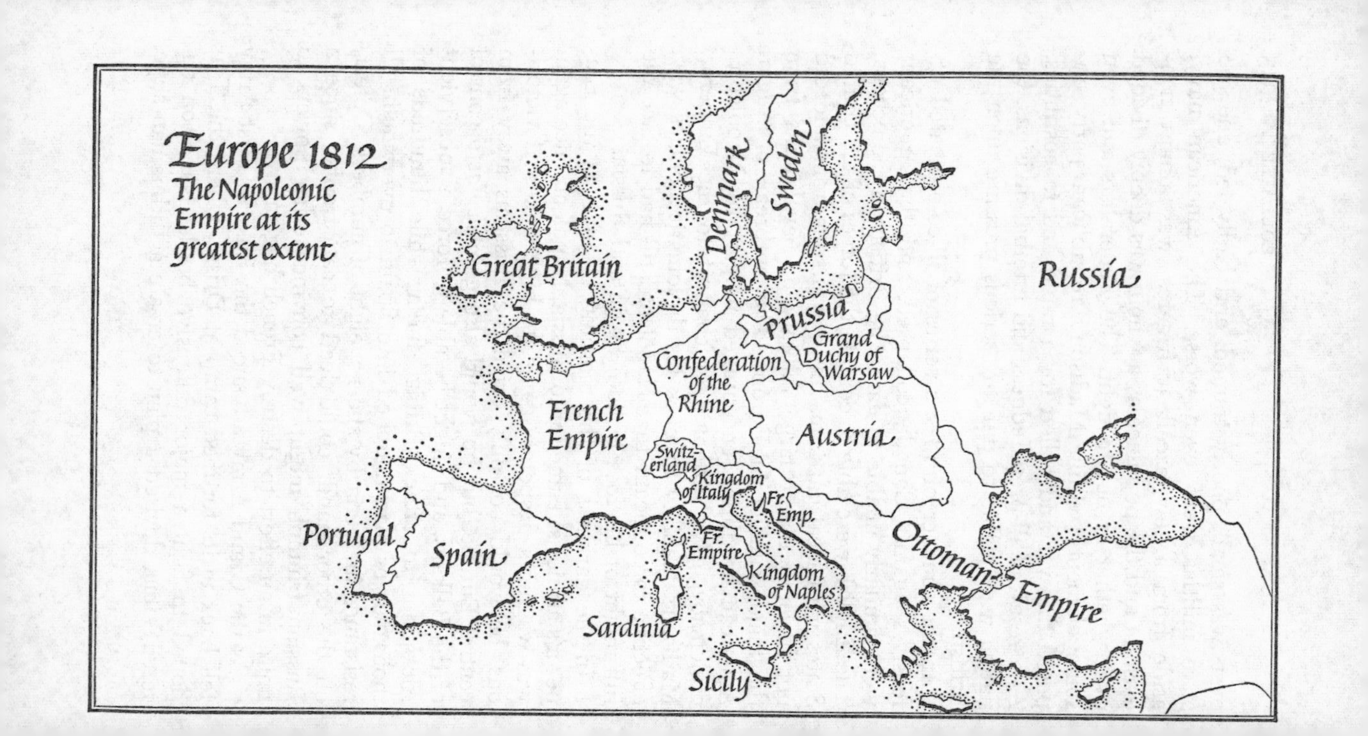
Europe 1812
The Napoleonic Empire at its greatest extent
Great Britain
Denmark
Sweden
Russia
Prussia
Grand Duchy of Warsaw
Confederation of the Rhine
French Empire
Austria
Switzerland
Kingdom of Italy
Fr. Emp.
Fr. Empire
Kingdom of Naples
Ottoman Empire
Portugal
Spain
Sardinia
Sicily

which he intended to place under Davout's control in order to limit Polish ambitions, and pushed on after the Russians. Occasional rains turned the roads into seas of mud, slowing his advance and causing serious delays in the arrival of supplies at the front. Nevertheless, the advance continued, and the Russians decided to evacuate Drissa without a fight because the First and Second armies had not yet linked up. The First Army fell back to Smolensk and the Second Army, after grueling forced marches, managed to avoid entrapment and joined them. The Emperor meanwhile entered Vitebsk at the end of July and halted to rest his troops and to bring up his artillery and supply trains. He had forced the Russians to abandon their fortified camp and conduct a hasty withdrawal, but he had so far failed to accomplish his major objective, the defeat of Alexander's field armies.

As the Russians successfully avoided defeat in detail, the British in Spain were winning important victories. After the battles on the frontier, Wellington with forty-five thousand men advanced toward Madrid, taking Salamanca, a little more than a hundred miles northwest of the Spanish capital, on June 27. Marshal Marmont gathered forty-three thousand troops to stem the British advance. In mid-July Marmont moved south in an effort to place his army across Wellington's line of communications with Portugal. The British had no option but to conform to the French movement, and for several days the two forces marched west in parallel columns. Near Salamanca on July 22 Marmont, confident that he had outmaneuvered his adversary, opened a gap in his line in order to detach a division for a flanking march against what he assumed was a British rear guard. Wellington, however, had his main army near at hand hidden in a fold of ground invisible to French scouts and decided to take advantage of Marmont's carelessness and initiate a general action. The British advanced and with rapid musket volleys, followed by hard-hitting bayonet attacks, crushed the French right wing. Wounded by a shellburst, Marmont was unable to organize effective counterattacks. His subordinates did manage to strike back and made some headway in the center, but their assaults were not well co-ordinated, and Wellington was able to transfer units to meet and check the French thrusts. The French army collapsed, and leaving behind some fourteen thousand casualties, the remnants fled eastward. Wellington followed his defeated foes and entered Valladolid the day after Napoleon marched into Vitebsk. Wellington had cleared the way for an advance on Madrid, and his victory at Salamanca also prevented the Emperor from transferring more veteran units from Spain to Russia.

In mid-August Napoleon struck at the Russian forces in and around Smolensk. After launching probing attacks on the seventeenth he attempted to outflank and surround Alexander's armies the next day. His troops were not fast enough, however. Despite heavy losses, nine thousand men, the Russians made good their escape to the east. Napoleon also lost about nine thousand men, and although he took Smolensk—a hollow victory, since his own artillery and Russian rear guards had set the city ablaze—he failed to entrap and destroy the Tsar's armed forces. The French Emperor now stood midway between the Prussian frontier and Moscow; nevertheless, the Russian army remained intact, and the Corsican had to decide whether to remain in Smolensk for the rest of the year and resume the campaign the following spring or to push on and try to win the war before the advent of winter.

If Bonaparte had scored a partial triumph on the Russian plains, his position in Spain continued to deteriorate. After Salamanca, Wellington pushed on into Castile. Joseph had almost no control over his generals, who were responsible for their conduct of operations to the French Emperor, and he could not gather sufficient forces to resist the British advance. To the south Soult refused to abandon his siege of Cádiz and come to Joseph's assistance. Consequently, on August 12, Wellington's forces entered Madrid, and as Napoleon marched into Smolensk, Wellington began to advance on Burgos, the last important French position south of the Ebro.

Meanwhile, in Russia Napoleon, against the advice of many of his marshals, decided to resume his advance into the Russian heartland. He felt that ruined Smolensk was unsuitable as a halting place, and that a withdrawal to an undamaged city would hurt his army's morale. Added to this, he did not wish to give the Tsar time to reorganize and expand his armies, but wanted to conclude his campaign as soon as possible.

As the Grand Army moved east it found the land deserted by its inhabitants and the houses and fields in flames. Due to the enormous distances involved, the Emperor's supply system was soon experiencing difficulties. Thousands of horses began to die of starvation, and troops started to leave their units in search of provisions. Peasant partisans and Cossack cavalry began to fall upon isolated patrols, and guerrilla activity flared along the entire French line of march.

Constantly retreating, the Russian forces also suffered privation and underwent a sharp decline in morale. High-ranking generals began to argue that the Tsar's army had retreated far enough and called for a battle. Michael Barclay de Tolly, the cautious Russian commander, refused to heed these appeals and ordered a further retreat —not because of a conscious strategy of pulling the French deeper into Russia but because he was unwilling to risk an encounter with the Grand Army. To halt the rising tide of denunciation, Alexander on August 20 removed Barclay and replaced him with Kutusov, the obese, drunk, and crafty officer who had played such a large role in the Austerlitz debacle. Owing his command to the support of those generals who wished to fight, Kutusov was morally committed to engage in a major battle.[6]

[6] *Min. de la Guerre A.H., M.h., Campagne de Russie* 677. See also E. Tarle, *Napoleon's Invasion of Russia* (New York, 1942) for a Russian historian's view of the campaign.

He pulled back to a defensive position near Borodino, a hamlet about sixty miles west of Moscow. His troops held a line four miles long with redoubts located at critical points. There, on the morning of September 7, 1812, the Russian army, 120,000 strong, prepared to do battle with Napoleon's army, which after subtracting casualties and men detached for garrison duty numbered approximately 130,000.

The Emperor opened the battle with a heavy cannonade that wreaked havoc among the tightly packed Russian units. Ney and Davout then led their corps against Kutusov's left center. Bitter fighting ensued, some positions changing hands as many as nine times as Kutusov drew reinforcements from his flanks and hurled them into the fight while French guns continued their bloody executions. Late in the morning a great assault against the Russian center pounded a hole in Kutusov's lines, and French field guns moved onto the newly conquered terrain and began to pour a withering flanking fire into Russian units on either side of the breakthrough. Polish troops then pushed in the Russian left, and French troops on the right captured one of Kutusov's main redoubts. Kutusov counterattacked and retook the position, only to lose it again to new French assaults. Having severely shaken the Russian army, Napoleon's marshals called upon him to throw the Imperial Guard and other units held in reserve into the fray. The marshals believed that the advance of thirty thousand fresh troops would enable them to shatter the Russian army and give the Emperor the military triumph he had been seeking since the start of the campaign. Bonaparte, however, refused to commit his Guard units. Suffering from a fever, he seemed to have lost his power of rapid decision. Moreover, the idea of sending forward his last fresh units while he was hundreds of miles from any reinforcements also influenced him to stay his hand. Consequently, the battle continued with some of Napoleon's best units participating only as observers.

Kutusov continued to mount counterattacks. His infantry moved forward in dense columns; French artillery slaughtered them, and they re-formed and attacked again. French infantry and cavalry, covered by massed field batteries, also attacked, gradually forcing Kutusov to abandon his entire line and fall back to a ridge line behind Borodino. Napoleon claimed Borodino as a victory for his army, which managed to gain possession of the battlefield and inflicted forty-five thousand casualties upon the Russians. On the other hand, the French had lost over twenty-five thousand men and had failed to shatter Alexander's main fighting force. Though battered, the Russian army was still intact, and on September 9 it withdrew in good order toward Moscow. The Emperor's tactical victory could not hide the fact that he had failed in his major objective—the destruction of Russia's fighting forces—and the occupation of territory even when coupled with major tactical triumphs was without significance as long as the Tsar's armies and his will to resist remained unbroken.

Meanwhile, Kutusov withdrew to the environs of Moscow, where he called a council of war to decide the army's next move. The council offered divided opinions, and the Russian commander in chief, unwilling to risk another major engagement, took it upon himself to order the evacuation of Russia's Holy City. He then led his army south into the rich Kaluga province, an excellent position where the Russians could rest and reorganize, protect the important arsenal at Tula, watch the Grand Army, and pose a constant threat to its flanks and communications. As the army retreated, the governor of Moscow ordered the populace to leave the city. He also carried off or destroyed all available fire-fighting equipment, released prisoners from the jails, and gave his subordinates instructions to start burning the metropolis rather than allow the French to capture it intact.[7]

[7] A. Palmer, *Napoleon in Russia* (New York, 1967), Ch. 9 deals

Napoleon's army meanwhile advanced toward Moscow, reaching its outskirts by September 14. After waiting in vain for a delegation to surrender the city, the Emperor moved into the deserted Kremlin on the fifteenth. Isolated fires had already broken out on the fourteenth, and the carelessness of the French and the activities of Russian incendiaries added to them. A stiff breeze then fanned the blazes into a major holocaust, and within three days most of Moscow burned to the ground. Amid the smoke and flames of the dying city, the Corsican ruler of the west waited for the monarch of the east to surrender, but no offer of capitulation or even a request to negotiate emanated from St. Petersburg. On September 20, Napoleon took the initiative and made overtures to the Tsar. Insisting that Alexander withdraw to the frontiers of 1772, rejoin the continental system, accept French terms for the partition of the Balkans, and seek compensation for his sacrifices by marching on India, he threatened to impose even more drastic terms if Alexander remained silent.[8]

The Tsar, however, did remain silent. He had come to realize that the loss of a battle did not mean total defeat. His army was intact and was receiving reinforcements. Moscow was useless to the French, and all along the Grand Army's line of communications irregular troops were harassing Napoleon's convoys. Finally, fresh Russian armies in the Baltic and south of the Pripet marshes were preparing a counteroffensive. Thus, despite the defeat at Borodino and the loss of Moscow, Russia's military position was by no means impossible, and the Tsar realized that the onset of winter would work in his favor. Alexander's refusal to negotiate and his determination to

---

with the problem of the Moscow fire. Palmer feels that most of the fires were started purposely to deny the city to the French.

[8] E. Driault, *Le Grand Empire (1809–1812)* (Paris, 1924), pp. 406–10; and Nesselrode, *Lettres et papiers de Nesselrode*, V, p. 205. In a memorandum of May 2 the Tsar had predicted Napoleon's diplomatic objectives with almost complete accuracy.

continue the war in turn forced the French Emperor to prepare for a winter campaign.

Napoleon concluded that his logistical situation precluded remaining in Moscow for the winter. Nor could he advance south into the Ukraine, for Kutusov's army barred his way. A march north on St. Petersburg was also out of the question, for the Russian army would then fall upon the Grand Army's rear. The Emperor therefore decided to retreat to Smolensk, spend the winter there, and launch a new campaign in the spring. The retreat, the most famous and one of the most terrible of any modern campaign, began on October 19 while on the other side of the Continent another withdrawal was about to begin.

After taking Madrid, Wellington had laid siege to Burgos, but lacking heavy artillery his army could make no headway against the strong French garrison. As the French gathered a large relieving force, Wellington decided that he could no longer safely maintain his army deep in Spanish territory and ordered his divisions to pull back to the Portuguese frontier. Three days after the Grand Army left Moscow, the British army abandoned their trenches before Burgos. Bad weather and bad terrain made the retreat difficult, but the French did not launch a vigorous pursuit, and the British army regained the safety of Portugal with its well-organized supply bases without heavy losses. Wellington was therefore able to plan with confidence a new offensive in 1813.

The retreat in Russia was by contrast chaotic and disastrous. Napoleon first ordered his army to move by a southerly route through terrain untouched by the previous months of campaigning, but Kutusov moved to intercept him. After several sharp clashes that indicated the Russians had replaced the losses suffered at Borodino and were spoiling for a fight, the Emperor decided not to risk a major battle and ordered his soldiers to retreat along their original line of advance. Lack of horses slowed the retreat, and supply shortages caused a rapid collapse of discipline as thousands of men straggled over the countryside in search of food and drink. Cossacks and peasant irregulars killed or captured thousands of these foragers. Heavy snow began to fall on November 4, adding to the miseries of the retreat. Troops abandoned their wagons, artillery, and even their muskets, Kutusov's army harassed the rear guard, and the wide-ranging Cossacks continued to round up thousands of starving men who could not keep pace with their units.[9]

Between November 9 and 13 some fifty thousand men, the survivors of those units that had reached Moscow, entered Smolensk, only to find that the city's garrison had consumed most of the reserve rations. The first units to reach Smolensk did manage to loot the few remaining depots, but most of the army found nothing. Napoleon had no choice but to resume his retreat, and directed his forces to head for Minsk, another of his supply bases. Plunging through the nightmarish weather, the Grand Army brushed aside a Russian force that attempted to block its line of retreat while Marshal Ney, commanding the rear guard with dash and brilliance, successfully threw back his pursuers. The Emperor discovered, however, that on November 16 the Russian army south of the Pripet marshes had seized Minsk, leaving the Grand Army with no choice but to take a more northerly route and head for Vilna.[10]

Once again the army lurched westward, with hunger, cold, and the Russians' harassing attacks taking an ever increasing toll. Meanwhile, the Russian armies began to close in on the shattered imperial forces. To reach Vilna

[9] *Min. de la Guerre A.H., M.h.*, 677. Augereau maintains that demoralization did more damage to the army than physical privation and that bad weather was not at first a major factor in the French army disintegration.

[10] *Min. de la Guerre A.H., M.h., Retraite du maréchal Ney depuis Smolensk jusqu'à Orcha* 676. For a series of accounts of the retreat see A. Brett-James, *1812 Eye Witness Accounts of Napoleon's Defeat in Russia* (New York, 1966).

the French had to cross the Beresina River, a tributary of the Dnieper. The Russian force at Minsk moved north, burned the only bridge across the river, and planted itself firmly athwart Napoleon's line of retreat while Kutusov closed in from behind it. A sudden thaw made it impossible to cross the river on foot, and the Emperor ordered his engineers to find other fords and build new bridges. On November 25 the engineers, working in the freezing water, managed to throw two bridges across the Beresina. During the next two days, as a few disciplined units held back Russian assaults on both banks, the army poured across the bridges. Choked with a seething mass of men, horses, women, and vehicles, the bridges frequently broke, throwing hundreds to their deaths in the icy waters. Russian artillery ranged in on the pontoons, adding to the carnage. Nevertheless, by November 29 the French rear guard crossed the bridges and burned them. The Grand Army had escaped total annihilation, but as a fighting force it was useless. Thousands of corpses lined both banks of the Beresina, and only twenty-five thousand men survived the murderous river crossing. On December 5, Napoleon left the remnants of his army and returned to his capital, there to quash an outbreak of political agitation and to raise new armies. Losing men to hunger and cold, the Grand Army pushed on, and by December 14 the last of the invaders had departed from Alexander's domains.

The defeat in Russia was a strategic and diplomatic catastrophe for Napoleon. By the winter of 1812 it was no longer a question of how far the Emperor would expand his domains but rather how much of his existing power and influence he would manage to retain. Some 270,000 imperial troops had died in battle or perished from disease, cold, and starvation, and an additional 200,000 men remained in Russia as prisoners. Moreover, the loss of 200,000 horses and 1000 cannon rendered the task of re-forming the Grand Army even more difficult. Napoleon, of course, threw himself into the task of raising new forces with his usual furious energy; he called conscript classes to the colors ahead of time, obtained volunteers from the national guards, and pressured his allies for additional contingents. He could not, however, remount his cavalry or replace the veterans who fell in Russia. Furthermore, the myth of invincibility that had hitherto surrounded him was gone, and his enemies were closing in from all sides. Alexander's armies were advancing from the east, and Wellington was preparing to launch another offensive into Spain. The Emperor of the French was still a formidable foe, but by the end of 1812 he was fighting not for conquest but for preservation of his empire and his dynasty.

While Bonaparte organized his new levies, Alexander was debating whether or not to carry the war across the Vistula. Kutusov favored halting the Russian advance, but Baron von Stein, a former imperial knight and Prussian official who because of his efforts to revitalize the Hohenzollern kingdom after 1806 had been forced to flee to Russia to avoid Napoleon's wrath, plus a number of diplomats and military men, urged the Tsar to advance into central Europe. Anxious to "liberate" Germany and expand his influence westward, the Tsar took the advice of his more bellicose counselors, but he first sought to detach Prussia from its ties with France.

General von Yorck, commander of the Prussian contingent serving with the Grand Army, gave Alexander his chance to influence Berlin's policy by signing on December 31, 1812, the Convention of Tauroggen. Acting on his own, Yorck agreed to an armistice between himself and the Russian army. This act of treason, regarded by many Germans as the patriotic gesture that began the War of Liberation that freed Prussia from French domination, enabled Russian troops to enter East Prussia without opposition and forced the French to fall back behind the Vistula. In January 1813 Alexander placed Stein in charge of organizing East Prussia for war. Working with the local government, Stein and Yorck created a Landwehr, a citizen militia, based on the principle of universal military obligation to the state. This move, with its revolutionary implications—for universal obligations implied universal rights—placed Frederick William III in a quandary. He was still afraid of Napoleon, but he was also suspicious of Alexander's intentions concerning the ultimate fate of East Prussia and frightened at the prospect of liberal reforms coming from a locus of power other than that of his own court. Frederick William therefore played a double game. He told Napoleon that he was going to Breslau to raise more troops to fight alongside the Grand Army, left Berlin on January 22, and once in Silesia created a Landwehr system for his entire kingdom, thereby strengthening his military position and keeping the process of mobilization in his own hands.[11] As the ranks of his army gradually expanded, the Hohenzollern King entered into secret talks with the Tsar. Alexander assured Frederick William that Russia would assist him in restoring his kingdom to a position as strong as that it held in 1806. Although he suspected that Berlin was about to turn against him, Napoleon failed to make an equally attractive offer, and Frederick William decided to join the Russians. He signed a military alliance with Alexander and on March 17, 1813, declared war upon France. Bernadotte also joined the anti-French coalition. After securing promises from England and Russia that Sweden would obtain Norway and Guadeloupe, the Crown Prince agreed to send thirty thousand men to fight with the allies.

Meanwhile, Clemens von Metternich, the handsome, vain, prolix, and linguistically versatile Austrian Foreign

[11] See G. S. Ford, *Stein and the Era of Reform in Prussia 1807–1815* (New York, 1922) for a discussion of Stein's reform efforts. W. Shanahan, *Prussian Military Reforms, 1786–1813* (New York, 1945), and P. Paret, *Yorck and the Era of Prussian Reform* (Princeton, 1966) discuss Prussia's military reforms. See also E. Botzenhart and W. Hubatsch, eds., *Freiherr vom Stein: Briefe und Amtliche Schriften* (Stuttgart, 1963), IV, pp. 13–14.

Minister, decided that the time had come for Austria to reassert itself as an independent great power. The son of a count of the Holy Roman Empire who had migrated to Bohemia after the French occupation of the Rhineland, Metternich married a daughter of Kaunitz, perhaps the most famous Hapsburg diplomat of the eighteenth century, and in 1801 began his own diplomatic career. In the following years he represented Vienna at Dresden, Berlin, St. Petersburg, and Paris. In 1809 just before the disaster at Wagram, Francis appointed him Foreign Minister, but before he could grasp fully the reins of office Austria lost the Battle of Wagram and signed the catastrophic 1809 treaty. Afterward, Metternich set out to restore Austria's power and influence. Realizing that for the moment the Hapsburg state was too weak to challenge Napoleonic hegemony, he played the role of an obedient satellite, biding his time until the French Emperor made a blunder of sufficient magnitude to enable Austria to seize the opportunity to reassert herself. In his role as satellite he helped arrange the marriage in 1810 between Napoleon and Marie Louise, a daughter of Emperor Francis, and sent in 1812 an Austrian corps into Russia.

The Russian disaster, Alexander's advance into Germany, and the re-emergence of Prussia as a foe of France presented Metternich with his long-awaited opportunity to act. He realized that despite all the recent defeats, Napoleonic France was still powerful and dangerous, and he decided to move with great care. First, he planned to build up his military strength. Secondly, he would employ his enlarged military capacity to compel the French Emperor to recognize Austria as an independent neutral power, his assumption being that Bonaparte, already hard pressed in Germany and Spain, would be reluctant to add another power to the ranks of his enemies, and would, therefore, consent to an end to the Austro-French alliance and agree to recognize the Hapsburgs' enhanced status. Finally, the Austrian Foreign Minister intended to bargain with all belligerents and support the side giving him the best terms. His ultimate objective was to enhance Austrian power, severely reduce but not destroy French influence, and prevent any other state from replacing France as Europe's dominant power.

Putting these schemes into action in December 1812, Metternich first assured the French of his loyalty and then in January 1813 arranged a secret military convention with the Russians providing for the retreat of the Austrian auxiliary corps from Poland to Bohemia. In Bohemia the corps served as a cadre for a general mobilization while Metternich continued to reassure France that he was enlarging his armed forces for the purpose of supporting her. Believing that Austria would indeed fight on his side, Napoleon encouraged Vienna to enlarge its army. As his military strength grew, Metternich put into action the second phase of his plan. In reply to a French demand of April 7 calling for Austria's active participation against the allies, Metternich replied that his master, Francis, would not consider himself bound by earlier treaties if the reasonable peace proposals he intended to make were rejected. This reply, while it did not say so specifically, indicated that Austria no longer considered herself bound to France, but would assume the stance of a mediator between Napoleon and the allies. On April 20 Metternich rejected a French demand for full military support and stated, this time in unambiguous terms, that Austria would henceforth act as an independent mediator. Repeated French calls for armed assistance met the same response. On May 1, Metternich sent a final reply to Napoleon's calls for military cooperation, again informing the French Emperor that Austria would act as a mediator between France and the allies, and this time adding that Francis possessed sufficient armed might to assure his independence. As Metternich had calculated, Napoleon was unwilling to add

Austria to the ranks of his enemies and had no choice but to accept the Hapsburgs' new status.

While dealing with the French, Metternich was also bolstering his position with the allies, and he obtained from Russia an offer to restore Austria to the limits of 1805 plus a guarantee of a free hand in settling the fate of southern Germany.[12] Thus by the spring of 1813 Metternich had freed Francis from his French alliance, built up Austria's army, convinced the Tsar to support a restoration of Hapsburg power, and because he had refused to commit his state to active military co-operation with either France or the allies, was in a position to demand a high price from the other belligerents for his support.

Unwilling to pay the cost in territory and influence that would result from an effort to negotiate a peace, Napoleon, who typically sought rapid military solutions to complex diplomatic issues, decided to strike quickly and dislocate the coalition. He planned to fall upon the Prussians before their mobilization was complete, drive them from the war, frighten Vienna into renewing its ties with Paris, and force the Russians back across the Niemen.

Concentrating a striking force of some eighty-five thousand men in Franconia, Napoleon led it north through Thuringia and into Saxony. By April 30, the striking force linked up with a sixty-thousand-man army that was guarding the line of the Elbe and Saale rivers, and together the united forces began to advance on Leipzig. On May 1 Napoleon's army came into contact with Prussian and Russian patrols, the advance guard of the main allied force, which was moving through Saxony. On May

[12] C. von Metternich, *Mémoires du Prince de Metternich* (Paris, 1959), I, p. 124. For a modern secondary account see H. A. Kissinger, *A World Restored* (New York, 1964), pp. 62–67. Additional studies of Metternich's diplomacy include H. von Srbik, *Metternich, der Staatsmann und der Mensch,* 2 vols. (Munich, 1925), and E. Kraehe, *Metternich's German Policy,* 2 vols. (Princeton, 1963).

2, near Lützen, the site of Gustavus Adolphus' great triumph and death in 1632, the Grand Army encountered the main 68,000-man Russo-Prussian force. After hard fighting, Napoleon brought up an eighty-gun battery, blasted a gap in the allied center, and launched an attack with sixteen battalions of the Young Guard. The allied ranks, though battered, did not collapse, and the Russo-Prussian force managed to retreat in reasonably good order. The allies lost some twenty thousand men and the French twenty-two thousand. For lack of cavalry, the French did not pursue, and the allies, abandoning Leipzig and Dresden, retired behind the upper Spree River near Bautzen.

Napoleon followed and on May 21 assailed his opponents. Three corps attacked frontally while a fourth led by Marshal Ney moved round the allied right flank. Napoleon ordered Ney to wheel southeast after turning the allied line and thereby cut their avenue of retreat, but the marshal failed in his mission. He delayed his advance and then pushed the allies east instead of southeast into the trap. Consequently, the allied army, though losing 20,000 men, escaped annihilation, and the Emperor's victory, bought at the price of 13,500 casualties, was a barren one.

While the allies were falling back into Silesia, Metternich proposed an armistice during which time Austria would attempt to mediate a peace. To gain time to reorganize and reinforce their armies, Alexander and Frederick William accepted the proposal on June 4. For similar reasons, Napoleon agreed to an armistice. The belligerents were less interested in negotiating a peace settlement than in the military advantages they could glean from the pause in hostilities. Napoleon brought up reinforcements for his battered units, but the allies, who needed the armistice more than the French, made better use of it. The Prussians completed their mobilization; the Russians brought forward fresh troops and on June 14 and 15 obtained English support. The allies signed treaties with the British obtaining financial subsidies in return for promising not to undertake separate talks with the French.

Meanwhile, the Austrians completed their mobilization, and Metternich presented to the allies the conditions he was prepared to offer the French Emperor as the basis of a preliminary peace. He called for the dissolution of the duchy of Warsaw, the enlargement of Prussia, the return of the Illyrian provinces to Austria, and the re-establishment of Hamburg and Lübeck as free cities. The allies had additional demands, including the dissolution of the Rhine Confederation, the restoration of Prussia to the status of 1806, and the liberation of Spain, Holland, and Italy. Not wishing to present Napoleon with harsh terms that would enable him to rally domestic support for his regime, Metternich persuaded the allies to withhold their maximum program until the final peace conference. On June 27 at Reichenbach, Austria, Russia, and Prussia signed a secret treaty calling for Austria to join the allies if Napoleon rejected the allied minimum program. Metternich had thus transformed Austria from a French ally into a neutral, and finally into a *de facto* member of an anti-French coalition. If the Emperor rejected Metternich's mediation terms, he would find all the major powers of Europe ranged against him.

In a final attempt to draw Austria into the war on his side or at least keep Francis neutral, Napoleon met with Metternich at Dresden at the end of June. In a stormy interview filled with bluster and threats, the Emperor failed to budge the imperturbable Austrian chancellor, who refused to divulge the conditions of mediation and insisted that Napoleon accept the principle of *armed* mediation, which meant that Austria had the option of declaring war against whichever side refused to accept a peace proposal. In this particular instance Metternich realized that Napoleon would be unwilling to make concessions, and Austria would therefore have a valid excuse for openly joining the allies. Since he had already obtained allied agreement to terms favorable to Hapsburg interests, he was willing to fight. To retain Austrian neutrality and to gain an extension of the armistice the Emperor agreed to Metternich's terms. He released Austria from its alliance to France, accepted the principle of armed mediation, and agreed to participate in a peace congress at Prague.[13]

The ensuing conference was basically a charade since none of the participants had any serious intention of concluding a peace treaty. Metternich planned to use the failure of the congress as a *casus belli* against France, and Napoleon had no plan to make any major concessions to the allies in return for peace. He did not send a delegate to Prague until the end of July and offered no concessions to the allies until August 9. Even those he did make were minimal: The Emperor agreed to give up Warsaw and Illyria and to re-establish Prussia's prewar power, but at the same time he insisted upon retaining Danzig, Trieste, and Istria, and demanded extensive territorial compensation for his Saxon ally. Even these concessions came too late, however, for at midnight on August 10 Metternich pronounced the cloture of the congress, and on August 12 Francis declared war upon Napoleon. Thus for the first time in the history of the Revolutionary and Napoleonic Era *all* of Europe's major powers were ranged against France.

By agreeing to the armistice yet at the same time refusing to seek peace seriously the French Emperor had weakened his position. He had given Austria the time and opportunity to join the allies and had granted the other members of the coalition the chance to improve their armaments. Consequently, when hostilities resumed, 442,000 French faced 512,000 allied troops.

[13] Metternich, *Mémoires*, II, pp. 187–89. For views more sympathetic to Napoleon see E. Driault, *La chute de l'Empire* (Paris, 1927), and A. Sorel, *L'Europe et la Révolution française* (Paris, 1904), VIII.

Meanwhile, in Spain, the Emperor's position continued to worsen. Joseph had reoccupied Madrid when Wellington pulled back to Portugal, but once again the French had to divert much of their strength to the brutal and indecisive tasks of antipartisan activity. Napoleon's withdrawal of fifteen thousand troops to bolster his forces on the Elbe further weakened the French position south of the Pyrenees. At the same time the Emperor refused to allow Joseph to abandon central Spain and concentrate his forces behind the Ebro, a refusal that exposed his troops to a concentrated blow from Wellington's 81,000-man army.

On May 22 the Anglo-Portuguese army, supported by twenty-one thousand Spanish troops, launched a two-pronged attack into Spain. Taken by surprise, the French fell back to Burgos, but Wellington marched quickly and threatened Joseph's exposed northern flank. Unable to gather enough men for a stand near Burgos, the "intrusive King" decided to fall back behind the Ebro. Wellington pursued him closely, and by the sixteenth his army had crossed the river. Wellington then drove toward Vitoria to cut the main road to France. In despair Joseph gathered fifty-seven thousand men for a last effort to save his crown, but on June 21, 1813, Wellington threw seventy-five thousand men against him. The British and Portuguese quickly cut the road to Bayonne and forced the French to evacuate Vitoria. The French then tried to retreat via a secondary road to Pamplona, but continued English pressure transformed the retreat into a rout. Leaving eight thousand casualties and most of their heavy equipment behind, Joseph's troops fled all the way across the Pyrenees.

The Battle of Vitoria marked the effective end of the Napoleonic dynasty in Spain, for by the first week of July the French held no more than a few fortresses and a frontier strip along the Pyrenees and some exposed positions in Catalonia. Late in July, Marshal Soult took command of the Spanish front and launched a series of desperate attacks to relieve Pamplona and drive Wellington back from the French frontier. But the attacks failed, Pamplona fell, and in August the British successfully stormed San Sebastián, the last important French post in Spain. Defeat in Iberia also had its impact on the coming battles in Saxony, for the Emperor had to continue to station thousands of first-rate troops along the Pyrenees to protect southern France from invasion at a time when he desperately needed them in Germany. Thus the two-front war that had so seriously hampered him in 1812 continued to plague Napoleon in 1813.

Despite the deteriorating military situation, the Emperor refused to believe he was beaten and in the summer prepared to risk the future of his empire upon his talents as a warrior. The bulk of his army, 240,000 men, he concentrated around Dresden. While this force prepared to fall upon any allied advance from Silesia or Bohemia, a second army, 66,000 men strong, prepared to strike north at Berlin, and Davout with a small force was to move east from Hamburg. The allies, however, had a strategic plan of their own. Recognizing their inability to defeat an army commanded by the French Emperor, the three sovereigns and Prince Karl Philipp Schwarzenberg—a veteran of numerous campaigns stretching back to the Turkish War of 1788, a competent if not a brilliant strategist, and who in 1813 led the Austrian army and served as commander in chief of the allied forces—decided to advance cautiously into Saxony from Bohemia, Silesia, and Brandenburg, avoid battles with Napoleon, and seek engagements with detached corps. After wearing down the French army, the allies with overwhelming superiority would concentrate their forces and risk a general battle with the Corsican.

The Prussians opened the summer campaign by advancing from Silesia, but Napoleon struck on August 21 and forced Gebhard von Blücher—the uneducated, wild, frequently drunken Prussian commander who, despite his personal failings, hated the French and never admitted defeat—to retreat in order to re-form his shaken army. The Emperor's detached force led by Marshal Oudinot advanced toward Berlin, but Schwarzenberg debouched from Bohemia and advanced north along the Elbe in an effort to take Dresden while Napoleon was chasing the Prussians. Reacting quickly, Bonaparte left Macdonald to continue the pursuit of the Prussians and led the Guard and a cavalry corps in a lightning three-day march back to Dresden. He arrived on August 26, the very day the allies were intending to attack, and his appearance caused instantaneous panic at Schwarzenberg's headquarters. The allied sovereigns thereupon decided to retreat, but before the orders reached the front the army followed its original orders and attacked the French positions. The Dresden garrison, bolstered by Napoleon's reinforcements, held off the allied advance, and on August 27 the Emperor launched an offensive of his own in which he captured fifteen thousand and killed and wounded twenty-three thousand enemy troops.

Napoleon's last major victory on foreign soil did not produce decisive results. The allied army escaped intact, and the coalition's high command, reverting to the original strategy of doing battle with Napoleon's subordinates, soon regained the initiative. In Silesia, Blücher inflicted a sharp defeat upon Macdonald; Oudinot, checked before Berlin, had to retreat south, a move that forced Davout to fall back to Hamburg, and in Bohemia the retreating allied army turned on its pursuers. Striking at a corps led by Vandamme, the allies ambushed it, inflicted over fifteen thousand casualties on the French, and even captured the corps commander. Allied success in the last days of August canceled the psychological and physical impact of the French victory at Dresden and enabled the forces of the coalition to regain the strategic initiative. Consequently, in the first weeks of September the allied armies resumed their concentric advance into Saxony.

From Dresden, Napoleon lunged desperately at the

allied armies, but they managed to avoid decisive encounters with him, and while the Emperor was marching against one foe, others took advantage of his absence to tighten further the armed ring about the Grand Army. Napoleon sent Ney against Bernadotte's army in Brandenburg, but Blücher advanced from Silesia and Napoleon had to call off his thrust at Berlin. He marched instead against the Prussians, who withdrew, but Schwarzenberg seized his opportunity to move north against Dresden. The Emperor turned about and drove the Austrians back, but while he fought near Bohemia, Bernadotte attacked in Brandenburg and defeated an isolated French corps. Growing losses, the failure to achieve a decisive victory, and the difficulty of maintaining his line of communications under constant attacks by Cossack cavalry finally convinced Napoleon to abandon Dresden and retire to the west bank of the Elbe. Allied strategy had thus prevented the French Emperor from winning a decisive victory and disrupting the alliance, and by the end of September it was the Prussian, Russian, and Austrian armies that were taking the offensive and seeking a major battle.

After bringing up reinforcements to hold Silesia, Blücher marched north to join Bernadotte. The two commanders then planned to march south on Leipzig, where Napoleon, having left a garrison in Dresden, had concentrated the bulk of his army. At the same time Schwarzenberg was to move on Leipzig from the south, and the allied generals also planned to send out flanking units that would link the two armies west of Leipzig, cut Bonaparte's line of retreat to France, and force him to accept combat against overwhelming odds.

Weakened by short rations and delayed by bad weather, French forces failed to disrupt Blücher's march to the Elbe. By the first week of October, Blücher and Bernadotte had joined forces. With Blücher's army in the lead the combined force crossed the Elbe, escaped a French counterthrust, and moved southwest. Schwarzenberg meanwhile had moved north and on October 12 one of his divisions established contact with Blücher west of Leipzig.

Napoleon still had the option of breaking through the allied cordon, which was quite weak where Blücher's and Schwarzenberg's armies met, but rather than abandon all of Saxony, the Emperor elected to fight. With 175,000 men in a central position, Bonaparte hoped to defeat the 345,000 allied troops by attacking them separately as they closed in on the city.

The Battle of Leipzig, also known as the Battle of Nations, opened on October 16 with heavy fighting around the hamlets north and south of the city. Entering the battle piecemeal, the allied forces could make no headway and suffered heavy casualties; but the French on the other hand, also suffered heavily and did not succeed in breaking any of the coalition's armies. Under existing circumstances these local French victories were little better than defeats.

Both sides rested on the seventeenth, but Bernadotte's army finally arrived on the battlefield north of the city, and new Russian and Austrian troops arrived and took up positions east of Leipzig, thus completing the encirclement. Napoleon in turn found that the weight of numbers was too great for him to attempt new attacks. Consequently, when combat resumed on October 18 the French army had no choice but to fight a defensive battle. The allies attacked on all sides of the city. They took grievous losses, but their great superiority in men and guns gradually wore down the French, who had to fall back into an ever narrowing perimeter. Unable to withstand further attrition, which would lead inevitably to the total annihilation of his army, Napoleon decided to fight his way out of Leipzig and withdraw to central Germany.

The French retreat began on October 19, the first anniversary of the flight from Moscow. The Grand Army fought its way through the allied units covering Leipzig's western exits, but men, guns, and wagons coming from the eastern part of the perimeter got tangled up and delayed in the city's narrow, winding streets. The sudden defection of Saxon troops who turned and began firing upon their former French comrades added to the growing confusion. At this juncture, the officer in charge of the team that was to demolish the only bridge over the Elster River, flowing along the western walls of the city, left his post ostensibly to get new orders from the rear-guard commander. A young corporal left in charge heard firing from the eastern suburbs, panicked, and blew up the bridge while it was still crowded with retreating troops. This piece of murderous incompetence also stranded some twenty thousand men of the rear guard, who were then overwhelmed by the allies.

In the three days' fighting the allies lost fifty-two thousand men, but Napoleon lost sixty-eight thousand and with them his power in Germany. He had no choice but to retreat to the Rhine, leaving garrisons in Hamburg, Dresden, and a number of other cities. The Grand Army slashed its way through the Bavarian army, whose King Maximilian I had undertaken secret talks with the Austrians in September and had openly joined the coalition on October 8, and on October 31, 1813, some ninety-five thousand Frenchmen recrossed the river.

For the second time in a year the Emperor had lost an army, and his defeat at Leipzig marked the end of his influence in central Europe. Napoleon's persistent refusal to accept limitations or to make concessions was the prime cause of his defeat. Had he negotiated seriously in the summer, he might have attained a favorable peace or at least sown confusion in the allied ranks. Instead he chose to risk his power on another throw of the military dice. The allies, however, devised a minimum diplomatic program that served effectively to hold the coalition together. They also developed a military strategy sufficient to hold the French in check and ultimately to defeat them. Consequently, by the end of 1813 France was, for the first time since 1799, threatened with invasion. Napoleon could no longer hope to preserve French influence beyond the Rhine, and the next campaign would decide not the extent of Bonaparte's empire but his regime's very existence.

CHAPTER 11

THE DESTRUCTION OF FRENCH HEGEMONY

As the main allied armies were advancing to the Rhine, Austrian troops reoccupied Illyria and Venetia, and Wellington's army crossed the Pyrenees into France, compelling Soult to evacuate a series of entrenched positions, and forcing the French back to the outskirts of Bayonne.

Despite defeat on all fronts Napoleon received yet another opportunity to salvage a reasonable portion of his defunct Grand Empire. This opportunity arose out of Metternich's growing fear that Alexander was about to attempt to replace French hegemony with Russian domination. The Tsar, a cunning mystic and a Machiavellian idealist, who was convinced that his goals were identical with universal justice and that universal justice was identical with Russian strategic and diplomatic interests, apparently was planning to organize what he regarded as inevitable victory in such a manner as to leave Russia the arbiter of Europe. He had already promised his loyal satellite, Frederick William, the restoration of Prussia to its 1806 status, but he did not intend to re-establish the exact pre-Jena frontiers. Rather, Alexander wished to compensate Prussia with Saxony, keep Berlin's former Polish provinces for himself, create a Polish state attached to the Romanov crown, and thereby establish his frontier within easy marching distance of the Oder River. By deflecting Prussia westward he would also rekindle Austro-Prussian rivalry in Germany, which in turn would limit Vienna's ability to counter Russian schemes for Balkan expansion. The Tsar further contemplated driving Bonaparte from France and replacing him with his own client, Bernadotte, becoming protector of the Swiss Confederation, and restoring the prerevolutionary *status quo* in Italy, thereby preventing the Hapsburgs from gaining compensation in the Po Valley region.[1]

To limit Russian expansion, Metternich desired to retain a powerful French state. He had wanted to exclude Napoleonic influence from areas east of the Rhine, and in September had joined with Russia and Prussia in calling for Germany's liberation up to that river. The three powers had also agreed to ignore proposals advocating a unified Germany or the creation of a federal structure that would limit the independence of the member states. They agreed to reorganize Germany as a collection of independent sovereign states each in full control of its foreign and domestic policy. Austria thereby eliminated the possibility that any of her allies would carry out sweeping changes in Germany in the name of nationalism or provide massive compensation to the victors at German expense. The three had not decided the fate of the Rhineland, however, and after Leipzig and the French retreat from central Germany, Metternich convinced his allies to make another peace offer to the Emperor. Thus at Frankfurt on October 29, the coalition at Metternich's insistence reluctantly agreed to reply to a peace offer Napoleon had made during the Leipzig campaign in a futile effort to divide the allies, and on November 9 Metternich presented the allied terms to the French chargé to Weimar, who was at this time an allied prisoner. The Frankfurt proposals called for Napoleon to abandon Italy, Germany, Spain, and Holland, but they left him Savoy, Belgium, and the Rhineland, the famous "natural frontiers" originally conquered by the Republic. The Austrian Foreign Minister urged the Emperor to accept the proposals, since new allied victories would lead inevitably to more extensive demands, while French triumphs could not compel the coalition to reduce its

[1] A. de Nesselrode, ed., *Lettres et papiers du Chancelier Comte de Nesselrode* (Paris, 1905), IV, p. 288.

terms. The Frankfurt proposals, then, were the Emperor's last opportunity to retain a significant portion of the fruits of two decades of warfare.

The Corsican, however, refused to accept the fact that the balance of power in Europe had shifted decisively against him, nor did he believe that he could no longer impose his will upon his enemies. Rather than accept the status of one major power among others or use the proposals to drive a wedge between the continental allies and Britain, whose leaders objected to leaving Belgium in French hands, Bonaparte employed Metternich's offer as an armistice that would give him time to reorganize his shattered regiments. On November 23 he replied to the proposals by suggesting Mannheim as a conference site but made no reference to the allied conditions other than to express interest about the possibility of British concessions on maritime questions, which was probably the one issue that England, with goods flooding back to the Continent in the wake of the continental system's collapse, would refuse even to discuss.

Although the allied armies were preparing to cross the Rhine, were advancing in southern France, and had already forced the French out of most of Holland, the Emperor refused to conduct a serious effort to conclude a compromise peace. Fear that anything short of total victory would tarnish his domestic prestige and lead to the collapse of his regime may, indeed, have influenced his decision, but the French people's desire for peace indicates that popular sentiment would not, in all probability, have turned against the Emperor if he had brought the war to its end on reasonable terms. It was not, then, the Emperor's concern for public opinion that led him to persist in seeking military solutions, but rather his belief in his own genius and his refusal to accept limitations. He simply assumed that despite all odds he would ultimately triumph.

Metternich replied to Napoleon's suggestion concerning a conference at Mannheim by telling him that the allies would not negotiate unless the French first accepted the Frankfurt proposals. Receiving no reply, the allies on December 1 issued a manifesto declaring that it was not their intention to wage war upon the French people but only to end Napoleonic preponderance outside of France. The unshaken unity of the coalition plus their continued military preparations finally convinced the Emperor to accept the Frankfurt proposals. In a note to the allies dated December 5, he accepted the proposals as a basis for negotiation, but he was too late. His earlier offer had revealed his true intentions, and the allies decided to invade France and dictate future French frontiers only after achieving military victory.

While talking with his foes, Bonaparte had also been busy trying to raise new armies. The French were, however, tired of the perpetual war, and thousands of conscripts refused to respond to their mobilization orders. Royalist bands composed primarily of deserters once again took up arms in the western and northern departments, while in Paris a band of politicians led by the former Foreign Minister Talleyrand began to prepare for the downfall of the imperial regime. Napoleonic appeals to national patriotism resembling the rallying cries of '92 and '93 went almost unnoticed in the provinces, and the imperial armies were ill prepared to meet the new allied offensive. On December 29, 1813, Blücher's army crossed the Rhine and advanced into Lorraine. On New Year's day 1814 Schwarzenberg's forces, having traversed Switzerland, entered France. To meet the 250,000-man invasion Napoleon had but 67,000 men ready to take the field.

As the allied armies marched, statesmen were deciding the future of France. Castlereagh, Britain's Foreign Secretary, arrived on the Continent armed with a Memorandum of Cabinet of December 26, 1813, which set forth his government's objectives. The British aims closely resembled Pitt's plans of 1799 and 1805 and included demands for the expulsion of France from the Low

Countries, the enlargement of Holland, independence for Spain and Portugal, and extensive colonial compensations for England. Stopping first at The Hague, Castlereagh arranged for a marriage between the hereditary Prince of Orange and the Princess of Wales, promising the Prince compensation in Belgium plus a cash payment in return for Dutch renunciation of the Cape Colony. Having re-established British influence in the Netherlands, the Foreign Secretary traveled to Basel to meet Metternich and discuss future plans.

The two ministers met on January 18 and soon reached accord upon a number of critical issues. Both men were worried about the Tsar's ambitions and about his refusal to discuss any peace terms until the conclusion of final victory. By refusing to set peace conditions before victory, Alexander was attempting to retain as many options as possible in order to expand Russian influence westward. Metternich was as determined to oppose Russian hegemony as he was to combat French dominance, and prior to his meeting with Castlereagh, he directed Schwarzenberg to halt military operations until further notice. He then described Alexander's schemes to the British minister, who in the interests of allied unity agreed to accept either Napoleon or a Bourbon restoration in France, and to exclude all other alternatives, including Bernadotte or a regency under Marie Louise. In return for British backing Metternich agreed to allow England to have her way on the questions of maritime rights and the fate of the Low Countries. The two diplomats also agreed to explore again the possibility of concluding a peace with Napoleon by opening talks with the French Foreign Minister, Armand de Caulaincourt, who had on January 9 presented himself before the allied lines, armed with the power to conclude a peace. The Austrian and British statesmen then met with the Tsar, who had to bow to their insistence upon further peace talks in order to keep the coalition united. In the Langres Protocol of January 29 the allies agreed to negotiate with Napoleon on the basis of the French frontiers of 1792, to unite Belgium to Holland, and to exclude maritime issues from all future discussions. Metternich and Castlereagh not only preserved the coalition's internal cohesion but also convinced Alexander and Frederick William to negotiate and fight simultaneously and to pursue relatively moderate goals. They thereby deprived Bonaparte of the chance to rouse the French people to defend their national existence and limited his opportunity to divide the allies by means of separate peace parleys and special concessions to one set of his foes.

Meanwhile on the battle front the allies continued to advance. By January 22 Blücher's army had crossed the Meuse and on the following day it seized a bridgehead on the Marne. Schwarzenberg's forces also moved forward, and as Blücher crossed the Marne the Austrian commander in chief was advancing on Troyes, which lay athwart the southern approach to Paris. On other fronts Murat in order to remain in power deserted his Emperor and joined the allies on January 11, and Denmark left the war three days later. In the south Wellington's forces beat off a series of desperate counterattacks and inflicted severe losses on Soult's tired and depleted forces.

Convinced that he could still turn the tide of battle, the French Emperor prepared to mount a fast-moving, hard-hitting campaign to take advantage of the facts that he held a central position and that his foes moving against him from the southeast were operating as two separate armies with virtually no units linking them together. By defeating each in detail the Corsican hoped to repeat his earlier Italian triumphs, which he had won by means of maneuver and shock power.

Leaving screening units on the Seine to delay Schwarzenberg's march on Troyes, Bonaparte concentrated thirty-four thousand men near the Marne for a blow against Blücher. On January 26 Napoleon pounced on St. Dizier, a town lying behind Blücher's line of march. French troops took the town after a sharp fight with

Blücher's rear guard but soon discovered that the main Prussian force had crossed the Marne and entered Brienne. Bonaparte pushed on to Brienne, where Blücher had concentrated a sizable force, and on January 29 the French forced him to evacuate the village and retreat south to a position near La Rothière, close by the Aube River. Blücher then received reinforcements from Schwarzenberg, and on February 1 the energetic Prussian general advanced back toward La Rothière. In bitter fighting in which each side lost some six thousand men, Blücher forced the Emperor to retreat. The French army limped back to Troyes, badly hurt but still dangerous.

At this moment the coalition gave Napoleon still another chance to save his throne. On February 5 the peace conference that the allies had previously agreed to hold opened at Châtillon. Two days later they presented their terms, which called upon the French Emperor to accept the reduction of France's frontiers to the limits of 1792 as a preliminary step to a general settlement. Caulaincourt wanted to accept the allied offer, but he felt that his master would refuse, and although he had full power to conclude a treaty, he decided to request further instructions from the imperial headquarters. Meanwhile, a dangerous split developed within the allied ranks as the Tsar, convinced that the victory at La Rothière was decisive, decided to march on Paris, overthrow Napoleon, and summon an assembly of notables to provide France with a new regime. The assembly would deliberate under close Russian supervision, and the Tsar would thereby play a major if not dominant role in selecting Napoleon's successor. On February 12 a Council of Ministers met to discuss Caulaincourt's offer, made without Napoleon's approval, to accept the allied terms. There the Tsar's delegate stated that the objective of the coalition was the overthrow of Napoleon. Austrian and British statesmen insisted that Caulaincourt's offer was an acceptable basis for peace talks and that if all negotiations failed and further campaigning brought about

Bonaparte's fall from power a Bourbon restoration was the only acceptable alternative. The next day Metternich declared that if Alexander persisted in his intention to impose his own solution upon France and his own allies, Austria would withdraw from the coalition and seek a separate peace with Napoleon. Castlereagh supported his Austrian colleague and called for a renewal of the Châtillon talks. The Tsar, however, remained adamant, and a coalition within the coalition developed as Austria and England ranged themselves against Russia. On this occasion Prussia, wishing to avoid renewed fighting and possible new defeats, deserted the Tsar and on February 14 agreed with England and Austria to regard the Châtillon terms as adequate guarantees of the future security of Europe. The three powers also undertook to negotiate only with Napoleon or a Bourbon king.[2]

Napoleon, however, did not take advantage of the allied peace offer or of the growing tensions within the coalition. In the aftermath of his defeat at La Rothière he had concluded that his situation was desperate and had actually drawn up a letter accepting the Châtillon conditions. He then learned that the allied commanders were repeating their mistake of January by marching toward Paris along separate routes without sufficient flanking units to link the two forces. Always more prone to fight than to negotiate and still convinced that his genius would enable him to triumph against almost any odds, the French Emperor disavowed Caulaincourt's unilateral acceptance of the Châtillon terms and abandoned diplomacy in favor of war.

Leaving a corps to hold Schwarzenberg in check near Troyes, Bonaparte gathered seventy thousand troops and descended upon Blücher. On February 10 at Champaubert, Napoleon struck and nearly destroyed a five-thousand-man Russian unit. He then swung west behind

[2] J. Hanoteau, ed., *Mémoires du général de Caulaincourt* (Paris, 1933), III, Ch. I; and Metternich, *Mémoires,* I, pp. 181–83.

Blücher's army, and at Montmirail on the eleventh the French severely mauled two enemy corps, inflicting four thousand casualties upon them. Blücher ordered a general retreat, but upon receiving news that Schwarzenberg was on the move, he stopped his retreat and ordered a renewed westerly advance. Napoleon was ready for him, and on February 14 near Vauxchamps he struck, shattering a division with a vicious cavalry charge and forcing the Prussian to order a new retreat. Harassed by the French, Blücher fled for Châlons, leaving behind seven thousand casualties.

Bonaparte then marched forty-seven miles in thirty-six hours and threw himself upon Schwarzenberg's army, destroyed a small detachment, and forced the rest into a hasty retreat all the way back to Bar-sur-Aube. Military victories, however, had an effect opposite to the one sought by the Emperor, for instead of deepening the rift in the coalition, they actually helped to heal it. Alarmed by Napoleon's demonstration of his continued capacity to wage war, Alexander on February 15 dropped his plans to impose his own solutions on France and accepted the policy of his allies. Nor did he object when Schwarzenberg offered to conclude an armistice with the French on February 17.

Once again, though, Napoleon misinterpreted the over-all situation. He assumed that his victories were strategic rather than tactical and began to contemplate not only the expulsion of his enemies from France but also a new campaign in Germany. Assuming that he was the master of events, he instructed Caulaincourt to conclude no agreement whatsoever without imperial sanction, and on February 21 he wrote to Francis I offering to sign a separate peace with Austria on the basis of France's "natural" frontiers. This effort to divide the coalition came too late and demanded too much, and on February 25 the allies insisted upon a reply to their offer of France's ancient limits as a preliminary to a general peace, but they received no answer.

Metternich then concluded that he could never convince Bonaparte to accept reasonable peace terms and that he could not balance Napoleon against the Tsar to secure the future European balance of power. He therefore agreed to join Castlereagh in signing a treaty of general alliance, thereby fulfilling the British minister's long-sought ambition to accomplish England's objectives through rather than in spite of the wishes of a coalition. The Prussians and Russians, in need of British subsidies and the co-operation of the Austrian army and desirous of maintaining allied unity until Napoleon's final defeat, readily agreed to join a Grand Alliance. Consequently, the four powers signed on March 1 and published on March 9 the Treaty of Chaumont. According to the terms of the treaty the four powers pledged themselves to continue the war against France until they achieved their objectives. They defined their goals as the creation of an enlarged and independent Holland, a confederated Germany, a free Switzerland, a liberated Italy, and the restoration of the Spanish Bourbons. The allies undertook to place a stipulated number of troops in the field, and England promised subsidies to the other powers. The members of the Grand Alliance also agreed that no one party would conclude a separate peace with Napoleon and that the alliance would last for twenty years after the conclusion of hostilities to insure against possible renewed French aggression. Finally, the four powers consented to assist each other in the event of any French effort to disrupt the arrangements made at the forthcoming peace. The allies had solidified their positions, insured themselves against the possibility of defection, and attained greater unity against the ever dangerous Corsican. Thus Napoleon's refusal to follow his tactical victories with sincere peace efforts, by convincing the allies to conclude the Treaty of Chaumont, had enhanced their military and diplomatic unity.

In addition to cementing their diplomatic unity the allies also regained the military initiative. Blücher added to his command an additional thirty thousand troops who had advanced into northern France, occupied Soissons, and then withdrawn toward Rheims to conform to Blücher's retreat. On February 24 the Prussian general began to advance north against Paris, and Napoleon decided to lead the bulk of his army away from Schwarzenberg's front, fall on the Prusso-Russian force, destroy it, sweep east, collect the garrisons of Metz and Verdun, and, finally, descend upon Schwarzenberg's line of communications. Blücher did not, however, move directly on Paris. Instead he marched toward Rheims seeking to link up with his new contingent, which had in the interim begun a new advance on Soissons. Napoleon tried to cut the Prussian off from Rheims, but Blücher eluded him, and on March 5 joined up with the other segment of his army near Laon. He thus had some eighty-five thousand troops under his command, concentrated and ready to strike at Paris. In the south Schwarzenberg lurched forward against the outnumbered French units left around Troyes. The French could do little but fight rear-guard actions, and by March 5 the Austro-Russian forces had entered the city.

Undaunted by the growing pressure south of Paris, Bonaparte pushed on in his effort to destroy Blücher. On March 7 near Craonne the French attacked one of Blücher's corps, and in confused fighting each side lost some five thousand men. Blücher then withdrew to Laon, where he concentrated all of his available units and prepared for a full-scale battle with the Emperor. On March 9 Napoleon with 37,000 men assaulted Blücher's 85,000-man force. No longer contemplating a great sweep into eastern France, Bonaparte wanted only to drive the Prussians and Russians away from Paris and then march to bolster his crumbling front south of the capital. French frontal attacks, however, made no progress, and even the arrival of ten thousand more troops failed to alter the situation. The day's fighting ended in a bloody stalemate, but at night Blücher launched a sudden attack that

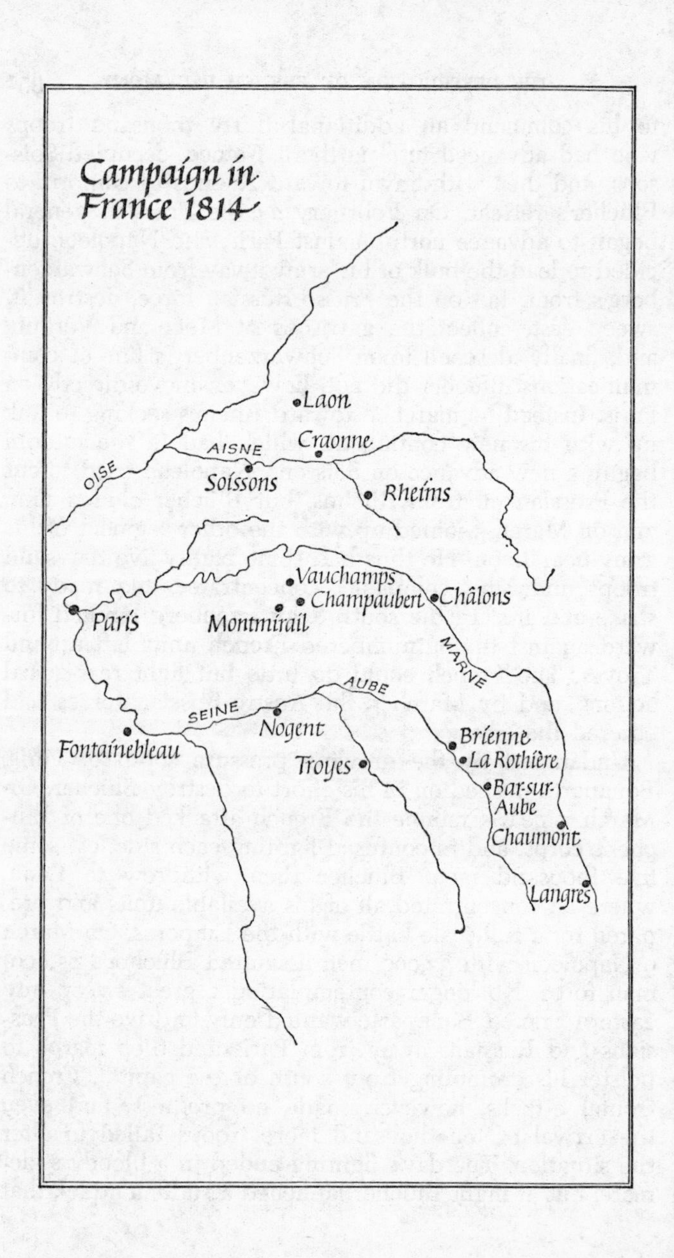
Campaign in France 1814
Laon
Craonne
AISNE
OISE
Soissons
Rheims
Vauchamps
Champaubert
Châlons
Paris
Montmirail
MARNE
AUBE
SEINE
Nogent
Fontainebleau
Brienne
La Rothière
Troyes
Bar-sur-Aube
Chaumont
Langres

left one of the Emperor's corps severely shaken. Blücher then collapsed from exhaustion but his chief of staff, Gneisenau, resumed the battle on the morning of the tenth. Outnumbered, the French finally had to disengage and fall back toward Paris. The allies had lost four thousand men, but Napoleon suffered six thousand casualties, losses that he could ill afford. In the far south of France the Emperor's forces also suffered defeat. On February 14 Wellington had led sixty thousand troops toward Bordeaux. After detaching a division to screen Bayonne, the British defeated Soult's forces, and on March 12 Wellington's men entered Bordeaux as the French fell back to Toulouse.[3]

Despite his defeat at Laon Napoleon was still a dangerous opponent, and without hesitation he issued orders to fortify Paris and prepared to march against Schwarzenberg. On March 13 the French army broke an allied division near Rheims, a blow that produced panic in the coalition's ranks. Blücher, having recovered from his collapse, led his army back to Laon, and Schwarzenberg not only halted his crossing of the Seine but also began to withdraw toward Troyes.

The Corsican then tried to profit from his tactical victory by replying to the allied peace offer of February 25. He agreed to surrender all of his conquests beyond France's frontiers, to evacuate Holland, and to establish Belgium as an independent state under the rule of a French prince. Since Holland, Belgium, and Bonaparte's conquests were already in allied hands save for a few garrisons, the coalition could not and did not take Napoleon's concessions seriously. Moreover, the French Emperor made no mention of the Rhineland, implying that he meant to retain that region, and thereby reinforced most allied statesmen in their view that it was impossible to deal with him. Metternich made a last appeal to Cau-

[3] Wellington fought a final battle with Soult at Toulouse, but it took place on April 10, after Paris had fallen.

laincourt to bring his master to a sense of reality, but the French Foreign Minister could do nothing. The allies then began to take the first steps toward overthrowing the Bonapartist dynasty and restoring the Bourbon monarchy. The leaders of the Grand Alliance received a royalist emissary, the Baron Vitroles, at their headquarters and encouraged him to organize a pro-Bourbon movement in those parts of France occupied by the invading armies. The British Cabinet meanwhile directed Castlereagh not to conclude a final peace with Napoleon, and in Bordeaux, with British blessings, local officials and citizens began sporting the white cockade and calling for the return of Louis XVIII.

On the battlefield Napoleon, still confident of his strategic abilities, advanced on Arcis-sur-Aube on the way to the upper Marne, where he intended to strike at the communications of both allied armies. Schwarzenberg for once did not react predictably, for instead of retreating he ordered his troops to concentrate between Troyes and Arcis. Nevertheless on March 20 Napoleon's leading corps took Arcis, crossed the Aube, and advanced on the hamlet of Torcy. There a bitter fight developed in which the French repulsed several allied cavalry charges. On the following day twenty-eight thousand French soldiers resumed their advance but soon discovered that they were trying to dislodge Schwarzenberg's entire army, which vastly outnumbered them. Napoleon therefore fell back; Schwarzenberg cautiously followed him, and a stiff rear-guard action ensued. The French Emperor, however, made good his withdrawal and marched for St. Dizier on the Marne.

The allies then decided to concentrate both their field armies for a final blow. Blücher moved east, retaking Rheims, and Schwarzenberg advanced north. At this moment cavalry pickets intercepted several French messengers who carried information indicating that the Parisians were in a state of panic and that the city's defenses were disorganized and incomplete. Acting on this news, the

Tsar virtually forced Schwarzenberg to order a general advance on the French capital, ignoring whatever threats Napoleon might pose to the allied flanks and communications.

On March 25 Schwarzenberg and Blücher began to move on Paris, and three days later the two armies joined together at Meux, a town on the very threshold of the French capital. The next day the Empress and her son, the King of Rome, left Paris for the south. On March 30 Joseph, who had fled to France after the Battle of Vitoria, and part of the government followed, while Talleyrand and his faction remained in the city to prepare for the arrival of the Tsar. Meanwhile, Marmont and Mortier, whose corps had been fending off the Prussian army, fell back to the outskirts of the metropolis, and after a series of rear-guard actions against overwhelming odds, the two marshals withdrew to defensive positions along the heights of Montmartre, the last bastion protecting Paris.

At 2 A.M. on the morning of March 31, 1814, Marshal Marmont deserted his Emperor. Feeling that further resistance was futile and would lead only to useless bloodshed, and desiring to carve a niche for himself with the allies and Bourbons, Marmont signed an armistice with the allies and withdrew his troops to a position south of Paris. The coalition's army then entered the city. Napoleon meanwhile had raced north from St. Dizier in a desperate attempt to save his capital. Outdistancing both his army and his personal escort, the Emperor passed through Fontainebleau and arrived at the village of Essonnes, where in the early hours of the thirty-first he encountered a courier bearing news of the surrender of Paris. Bonaparte then returned to Fontainebleau, where he began to amass troops for a counterattack and where he was to play out the last desperate hours of his reign.

In Paris royalist demonstrators took to the streets while Talleyrand kept in touch with the Tsar and the royalists and called the imperial Senate into session. On April 3 the Senate formally deposed Napoleon and released the army from its oath of loyalty to the Emperor. On April 4 the Corsican sent Caulaincourt and Ney to Paris, bearing an offer of abdication in favor of his infant son, the King of Rome. The two delegates reached the city on the fifth and obtained an audience with Alexander, the only allied ruler who had entered Paris. At first the Tsar seemed receptive to Napoleon's proposal, but in the midst of the talks news that Marmont had marched his corps to Versailles and placed himself and his men at the coalition's disposal changed Alexander's mind. The Russian ruler thereupon insisted that Napoleon abdicate without conditions, and on the following morning a dejected Caulaincourt returned to Fontainebleau and informed his Emperor of his final defeat.

Later that day the Senate, guided by Talleyrand, issued a charter, the second article of which recalled the brother of the last Bourbon king to ascend the throne of France as Louis XVIII. The allies and the provisional French regime then signed the Treaty of Fontainebleau, which called upon Napoleon, who had not yet given up hopes of retaining his throne and did not recognize the provisional government in Paris, to renounce sovereignty over France and Italy for himself and all members of his family. In return the allies promised him the island of Elba and an annual subsidy. Caulaincourt had returned to Paris, and although he lacked the authority to agree to end the Bonapartist regime, he signed the treaty in Napoleon's name and departed again to present the allied terms to his master. The Emperor then tried to rally his army for another campaign to save his throne, but this time his marshals, seeing no hope of victory, refused to march. He thereupon made a suicide attempt, but a doctor saved him. The Corsican then bowed to the inevitable and ratified the treaty signifying his downfall. A few days later allied commissioners arrived at Fontainebleau to escort him into exile. On April 20, 1814, the Imperial Guard paraded in the courtyard of the Fontainebleau château. Napoleon selected his personal escort, made a short address, embraced the commander of the Guard and the Imperial Guard standard, entered his carriage, and drove off into exile.[4]

By refusing to accept the fact that he could not triumph against the combined forces of the great powers of Europe, by relying on armed might rather than diplomacy, and by failing to accept allied peace offers in time, Napoleon had lost his empire and his throne. His last campaigns were gallant and brilliant but ultimately futile. He had risked total defeat in pursuit of the elusive dream of complete victory, and his gamble had failed. In the wake of his collapse he left behind a growing legend of genius, bravery, and military glory. He also left the victors the difficult if prosaic task of reorganizing a Continent shaken by decades of war and revolution and of re-establishing the conditions of normal international relations.

In concluding peace with France, the great powers decided to deal mildly with the restored Bourbon regime. Allied statesmen regarded the monarchy as a nonaggressive power since Louis XVIII owed his throne to the coalition's arms. Furthermore, the allied leaders realized that the monarchy was not popular in France and that to impose harsh terms of peace would only erode its already rather narrow base of support. Consequently, the First Peace of Paris, signed on May 3, 1814, established France's frontiers as they existed on January 1, 1792. In addition, France retained Avignon, the Saar, and part of Savoy without having to grant either financial or territorial compensation to the former owners. Finally, the victorious powers did not impose an indemnity or an occupation army upon their prostrate rival. Thus if France lost her dominant European position, her national integrity remained intact, and her status as a major

[4] Hanoteau, *Mémoires du . . . Caulaincourt*, III, Ch. IX; and G. Lacour-Gayet, "Napoléon à Fontainebleau en 1814," in *Revue des études napoléoniennes* (1922), XIX.

power, although not *the* major power, remained unquestioned.

In the Low Countries and in portions of Italy and the non-European world, the British imposed their policies of creating barrier states against the possibility of future French aggression, and London also expanded its imperial domain. The House of Orange returned to Holland; the Stadtholder became a king, and he annexed Belgium. He allowed the British to retain the Cape Colony and received from London a cash compensation, which he agreed to employ in the construction of fortresses along the Franco-Belgian frontier. The King of Sardinia returned to the Italian mainland, resumed control of Piedmont and Savoy, and enlarged his kingdom by taking Genoa. Sardinia-Piedmont, like Holland, could act as a barrier against an aggressive France, a barrier strengthened by the fact that Austria intended to enlarge her frontiers by taking extensive compensation in northern Italy. The British also kept for themselves a number of small but strategically vital territories, including Heligoland, Malta, and the Ionian Islands. Possession of these regions gave London excellent bases from which to extend its naval, commercial, and diplomatic influence into the Baltic and eastern Mediterranean.[5]

Even after the conclusion of the Peace of Paris the powers had to resolve a number of issues—the exact nature of German reorganization, the fate of Poland, Saxony, and Italy, and the future of the Grand Alliance. In the Paris Treaty the allies had agreed to hold a congress to decide upon the future settlement of these and other issues. The congress convened at Vienna on September 15, 1814, and the assemblage of kings, princes, generals, and statesmen was indeed impressive. Representatives

[5] Provisions dealing with the enlargement of Holland and the future of Malta were included in the Treaty of Paris. See also F. Murhard, ed., *Nouveaux suppléments au recueil de traités et d'autres actes remarquables des puissances et états de l'Europe depuis 1761 jusqu' à présent* (Gottingen, 1839), I, pp. 330–31.

of great and small powers and even spokesmen for defunct states seeking re-establishment flocked to the Hapsburg capital.

Of course, the members of the Chaumont alliance had no intentions of giving the lesser powers an equal voice in the forthcoming deliberations. In fact, they fully intended to retain the decision-making process in their own hands. Despite this fundamental agreement, however, divisions within the ranks of the great powers persisted. Russia and Prussia intended to resist. England, moreover, was suspicious of Russo-Prussian intentions, and Castlereagh feared that Vienna might bow to pressure from Berlin and St. Petersburg. The existence of rivalries within the coalition gave Talleyrand, once again Foreign Minister of France, an opportunity to seek admission into the inner councils of the coalition and thereby end French diplomatic isolation and restore his nation's status as one of Europe's leading states. Even before the congress assembled, Talleyrand had launched his campaign to restore French influence. He began to write flattering letters to the Tsar in the name of Louis XVIII. These notes hinted at the existence of a community of interests between France and Russia. Rumors of these notes filtered back to London, as Talleyrand intended. Fearing the development of a Franco-Russian entente, which would make any balance of forces completely uneven, Castlereagh decided to accept a French invitation to stop off at Paris on his way to Vienna. Arriving in Paris at the end of August, Castlereagh soon discovered that Talleyrand and Louis XVIII agreed with his view concerning the necessity of establishing a European balance in which no single state or coalition could dominate the rest. He found that the French were suspicious of Russian and Prussian intentions as well. Although the two statesmen did not conclude any formal agreements at Paris, and France remained in theory an isolated, defeated state with no power to influence the decisions of the great powers, they did, however, arrive at the tacit understanding that they had mutual interests. Consequently, at Vienna the French were able to rely upon British approval of their continued efforts to gain admission into the highest councils of the congress.

Procedural and legal technicalities concerning the organization and structure of the congress gave Talleyrand an opening to demand a major role in the deliberations. Although the four great powers had stated in a secret article in the Peace of Paris their intention to control the congress, the lesser powers were not bound either legally or morally to accept this decision. Talleyrand seized upon this fact to mount an attack against the projected structure of the deliberations. On September 30 in a meeting with representatives of the great powers, he denounced the absence of other states that had signed the Peace of Paris. That same evening he addressed an official note to the four ministers in which he argued that all eight signatories of the Peace of Paris—the great powers plus Portugal, Spain, Sweden, and France—should jointly direct the congress. Moreover, he asserted that a plenary session of the whole congress had to sanction the actions of the eight.[6]

Talleyrand then held a meeting of the small powers and obtained their ardent backing. The four leading powers were in a quandary. They did not wish to include all of the minor powers in their deliberations, but neither did they wish to impose their will on the rest of Europe, since any future revisionist power would thereby be able to find numerous allies. Furthermore, the major powers were not themselves in accord, and Castlereagh was more than willing to enlarge the decision-making body

[6] Murhard, *Nouveaux suppléments*, I, pp. 334–37 gives the protocol of September 22 wherein the four great powers agreed to retain real decision-making powers in their own hands. For Talleyrand's policy see G. Ferrero, *The Reconstruction of Europe: Talleyrand and the Congress of Vienna* (New York, 1963), pp. 142–43; D. Cooper, *Talleyrand* (Stanford, 1967), Ch. X; and G. Pallain, ed., *The Correspondence of Prince Talleyrand and King Louis XVIII during the Congress of Vienna* (New York, 1881).

of the congress in order to find counterweights to Russia and Prussia. Therefore, on October 30 the members of the Quadruple Alliance plus the four other parties to the Treaty of Paris agreed to postpone indefinitely the plenary sessions of the congress, and such a session never met except to ratify the final act. The eight powers then proceeded to direct the workings of the Vienna negotiations while the great powers plus France retained control of major questions and critical decisions. Talleyrand thus prevented the great powers from exercising complete control over the congress, and although he did not gain complete acceptance for France as an equal partner with the major states, he did gain admission to their councils. Henceforth the allies consulted with the French instead of dictating to them.

In the ensuing negotiations the rulers and statesmen of the leading powers readily agreed that their basic objective was to restore a state system in which a number of independent and sovereign states could exist without fear of domination or conquest by another power. Despite this general consensus the leading nations of Europe were nevertheless deeply divided over specific issues.

The major divisive problem concerned Russian and Prussian designs in eastern Europe and the fate of Poland and Saxony. Alexander and Frederick William had agreed before the congress that Russia would take control of the former duchy of Warsaw, add to this region the Polish provinces seized in earlier partitions, and create a Kingdom of Poland linked to Russia by a personal union wherein Alexander would remain the autocratic Tsar of Russia and simultaneously become the constitutional monarch of Poland. In return for sacrificing his Polish provinces Frederick William was to take all of Saxony. Metternich naturally was horrified by these plans. Having fought against French hegemony, he had no intention of passively watching its replacement with Russo-Prussian domination. The expansion of Russia from the Vistula almost to the Oder and the enlargement of

Prussia along Austria's strategic Bohemian frontier was such a severe threat to Hapsburg security that Metternich was determined to counter it by any means necessary.

Castlereagh shared many of Metternich's views and had no desire to substitute a Romanov for a Bonapartist hegemony. His appeals to the Tsar to renounce Russian claims to all of Poland in the interests of allied unity and a stable continental peace were fruitless;[7] the Tsar informed him that a large Russian army held Poland and that only superior force would prevent him from dealing with Poland as he saw fit. Castlereagh also failed to convince the Prussians to abandon their eastern ally. Metternich then joined with him in a promise to the Prussians to support their claims to Saxony if they would abandon their backing of Russian designs on Poland. Shortly afterward Metternich offered to accept Russian plans for Poland if the Tsar abandoned his Prussian ally. The Tsar, however, uncovered this stratagem, rejected the Austrian proposals, and exposed the scheme to the Prussians, thereby bringing about the collapse of efforts to divide the Russo-Prussian entente. As a next step Castlereagh proposed that the great powers place the Polish issue before the Vienna congress as a whole, but Alexander rejected this gambit also. The Prussians in turn made a compromise proposal. They advocated that the Tsar dispose of Poland as he wished but that the important military and commercial centers, Thorn and Cracow, remain independent and neutral. They also demanded all of Saxony for themselves and suggested that the deposed King, Frederick Augustus, find compensation in the Rhineland or Westphalia. Metternich quickly rejected this solution and thereby brought about a complete deadlock in the negotiations.

Growing tensions between England and Austria on the

[7] Murhard, *Nouveaux suppléments*, I, pp. 338–40; and Great Britain Foreign Office, *British and Foreign State Papers 1812–1814* (London, 1841), II, pp. 1173–80.

one hand and Russia and Prussia on the other grew more serious in November when the Russian occupation army in Saxony handed over the administration of the kingdom to Prussian authorities in an effort to present England and Austria with a *fait accompli.* At the same time Grand Duke Constantine, the Tsar's brother, issued a proclamation in Warsaw calling upon the Poles to fight for their independence, a clear indication that the Russians intended to stay in Poland with or without the consent of London and Vienna. The Austrians then moved troops to Galicia, and a new war became a distinct possibility.

Talleyrand, still anxious to gain full admittance for France into the ranks of the great powers, undertook to use the crisis to gain recognition of French equality from at least one of the rival factions. He agreed to support Metternich and Castlereagh while Hardenberg, Prussia's representative at Vienna, announced that the Hohenzollern kingdom was prepared to fight in order to gain control of Saxony. The response to this overt threat was the creation of a coalition within the coalition. On January 3, 1815, England, Austria, and France signed a treaty of mutual defense against Prussian or Russian attack.[8] The contracting parties agreed to furnish 150,000 men each or the equivalent in cash. The treaty ended French isolation and gained for the Bourbon regime equal status with the other major powers. The treaty also placed Frederick William and Alexander on notice that if they persisted in their aggressive designs they would have to face the prospect of war.

Neither the Tsar nor the Prussian King was in the last analysis willing to undertake a new war. Consequently, at the end of January the Prussians accepted Metternich's proposal that Berlin and Vienna co-operate to establish a mutually satisfactory Polish border and that Prussia should obtain part but not all of Saxony. In February

[8] Murhard, *Nouveaux suppléments,* I, pp. 368–72; and Pallain, *Correspondence of Prince Talleyrand,* p. 242.

Russia accepted the Austrian plan, and a drafting committee received instructions to implement Metternich's general plan and put it into a concrete treaty form. The committee worked rapidly, and the powers signed a final agreement on February 11. The treaty provided that Prussia should receive Posen and Thorn, that Austria should retain Galicia, and that Cracow should become a free city. The rest of Napoleonic Warsaw passed into the hands of Tsar Alexander, who transformed his new acquisition into a Kingdom of Poland, where he reigned as a constitutional monarch. Prussia received about 40 per cent of Saxony, the remainder being returned to the Saxon ruler, and Swedish Pomerania plus extensive Rhineland territories, including the cities of Mainz and Cologne. Austria retook the Tyrol and Salzburg, gained back the Illyrian provinces, and received promises of extensive gains in Italy.[9]

After the settlement of the Polish-Saxon issue the powers dealt with other questions with relative ease. Most of the new territorial arrangements were in fact either already in existence or previously agreed upon, and the congress had only to elaborate the details, which it did with reasonable speed and efficiency. In Italy, Austria received Venetia and Lombardy, and Hapsburg princes ascended the thrones of Parma and Tuscany. The Pope regained his former domains in central Italy; Sardinia retook Piedmont and Savoy and annexed Genoa, and in return for his betrayal of Napoleon the allies allowed Murat to retain the Neapolitan throne while Ferdinand, the former Bourbon monarch, kept the island of Sicily. In other areas the powers recognized the Swiss Confederation as perpetually neutral, a status that has remained unchanged to this day. Sweden took Norway, retained it

[9] These provisions were incorporated into the final act of the Vienna congress. See G. F. Martens, *Nouveau recueil de traités d'alliance, de paix, de trève, de neutralité, de commerce de limites d'échange etc. des puissances et états de l'Europe* (Gottingen, 1817), II, pp. 379–431.

until 1905, and the German states formed a new confederation. The eighteenth-century gothic wonderland of over three hundred separate states was not restored, and the "Napoleonic revolution" that reshaped Germany into some thirty-nine sovereignties was retained. Liberals from every part of Germany hoped to go further and create a unitary constitutional Germany in 1815, but the Germanic princes, including Austria and Prussia, frustrated their designs. Each member state retained full sovereignty, and the Federal Diet, which met at Frankfurt under permanent Austrian presidency, represented the member states. The Diet had the right to declare war and make peace, and each member of the Confederation agreed not to make hostile alliances or go to war against another participant. The princes thus protected their sovereign rights, for the German liberals, drawn mainly from the middle classes, lacked the strength and popular support to impose their own solution. But because none of the German rulers wished to limit his authority by strengthening the Confederation, the Diet was destined to remain a conference of ambassadors and never became a focal point for the evolution of a unified Germany. German and Italian unity thus remained a dream—only later when one of the princely states decided to use nationalism to enhance its own power did the dream become reality. The various committees of the congress also solved several minor but vexing issues, including a new set of rules of diplomatic procedure. In fact, the rules of determining classification of diplomatic officials, precedence in ceremonial matters, and the order of signing a treaty functioned with a minimum of confusion for more than a century.[10]

The congress did not attempt to resolve international conflicts outside the Continent—an implicit recognition of England's mastery of the seas. The Anglo-American conflict had raged throughout the last years of the Napole-

[10] Ibid.

onic wars. In 1813 the Royal Navy launched a series of successful hit-and-run raids in the Chesapeake Bay area and the Delaware capes. For their part the Americans gained control of Lake Erie. The Americans also recaptured Detroit, which they had lost in 1812, and took and burned York, the capital of Upper Canada. British troops raided western New York state, took Fort Niagara on the south shore of Lake Ontario, and beat off an assault on Montreal.

In 1814 after Napoleon's defeat, the British stepped up their war effort against the United States. They planned to invade the United States from Niagara, Lake Champlain, and New Orleans, and raid the Chesapeake area. On the Niagara front the Americans attacked first, and in hard fighting defeated the British. In a second clash the Americans gained a second triumph, thus preventing a British offensive from Niagara. On Lake Champlain the Americans won a murderous naval engagement, thereby foiling the British on their second front. In the Chesapeake area the British were more successful for a time. They captured Washington, D.C., and burned it in revenge for the destruction of York. American forces at Baltimore were better prepared, however, than the troops in Virginia. They repulsed the English expedition, an event that became enshrined in a poem that in turn became the American national anthem. In the south, American forces led by Andrew Jackson achieved a striking success by defeating fifty-three hundred veterans of the Spanish campaign as they attempted to march on New Orleans. Though striking, the American victory was not really necessary since the British and Americans had already concluded a peace treaty.

Negotiations in fact had begun soon after the outbreak of hostilities with an offer from the Tsar, who was deeply involved in hostilities with Napoleon and hoped to free British military and financial resources for use against France, to act as mediator. Reluctant to deal with a British ally, the Americans did little until January 1814, when

British and United States representatives met face to face at the Belgian city of Ghent. At first the English put forth extensive demands. They refused to discuss impressment or maritime rights, demanded that the Americans abandon claims to use the Newfoundland fisheries, insisted upon frontier rectifications in favor of Canada, and called for the creation of an Indian state north of the Ohio River. Naturally the Americans rejected these terms, and the British soon dropped their Indian state project. News of the American victory on Lake Champlain and the repulse of their attack on Baltimore caused the British to scale down their demands even further by agreeing to a restoration of the prewar territorial *status quo*. The Treaty of Ghent, signed on December 24, 1814, ended the war, restored the prewar frontiers, created commissions to resolve boundary disputes between the United States and Canada, and said nothing about British policies on the high seas.

The second Anglo-American war thus ended in compromise. Despite their military and naval reverses the Americans did not have to relinquish any territory, and the British despite their failure to inflict decisive defeats upon the United States did not have to sacrifice their prerogatives on the high seas, although they did tacitly agree to abandon impressment since it was no longer vitally necessary to their security. England and America never fought again, and despite occasional tensions and disputes between the two nations, London never again had to face the prospect of a war with a European foe and America.

Meanwhile, revolution continued in Latin America. The South American rebellions had begun soon after Bonaparte dethroned the Spanish Bourbons. Previous revolutionary efforts in the late 1790s and Miranda's attempts to invade Venezuela in 1806 had failed, but the coup at Bayonne gave the Creoles, native-born South Americans of Spanish descent who dominated the economic and social life of the colonies and objected to peninsula control, another opportunity to seek independence. Like the Spaniards, the Creoles began to form juntas, but these organizations refused to recognize the authority of Joseph or of the revolutionary Spanish juntas. By the end of 1810 all the capitals of Spanish America except for Lima and Guatemala had established independent governments. Pro-Spanish groups resisted, and long and frequently bitter wars ensued. Hostilities continued long after the collapse of the Bonapartist dynasty in Europe. The revolutionaries found effective political and military leaders in men like Bolivar, San Martín, and O'Higgins and ultimately obtained British and American support.[11] Thus Latin American independence for better or worse was a direct outgrowth of the French Revolution and Napoleonic wars.

Napoleon was not, of course, willing to sit on Elba and passively observe the effects of his decades of power. Reports soon reached him revealing the general unpopularity of the Bourbons and the fears aroused by the extravagant claims of the ultraroyalists, who sought to restore the political power of the aristocracy and publicly called for a return to the pre-1789 social *status quo*. Always willing to gamble for high stakes, Bonaparte and a handful of followers escaped from Elba at the end of February and landed in France on March 1. Army units, composed largely of imperial veterans, that were sent to capture him promptly deserted the Bourbons, and on March 10 the Corsican entered Lyons. Louis XVIII declared that he would if necessary die in defense of his throne, but on March 19 he fled Paris. On March 20, 1815, Napoleon, escorted by his Polish lancers, re-entered his capital.

News of Bonaparte's escape reached the Vienna congress on March 7, and the allies reacted quickly. Francis,

[11] See J. B. Trend, *Bolivar and the Independence of Spanish America* (New York, 1965); F. A. Kirpatrick, *Latin America, A Brief History* (Cambridge, 1938); and C. Webster, *Britain and the Independence of Latin America 1812–1830*, 2 vols. (Oxford, 1938).

Frederick William, and Alexander immediately agreed to resume the war, and on March 13 the sovereigns of France, England, Prussia, Russia, Spain, Portugal, and Sweden issued a joint declaration proclaiming Napoleon a disturber of world peace and an outlaw. The powers stated that they would fight until they had restored the legitimate government of France and general tranquillity. Moreover, the powers signed another treaty on March 25, reaffirming the Grand Alliance and agreeing to fight until they rendered Napoleon incapable of stirring up further trouble.

Meanwhile, Bonaparte with his usual dynamic energy began to organize his government, raise armies, and inaugurate diplomatic overtures designed to divide his enemies. He proclaimed an additional article to the imperial constitution that promised to provide the nation with a two-chambered legislative body. On June 1 a plebiscite gave a favorable if limited response to that act. In military matters Napoleon overcame supply shortages, war weariness, and royalist outbreaks to raise some 284,000 men. He sent detachments to the frontiers and gathered 128,000 troops into a single striking force that he planned to lead into Belgium. His diplomacy, however, failed to rupture the coalition. He made secret overtures to Francis of Austria and revealed to the Tsar the Bourbon French, English, and Austrian design to check Russian influence in Poland. He sent to Alexander a copy of the secret treaty signed by these powers in January 1815 that Louis XVIII had left behind in his hasty flight from Paris. The Tsar did indeed become enraged, but the threat of renewed French aggression appeared so great that the allies refused to allow peripheral issues to divert them from their main task of crushing Napoleonic power. Consequently they set their armies in motion and on June 9, 1815, ratified the 121 articles of the final act of the Congress of Vienna. The allies thus remained united, and the Emperor of the French had to confide his fortunes to the force of his arms.

The task before Napoleon bordered on the impossible. Wellington with a composite force of English, Dutch, and German units, a total of 92,000 active troops, covered Brussels, and Blücher's 121,000-man army was within supporting distance of Wellington's left flank. Schwarzenberg, with 225,000 men, moved toward Alsace followed by a 168,000-man Russian army. In Italy the Austrians dispatched 25,000 men against Murat, who had deserted the allies and sought to rally the Italian people to his own, and incidentally to Bonaparte's, cause, and ordered 60,000 soldiers to advance through the Alps into southeastern France. Along the Pyrenees the Spanish and Portuguese armies slowly gathered their strength for a thrust into France's southern departments. The allies had over 650,000 men, not counting the Spanish and Portuguese forces, to deal with fewer than 300,000 Frenchmen. Furthermore, the coalition's leaders were determined to win and remove forever the threat of Napoleonic aggression.

Undaunted, the French Emperor decided to launch a lightning blow into Belgium in order to defeat Wellington and Blücher, the most famous allied generals, whose armies also posed the most immediate threat to Paris. Napoleon was also fully aware of the psychological impact on both the French people and the allies of a major imperial victory early in the war. Even a great military triumph in the Low Countries could not, however, guarantee diplomatic success. Given the coalition's determination to resist any form of Napoleonic rule, their numerical superiority, and their knowledge that as in past campaigns persistence would sooner or later enable them to trap and defeat the Emperor, it is doubtful that one or even several French victories would have shaken either the allies' resolve or their ability to win a final triumph.

The question of the coalition's reaction to an initial French success was never answered, for on June 18, 1815, nine days after the conclusion of the Vienna congress, the

French Emperor met Wellington and Blücher in battle near the hamlet of Waterloo.

The Battle of Waterloo, perhaps the most famous in the annals of modern warfare, developed after Napoleon had raced north into Belgium and crossed the Sambre River at Charleroi. Attaining initial surprise, he had sent Ney to drive the British from Quatre Bras and directed Grouchy to attack the Prussians at Ligny. In confused combat Ney's assaults had failed, but Grouchy, closely supervised by the Emperor, succeeded in defeating the Prussians. On the seventeenth Napoleon sent Grouchy with thirty-three thousand men, nearly a third of his total forces, to pursue Blücher and interpose his force between the Prussians and the British, who had retreated to a new position south of Waterloo on the Brussels road. On the morning of June 18 the Emperor ordered a series of frontal attacks on Wellington's lines. Despite great dash and heroism the French failed to pierce the British lines, while on the right Blücher marched to Wellington's assistance as Grouchy followed him instead of keeping his force between the Prussian army and Napoleon's right flank. Late in the afternoon the first of Blücher's men reached the field of battle, but Napoleon detached troops to hold them back.

Napoleon realized at this point that he had to destroy the British or Prussian reinforcements would overwhelm him. Consequently, he launched two full cavalry corps against the British infantry. The English, however, formed squares, did not break under a furious cannonade, and aided by their own cavalry drove back the French horsemen in a series of grim and deadly encounters. In the evening the Emperor launched his final attack. Eight battalions of the Old Guard covered by a heavy barrage charged the British lines. Wellington's men stood firm despite heavy losses and then delivered a volley that shattered the Emperor's assault and his last hopes of victory. Napoleon had expended his last reserves and had no choice but to retreat. As the Prussians and English pursued, the retreat degenerated into a rout. Units of the Guard stood and perished in a futile effort to cover the withdrawal, but Napoleon's army was finished as an effective fighting force.

With his army, Napoleon's power of further resistance disappeared. He returned to Paris, and after a few feeble efforts to reorganize his forces he abdicated in favor of his son. Scattered French units continued to offer resistance to the allied advance, and even won a few skirmishes, but their efforts were not sufficient to revitalize the total war effort. Bonaparte abandoned Paris, and Louis XVIII re-entered the city on July 8.

The Corsican fled south looking for a ship to carry him away from France and away from the Prussians, who had vowed to execute him. Finally he took refuge on a British vessel, H.M.S. *Bellerophon,* which carried him to Plymouth. Bonaparte asked for asylum in England; many political figures favored the idea of granting the former Emperor refuge in their country, but the Cabinet, fearful of future Bonapartist attempts to regain power in France, decided to transport him to the south Atlantic island of St. Helena, where, living under constant guard, he could never again pose a threat to Europe's *status quo.*

Bonaparte thus spent the remaining years of his life as a British prisoner. He died in 1821 on St. Helena, where he proceeded to fashion and elaborate his own legend. His picture of himself as the little corporal, the friend of the common soldier, the Great Commander, the crowned personification of the will of the French people, the preserver of the positive aspects of the Revolution, and the father of European nationalism won a large measure of acceptance both in France and in the world at large. People soon forgot that Napoleon lost his empire, that millions had perished in his ultimately futile wars, that because of his wars the French nation fell far behind England in the process of industrialization, and that France was smaller and less powerful in 1815 than she had been in 1799. People, especially the French people, preferred to remember the ephemeral glory, the

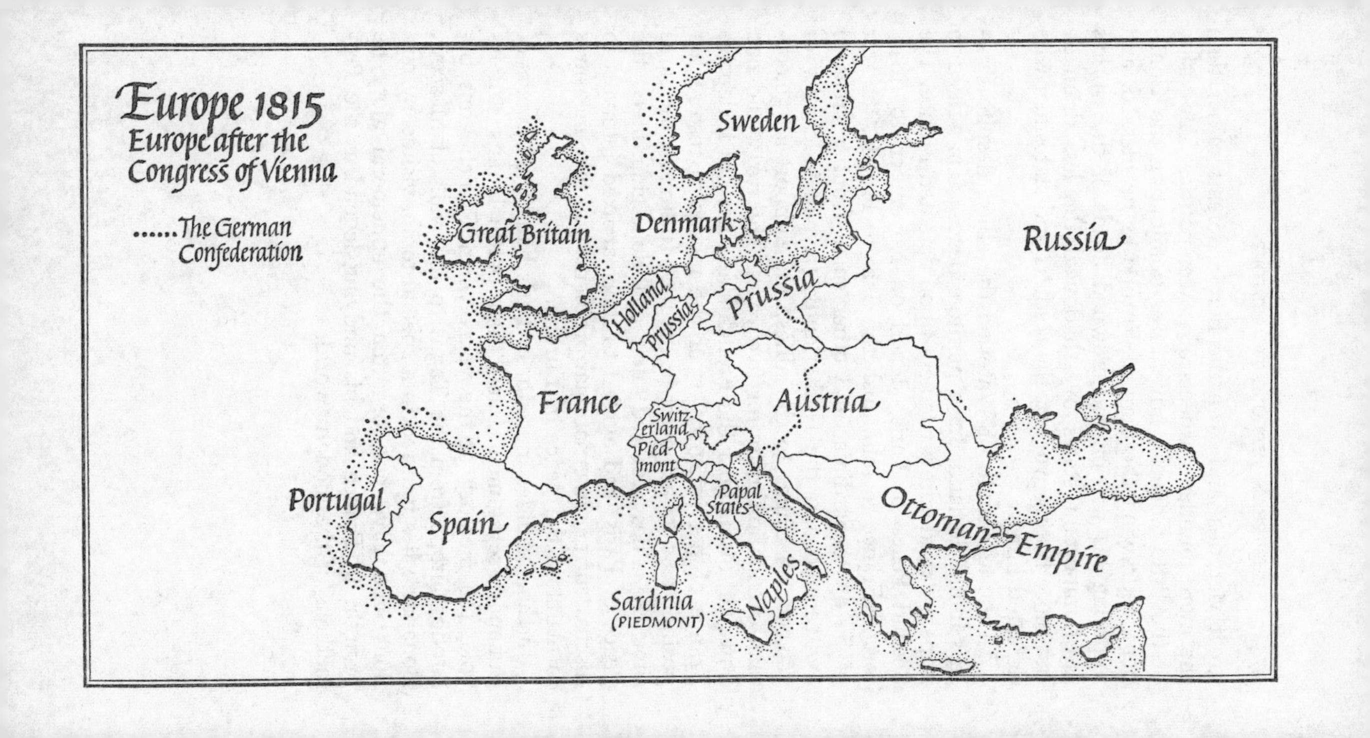
Europe 1815
Europe after the
Congress of Vienna
......The German
Confederation
Sweden
Great Britain
Denmark
Russia
Holland
Prussia
Prussia
France
Austria
Switz-
erland
Pied-
mont
Portugal
Spain
Papal
States
Ottoman Empire
Sardinia
(PIEDMONT)
Naples

great victories, and even the heroic defeats rather than the more mundane aspects of power politics. The vision of the little Corsican adventurer dominating the Continent, redrawing the map of Europe as he pleased, and imposing his will on the crowned heads of the world's most important states overshadowed the less dramatic but more lasting work of the soldiers and statesmen who defeated him.

In the aftermath of Waterloo the allies, despite Prussia's initial demands for a punitive peace, soon agreed to impose a moderate settlement upon defeated France. The Second Peace of Paris, signed on November 20, 1815, forced France to relinquish the Saar to Prussia, the rest of Savoy to Sardinia, and other small frontier areas to Switzerland and the Netherlands, pay an indemnity of 700,000,000 francs to the allies, and support a 150,000-man occupation army for five years. The treaty did not, however, dismember the French state, nor did it deprive France of her integrity or of the means to restore her position as a great power in the near future. At the same time the allies renewed their coalition, guaranteed the Peace of Paris, and agreed to meet at fixed intervals to discuss current international problems and take measures to maintain the peace of Europe.

In the Invalides museum in Paris hang the banners of Bonaparte's regiments, and their battle honors still invoke the memory of the years when French arms bestrode Europe from the Tagus to the walls of Moscow. Bonaparte lies interred in a special tomb, visited by millions who have not forgotten the ephemeral glory he brought to France and his undying legend as the Prometheus of the modern world.

CONCLUSION

The French Revolution caused no essential changes in diplomatic techniques or objectives. There was of course a significant increase in the tempo of diplomacy and war. The European equilibrium underwent severe shocks delivered by the powerful expansionist French state, and the efforts of the other great powers to readjust and restore some sort of balance necessarily took an extremely violent form. Threatened with the loss of souls, provinces, and even real sovereignty, statesmen reacted as they had in the days of Louis XIV, forming a series of coalitions that finally blunted the second French bid for hegemony.

The drama and excitement of the Revolutionary and Napoleonic Era should not, however, be allowed to obscure the existence of striking similarities between the policies of republican and imperial France and those of the Sun King and his Bourbon successors. The military reforms of Le Tellier and Louvois had provided Louis XIV with a highly effective military machine in the form of large and well-trained forces, which Louis employed in pursuit of an aggressive and expansionist foreign policy. Similarly, the military innovations of 1793 and 1794 gave republican leaders a superior military instrument that they used to defend the state and expand French power well beyond the prewar frontiers.

The great Bourbon monarch also had frequently encouraged revolt and rebellion in the lands of his international rivals. He supported the estates faction against William of Orange in the United Provinces, backed Hungarian rebels against their Hapsburg monarch, and assisted with ships, men, and money an armed rising in Ireland. His successors continued to support foreign revolutions against the enemies of France, and units of the Royal Army played a leading role in securing the independence of the North American colonies from British rule. Republican France pursued a similar policy, working with local revolutionaries in Belgium, the Dutch Republic, Germany, Switzerland, Italy, and Ireland. Despite the existence of ideological rhetoric, those who guided French foreign policy, royalist and republican alike, never allowed their universal ideals to blind them to the specific interests of the French state. Bourbon rulers had never supported revolutions for the sake of ideological principles. Rather, they promoted rebellion only when it was in their own state's interest. French republicans regarded foreign upheavals in a similar light. The Republic excluded neutrals from the impact of the Propaganda Decrees; and the Directory refused to create a unitary Italian republic that might have been able to pursue an independent policy, manifested a willingness to desert local revolutionaries when established regimes accepted peace on French terms, and assisted revolutions with the intent of using the resulting satellites as pawns in talks with important rivals.

The enemies of France were equally pragmatic. Despite a genuine distaste for the principles of the Revolution, representatives of the old order practiced many of the policies pursued by the radical French. Monarchs seized church lands; nobles conspired against and even murdered kings; and all rulers were interested in expanding the frontiers and power of their kingdoms. When the monarchs of Europe fought the Republic, they were less interested in combating subversion than in expanding their own territories. They did of course employ antirevolutionary rhetoric for propagandistic purposes and because they believed in it, but principle always bowed to the reality of diplomacy and strategy. They fought the Republic and the Empire out of fear of a loss of power and territory, and in hope of concrete gains in the form of new subjects and dominions, and whatever their opinion of Revolutionary and Napoleonic France, they showed themselves willing to negotiate and even ally themselves with their ideological foes when the interest of their state so dictated.

Ideology did of course play an important role during the Revolutionary and Napoleonic Era, but its impact was less direct than the overly simple view that the political and social upheaval in France ushered in a new era in the diplomatic history of Europe would have it. Leaders pushed to the fore in the course of the Revolution quickly learned to conduct diplomacy in a manner little different from their Old Regime predecessors. But when defending France from invasion, various republican factions did devise a radically new form of national defense consisting in the application of republican principles to military problems. The revolutionaries implicitly assumed that since the state guaranteed the civic and political rights of the citizens, the citizens had an obligation to defend the state. The result of this outlook was the *levée* of 1793 and the Conscription Act of 1798. The revolutionary principle of career open to talent coupled with the refusal of the vast majority of aristocratic officers to serve the Republic led the government to pick military leaders on the basis of loyalty and ability and to disregard almost entirely questions of social status. The result was the creation of a corps of first-rate commanders who led the new citizen armies to victory.

The areas conquered by the French during the Revolutionary Era underwent extensive social, political, and economic changes, in contrast to the period of the Old Regime, when a change of political sovereignty produced relatively few alterations in the *status quo,* and these came about only gradually. In the interest of easing their tasks as occupying forces and to exploit more effectively conquered regions, French armies in the 1790s and early 1800s brought with them a whole complex on innovations, including the abolition of feudalism, the disestablishment of churches, legal reform, the destruction of guild and caste privileges, the introduction of representative political institutions, and frequently extensive territorial changes. Such blows to the *status quo* often led to violent counterrevolutions and guerrilla wars, proof that old religious and political institutions had not lost their hold on large numbers of Europeans. Genuine fear of revolution also existed among supporters of the old order, and fear of rebellion on several occasions prevented incumbent regimes from attempting to create a mass army to check the French. These governments were too frightened of their own subjects to put arms in their hands. Thus the implementation of revolutionary doctrine within France enabled French leaders to pursue the traditional goals of foreign policy—security, power, aggrandizement—with tremendous effectiveness, while the application of republican principles abroad transformed the results of French conquest from a simple change of sovereignty into a shattering upheaval of the old order. But, as stated above, French leaders rarely thought in terms of ideological war or of a crusade to revolutionize the globe. Their prime concern was the interest of the French state, and their methods and techniques led them only secondarily to export their revolution, as a means to political power. Old Regime governments were also interested primarily in security and expansion, but the requirements of internal security and fear of subversion often limited their range of available responses for countering French assaults.

Ironically the wars of the Revolutionary and Napoleonic Era did not have their origins in a policy of calculated aggression. Rather, the belligerents sought war to solve limited problems, but soon found themselves engaged in hostilities whose magnitude went far beyond their initial calculations, a frequent occurrence in the course of diplomacy and war. French political factions looked upon war primarily as an instrument in the domestic political struggle for power. The Hapsburg and Hohenzollern monarchs were not primarily concerned with crushing the center of revolutionary subversion, but intended to use the war as part of their traditional search for new subjects and provinces. They expected to fight a limited war and make limited gains. Thus both France and her enemies expected to fight a war of short duration. Neither side anticipated committing a large percentage of its human and material resources.

But as the war grew in extent and intensity the objectives of the statesmen underwent a similar transformation. The French success in blunting the initial allied offensive, the successful but short-lived republican counterthrust into Belgium and the Rhineland, the entrance of additional states into the coalition, the successful allied offensive in 1793, and the French military innovations of 1793–94 drastically altered the nature of the war. The large new French armies began to win victories, and French leaders became determined to obtain compensation for their military expenses and sought additional territory to balance out Austro-Prussian gains in Poland. For their part the British Government were equally determined to deny the Low Countries to France and to expand their colonial empire at French and Dutch expense, and the Hapsburgs refused to abandon Belgium or the Rhineland.

In 1795 Prussia and Spain concluded peace with the French Republic, further proof that neither France nor her enemies fought primarily for ideological principles. But in the following year Bonaparte's actions in Italy reversed the trend toward peace. At the outset of his campaign, the French Government had not wished to make permanent conquests in Italy, and although it authorized its general to deal with Italian democrats, the Directory fully intended to desert its allies and use its conquests as bargaining counters in peace talks with Vienna. But with its popular support resting upon a very narrow basis and with a large percentage of the French populace regarding the regime as a transitional one, the Directory did not even have full control over its generals and, in fact, was forced to rely upon the military to protect the regime from domestic opposition. Consequently, the government had to accept Bonaparte's treaty with the Hapsburgs, a treaty that extended French influence into Italy, did not fully secure the Rhineland for the Republic, and deepened Vienna's resolve to exact revenge. The weakness of the French Government also played a major role in the collapse of peace talks with England. At the Lille negotiations the British received conflicting reports of French intentions and decided to negotiate on the basis of the most favorable reports. The Directory pursued a fluctuating policy because of factional disputes within the executive and legislative branches of the government, and by the time it developed a consistent set of terms and objectives, the British position had hardened, so that constructive talks were no longer possible. Burdened with a strong army and factionalized political leadership, France failed to conclude her war with her most dangerous foe and was by 1798 faced with the gloomy prospect of devising a means to defeat England or risking perpetual war.

The Directory's attempts to employ naval power and overseas expeditions in an effort to defeat England led to major strategic and diplomatic catastrophes. The Republic's policy enabled the British to fight in their chosen element, inflict serious reverses upon the French, and convince other powers to renew hostilities against the Directory. The Second Coalition, although not including as many members as the first, was nevertheless in many respects stronger than its predecessor. Though plagued by internal rivalries and conflicting objectives, problems common to all alliances, the allies did manage at the outset to establish a basic strategy and a minimal set of political goals. Furthermore, the coalition's armies were large and ably led, and the Polish issue, which had proven so divisive during the First Coalition, was no longer a serious problem. Consequently, the allies scored a whole series of major victories in 1799, bringing France to the brink of disaster. The Directory, however, managed to recover its balance and, taking advantage of growing rivalries within the coalition's ranks, turned the tide of battle. Thus when Bonaparte seized power at the end of the year he took control of a victorious nation that was preparing a massive offensive designed to shatter the remnants of the coalition's military and diplomatic strength. Bonaparte successfully concluded the war and won a favorable if short-lived peace.

Supremely confident of his own abilities, Bonaparte, in the years following the Amiens peace, continued to consolidate and expand French power. He did not actively seek a new war but was so unwilling to limit his objectives and make opportune concessions in order to keep the peace that he convinced other powers the only way to avoid French domination was to offer armed resistance.

In the next few years Bonaparte proved that he was a consummate master of the art of war. With a brilliant combination of force and diplomacy Napoleon destroyed the Third Coalition before it could organize an effective offensive or find additional allies. He then reorganized central Germany according to his own wishes, virtually compelled Francis to put an end to the Holy Roman Empire, and destroyed Prussia. He went on to defeat Russia in battle and convince the Tsar to switch alliances and become a French ally.

Thus by 1807 the Emperor of the French, always prone to seek quick, sharp military solutions to complex diplomatic issues, had won a series of amazing and impressive victories. The Continent lay at his feet. No power east of the Channel dared openly defy him. Despite these triumphs, however, Napoleon had failed to establish the basis for a lasting peace. He forced his victims into submission by the imposition of peace terms so rigorous that the treaties invariably were little more than truces under which the defeated powers thirsted for revenge and constantly sought a favorable opportunity to resume their contest of arms. This was due in part to the fact that Bonaparte persistently ignored advisers who advocated a "soft peace," which would have created the option of transforming opponents into useful allies, but rather, transferred his battlefield technique to the diplomatic arena. In combat he sought to obliterate the enemy and render it incapable of offering further resistance to the Grand Army; at the conference table he attempted to weaken his rivals and prevent them from challenging the supremacy of the Grand Empire. He thus surrounded himself with restless satellites and reluctant allies rather than with neutrals and true partners, and he had no alternative other than to maintain the supremacy won in battle by the constant application of armed force. His inability to defeat England, moreover, meant that the British stood ready to help any power that wished to resume hostilities. Napoleon realized that in order to transform his victories into a permanent French hegemony it was necessary to defeat Britain, but like his predecessors he could never overcome her naval supremacy. Direct invasion was therefore out of the question, and his alternative policy, economic strangulation, suffered from the defects of poor enforcement, lack of co-operation from his allies, and underestimation of the ability of British businessmen to find loopholes in the continental system and exploit new markets. Thus, if the Emperor's policy of attaining economic supremacy for his own kingdom by means of protective tariffs and favorable commercial agreements attained occasional successes, it failed to disrupt completely the British economy and antagonized France's allies and satellites, who suffered serious economic setbacks due to their loss of trade with the island kingdom. It was just another imposition upon them and added to the growing discontent with French domination.

So onerous did the continental system become that Russia, already alarmed by continued French expansion after 1807 and by Napoleon's refusal to grant her equal compensation, deserted him. The Emperor then began to plan a massive campaign to force the Tsar back into the

French economic bloc and reduce Russia to the status of a second-rate power. By the time the Grand Army marched east, however, Napoleon was already deeply involved in war south of the Pyrenees. Confident that he could reorganize Spain according to his wishes, he soon found himself engaged in a long, expensive, brutal, and fruitless guerrilla war. Seizing their opportunity to strike directly at France, the British sent an army to Portugal and the Austrians renewed the war on the Danube. Although the Austrians suffered another defeat, the British not only continued to maintain their foothold in Europe but also inflicted severe reverses on the best of Napoleon's marshals and men. Consequently, when the Russian campaign opened Napoleon found himself engaged in a two-front war.

Defeated on both fronts, the Emperor nevertheless refused to sue for peace. He seemed unable to comprehend that any power or alliance could defeat him and constantly subordinated diplomacy to strategy, continuing to seek to impose battlefield techniques upon diplomatic strategy long after purely military solutions were out of the question. The allies, on the other hand, finally formed an effective coalition. Heretofore, the great powers had failed to act together. During the First Coalition, Russia had remained on the sidelines; Prussia had refused to join the Second and Third coalitions, Austria remained aloof from the Fourth, and neither Russia nor Prussia came to Austria's assistance in 1809. In 1812 Prussia and Austria were allies, although reluctant ones, of France, and it was not until 1813 that all the major powers found themselves at war with Napoleon at the same time. Despite divergent objectives, the Fifth Coalition managed to retain its unity and to devise an effective military strategy. Furthermore, the allies had learned not to become disheartened by tactical defeats, doubtless having been affected by the vital lesson of the Spanish and Russian campaigns: A defeat in the field, even several defeats, did not necessarily mean that effective resistance and future counteroffensives were impossible. They were thus able to wear down French strength, bring the Grand Army to battle, defeat it, and drive it from Germany.

The coalition had not at first been dedicated to the total extinction of the Napoleonic dynasty. The Austrians desired to maintain a powerful French state as a counterweight to the growth of Russian influence. And on several occasions the allies made serious peace offers to the French Emperor. Once again, however, Napoleon's supreme confidence in his own genius led him to reject these offers or accept them too late. He persisted in the belief that sooner or later he would turn the tide of the war on the field of battle, and he virtually compelled the allies to fight on to total victory. The Corsican's last campaign was brilliant but futile. The allies finally overwhelmed him and compelled him to abdicate. The Hundred Days and the Battle of Waterloo only reinforced their decision of 1813 and 1814. Banding together, the great powers brought to bear overwhelming strength, and put an end to the threat of French hegemony.

The Congress of Vienna, the Second Peace of Paris, the Quadruple Alliance, and the congress system provided Europe with one of the longest eras of relative peace in its dark and bloody history. The 1815 settlement constructed a balance of power that largely satisfied the major states, and no power sought drastic revisions of the new situation. England retained and expanded her maritime and colonial ascendency. Austria retained her great power status, attained a predominant position in Italy, and shared with Prussia a controlling influence in German affairs without having to grant significant concessions to liberal and nationalist sentiment. Prussia recovered her former status and gained new territories, and Russia gained Finland, Bessarabia, and most of Poland. Alexander, moreover, became one of the more influential European statesmen, and he was even able to convince most continental rulers to subscribe to his Holy Alliance of September 1815, under which princes and monarchs except for the Regent of England, the Sultan, and the Pope agreed to conduct their foreign policy according to the precepts of the New Testament. The Holy Alliance was perhaps not the most practical policy guide, but nevertheless it indicated the extent of Alexander's influence and the general willingness of the powers to try and live in peace. The 1815 settlement also built a series of barrier states around France to check any possible renewal of French aggression. Thus the treaties and agreements of 1815 created a continental balance of power in which the major states could live in reasonable security and no single power was strong enough to threaten the sovereignty of the others. Thus, as in the days of Louis XIV when France had threatened to dominate the Continent, the states of Europe banded together to halt French expansion. After the fall of Napoleon, France never again threatened to dominate the Continent, and the attempt to unify Europe by force remained in the realm of the hypothetical.

The 1815 settlement did not, of course, bring complete European tranquillity, nor did it provide solutions to all problems. Liberals and nationalists throughout the Continent were dissatisfied with the *status quo*, and the numerous rebellions and revolutions of the ensuing half century—in England, France, Belgium, Austria, Spain, Italy, Germany, the Balkans, Poland, and Russia—testified to the extent and growth of this distaste for the old order. Not all were successful, but they did testify to the extent of the dissatisfaction with the political and social system. Furthermore, despite the efforts of the peacemakers, Europe continued to be beset with constant diplomatic rivalries, alarms, threats of war, and real hostilities. The balance of power also underwent a number of significant alterations. Turkish power continued to deteriorate; Spain lost most of her Latin American empire; England continued to enlarge her overseas domains, and France soon recovered her great power status and, led by Napoleon III, nephew of the great Emperor, resumed her policy of expanding her influence into surrounding regions. Russian influence suffered a temporary eclipse after 1855, but the Romanovs soon recovered their prestige and resumed their expansionist policies in the Balkans, central Asia, and the Far East. Austria suffered a number of major reverses, losing control of Italy and influence in Germany, but as in previous eras, defeats did not deprive the Hapsburgs of their status as one of Europe's leading powers. Italy attained unification and admittance into the ranks of the leading powers, and Prussia united Germany by conquest, replacing France as the single most powerful state in Europe. Nevertheless, despite all changes and wars, the nineteenth century was one of relative peace. Europe managed to avoid a major war until 1854. The wars of 1859, 1865, 1866, and 1870–71 were limited in scope, if not in impact, and none was as prolonged or as bloody as the American Civil War. Germany's appearance as Europe's greatest land power was of momentous significance, but even the shift of power from Paris to Berlin and the consequent diplomatic realignments did not automatically produce conditions that led to a war involving all of the powers. Despite numerous alarms and confrontations it was not until 1914 that all the great powers became immersed in a major conflict. In an imperfect world in which suspicion and hostility are standard aspects of international relations and war is a normal function of national policy, the Vienna settlement indeed stands as an impressive achievement.

BIBLIOGRAPHY

I. MANUSCRIPT SOURCES

A. Archives des Affaires Étrangères

1. Correspondance politique vols: 363, 364, 586, 651, 668.
2. Mémoires et documents vols: 28, 321, 652, 655.

B. Archives Nationales

1. AF II cartons: 3, 9, 27, 77, 212, 214^{A}, 214^{B}, 281.
2. AF II* carton: 24.
3. AF III cartons: 13, 23, 56, 57, 59, 61, 69, 76, 149, 150^{A}, 150^{B}, 151^{A}, 151^{B}, 152^{A}, 331, 332, 333, 334.
4. AF III* cartons: 1, 2, 13, 14, 16, 18, 19, 20, 202.
5. DP II cartons: 4, 5.
6. F^{9} carton: 48.
7. Archives de la Marine, cartons: BB^{4} 129, 139.

C. Ministère de la Guerre État-Major de l'Armée Archives Historiques

1. Correspondance

   Armées du Nord et des Ardennes, 1793, cartons: $B^{1}18$, $B^{1}19$, $B^{1}20$.

   Armées du Nord et de Sambre et Meuse, 1794, cartons: $B^{1}32$, $B^{1}33$, $B^{1}34$.

   Armée de Batavie, 1799, cartons: $B^{1}92$, $B^{1}93$.

   Armées de Mayence, du Rhin, et d'Helvétie, 1798–1799, cartons: $B^{2}63$, $B^{2}64$, $B^{2}65$, $B^{2}66$, $B^{2}67$, $B^{2}68$, $B^{2}69$, $B^{2}70$.

   Armée de Mayence devenue Armée du Danube et d'Helvétie, 1799, cartons: $B^{2}71$, $B^{2}72$.

   Armée du Danube, 1799, cartons: $B^{2}73$, $B^{2}74$.

   Armée du Rhin et du Danube, 1799, cartons: $B^{2}75$, $B^{2}76$, $B^{2}77$, $B^{2}78$, $B^{2}79$.

   Armée d'Italie, 1798, cartons: $B^{3}55$, $B^{3}56$, $B^{3}56^{bis}$.

   Armées d'Italie et de Rome, 1799, cartons: $B^{3}57$, $B^{3}58$, $B^{3}58^{bis}$.

   Armées d'Italie et de Naples, 1799, cartons: $B^{3}59$, $B^{3}60$, $B^{3}61$, $B^{3}62$, $B^{3}63$, $B^{3}64$.

   Indes orientales, 1797–1799, carton: $B^{8}1$.

   Grandé Armée, 1805–1813, cartons: $C^{2}9$, $C^{2}10$, $C^{2}11$, $C^{2}27$, $C^{2}28$, $C^{2}127$, $C^{2}158$.

   Correspondance particulière du général Moreau, 1792–1803, carton: $B^{2}98$.

   Correspondance du général Jourdan, 1798–1799, cartons: $B^{2*}260$, $B^{2*}262$.

Correspondance du ministère de la guerre avec les armées d'Italie et de Naples, 1799, carton: $B^{3*}221^{*}$.
Correspondance de Macdonald, 1799, carton: $B^{3*}322^{*}$.
Correspondance du ministère de la guerre avec la Convention et le Comité de Salut Public, 1792–1794, carton: $B^{12}53$.
Rapports du ministre de la guerre au Directoire exécutif, 1799, cartons: $B^{12*}37$, $B^{12*}39$, $B^{13}105$, $B^{13}106$.
Correspondance du ministre de la guerre avec les armées, 1799, carton: $B^{2*}171^{*}$.

2. Situations and ordres de bataille
Registre de l'Etat-Major général, 1793–1794, carton: $B^{1}110$.
Armées de la République situations générales, 1791–1802, cartons: $B^{1}244$, $B^{1}245$, $B^{2}339$, $B^{2}340$, $B^{2}342$, $B^{6}190$, $B^{3}381$.
Grandé Armée situations, 1802–1814, cartons: $C^{2}522$, $C^{2*}697$, $C^{2}724$, $C^{2}736$.
Ordres de bataille des armées en campagne, 1792–1815, cartons: $X^{p}3$, $X^{p}5$, $X^{p}33$, $X^{p}34$, $X^{p}81$.
Organisation générale de l'armée, 1793, carton: $X^{s}4$.

3. Inventaire analytique de la correspondance militaire
Armées du Nord et des Ardennes, janvier–mars 1794.
Armées du Nord et des Ardennes, avril–juin 1794.
Armées du Rhin et de la Moselle, janvier–juin 1795.
Armées du Rhin et de la Moselle, juillet–décembre 1795.
Armées du Nord et de Sambre-Meuse, octobre–décembre 1795.
Armées des Alpes et d'Italie, mai–juin 1796.
Armées des Alpes et d'Italie, juillet–septembre 1796.
Armées des Alpes et d'Italie, avril–juin 1797.
Armées des Alpes et d'Italie, octobre–décembre 1797.

4. Mémoires historiques
Relation de la bataille de Fleurs livrée le 8 messidor an 2 (26 juin 1794) no. 274.
Exposé des opérations des Armées du Nord et de Sambre-Meuse, 1794–1795, no. 280.
Journal de la campagne de l'an IV sous le Commandement du général en Chef Jourdan no. 287.
Campagne des Armées du Nord, des Ardennes et de Sambre-Meuse (5 mai 1794–18 Mars 1795) no. 293.
Précis de la campagne de l'Armée de Sambre et Meuse pendant l'an 4 no. 298.
Campagne de 1796 sur le Rhin no. 301.
Campagne de 1796 sur le Rhin no. 302.
Armée du Rhin journal général des opérations 28 septembre 1792 jusqu'au 8 janvier 1794 no. 322.
Campagne de 1796 sur le Rhin no. 333.

Précis des opérations des Armées de Rhin et Moselle et de Sambre et Meuse pendant la Campagne de 1796 no. 342.
Bulletin des opérations de l'Armée de Rhin et Moselle, 1796–1797, no. 348.
Bataille de Hohenlinden 3 décembre 1800 no. 384.
Situation de l'armée enemie 1800 no. 386.
Précis des campagnes de l'an 8 et l'an 9 de l'Armée du Rhin no. 387.
Précis historique sur le siège de Toulon en 1793 no. 400.
Armée d'Italie campagnes de l'an IV et de l'an V no. 417.
Campagne de l'an 5 en Italie no. 423.
Journal historique de quelques opérations militaires de l'Armée d'Italie commandée par Bonaparte en l'an IV no. 426.
Campagne de l'armée autrichienne russe en Italie en 1799 no. 438.
Précis des opérations de l'Armée d'Italie depuis l'affaire de l'Adda jusqu' à la bataille de Novi no. 443.
Précis historique de la Campagne de l'Armée napolitaine par le général Mack no. 453.
Armée des Pyrénées orientales campagne de 1793 no. 474.
Mémoires militaires du Maréchal Jourdan, campagne de 1793 no. 608^{1}.
Mémoires militaires du Maréchal Jourdan, campagne de 1794 no. 608^{2}.
Extrait de la relation de la prise d'Ulm no. 632.
Relation de la Bataille d'Austerlitz par le général Berthier no. 633.
Récit de la bataille de Preussich-Eylau no. 647.
Bulletin de la Grande Armée 58 no. 648.
Campagnes de Prusse et de Pologne 1806–1807 no. 659.
Relation sur la bataille près de Wagram no. 672.
Passage de la Berezina no. 673.
Retraite du Maréchal Ney depuis Smolensk jusqu' à Orcha no. 676.
Campagne de Russie par le Maréchal Augereau no. 677.
Campagne de 1813 no. 688.
Campagne de 1813 no. 690.
Campagne de France 1814 no. 715.
Notice sur la campagne de Portugal en 1810 et 1811 no. 748.
Bataille de Albuera no. 768.
Retraite des armées françaises d'Espagne et bataille de Vitoria no. 774.
Campagne de 1800 en Italie no. 900^{bis2}.
Campagne de 1809 no. 900^{bis2}.
Campagne de 1815 no. 900^{bis2}.

Notes diverses sur l'Espagne en août, septembre, et octobre 1812 et février 1813 no. 902[1].
Lutzen et Bautzen en mai 1813 no. 902[2].
Bataille de Laon 9 et 10 mars 1814 no. 902[3].
Bataille des Pyramides le 3 Thermidor an 6 (27 juillet 1798) par le général Berthier no. 908[1].
Campagne de Syrie an VII no. 908[1].
Bataille d'Essling no. 910[3].
Bataille de Wagram no. 910[3].
Début détaillé de la Campagne de Russie no. 910[4].
Journal historique de la Campagne de Portugal (du 15 septembre 1810 au 12 mai 1811) no. 916.
Campagne de Portugal 1810 et 11 no. 918[1].
Opérations des armées françaises et anglaise sur la Tormes en novembre 1812 no. 918[1].
Commencement de la Campagne de 1812 en Espagne no. 918[1].
Armée du Portugal situation 1811 no. 919.

5. Reports
Rapport fait par le général Masséna au Directoire exécutif sur les opérations du 3 au 18 vendemiaire an 8.
Rapport fait par le ministre de la guerre L. de Narbonne à l'Assemblée Nationale le 11 janvier 1792.

II. PUBLISHED DOCUMENTS, LETTERS, AND MEMOIRS

Angers, D. d', ed., *Memoires de Larevellière-Lepaux,* 3 vols. (Paris, 1895).

The Annual Register or a View of the History, Politics and Literature for the Year 1798 (London, 1800).

The Annual Register or a View of the History, Politics and Literature for the Year 1799 (London, 1801).

Archdukes, eds., Albrecht and Wilhem, *Ausgewählte Schriften des Erzhogs Karl,* 4 vols. (Vienna, 1893).

Arenth, A. R. ven, *Marie Antoinette, Joseph II, und Leopold II ihr Briefwechsel* (Leipzig, 1866).

The Asiatic Annual Register; or a View of the History of Hindustan and of the Politics, Commerce, and Literature of Asia for the Year 1799 (London, 1800).

Aulard, A., ed., *Recueil des actes du Comité de Salut Public avec la correspondance officielle des représentants en mission,* 28 vols. (Paris, 1889–1951).

Bailleu, P., ed., *Preussen und Frankreich von 1795 bis 1807 Diplomatische Correspondenzen,* 2 vols. (Leipzig, 1880–87).

Barrow, J., ed., *The Life and Correspondence of Admiral Sir William Sidney Smith,* 2 vols. (London, 1848).

Bartenev, P., ed., *Papers of Mikhail Larionovich Vorontsov and Other Members of the Family,* 38 vols. (Moscow, 1876–80).

Beer, A., ed., *Joseph II, Leopold II and Kaunitz* (Vienna, 1873).

Berthier, A., *Relation des Campagnes du général Bonaparte en Egypte et en Syrie* (Paris, 1800).

Bertrand, H., ed., *Guerre d'orient campagnes d'Egypte et de Syrie 1798–1799, mémoires pour servir à l'histoire de Napoléon dictées par lui-même à Sainte-Hélène,* 2 vols. (Paris, 1847).

Bishop of Bath and Wells, ed., *The Journal and Correspondence of William, Lord Auckland,* 4 vols. (London, 1861).

Bonaparte, N., *Correspondance inédite officielle et confidentielle de Napoléon Bonaparte,* 7 vols. (Paris, 1819–20).

Botzenhart, E. and Hubatsch, W., eds., *Freiherr von Stein Briefe und Amtliche Schriften,* 6 vols. (Stuttgart, 1963).

Bouloiseau, M., Lefebvre, G., and Soboul, A., eds., *Oeuvres de Maximilien Robespierre,* 9 vols. (Paris, 1953).

Bourrienne, L-A., ed., *Memoirs of Napoleon Bonaparte,* 5 vols. (London, 1961).

Broglie, Duc de, ed., *Memoirs of the Prince de Talleyrand,* 5 vols. (London, 1891–92).

Caulaincourt, A., *With Napoleon in Russia* (New York, 1935).

Charavay, E., *Correspondance générale de Carnot,* 3 vols. (Paris, 1892–97).

Clercq, A., ed., *Recueil des traités de la France,* 21 vols. (Paris, 1864–1900).

Cobbett, W., ed., *The Parliamentary History of England from the Earliest Period to the Year 1803,* 36 vols. (London, 1818).

Colenbrander, H. T., ed., *Gedenkstukken der Algemeene Geschiedenis van Nederland van 1795 tot 1840,* 22 vols. (The Hague, 1907).

Conches, F. de, ed., *Louis XVI, Marie-Antoinette et Madame Elisabeth lettres et documents inédits,* 6 vols. (Paris, 1864–73).

Congress at Rastadt Official Correspondence from the Original Papers (London, 1800).

Corbett, J., ed., *Private Papers of George Second Earl Spencer First Lord of the Admiralty 1794–1801,* 4 vols. (London, 1914).

Coupland, R., ed., *The War Speeches of William Pitt the Younger* (Oxford, 1916).

Debidour, A., *Recueil des actes du Directoire exécutif,* 4 vols. (Paris, 1910).

Desbrière, E., ed., *1793–1805 projets et tentatives de débarquement aux Iles Britanniques,* 4 vols. (Paris, 1900).

Dunferline, J., ed., *Lieutenant-General Ralph Abercromby* (Edinburgh, 1861).

Duruy, G., ed., *Mémoires de Barras,* 4 vols. (Paris, 1896).
France, Ministre de la guerre, *Correspondance militaire de Napoléon Ier,* 32 vols. (Paris, 1876).
Galli, H., ed., *Journal d'un officier de l'armée d'Egypte* (Paris, 1883).
Great Britain Foreign Office, *British and Foreign State Papers 1812–1814,* 2 vols. (London, 1841).
Gurwood, Lieut.-Col., ed., *The Dispatches of Field Marshal the Duke of Wellington during his various Campaigns,* 13 vols. (London, 1837).
Hanoteau, J., ed., *Mémoires du général Caulaincourt,* 3 vols. (Paris, 1933).
Historical Manuscripts Commission, *Report on the Manuscripts of J. B. Fortescue, Esq., preserved at Dropmore,* 10 vols. (London, 1905).
History of the Campaign of 1799 in Holland (London, 1801).
Jonquière, C. de la, ed., *Journal de l'expédition d'Egypte 1798–1801,* 5 vols. (Paris, 1899–1907).
Kaye, J., ed., *The Life and Correspondence of Major-General Sir John Malcolm. G.C.B.,* 2 vols. (London, 1856).
Koch, le général, ed., *Mémoires de Masséna rédigés d'après les documents qu'il à laissés,* 7 vols. (Paris, 1848–50).
Lloyd, C., ed., *The Keith Papers,* 2 vols. (London, 1950).
London Gazette, Bulletins of the Campaign of 1799 (London, 1800).
Macdonald, A., *Souvenirs du Maréchal Macdonald* (Paris, 1892).
Mangourit, M. A. B., *Defénse d'Ancone et des départments romains, Le Toronto, Le Musone, et Le Metauro, par le général Monnier aux années VII et VIII,* 2 vols. (Paris, 1802).
Martens, F., ed., *Recueil des traités et conventions conclus par la Russie avec les puissances étrangères,* 13 vols. (St. Petersburg, 1875–83).
Martens, G. F., ed., *Recueil des principaux traités d'alliance, de paix, de trêve, de neutralité, de commerce, de limites, d'échange conclus par les puissances de l'Europe,* 8 vols. (Gottingen, 1817–35).
——, ed., *Nouveau recueil de traités d'alliance, de paix, de trêve, de neutralité, de commerce, de limites, d'échange conclus par des puissances et états de l'Europe,* 16 vols. (Gottingen, 1817–41).
Meredith, W., ed., *Memorials of Charles John, King of Sweden and Norway* (London, 1829).
Metternich, C. von, *Mémoires du prince de Metternich,* 4 vols. (Paris, 1959).
Michon, G., ed., *Correspondance de Maximilien et Augustin Robespierre,* 2 vols. (Paris, 1926–41).

Minto, Countess, ed., *Life and Letters of Sir Gilbert Eliot First Earl of Minto from 1751 to 1806*, 3 vols. (London, 1874).

Montarlot, P., and Pingaud, L., eds., *Le Congrès de Rastatt (11 juin 1798–28 avril 1799) Correspondance et documents,* 3 vols. (Paris, 1912).

Moore, Sir John, *Diary* (London, 1904).

Murhard, F., ed., *Nouveaux suppléments au recueil des traités et autres actes remarquables des puissances et états de l'Europe depuis 1761 jusqu' à nos jours,* 3 vols. (Gottingen, 1839).

Nabonne, B., *La diplomatie du Directoire et Bonaparte d'après les papiers inédits de Reubell* (Paris, 1951).

Naish, G. P., ed., *Nelson's letters to his Wife and Other Documents* (London, 1958).

Naradounghian, G., ed., *Recueil des actes internationaux de l'Empire ottoman,* 4 vols. (Paris, 1900).

Nesselrode, A., ed., *Lettres et papiers du Chancelier comte de Nesselrode,* 4 vols. (Paris, 1905).

Neumann, L., ed., *Recueil des traités et conventions Conclus par l'Autriche avec les puissances étrangères depuis 1763 jusqu' à nos jours,* 32 vols. (Leipzig, 1855).

Nicolas, N., ed., *The Dispatches and Letters of Vice-Admiral Lord Viscount Nelson,* 6 vols. (London, 1845).

Owen, S. J., ed., *A Selection from the Dispatches, Treaties and Other Papers of the Marquess Wellesley, K.G. during his Government of India* (Oxford, 1877).

Pallain, G., ed., *Le ministère de Talleyrand sous le Directoire* (Paris, 1891).

——, ed., *The Correspondence of Prince Talleyrand and King Louis XVIII during the Congress of Vienna* (New York, 1881).

Pearce, R. R., ed., *Memoirs and Correspondence of the Most Noble Richard Marquess Wellesley,* 3 vols. (London, 1846).

Perroud, C., ed., *J.-P. Brissot Mémoires (1754–93),* 2 vols. (Paris, 1912).

Pettigrew, T. J., ed., *Memoirs of the Life of Vice-Admiral Lord Viscount Nelson,* 2 vols. (London, 1849).

Pitt, W., *The Speeches of the Right Honourable William Pitt in the House of Commons,* 4 vols. (London, 1806).

Plon, H., and Dumaine, J., eds., *Correspondance de Napoleon Ier,* 32 vols. (Paris, 1858–70).

Réimpression de l'Ancien Moniteur, 31 vols. (Paris, 1847).

Report of Committee of Secrecy of the House of Commons (London, 1799).

Richmond, H. W., ed., *Private Papers of George, Second Earl Spencer, First Lord of the Admiralty 1794–1801,* 4 vols. (London, 1924).

Ross, C., ed., *Correspondence of Charles, First Marquess of Cornwallis,* 3 vols. (London, 1859).
Saint-Cyr, G., *Mémoires pour servir à l'histoire militaire sous le Directoire, le Consulat et l'Empire,* 4 vols. (Paris, 1831).
Saint-Pierre, L., *Mémoires du Maréchal Soult, Espagne et Portugal* (Paris, 1955).
Soult, N., *Mémoires du Maréchal-Général Soult Duc de Dalmatie,* 3 vols. (Paris, 1854).
Stewart, J. H., *A Documentary Survey of the French Revolution* (New York, 1951).
Vaccarino, G., ed., *I Patrioti "Anarchistes" E L'Idea Dell' Unità Italiana 1796–1799* (Milan, 1955).
Vane, C., ed., *Memoirs and Correspondence of Vicecount Castlereagh Second Marquess of Londonderry,* 8 vols. (London, 1848).
Vivenot, A. R. von, ed., *Quellen zur Geschichte der Deutschen Kaiserpolitik Oesterreichs,* 5 vols. (Vienna, 1873–90).
——, ed., *Vertrauliche Briefe des Freiherrn von Thugut,* 2 vols. (Vienna, 1872).
Weil, M. H., ed., *Un agent inconnu de la Coalition le général Stamford d'aprés sa correspondance inédite (1793–1806)* (Paris, 1923).
Wellesley Papers, 2 vols. (London, 1914).
Wellington, Duke of, *Supplementary Despatches and Memoranda of Field Marshal Arthur Duke of Wellington K.G.* (London, 1858–72).
Wickham, W., ed., *The Correspondence of the Right Honorable William Wickham from the Year 1794,* 2 vols. (London, 1870).
Wolfe, Tone, W. T., ed., *Life of Theobold Wolfe Tone,* 2 vols. (Washington, 1826).

III. SECONDARY WORKS

Acton, H., *The Bourbons of Naples (1734–1825)* (London, 1956).
Adams, E. D., *The Influence of Grenville on Pitt's Foreign Policy 1787–1798* (Washington, 1904).
Aimond, C., *L'enigme de Varennes* (Paris, 1936).
Andersson, I., *A History of Sweden* (London, 1956).
Artola, M., *Los Origenes de la España contemporánea,* 2 vols. (Madrid, 1959).
Augustin-Thierry, A., *Masséna* (Paris, 1947).
Azoux, A., "La France et Muscate aux dixhuitième et dix reuvieme siècles," in *Revue d'histoire diplomatique* (1910), XXIV.
Ballot, C., *Les négociations de Lille (1797)* (Paris, 1910).
Beer, A., *Die orientalische Politik Oesterreichs seit 1774* (Prague, 1883).

Biro, S., *The German Policy of Revolutionary France; A Study in French Diplomacy during the War of the First Coalition 1792–1797*, 2 vols. (Cambridge, 1957).
Blácam, A. de, *The Life Story of Wolfe Tone* (London, 1935).
Bonnefons, A., *Marie-Caroline reine des Deux-Sicilies (1768–1814)* (Paris, 1905).
Boulay de la Meurthe, A., *Le Directoire et l'expédition d'Egypte* (Paris, 1885).
Bourdeau, E., *Campagnes moderns*, 3 vols. (Paris, n.d.).
Bourgeois, E., *Manuel historique de politique étrangère, II, les révolutions (1789–1830)* (Paris, 1913).
Bourniseaux, P., *Histoire des guerres de la Vendée et des Chouans*, 3 vols. (Paris, 1819).
Brace, R. M., *Bordeaux and the Gironde, 1789–1794* (Ithaca, 1947).
———, "Bordeaux's Opposition to Dictatorship in 1793," in *Journal of Modern History* (1942), XIV.
Brett-James, A., *1812: Eyewitness Accounts of Napoleon's Defeat in Russia* (New York, 1966).
Brian-Chaninov, N., "Alexandre I[er] et la paix," in *Revue d'histoire diplomatique* (1933), XLVII.
Brinton, C., *The Jacobins* (New York, 1930).
Brown, P., *The French Revolution in English History* (London, 1918).
Bruun, G., *Europe and the French Imperium 1799–1814* (New York, 1938).
Bunbury, H., *Narratives of Some Passages in the Great War with France, from 1799 to 1810* (London, 1854).
Burgoyne, J., *A Short History of the Naval and Military Operations in Egypt* (London, 1885).
Butterfield, H., *The Peace Tactics of Napoleon 1806–1808* (Cambridge, 1929).
Caron, P., *La défense nationale de 1792 à 1795* (Paris, 1912).
Chabert, A., *Essai sur les mouvements des revenus et de l'activité économique en France de 1789 à 1820* (Paris, 1949).
Chandler, D. G., *The Campaigns of Napoleon* (New York, 1966).
Charles-Roux, F., *Bonaparte, governeur d'Egypte* (Paris, 1936).
———, *L'Angleterre et l'expédition française en Egypte*, 2 vols. (Cairo, 1925).
———, *Les origines de l'expédition d'Egypte* (Paris, 1910).
Chevalier, E., *Histoire de la marine française sous la première république* (Paris, 1886).
Chuquet, A., *Dumouriez* (Paris, 1914).
———, *La première invasion prussiene (11 août–2 septembre 1792)* (Paris, n.d.).

——, *Jemappes et la conquête de la Belgique* (*1792–1793*) (Paris, n.d.).
——, *Valmy* (Paris, 1887).
Clapham, J. H., *The Causes of the War of 1792* (Cambridge 1899).
Clough, S., *France, a History of National Economics 1789–1939* (New York, 1939).
Clowes, W., *The Royal Navy*, 7 vols. (London, 1899).
Colin, J., *La tactique et la discipline dans les armées de la Révolution* (Paris, 1902).
Connelly, O., *The Gentle Bonaparte; a Biography of Joseph, Napoleon's Elder Brother* (New York, 1968).
——, *Napoleon's Satellite Kingdoms* (New York, 1965).
Cooper, D., *Talleyrand* (Stanford, 1967).
Coutanceau, H., *La campagne de 1794 à l'Armée du Nord*, 4 vols. (Paris, 1903–8).
Crouzet, F., *L'économie britannique et le Blocus Continental, 1806–1813*, 2 vols. (Paris, 1958).
Curtis, E. N., *Saint-Just* (New York, 1935).
Dallas, R. C., *The History of the Maroons*, 2 vols. (London, 1803).
Dard, E., *Le Comte de Narbonne* (Paris, 1943).
——, *Napoléon et Talleyrand* (Paris, 1935).
Daudet, E., *Les émigrés et la Seconde Coalition* (Paris, 1886).
Davies, G., *Wellington and His Army* (Oxford, 1954).
De Conde, A., *Entangling Alliance Politics and Diplomacy Under George Washington* (Durham, 1958).
——, *The Quasi-War, The Politics and Diplomacy of the Undeclared War with France 1797–1801* (New York, 1966).
Dejoint, J., *La politique économique du Directoire* (Paris, 1951).
Deschampes, J., *Les Iles britanniques et la Révolution française* (Paris, n.d.).
——, *Les colonies pendant la Révolution la Constituante et la réforme coloniale* (Paris, 1898).
Desdevises du Dezert, G., *L'Espagne de l'Ancien Régime*, 2 vols. (Paris, 1899).
Deutsch, H., *The Genesis of Napoleonic Imperialism* (Cambridge, 1938).
——, "Napoleonic Policy and the Project of a Descent upon England," in *Journal of Modern History* (1930), II.
Dodge, T. A., *Napoleon*, 4 vols. (Boston, 1904).
Douin, G., *La Campagne de Bruix en Méditerranée mars–août 1799* (Paris, 1923).
——, *La flotte de Bonaparte sur les côtes d'Egypte* (Paris, 1922).
Driault, E., *La chute de l'Empire* (Paris, 1927).
——, *Le Grand Empire* (Paris, 1924).

———, "La politique exterieure de Napoléon Ier," in *Revue des études napoléoniennes* (1915), VII.

Droz, J., *L'Allemagne et la Révolution française* (Paris, 1949).

Ducéré, E., *L'Armée des Pyrénées occidentales* (Bayonne, 1882).

Dugan, J., *The Great Mutiny* (London, 1966).

Dunana, M., "Napoléon et le système continental en 1810," in *Revue d'histoire diplomatique* (1946), LX.

Dunfermline, J., *Lieutenant-General Ralph Abercromby* (Edinburgh, 1861).

Edwards, F. L., trans., Lachocque, H., *The Last Days of Napoleon's Empire* (New York, 1967).

Ellery, E., *Brissot de Warville* (New York, 1915).

Esposito, V., *The West Point Atlas of American Wars* (New York, 1959).

Esposito, V., and Elting, J., *A Military History and Atlas of the Napoleonic Wars* (New York, 1964).

Falkiner, C. L., *Studies in Irish History and Biography* (London, 1902).

Faverie, A. S. de la, *Napoléon et l'Amérique* (Paris, 1917).

Ferrero, G., trans. by B. Pritchard and L. C. Freemen, *The Gamble; Bonaparte in Italy 1796–1797* (London, 1961).

———, trans. by Theodore Jaeckel, *The Reconstruction of Europe* (New York, 1963).

Ferval, J., *Campagne de la Révolution française dans les Pyrénées orientales,* 2 vols. (Paris, 1851–53).

Fisher, H., *Napoleon* (London, 1913).

———, *Studies in Napoleonic Statesmanship: Germany* (London, 1903).

Flammermont, J., *Négociations secrètes de Louis XVI et du baron Breteuil avec la cour de Berlin décembre 1791–juillet 1792* (Paris, 1885).

Ford, G. S., *Stein and the Era of Reform in Prussia* (Princeton, 1922).

Fortescue, J. W., *A History of the British Army,* 13 vols. (London, 1906).

———, *Wellington* (New York, 1925).

Franchetti, A., *Storia d'Italia dal 1789 al 1799* (Milan, 1907).

Froude, J. A., *The English in Ireland in the Eighteenth Century,* 3 vols. (London, 1874).

Fugier, A., *Histoire des relations internationales, la Révolution française et l'Empire napoléonien* (Paris, 1954).

Gabroy, E., *La Révolution et la Vendée,* 2 vols. (Paris, 1925).

Gachot, E., *Les campagnes de 1799 Jourdan en Allemagne et Brune en Hollande* (Paris, 1906).

Gayer, A., Rostow, W., and Schwartz, A., *The Growth and Fluctua-*

tion of the British Economy 1789–1850, 2 vols. (London, 1953).
Gershoy, L., *Bertrand Barere A Reluctant Terrorist* (Princeton, 1962).
Glover, M., *Wellington as Military Commander* (London, 1968).
——, *Wellington's Peninsular Victories* (London, 1963).
Godechot, J., *Les commissaires aux armées sous le Directoire*, 2 vols. (Paris, 1937).
——, *La contre-révolution doctrine et action 1789–1804* (Paris, 1961).
——, *La Grande Nation*, 2 vols. (Paris, 1956).
——, *Histoire de Matte* (Paris, 1952).
——, *Les institutions de la France sous la Révolution et l'Empire* (Paris, 1951).
Goetz-Bernstein, H.-A., *La diplomatie de la Gironde Jacques-Pierre Brissot* (Paris, 1912).
Gooch, G. P., *Germany and the French Revolution* (London, 1920).
Goodwin, A., "Counter-Revolution in Brittany: the Royalist Conspiracy of the Marquis de la Rouerie 1791–1793," in *Bulletin of the John Rylands Library* (1957), XXXIX.
Grant Duff, J., *A History of the Mahrattas*, 3 vols. (Calcutta, 1918).
Greer, D., *The Incidence of the Emigration during the French Revolution* (Cambridge, 1951).
——, *The Incidence of the Terror during the French Revolution* (Cambridge, 1935).
Guillon, E., *La France et l'Irlande pendant la Révolution* (Paris, 1888).
Guyot, R., *Le Directoire et la paix de l'Europe* (Paris, 1912).
Hall, W., *British Radicalism 1789–1797* (New York, 1912).
Handelsman, M., "Napoléon et la Pologne," in *Revue des études napoléoniennes* (1914), V.
——, "The Duchy of Warsaw," in *Cambridge History of Poland* (Cambridge, 1941).
Hardman, W., *A History of Malta* (London, 1909).
Harris, S. E., *The Assignats* (Cambridge, 1930).
Hartmann, L., *Les officiers de l'armée royale et la Révolution* (Paris, 1910).
Hawtrey, R. G., *Currency and Credit* (London, 1919).
Heckscher, E. F., *The Continental System; an Economic Interpretation* (London, 1922).
Heidrich, H., *Preussen im Kampfe gegen die französiche Revolution bis zur zweiten Teilung Polens* (Berlin, 1908).
Hennequin, L., *Zurich Masséna en Suisse* (Nancy, 1911).
Herr, R., *The Eighteenth Century Revolution in Spain* (Princeton, 1958).

Heyman, N. M., "France against Prussia: The Jena Campaign of 1806," in *Military Affairs* (1966–67), XXX.
Hibbert, C., *Corunna* (New York, 1961).
Holborn, H., *A History of Modern Germany 1648–1840* (New York, 1966).
Hueffer, H., "Fin de la République napolitaire," in *Revue historique* (1903–4), LXXIII, LXXIV.
Huntington, J., trans. J. Chastenet, *Godoy Master of Spain 1792–1808* (London, 1953).
Jacob, R., *The Rise of the United Irishmen 1791–1794* (London, 1937).
James, C. L. R., *The Black Jacobins* (New York, 1938).
Jones, E. H. S., *An Invasion that Failed* (London, 1950).
——, *The Last Invasion of Britain* (London, 1950).
Jouan, L., *La Conquête de la Belgique mai-juillet 1794* (Paris, 1914).
Jouvenal, B. de, *Napoléon et l'économie dirigée* (Paris, 1942).
Kirpatrick, A. F., *Latin America, a Brief History* (Cambridge, 1938).
Korngold, R., *Citizen Toussaint* (New York, 1944).
Kraehe, E., *Metternich's German Policy*, 2 vols. (Princeton, 1963).
Krieger, L., *The German Idea of Freedom* (Boston, 1957).
Kukiel, M., "Kosciuszko and the Third Partition," in *Cambridge History of Poland* (Cambridge, 1941).
Kuscinski, A., *Les députiès à l'Assemblée legislative* (Paris, 1900).
Labovchére, G., "L'annexation de la Luisiane aux Etats-Unis," in *Revue d'histoire diplomatique* (1916), XXX.
Lacour-Gayet, G., "Napoléon à Fontainebleau en 1814," in *Revue des études napoléoniennes* (1922), XIX.
Lacouture, J., *Le mouvement royaliste dans le sud-ouest (1797–1800)* (Paris, 1932).
Lacroix, D., *Bonaparte en Egypte (1798–1799)* (Paris, 1899).
Langsam, W., *The Napoleonic Wars and German Nationalism in Austria* (New York, 1930).
Laprade, W. T., *England and the French Revolution* (Baltimore, 1909).
Latreille, A., *L'Eglise catholique et la Révolution française* (Paris, 1946).
Lavigne, B., *Histoire de l'insurrection royaliste de l'an VII* (Paris, 1887).
Lebon, A., *L'Angleterre et l'émigration française de 1794 à 1801* (Paris, 1882).
Lechartier, G., *Les soldats de la Révolution et de l'Empire* (Paris, 1902).
Lecky, W., *A History of England in the 18th Century*, 8 vols. (London, 1887–90).

Lefebvre, G., *Le Directoire* (Paris, 1946).
——, *Etudes sur la Révolution française* (Paris, 1954).
——, *Napoléon* (Paris, 1953).
——, *La Révolution française* (Paris, 1951).
Léger, J. N., *Haiti, Her History and Her Detractors* (New York, 1907).
Lipinska, A., "La Lithuanie en 1812," in *Revue des études napoléoniennes* (1915), VII.
Lloyd, C., *St. Vincent and Camperdown* (London, 1963).
Lobanov-Rostovsky, A., *Russia and Europe 1789–1825* (Durham, 1947).
Lord, R. H., *The Second Partition of Poland* (Cambridge, 1915).
Lovett, G. H., *Napoleon and the Birth of Modern Spain*, 2 vols. (New York, 1965).
Lutostanski, K., *Les partages de la Pologne et la lutte pour l'indépendance* (Paris, 1918).
MacDermot, F., *Theobold Wolfe Tone, A Biographical Study* (London, 1939).
Mackesey, P., *War in the Mediterranean 1803–1810* (London, 1957).
Madden, R., *The United Irishmen, Their Lives and Times*, 7 vols. (Dublin, 1842–46).
Madol, H., "De Bâle à Bayonne: Napoléon et Godoy," in *Revue d'histoire diplomatique* (1935), XLIX.
Mahan, A. T., *The Life of Nelson*, 2 vols. (Boston, 1897).
Mahon, P., *Etudes sur les armées du Directoire* (Paris, 1905).
Majumdar, R., Raychaudhuri, H., and Datta, K., *An Advanced History of India* (London, 1948).
Manceron, C., *Austerlitz* (Paris, 1963).
——, *Napoléon reprend Paris* (Paris, 1965).
Marshall-Cornwall, J., *Marshal Masséna* (London, 1965).
——, *Napoleon as Military Commander* (London, 1967).
Masson, F., *Les diplomates de la Révolution* (Paris, 1882).
Matheson, C., *The Life of Henry Dundas First Viscount Melville 1742–1811* (London, 1933).
Mathiez, A., *Le Club des Cordeliers pendant la Crise de Varennes* (Paris, 1910).
——, *Le dix août* (Paris, 1934).
——, *Etudes sur Robespierre* (Paris, 1958).
——, *La Révolution et les étrangères* (Paris, 1918).
——, *Rome et le clergé français sous la Constituante* (Paris, 1910).
Maxwell, C., *Country and Town in Ireland under the Georges* (London, 1940).
McDowell, R. B., *Irish Public Opinion 1750–1800* (London, 1937).
Melvin, F. E., *Napoleon's Navigation System* (New York, 1919).

Michon, G., *Essai sur l'histoire du parti feuillant Adrien Duport* (Paris, 1924).
Moran, C., *Black Triumvirate* (New York, 1957).
Mowat, R. B., *The Diplomacy of Napoleon* (London, 1924).
Muret, P., "L'affaire des princes possessionnés d'Alsace et les origines du conflict entre la Révolution et l'Europe," in *Revue d'histoire moderne* (1899–1900), I.
Naylor, J., *Waterloo* (London, 1960).
Nussbaum, F. L., *Commercial Policy in the French Revolution* (Washington, D.C., 1923).
Oman, C., *A History of the Peninsular War,* 8 vols. (Oxford, 1902–30).
——, *Wellington's Army* (London, 1913).
Osipov, K., *Alexander Suvorov* (New York, 1941).
Palmer, A., *Napoleon in Russia* (New York, 1967).
Palmer, R. R., *The Age of the Democratic Revolution,* 2 vols. (Princeton, 1959 and 1964).
——, "Fifty Years of the Committee of Public Safety," in *Journal of Modern History* (1941), XIII.
——, "Much in Little: The Dutch Revolution of 1795," in *Journal of Modern History* (1954), XXVI.
——, "A Revolutionary Republican: M. A. B. Mangourit," in *William and Mary Quarterly* (1952), IX.
——, *Twelve Who Ruled* (Princeton, 1941).
Pappas, S., "Un point d'histoire ignoré l'agence de commerce français d'Ancône (1799)," in *Revue d'études historiques* (1902), LXVIII.
Paret, P., *Internal War and Pacification, The Vendée 1789–1796* (Princeton, 1961).
——, *Yorck and the Era of Prussian Reform 1807–1815* (Princeton, 1966).
Paret, P., and Shy, J., *Guerrillas in the 1960's* (New York, 1962).
Parker, H. T., *Three Napoleonic Battles* (Durham, 1944).
Parkinson, C. N., *War in the Eastern Seas 1793–1815* (London, 1954).
Perkins, B., *Prologue to War: England and the United States 1805–1812* (Berkeley, 1968).
Petrie, C., *Wellington, a Reassessment* (London, 1956).
Philippson, M., *Geschichte des preussischen Staatswesens vom Tode Frederichs des Grossen bis zu den Freiheitskriegen,* 2 vols. (Leipzig 1880–82).
Philips, C. H., *The East India Company 1784–1834* (Manchester, 1940).
Phipps, R. W., *The Armies of the First French Republic,* 5 vols. (London, 1926–39).

Pisani, P., "L'expédition russo-turque aux Îles ioniennes en 1798–1799," in *Revue d'histoire diplomatique* (1888), II.
Puryear, V. J., *Napoleon and the Dardanelles* (Berkeley, 1951).
Quimby, R., *The Background of Napoleonic Warfare* (New York, 1957).
Reinhard, M., *Le Grand Carnot*, 2 vols. (Paris, 1952).
Richard, C., *Le Comité de Salut Public et les fabrications de guerre* (Paris, 1922).
Rivière, C. de la, *Catherine II et la Révolution française* (Paris, 1895).
Rose, J. H., *The Life of Napoleon I*, 2 vols. (New York, 1907).
——, "Napoleon and English Commerce," in *English Historical Review* (1893), I.
——, "Napoleon and Poland," in *Cambridge History of Poland* (Cambridge, 1941).
——, *Napoleonic Studies* (London, 1904).
——, "The Political Reactions of Bonaparte's Eastern Expedition," in *English Historical Review* (1929), XLIV.
——, *William Pitt and the Great War* (London, 1911).
Rose, J. H., and Broadley, A. M., *Dumouriez and the Defense of England against Napoleon* (London, 1909).
Rose, R. B., "The French Revolution and the Grain Supply," in *Bulletin of the John Rylands Library* (1956), XXXIX.
Ruppenthal, R., "Denmark and the Continental System," in *Journal of Modern History* (1943), XV.
Sagnac, P., *Le Rhin français pendant la Révolution et l'Empire* (Paris, 1917).
Savary, J., *Guerres des Vendéens et des Chouans contre la République française*, 6 vols. (Paris, 1824–27).
Scott, F. D., "Bernadotte and the Throne of France 1814," in *Journal of Modern History* (1933), V.
See, H., *Histoire économique de la France, les temps modernes (1789–1914)* (Paris, 1942).
Segur, P., *Napoleon's Russian Campaign* (Boston, 1958).
Sen, S. P., *The French in India (1763–1816)* (Calcutta, 1958).
Shanahan, W., *Prussian Military Reforms 1786–1813* (New York, 1945).
Shupp, P. F., *The European Powers and the Near Eastern Question 1806–1807* (New York, 1931).
Sirich, J. B., *The Revolutionary Committees in the Departments of France 1793–1794* (Cambridge, 1937).
Six, G., *Dictionnaire biographique des généraux et admiraux français de la Révolution et de l'Empire*, 2 vols. (Paris, 1934).
——, *Les généraux de la Révolution et le l'Empire* (Paris, 1947).
Sorel, A., *L'Europe et la Révolution française*, 8 vols. (Paris, 1885–1904).

——, *La question d'orient du XVIIIe Siècle* (Paris, 1878).
Srbik, H. von, *Metternich der Staatsmann und der Mensch,* 2 vols. (Munich, 1925).
Stoddard, T. L., *The French Revolution in San Domingo* (New York, 1914).
Stulz, P., and Opitz, A., *Volksbewegungen in Kursachsen zur Zeit der französischen Revolution* (Berlin, 1956).
Surtees, J., *Twenty-five Years in the Rifle Brigade* (Edinburgh, 1831).
Sydenham, M. J., *The Girondins* (London, 1961).
Tarlé, E., *Napoleon's Invasion of Russia* (New York, 1942).
Tassier, S., *Les démocrats belges de 1789: étude sur le Vonckisme et la Révolution brabançonne* (Brussels, 1930).
——, *Histoire de la Belgique sous l'occupation française 1792 et 1793* (Brussels, 1934).
Thiry, J., *Eylau, Friedland, Tilsit* (Paris, 1964).
Thompson, J. M., *Robespierre,* 2 vols. (London, 1935).
——, *Napoleon Bonaparte* (London, 1952).
Tilly, C., "Some Problems in the History of the Vendée," in *American Historical Review* (1961), LXVII.
——, *The Vendée* (Cambridge, 1964).
Tramond, J., *Manuel d'histoire maratime de la France des origines à 1815* (Paris, 1927).
Trend, J. B., *Bolivar and the Independence of Spanish America* (London, 1965).
Valjavec, F., *Die Entstehung der politischen strömungen in Deutschland 1770–1815* (Munich, 1951).
Vandal, A., *L'avènement de Bonaparte,* 2 vols. (Paris, 1903).
——, *Napoléon et Alexandre Ier L'alliance russe sous le premier Empire,* 3 vols. (Paris, 1896–1903).
Viennet, O., *Napoléon et l'industrie française, la crise de 1810–1811* (Paris, 1947).
Vingtrinier, E., *Histoire de la contre-révolution,* 2 vols. (Paris, 1924–25).
Vingvier, J., "La réunion d'Avignon et du Comtat-Venaissin à la France," in *La Révolution française* (1891, 1892, 1894), XXI, XXIII, XXVI.
Wallon, H., *Les représentants du peuple en mission et la justice révolutionnaire dans les départments,* 5 vols. (Paris, 1889–90).
Ward, A. W., and Gooch, G. P., *The Cambridge History of British Foreign Policy,* 2 vols. (Cambridge, 1922).
Ward, S. G. P., *Wellington's Headquarters* (London, 1957).
Warner, O., *The Battle of the Nile* (London, 1960).
——, *Nelson's Battles* (New York, 1965).
——, *Trafalgar* (London, 1959).
Watson, S., *The Reign of George III 1760–1815* (London, 1960).

Watson, S. F., *Carnot* (London, 1954).
Webster, C., *Britain and the Independence of Latin America 1812–1830,* 2 vols. (Oxford, 1938).
——, *The Congress of Vienna* (New York, 1966).
Wheeler, H. F. B., and Broadley, A. M., *Napoleon and the Invasion of England,* 2 vols. (London, 1908).
——, *The War in Wexford* (London, 1910).
White, P. T., *A Nation on Trial; America and the War of 1812* (New York, 1965).
Wilkinson, S., *The French Army before Napoleon* (London, 1915).
——, *The Rise of General Bonaparte* (London, 1930).
Wilson, A., *The Persian Gulf* (Oxford, 1928).
Yonge, C. D., *The History of the British Navy,* 3 vols. (London, 1886).

INDEX

INDEX

ANCHOR BOOKS

HISTORY

AFRICA AND THE VICTORIANS: The Climax of Imperialism–Ronald Robinson and John Gallagher, A614
THE ANCIENT CITY–Fustel de Coulanges, A76
THE ARAB WORLD TODAY–Morroe Berger, A406
BAGEHOT'S HISTORICAL ESSAYS–Norman St. John-Stevas, ed., A451
THE BIRTH OF CIVILIZATION IN THE NEAR EAST–Henri Frankfort, A89
THE BOOK OF THE COURTIER: Baldesar Castiglione–Charles S. Singleton, trans., A186
THE BRUTAL FRIENDSHIP: Mussolini, Hitler and the Fall of Italian Fascism–F. W. Deakin, A508a
CRISIS AND COMPROMISE: Politics in the Fourth Republic–Philip M. Williams, A518
CRISIS IN EUROPE, 1560–1660–Trevor Aston, ed., A575
DARWIN, MARX, WAGNER–Jacques Barzun, A127
DISCOVERIES AND OPINIONS OF GALILEO–Stillman Drake, trans., A94
THE DISCOVERY OF INDIA–Jawaharlal Nehru, Robert I. Crane, ed., A200
THE EARLY CHRISTIAN CHURCH–J. G. Davies, A566
ENGLAND: From Pre-History to the Present–Martin J. Havran and Arvel B. Erickson, AO2
1848: THE REVOLUTION OF THE INTELLECTUALS–Lewis Namier, A385
THE ELIZABETHAN JOURNALS, Vol. I: Being a Record of Those Things Most Talked of During the Years 1591–1597–G. B. Harrison, ed., A458a
THE ELIZABETHAN JOURNALS, Vol. II: Being a Record of Those Things Most Talked of During the Years 1598–1603–G. B. Harrison, ed., A458b
THE ERA OF TYRANNIES–Elie Halévy; Robert K. Webb, trans., A463
ESSAYS ON OLD TESTAMENT HISTORY AND RELIGION–Albrecht Alt, A544
THE FALL OF PARIS–Alistair Horne, A562
FOUR STAGES OF RENAISSANCE STYLE–Wylie Sypher, A44
FROM HEGEL TO NIETZSCHE–The Revolution in Nineteenth-Century Thought–Karl Lowith; David E. Green, trans., A553

THE PURITAN REVOLUTION: A Documentary History—Stuart E. Prall, ed., A602
QUEEN ELIZABETH I—J. E. Neale, A105
THE RUSSIAN REVOLUTION—Leon Trotsky, F. W. Dupee, ed., A170
SEVENTEENTH CENTURY BACKGROUND—Basil Willey, A19
SEVENTEENTH CENTURY FRANCE—Geoffrey Treasure, A592
THE SIX HUNDRED DAYS OF MUSSOLINI—F. W. Deakin, A508b
THE SPLENDID CENTURY—W. H. Lewis, A122
STATES AND NATIONS—Benjamin Akzin, A493
THIRTY YEARS WAR—C. V. Wedgwood, A249
TODAY'S LATIN AMERICA—Robert J. Alexander, A327
TO THE FINLAND STATION—Edmund Wilson, A6
THE WANING OF THE MIDDLE AGES—John Huizinga, A42
THE YORKIST AGE: Daily Life During the Wars of the Roses—Paul Murray Kendall, A466

ANCHOR BOOKS

AMERICAN HISTORY AND STUDIES

AMERICAN HUMOR—Constance Rourke, A12
AMERICAN LIFE IN THE 1840S—Carl Bode, ed., AD4
THE AMERICAN LITERARY REVOLUTION 1783–1837—Robert E. Spiller, ed., AD6
THE AMERICAN NOVEL AND ITS TRADITION—Richard Chase, A116
AMERICAN POETRY AND POETICS—Daniel Hoffman, ed., A304
THE AMERICAN PURITANS: THEIR PROSE AND POETRY—Perry Miller, ed., A80
AMERICAN RACE RELATIONS TODAY—Earl Raab, ed., A318
AMERICAN SOCIAL PATTERNS—William Petersen, A86
AMERICAN STRATEGY: A New Perspective—The Growth of Politico-Military Thinking in the United States—Urs Schwarz, A587
THE AMERICAN TRANSCENDENTALISTS: THEIR PROSE AND POETRY—Perry Miller, ed., A119
CAN AMERICAN DEMOCRACY SURVIVE COLD WAR?—Harry Howe Ransom, A402
CASTE AND CLASS IN A SOUTHERN TOWN—John Dollard, A95
CAVALIER AND YANKEE: The Old South and American National Character—William R. Taylor, A351
CHRISTIAN SCIENCE: Its Encounter with American Culture—Robert Peel, A446
THE CIVIL WAR IN AMERICA—Alan Barker, A274
THE COMPLETE POEMS AND SELECTED LETTERS AND PROSE OF HART CRANE—edited with an Introduction and Notes by Brom Weber, A537
THE CONGRESSMAN—Charles L. Clapp, A426
CONSTRAINT AND VARIETY IN AMERICAN EDUCATION—David Riesman, A135
THE DEATH PENALTY IN AMERICA, Revised Edition—Hugo Adam Bedau, ed., A387
THE EMANCIPATION PROCLAMATION—John Hope Franklin, A459
THE EXPLODING METROPOLIS—the Editors of Fortune, A146
THE FEDERALIST PAPERS, Second Edition—Roy P. Fairfield, ed., A239

THE FIRST AMENDMENT: The History of Religious Freedom in America—William H. Marnell, A472
THE FIRST NEW NATION—The United States in Historical and Comparative Perspective—Seymour Martin Lipset, A597
IDEOLOGY AND POWER IN THE AGE OF JACKSON—Edwin C. Rozwenc, ed., AD1
THE IMMEDIATE EXPERIENCE—Robert Warshaw, A410
THE INDIAN AND THE WHITE MAN—Wilcomb E. Washburn, ed., AD2
KILLERS OF THE DREAM—Lillian Smith, A339
LITERATURE AND THE AMERICAN TRADITION—Leon Howard, A329
MAN-MADE MORALS: Four Philosophies That Shaped America—William H. Marnell, A613
MARGARET FULLER: AMERICAN ROMANTIC, A Selection from Her Writings and Correspondence—Perry Miller, ed., A356
THE NATURE OF PREJUDICE—Gordon Allport, A149
THE NEGRO AND THE AMERICAN LABOR MOVEMENT—Julius Jacobson, ed., A495
ON NATIVE GROUNDS—Alfred Kazin, A69
THE ORGANIZATION MAN—William H. Whyte, Jr., A117
POLITICS IN AMERICA—D. W. Brogan, A198
POPULAR CULTURE AND INDUSTRIALISM, 1865–1890—ed. by Henry Nash Smith, AD5
THE POSITIVE THINKERS: A Study of the American Quest for Health, Wealth and Personal Power from Mary Baker Eddy to Norman Vincent Peale—Donald Meyer, A525
PROTESTANT, CATHOLIC, JEW—Will Herberg, A195
PURITAN VILLAGE: The Formation of a New England Town—Summer Chilton Powell, A441
QUEST FOR AMERICA—Charles Sanford, ed., AD3
RACE AND NATIONALITY IN AMERICAN LIFE—Oscar Handlin, A110
RELIGIOUS CONFLICT IN AMERICA—Earl Raab, ed., A392
TEACHER IN AMERICA—Jacques Barzun, A25
THE THEOLOGY OF JONATHAN EDWARDS—Conrad Cherry, Introduction by Will Herberg, A542
WHITE MAN, LISTEN!—Richard Wright, A414
WHO DESIGNS AMERICA?—ed. by Laurence B. Holland, A523